EU LABOUR MIGRATION IN TROUBLED TIMES

This is much awaited and indeed valuable collection of analytical papers that examine the effects of on-going economic crisis on intra-EU worker mobility that ensued on the recent eastward enlargements. The book will not only meet the expectations of those interested in the European migration and outcomes of the extended freedom of labour movements but also in the management of those movements in the present turbulent period.

Marek Okolski, University of Warsaw and Warsaw School of Social Sciences and Humanities, Poland

This unique volume addresses some of the most fascinating and momentous developments characterising labour mobility in an enlarged and crisis-stricken EU. An innovative analysis of skill mismatches, return migration and selectivity of migration, and an analysis of how migration interacts with wage setting and trade union policies make this book a must read for anyone wishing to grasp post-enlargement mobility in the EU.

Martin Kahanec, Central European University, Hungary

T0300455

EU Labour Migration in Troubled Times

Skills Mismatch, Return and Policy Responses

BÉLA GALGÓCZI, JANINE LESCHKE AND ANDREW WATT

European Trade Union Institute, Brussels, Belgium

LONDON AND NEW YORK

First published 2012 by Ashgate Publishing

Published 2016 by Routledge
2 Park Square, Milton Park, Abingdon, Oxfordshire OX14 4RN
711 Third Avenue, New York, NY 10017, USA

First issued in paperback 2016

Routledge is an imprint of the Taylor & Francis Group, an informa business

Copyright © 2012 Béla Galgóczi, Janine Leschke and Andrew Watt

Béla Galgóczi, Janine Leschke and Andrew Watt have asserted their right under the Copyright, Designs and Patents Act, 1988, to be identified as the editors of this work.

All rights reserved. No part of this book may be reprinted or reproduced or utilised in any form or by any electronic, mechanical, or other means, now known or hereafter invented, including photocopying and recording, or in any information storage or retrieval system, without permission in writing from the publishers.

Notice:
Product or corporate names may be trademarks or registered trademarks, and are used only for identification and explanation without intent to infringe.

British Library Cataloguing in Publication Data
EU labour migration in troubled times : skills mismatch, return and policy responses.
1. Labor mobility–European Union countries. 2. Foreign workers–European Union countries. 3. Manpower policy–European Union countries. 4. Migration, Internal–Economic aspects–European Union countries. 5. Return migration–European Union countries.
I. Galgóczi, Béla. II. Leschke, Janine. III. Watt, Andrew.
331.6'2'094-dc23

Library of Congress Cataloging-in-Publication Data
Galgóczi, Béla
EU labour migration in troubled times : skills mismatch, return, and policy responses / by Béla Galgóczi, Janine Leschke, and Andrew Watt.
   p. cm.
Includes bibliographical references and index.
ISBN 978-1-4094-3450-4 (hardback : alk. paper)
1. Labor mobility–European Union countries. 2. Vocational qualifications–European Union countries. 3. Manpower policy–European Union countries. 4. Labor market–European Union countries. 5. European Union countries–Emigration and immigration.
I. Leschke, Janine. II. Watt, Andrew. III. Title.
HD5717.5.E85G35 2012
331.12'791094-dc23

                                                                              2012004144

ISBN 13: 978-1-138-27151-7 (pbk)
ISBN 13: 978-1-4094-3450-4 (hbk)

Contents

PART III: POLICY IMPLICATIONS OF, AND RESPONSES TO, CROSS-BORDER LABOUR MOBILITY IN THE EU AFTER 2004

List of Figures

List of Tables

List of Contributors

Marta Anacka is a PhD candidate at the Faculty of Economic Sciences, University of Warsaw and a doctoral fellow at the Centre of Migration Research, University of Warsaw. Up until now she has been involved in many research projects focusing on migration within the economic and demographic frameworks.

Giulia Bettin graduated from the University of Ferrara (Italy) in 2004 with a BA in Economics. She holds a PhD in Economics (2009) from the Polytechnic University of Marche, Ancona (Italy). She was appointed Marie Curie Fellow at the Hamburg Institute of International Economics in the context of the EU Marie Curie Research Training network TOM (Transnationality of Migrants) (2008–2009). She is currently a Postdoc Researcher at the Polytechnic University of Marche. Her main research interests are international migration, remittances, trade and labour economics.

Line Eldring, sociologist, University of Oslo, is a researcher at Fafo Institute for Labour and Social Research in Norway. During the last years her research has mainly been devoted to issues related to EU enlargement, labour migration, trade union responses and minimum wage setting mechanisms. She is responsible for the coordination of this research area at Fafo, and is currently involved in a number of projects on mobility of labour and services in Europe.

Agnieszka Fihel obtained her PhD in economic sciences from the University of Warsaw in 2009. She has been a researcher in the Department of Economic Sciences and in the Centre of Migration Research, both at University of Warsaw, and a post-doc researcher in the *Institut national d'études démographiques* in Paris. Her research interests include international migration in Poland and the European Union, as well as recent mortality changes in Poland.

Béla Galgóczi graduated in electronic engineering and then in sociology and philosophy in Budapest, subsequently gaining a PhD in Economics. He currently works as a senior researcher at the European Trade Union Institute, Brussels, Belgium. His fields of research include capital and labour mobility in an enlarged Europe in the global environment with a view to labour market developments, industrial relations and collective bargaining.

Mihails Hazans is a professor of econometrics at the University of Latvia and an independent labour market expert. He is research fellow at the Institute for the Study of Labour (IZA), Bonn, Germany. He has served as an expert, consultant or principal investigator in numerous projects for OECD, World Bank, USAID, European Commission, ILO, etc. Among others, he has extensively published on migration, commuting, economics of education and on active labour market policies.

Jason Heyes is reader in Human Resource Management at Birmingham Business School, University of Birmingham, UK. His main research interest is in the connections between employment relations, the labour market and public policy. His research has explored these issues in relation to minimum wages, vocational education and training, and migrant workers. He is currently researching the implications of the ongoing economic crisis for employment and social protection policies in Europe.

Peter Huber is a researcher at the Austrian Institute of Economic Research. He studied Economics at the University of Economics and Business Administration in Vienna, the University of Innsbruck and the Institute of Advanced Studies, Vienna where he also worked as a research assistant. His main research interests are in regional economics and the analysis of migration and commuting patterns in Europe. He has lectured, researched and lived in Brno, East Berlin, Kromeriz, Olomouc, Salzburg and Samara.

Mary Hyland is a senior researcher in the Office of Civic and Global Engagement at Dublin City University and is managing editor of the intra-university open-access research journal, *Translocations, Migration and Social Change*. Her research interests are in the areas of industrial relations, migration and political communication. She is currently completing her PhD in the Department of Law and Government in DCU where she is examining the response of the Irish trade union movement to contemporary labour migration and its implications for future trade union organisation.

Maarten van Klaveren is researcher at the Amsterdam Institute for Advanced Labour Studies (AIAS) at the University of Amsterdam and senior consultant at STZ consultancy and research, Eindhoven, the Netherlands. His research interests focus on the interrelations of work organisation, wages and working conditions, in particular in multinational enterprises. Recent publications cover employment in retail and call centres, women's work and employment in 14 developing countries, and the impact of foreign direct investment on wages and working conditions in EU countries.

Tomas Korpi works at the Swedish Institute for Social Research at Stockholm University. His areas of interest encompass structural change on the labor market, including processes linked to globalisation. In addition to international migration, he has also examined the labor market consequences of increasing international trade (e.g. M. Hällsten et al. 'Globalization and uncertainty', *Industrial Relations*,

2010) and international financial flows (e.g. H. Gospel et al. 'The impact of investment funds on restructuring practices and employment levels', *Eurofound*, 2010).

Janine Leschke, PhD, is a senior researcher at the European Trade Union Institute (ETUI). Her research focus is on interlinks between labour market and social policies. She is currently working on comparative projects on job quality, non-standard employment and cross-border labour mobility. From 2000 to 2006 she worked in the employment and labour market policy unit of the Social Science Research Center Berlin (WZB).

Thorsten Schulten is a senior researcher at the Institute for Economic and Social Research (WSI) within the Hans Böckler Foundation in Düsseldorf, Germany. His main research interests are on collective bargaining and wage policy, industrial relations and political economy in an international and European comparative perspective. He is currently involved in research projects on 'collectively agreed wages in Europe', 'extension of collective agreements' and 'labour clauses in public procurement'.

Kea Tijdens is a research coordinator at the Amsterdam Institute of Advanced Labour Studies (AIAS) at the University of Amsterdam, and a Professor of Women and Work at the Department of Sociology, Erasmus University Rotterdam. She is scientific coordinator of the continuous *WageIndicator* web-survey about work and wages, which is currently operational in 61 countries. Current research interests include gender-based wage differentials, working time-related issues, industrial relations, collective bargaining and the upgrading and downgrading of occupations. She has published several books, and contributed articles to books and to academic journals.

Andrew Watt is a senior researcher at the European Trade Union Institute (ETUI). His research focuses on European economic and labour market trends and policies, on which he has published widely. A particular interest is policy coordination and the interaction between wage setting and demand-side policies and its employment consequences in the context of EMU. He edits the ETUI's *European Economic and Employment Policy Brief* and is the coordinator of the European Labour Network for Economic Policy (www.elnep.org).

Chapter 1

EU Labour Migration and Labour Markets in Troubled Times[1]

Béla Galgóczi, Janine Leschke and Andrew Watt

1. Introduction

The accession of eight new central and eastern European countries (EU8) to the EU in May 2004 and the subsequent accession of Romania and Bulgaria in January 2007 (EU2) marked an important step in the history of European integration. It reunited a continent divided since (at least) 1945. An important consequence was the extension of the free movement of capital, goods, services and people to Central and Eastern Europe. European law guarantees these freedoms within the EU – in principle. However, there were fears of a massive influx of workers from the new Central and Eastern European member states (NMS) with expected negative impacts on the receiving countries' labour markets (and welfare systems); in many western European countries the 'Polish plumber' came to symbolise this threat. As a result, all but three countries (the United Kingdom, Ireland and Sweden) made use of so-called transitional measures in 2004. These transitional measures restricted – to varying degrees – the right to work for EU8 citizens in EU15 countries for a period of up to seven years.

EU15 countries successively opened their labour markets over the subsequent years, however, and only Germany and Austria made use of the entire seven-year transition period, fully opening up their labour markets only in May 2011. Workers from Bulgaria and Romania will not have complete freedom of movement until January 2014; currently, 11 Member States still have transitional measures in place with regard to EU2 workers, in several cases with simplified procedures or exceptions for certain groups of workers or certain sectors.[2] The darkening economic outlook from the summer of 2007 was a major factor here. Interestingly, Spain temporarily

The chapters of this book have been written as part of a research project of the European Trade Union Institute, which was made possible due to the financial support of the European Union. The European Union is not responsible for any use made of the information contained in this publication.

1   The authors would like to thank – with the usual disclaimer – Agnieszka Fihel and Jason Heyes for extremely useful comments on earlier drafts of this text.

2   The countries that still had transitional measures in place with regard to Bulgaria and Romania at the end of April 2011 are Belgium, Germany, Ireland, France, Italy,

re-introduced restrictions on Romanian workers in July 2011, a step that was justified with reference to the labour market impact of the crisis. Transitional measures do not apply to those Romanian workers and their families already employed or registered as jobseekers in Spain (European Commission 12 August 2011).

Post-2004 labour mobility constitutes a historically new phenomenon in a number of respects, exhibiting characteristics that distinguish it from its previous forms as a result of EU enlargements. First of all, it is a multifaceted process, with different forms of labour mobility coexisting in a rapidly changing environment, a factor whose importance has more recently has been further accentuated by the economic crisis. This is why a key focus of this book is on different *forms* of cross-border labour mobility, including commuting, short-term, circular and more permanent migration.

It is also new that migrants from low-wage countries have a comparably high educational profile in absolute terms and in relation to nationals in the target countries. Although a number of studies have pointed to a mismatch between immigrant workers' skills and the jobs they are performing, this essential issue has not received enough attention. It is, however, a focus of this study, in which we address such questions as: To what extent are skills transferable across borders? Does the length of stay in the receiving country improve the skills–job match of migrant workers? Do migrant workers experience human capital augmentation (or depreciation) during their time abroad and what does that imply for the jobs they get on their return? Do specific forms of cross-border labour mobility such as cross-border commuting lead to more positive outcomes in terms of skills–job match?

Free labour mobility within a heterogeneous economic and political union has been (progressively) introduced in a rapidly changing environment. The regulatory environment has changed as more and more countries opened their labour markets for intra-EU labour mobility, but the context remains one of different coexisting regulatory frameworks. The economic crisis further changed the environment for cross-border labour mobility, as both source and target countries were affected but with large intra-country differences and in waves that were not completely synchronised. Key questions addressed by this publication include the impact of the economic crisis on migrants' opportunities and perspectives. To what extent has the crisis led to increased return migration? Have those that have stayed been disproportionately affected by employment losses and unemployment? And what have been the policy responses in this context?

The approach taken in this book is primarily comparative, and the majority of chapters make use of quantitative data sources, among them European and national Labour Force Surveys, the *WageIndicator* data and the International Adult Literacy Survey. For more detailed information on these data sources, and their limitations, as well as on common definitions used in this book refer to Annex 1. Beyond the thematic unity, all the chapters take a predominantly 'macro' view, in other words, discussing the position of migrants on (national) labour markets in the aggregate

---

Luxembourg, Malta, Netherlands, Austria, the United Kingdom and Spain (reintroduced in July 2011) (compare: http://ec.europa.eu/social/main.jsp?catId=466&langId=en).

and, in some cases, by migrant category and sector. The chapters of this book are structured in three parts. The first part looks at the issue of jobs–skills mismatch with regard to migrant workers and cross-border commuters in the post-accession period and especially during the crisis. The second part deals with selectivity in return migration: in other words, what are the characteristics of migrant workers and of those returning to their home countries after a period working abroad. Part III analyses the policy implications of and responses to cross-border labour mobility.

This introduction proceeds as follows. We provide an overview of the existing literature on post-2004 labour mobility and situate the various chapters of this book within that context (2). Taking a birds-eye European perspective, we then present, in Section 3, an overview of relevant empirical developments using the latest ELFS data. We begin with overall population movements, and then turn to employment and unemployment trends, with a focus on the impact of the crisis. Finally, we look in a more disaggregated way at migrant stocks and flows, considering issues of sector, skill levels and types of employment contract. Section 4 presents the structure of this book and reports the main findings from its chapters.

2. Existing Research into the Key Topics of the Book

In this section we discuss the available evidence on the key topics covered in this book and situate its chapters in that context. We first discuss the different forms of labour mobility; second, we consider the as yet sparse evidence in the literature on the impact of the economic crisis on labour mobility, including return migration; and third, we look at the evidence on skills mismatch.

2.1 Different Forms of Labour Mobility Including Return Migration

One simple distinction is between temporary and permanent labour mobility.[3] Temporary labour mobility can be either a matter of choice of the migrant worker (leading to voluntary return migration) but it can also be due to limited residence or work permits (contract migration) (see, for example, Dustmann and Weiss 2007). The latter is becoming less important with the successive implementation of free movement of labour in Europe. Temporary migration is sometimes seen as a possibility to limit the brain drain on sending countries (compare, for example, OECD 2009: 155–60; Wickramasekara 2002; see also next section). In this regard, the role of policy measures from sending countries in incentivising return migration is also frequently pointed out (OECD Migration Outlook 2009: 155–60; for specific examples see Galgóczi, Leschke and Watt 2009).

A specific form of temporary labour mobility is circular migration, where migrant workers move back and forth between their home and their host country.

---

3   As we focus on intra-EU mobility within the post-enlargement context we leave aside topics such as migration for humanitarian reasons (asylum seekers and so on).

The most obvious example is seasonal migration in, for example, agriculture but non-seasonal circular migration may also have become more important in the light of frequent and cheap airline connections. Another form of labour mobility and, in a way, a substitute for full geographic mobility is cross-border commuting. Overall, its quantitative role is limited, but it is of great significance in border areas (see Huber in this book and Huber and Nowotny 2009).[4]

Particularly given the transitional measures applied to workers (which ended for EU8 workers between 2004 and 2011, depending on the destination country, and are still in place for EU2 migrants in the majority of EU15 countries) another important distinction is that between labour mobility and services mobility, including service provision by the self-employed and the posting of workers by foreign firms, as there is evidence that these have been used to circumvent transition measures (for a critical assessment of service mobility in the Nordic countries compare, for example, Dølvik and Eldring 2008: 36–49). Krings (2009) for Germany and Austria and Fellmer and Kolb (2009) for Germany address the relationship between the maintenance of transition measures and the recourse to and abuse of the freedom of services (for example, posting of workers and bogus self-employment) and likely incentives to irregular work as an alternative to regular labour market mobility. We look at this issue in Section 4.3 below.

Several studies on pre-enlargement migration have concluded that return migration of migrants from European countries working in other European countries is substantial (on the United Kingdom, see, for example, Dustmann and Weiss 2007). But the evidence on duration of migration is still very limited and sometimes inconclusive which, besides the abovementioned data deficiencies, also reflects the fact that it is still relatively early to assess this phenomenon comprehensively. Indeed, according to the European Integration Consortium (2009: 159) the existing studies on return migration rather show the methodological difficulties than provide reliable data. This is a notable gap that a number of the contributions to this volume help to fill.

Reviewing the existing research in this area, a number of authors present preliminary evidence on the duration of pre-crisis post-enlargement migration. Some (for example, OECD 2009: 5665) have suggested that the importance of temporary relative to permanent migration is greater than in previous migration waves. In this regard emerging labour shortages in sending countries, policies to incite migrants to come back home and changes in the size of the wage gap (also driven by currency appreciation in home countries) are pointed out, as are low travel costs. As an illustration, in 2007 59 per cent of A8 migrant workers reported in the British Workers Registration Scheme questionnaire that they intended to stay in the UK for less than three months and only 8 per cent said they intended to stay more than two years; about a quarter of respondents didn't know yet (Clark

4   Average cross-border mobility rates from new member states to the EU15 are around 0.6 per cent and thereby of a similar magnitude to commuting between EU15 countries (IZA 2008).

and Drinkwater 2008). Of course the period since accession is still relatively short and such *ex ante* expectations on the part of workers embarking on a spell of employment abroad may, but need not, be realised. Pedersen and Pytlikova (2008) look at return migration of EU10 migrants in the five Nordic countries using data from the national statistical offices of the receiving countries up to the year 2007. According to the authors a comparison of flows and stocks suggests that return migration plays a significant role in migration from Hungary, Slovenia, the Czech and Slovak Republics, and Poland (on Poland see also Anacka and Fihel in this volume), whereas they conclude that the figures for EU2 migrants show rather low return migration tendencies. Their results for the Baltic countries are inconclusive. (for more recent results see Hazans in this volume).

Dølvik and Eldring (2008: 31–2) note that a large part of the labour migration to the Nordic countries has been of a short-term and circular character, but that Norwegian data in particular point to a clear tendency towards longer periods of residence and growth in the numbers of those who have moved permanently, including a growing level of family reunification. Register figures still indicate that most migrants stay only for short periods. However, a specific survey of Polish migrants in Oslo showed that most respondents had a time frame for their stay of several years rather than months (Dølvik and Eldring 2008: 31–2). Ivlevs (2008a and 2008b), comparing net immigration to total immigrant flows separately for Sweden and Denmark, concludes that for the period 2003 to 2007 the majority of migrants from the new member states stayed until the end of that period. In general, the proportion of 'stayers' was higher in Sweden and in NMS comparison it was highest for Polish, Lithuanian and EU2 migrants. OECD (2009: 60) confirms that EU2 migrants are less likely to return (probably due to the fact that restrictions on movement are still in place in most countries and wage gaps remain high) than, for example, Polish workers.

Studies on return migration point to a range of reasons for return: family and other social bonds in the home country, higher purchasing power of the host country's currency in the home country; acquisition of human capital and/or financial capital in the host country that may increase earnings in the home country (for example, Dustmann and Weiss 2007: 246). Of course, return migration can also reflect the fact that the migration experience did not live up to the individual's private expectations (an issue addressed by Anacka and Fihel in this volume). These studies also highlight that the (planned) duration of stay is likely to determine the labour market outcomes in that those migrants that plan to return home within a short period of time may be more willing to accept lower paid and less fitting jobs, considering the purchasing power of their earnings in their home country, and they are less likely to invest in acquiring the specific human capital of the host country, such as the language (Clark and Drinkwater 2008).

2.2 Impact of the Economic Crisis on Cross-border Labour Mobility

Although intra-EU mobility is still relatively low in terms of the share of the non-national EU population in individual member states from a sending country perspective the magnitude of outward migration has reached high levels already, with around 5 per cent of the Baltic labour force in the United Kingdom (Dølvik and Eldring 2008) and even higher rates for outward migration for Romania (Ambrosini et al. 2011).

The European Integration Consortium has estimated that the stock of migrants from the EU8 in the EU15 could increase from 1.9 million in 2007 to 3.8 million in 2020 under the present institutional conditions, and to 4.4 million when the free movement is eventually introduced by all EU15 member states; for Bulgaria and Romania the stock is estimated to increase from almost 1.9 million in 2007 to 3.9 million in 2020 under current immigration conditions, and to slightly more than 4.0 million if the free movement of workers is introduced (European Integration Consortium, final report 2009: 40–53). Beyond the more general uncertainty surrounding such forecasts, these estimates may be affected by the economic crisis, as the authors also mention.

Severe recessions have historically had a negative impact on net migration flows, and particularly labour migration flows; on the other hand, they have not usually affected long-term migration trends (OECD 2009: 63). With regard to the recent economic crisis, the literature is still sparse and, at the time of writing, inconclusive.

Already in 2009, the European Integration Consortium (2009: 53) suggested that the current financial crisis may reduce short-term migration substantially as migration is largely determined by employment opportunities in destination countries and foreign workers are disproportionally affected by dismissals in an economic downturn. This was based on the view, which was in line with our findings in Galgóczi, Leschke and Watt (2009), that labour demand in the destination countries plays the predominant role as a driver. Simulations by Ahearne et al. (2009: 34–9) focus on the labour market situation in *sending* countries, as a push factor. Overall, they find that the crisis does affect net migration flows from new to old member states but the effects are relatively small, while pointing to some important country-specific differences. In the four countries that have been less affected by the crisis – namely Czech Republic, Poland, Slovakia and Slovenia – migration outflows are projected to be lower than if the crisis had not hit. By contrast, hard-hit countries like the Baltic states were expected to experience, after a brief decline in emigration as an immediate result of the crisis, a rapid expansion of emigration due to the worsening of their position relative to the EU15.

An important study by the OECD (2010) provides an overview of quantitative developments in the first period of the crisis (see also some of the chapters in Kahanec and Zimmermann 2010). Labour migration within the EU appeared to be particularly sensitive to economic changes. Migration from EU8 countries, especially Poland, has slackened significantly (see Section 3.1 for more detail). Heavy impacts were also evident on temporary migration as is manifest in the Spanish seasonal work programme (OECD 2010: 32).

Immigrant labour is particularly vulnerable to economic shocks. Migrant workers are usually concentrated in sectors such as manufacturing, construction, hotels and restaurants which are more sensitive to business cycle fluctuation, and they often have less secure contractual arrangements; migrant workers are often overrepresented in temporary (fixed-term) employment which was hard hit particularly in the first phase of the crisis. They have on average lower job tenure[5] and may be subject to discrimination in hiring and lay-offs (on these issues compare OECD 2009: 19–25; OECD 2010: 97–101).

We take up these issues in Section 4 below and they are treated in a number of chapters, including Heyes and Hyland, Bettin and Hazans.

2.3 Skills Mismatch: Brain Drain, Brain Gain and Brain Waste

While migrant labour is often discussed with regard to skills and education, the debate depends fundamentally on one's perspective. From a sending country perspective, the literature is often concerned with the brain drain which occurs when highly qualified people or workers with specific skills needed in the local labour market leave the country in disproportionately large numbers. A field that has received particular attention in this regard is the health sector (for example, Fihel et al. 2007; OECD 2007).

An important 'stylised fact' is that EU10 countries have significantly *higher* shares of medium and high skilled persons in their working age population than the EU15 countries. The share of persons having completed at least upper secondary education is almost 20 percentage points higher in the EU10 than in the EU15. Moreover, young migrants, who on average have higher education levels, have dominated post-accession cross-border movements. This implies that post-2004 migration is qualitatively different from previous migration waves (European Integration Consortium 2009 and 4.2 below).

In light of increasing human capital investment in the vast majority of EU10 countries, as evident for example in the increasing trend in enrolled tertiary education students, the brain drain hypothesis has been challenged for some NMS countries and it has been suggested that it should be interpreted rather in terms of a brain overflow: in other words, a lack of employment opportunities commensurate with the high skills that young people, in particular, have to offer (on this see, for example, Fihel et al. 2007; Kaczmarczyk and Okólski 2008).

From a receiving country perspective the discussion is about brain gain versus a brain waste. A brain gain occurs when migrant workers are recruited to fill gaps in the high skilled segment (for example, doctors) or in specific occupations experiencing shortages (for example, nurses or IT experts). Policy measures and initiatives of receiving countries are often geared to attracting high-skilled migrants (for example, points-based systems for managing labour immigration or programmes to retain international students, discussed by Korpi in this volume).

---

5   In 2008 in Ireland more than one-fourth and in Spain one-third of migrant workers had been recruited in the previous 12 months compared with less than 15 per cent of native born workers (OECD 2010: 99f).

However, as soon as free movement of labour applies most of these activities are no longer relevant for EU migrants. Specific programmes to attract high skilled labour and retain graduates from EU10 countries have been important, however, in for example Germany and Austria as part of their transitional measures (OECD 2010: 42–58). The same is true in several countries with regard to highly skilled EU2 migrants (for Italy, see Bettin in this volume). A form of brain gain can also apply from a sending country perspective if the migrant workers return to their home country with improved skills and qualifications (for example, language).

Over-qualification (sometimes termed 'brain waste') describes a situation in which migrant workers are employed in jobs that are substantially below their skill level. This was a key finding of our earlier study (Galgóczi, Leschke and Watt 2009). From a global perspective this risks misallocating scarce human capital and, on the individual level, challenges the hypothesis that returning migrant workers really have improved their human capital.

A number of studies find that Polish post-accession migrants to Germany have on average a lower educational attainment than the source population, whereas those who went to the United Kingdom have a higher average educational attainment (termed, respectively, negative and positive selection with regard to education) (Fihel and Okólski 2009; Kaczmarczyk and Okólski 2008). This might be due to the application of transitional measures in Germany, or may reflect differences between migration networks in different destination countries.[6]

In contrast to the United Kingdom, as Dølvik and Eldring (2008: 30–35) point out, in the Nordic countries unskilled or low skilled post-accession labour migration has predominated. They also point to the fact that Finland has gained considerably from the mobility of medical staff from the EU8, particularly from Estonia, which points to the importance of language bonds (see also Korpi in this volume)

Language is clearly one of the main barriers to achieving a good match between skills and occupation in the receiving country. According to Clark and Drinkwater (2008: 513) almost one-third of recent EU8 migrants to the United Kingdom who did not speak English at home reported that they had experienced language difficulties in finding or keeping a job. Other barriers mentioned in the literature are discrimination by employers, pressure to find work quickly, formalised recruitment procedures and a lack of recognition of qualifications (see Hardy 2010; *IZA* 2008: 111–13 and Tijdens and Klaveren in this volume).

A common finding is that post-2004 migrants from the new member states are employed well below their skill levels and thus that the returns to education are very low ('brain waste'). The European Integration Consortium (2009: 97–103) illustrates this convincingly for the United Kingdom, as do the chapters in

---

6 McKenzie and Rapoport (2008) as cited in European Integration Consortium provide theoretical and empirical evidence on the link between negative self-selection and size of migration networks.

Kahanec and Zimmermann (2010) and in Galgóczi, Leschke and Watt (2009) for a range of receiving countries. This point is taken up by Bettin in this volume.

The analysis also shows that post-2004 migrants fare considerably worse than pre-2004 migrants from the NMS, both as concerns occupation–skills match and wages (see, for example, Drinkwater, Eade and Garapich 2009). A simple explanation might be the fact that the amount of time spent abroad (learning languages, acquiring contacts and so on) is a crucial factor in facilitating the transferability of skills. The 'brain waste' hypothesis is also confirmed by Dølvik and Eldring (2008: 76–7) for Baltic and Polish migrants in the Nordic countries. Skills–occupation mismatch is one of the explanations of large wage gaps as identified with recent EU10 migrants, who earn on average 42.5 per cent less than natives (European Integration Consortium 2009: 101). The issue of wage gaps and the regulation of wages for migrant workers is a focus of the chapter by Eldring and Schulten in this volume.

All this suggests that the decision to emigrate is driven by absolute differences in wage levels across countries rather than by the relative returns to skills: migrants, particularly those who are planning to return at some point in time, are willing to take up jobs below their skill level as long as this allows them to accumulate savings (that can later be invested in the home country) or sent as remittances (see next section).

A conclusion from the existing literature would be that in most cases neither the 'brain drain' nor the 'brain gain' will have a strong overall impact on labour markets and the economies of the sending and receiving countries. However, for small countries with large outflows and in certain sectors (for example, medical staff) it may be a cause for concern. Various chapters in this book contribute additional evidence to this debate.

Regarding the question of whether migration develops or rather destroys human capital, there is as yet little evidence on how immigrants fare on returning to their home country. Hazans (2008), controlling for a range of characteristics states that return migrants to Latvia earn wages that are on average about 15 per cent higher than those of other Latvian workers; the earnings premium is higher for men than for women. Considering the low returns to education in the host country this finding points to the importance of the acquisition of other forms of human capital, such as language skills. These issues are a focus of Hazans's contributions to this volume.

2.4 Conclusions from the Literature

To conclude, we may identify three important aspects addressed by the literature with regard to post-enlargement labour mobility in the EU. A variety of different forms of labour mobility were identified (temporary, circular, return migration) with the additional channel of the self-employed. Changing environments in terms of the effect of transitional measures and the economic crisis resulted in subsequent shifts within these forms of mobility.

Three major factors have had an impact on migration flows during the crisis: labour market demand and characteristics of jobs by migrants in the target country (impact of the crisis on particular sectors, job security); labour market situation and welfare provision in the source country (as possible push factors) and finally, changing migration policy in target countries (with the accession of EU2 countries in 2007 under the services directive access became possible for the self-employed to EU15 labour markets, and countries are gradually opening their labour markets either fully or partially).

When examining the skills characteristics of EU10 migrant workers in the EU15, it has been empha*sise*d that the educational attainment of the EU10 migrant population tends to be significantly higher than in previous migration waves. Debates have addressed the issue of brain drain, brain overflow and brain waste from the point of view of sending countries. One conclusion seemed to crystallise: post-enlargement East-West labour mobility has not contributed to better human capital allocation due to large-scale skills–occupation mismatches affecting EU10 migrants on EU15 labour markets.

3. A Birds-eye View of Intra-EU Migration Trends During the Crisis

In this section we turn our attention to the main trends of intra-EU labour mobility since enlargement and particularly during the period of the crisis. The analysis draws on the most recent European Labour Force Survey data (LFS) Against the background of divergent labour market developments in source and target countries during the crisis, we highlight how EU10 migrant workers have been affected by the crisis in various countries, not least in comparison to native workers (3.1). Using a special extraction of the LFS data we are also able to present disaggregated results by sector, skill level and employment contract, which shed additional light on some of the still unresolved research questions mentioned in the previous section (3.2).

3.1 Major Trends in Cross-border EU Labour Mobility since Enlargement and the Impact of the Economic Crisis

Population Stocks and Flows
The broad developments of East–West labour mobility since enlargement in 2004 and up to the crisis show a marked increase of the EU8[7] migrant population in the two receiving countries (United Kingdom and Ireland) that opened their labour market from the beginning, as Figure 1.1 shows. In interpreting the figure it should be recalled that the Irish population is only about one-fifteenth that of the United Kingdom. Sweden (not included in this figure), the only other

---

7   In this section, which uses ELFS data, the EU8 and EU10 figures include Cyprus and Malta. The absolute numbers involved are so small that the differences can be ignored.

country that granted free access to EU8 migrants right from the start, did not experience any significant increase, demonstrating that labour demand is also a necessary condition for attracting labour migrants and that language can act as a barrier (cf. Galgóczi, Leschke and Watt 2009: 11). On the other hand, Germany – a traditional destination country for CEE migrants but which maintained restrictions until May 2011 – still shows a steady but moderate growth in its EU8 population without any visible effect of the crisis. In light of the fact that recent labour market developments in Germany were positive (Leschke and Watt 2010), in contrast to most other EU15 countries, one might even have expected a more pronounced positive trend in the past two years than the one observed. The impact of the crisis, however, is visible in the two receiving countries – United Kingdom and Ireland – that absorbed a large number of EU8 workers after enlargement.

The UK labour market shows initial signs of saturation from the crisis year of 2008, followed, however, by recent marked increases, while Ireland experienced a significant drop of EU8 population (cf. Heyes and Hyland in this volume). The crisis in the United Kingdom brought the previous dynamic growth of EU8 population to a halt in 2008 and led to an initial slight decline. The negative impact was short-lived, however, as marked increases in stocks of EU8 migrants are visible between 2009 and 2010 (Figure 1.1). More detailed data show that restructuring within the EU10 migrant group took place in the background. While total EU8 population in the United Kingdom stagnated, a wave of return migration of Polish citizens started to emerge from 2007. Polish data show that the number of Polish residents in the United Kingdom decreased by 135,000

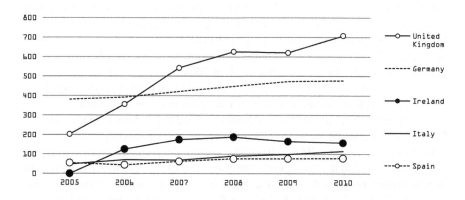

Figure 1.1   EU8 population in major EU15 receiving countries, 2005–2010 ('000s; stocks)

Note: Migration status defined by nationality.

Source: European Labour Force Survey.

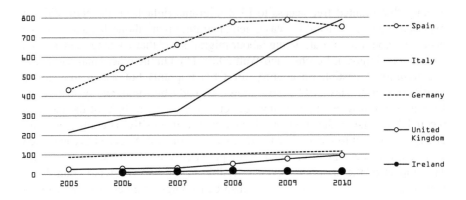

Figure 1.2   EU2 population in receiving countries, 2005–2010 ('000; stocks)

Note: Migration status defined by nationality.
Source: European Labour Force Survey.

between the end of 2007 and the end of 2009 (cf. Anacka and Fihel in this volume). Although new figures reveal that in 2010 Polish migrant stock increased slightly it remained well below the 2007 peak (Polish Statistical Office 2011). At the same time, the inflow of EU2 migrants to the UK has grown uninterruptedly during the crisis despite restrictions and has resulted in a net increase of all EU10 nationals on the UK labour market (Figure 1.2).

Ireland experienced a radical reversal of migration trends during the crisis. The number of EU8 nationals – which peaked in 2008 at 8 per cent of the Irish labour force – had decreased by 25 per cent by the end of 2010, (a trend also revealed by recent data from the Polish Statistical Office). Inflows of EU2 migrants were marginal and, in contrast to the United Kingdom, the stock figures substantially declined again after the onset of the crisis in 2008 (compare Figure 1.2).

The effect of pull factors in terms of existing labour market access and labour demand, as well as cultural and linguistic proximity and network effects is demonstrated by the case of EU2 migrants, as Figure 1.2 shows. Spain and Italy have seen a spectacular increase of their EU2 population in recent years (altogether 1.45 million migrants by 2009, falling little short of the 1.68 million EU8 migrants in the entire EU15 in the same year). The number of EU2 migrants was topping out in Spain from 2008 which can be explained by the severe impact of the economic crisis, particularly but not exclusively on the construction sector, with important shares of migrant workers (see also below). Between 2009 and 2010 stock figures fell and it is likely that the reintroduction of transitional measures for Romanians from mid-2011 onwards will have a further negative impact on migrant stocks. In contrast, the effect of the economic crisis on cross-border labour mobility from EU2 countries is not visible in Italy where the EU2 population continued to grow dynamically. In 2010 for the first time more EU2 migrants were resident in Italy than in Spain.

The number of EU2 migrants remained at a very low level in Ireland and the United Kingdom, showing, among other things, the effect of the transitional measures for workers that, in contrast to the first round of accession in 2004, were imposed on workers from Romania and Bulgaria in 2007. The same is true for Germany in the context of EU2 migrants. Both Germany and the United Kingdom have seen stocks of EU2 migrants increasing during the crisis, although with more pronounced developments in the United Kingdom. Looking purely at labour markets as pull factors the latter is somewhat surprising as the UK labour market was much more strongly affected by the economic crisis. This may be due to differences in the application of transitional measures applied to Romanians and Bulgarians in the two countries.

Whereas the number of EU2 migrants reached very high levels in Spain and Italy, EU8 migrants used the opportunity of the free access to the labour markets of these two countries which had lifted restrictions in mid-2006 only to a limited degree. Both Spain and Italy show comparatively low levels of EU8 population with a slight upward trend in Italy (Figure 1.1). This difference compared with the United Kingdom and Ireland can be explained, particularly for the pre-crisis period, by the much more favourable labour market conditions in these two countries, as well as by the language effect and network effects.

Impact of the Crisis on EU10 Migrants in Receiving Country Labour Markets
Comparing second quarter LFS data from 2008 and 2010, we now examine how the EU10 migrant population was affected by the crisis in the receiving EU15 countries compared to the local population. Subsequently, we use a special extraction of data from the LFS to delve into structural issues (sector, skill level, employment status) to shed further light on the impact of the crisis (Section 3.2).

Figure 1.3 shows that only two receiving countries, Spain and Ireland, saw a decrease of the EU10 working age population during the most intensive period of the crisis. This can be explained largely by the major impact of the crisis on their labour markets: the percentage loss of employment was greatest in these two countries (see also Leschke and Watt 2010: 12–18). The crisis notwithstanding, all other EU15 countries witnessed an increase with a spectacular rise of over 300,000 EU10 (overwhelmingly EU2) citizens in Italy.

As regards EU10 countries, their working age population (nationals) did not show significant changes; only Poland had a substantial increase. Between the second quarter of 2008 and the second quarter of 2010 the working age population rose by 342,000, of which a substantial proportion represents net return migration (European Labour Force Survey, not shown).

If net EU10 inflows in EU15 receiving countries have remained the predominant trend of labour mobility also during the crisis, an important question is how EU10 migrants were affected by the economic crisis. Were they hit to a higher or lesser

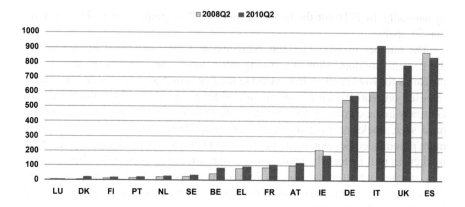

**Figure 1.3   Impact of the crisis on stocks of EU10 nationals in EU15
           countries, working age population ('000)**

Note: Migration status defined by nationality.
Source: European Labour Force Survey.

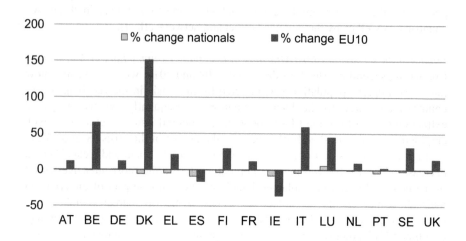

**Figure 1.4   Employment changes among nationals and EU10 citizens in
           receiving countries between the second quarter of 2008 and the
           second quarter of 2010 (percentage change)**

Note: Migration status defined by nationality.
Source: European Labour Force Survey.

extent by decreasing employment and increasing unemployment than the local population?

While the number of employed nationals showed a decrease during the crisis in all receiving countries except Germany and Luxemburg, the number of EU10 employed grew in all countries but Spain and Ireland (Figure 1.4). It must be borne in mind that the figures are percentage changes in order to make the countries comparable. In absolute terms, the change in native employment is much larger than that of foreign-national employment. In the two receiving countries where EU10 employment fell in absolute terms, however, migrants were more affected than natives, who suffered a smaller setback in employment.

From considering absolute numbers of working age migrant populations and employees, we now turn our attention to the *proportions* of these populations in employment and unemployment in the receiving countries; that is, to employment and unemployment rates.

Figure 1.5 shows how the employment rate of nationals and EU10 migrants developed on receiving country labour markets during the crisis. Prior to the crisis EU10 migrant workers had higher employment rates than nationals in most receiving countries. Exceptions in this regard are France, Germany, Austria, Sweden and Denmark.

In the course of the crisis the relations between the employment rates of native and EU10 workers changed in the various countries.

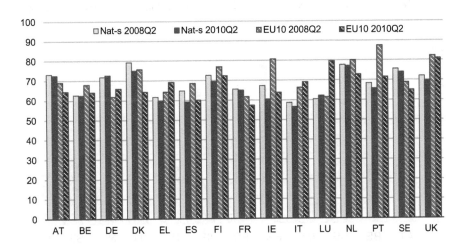

Figure 1.5   Employment rate of nationals and of EU10 citizens before and after the crisis (%)

Note: Migration status defined by nationality.

Source: European Labour Force Survey.

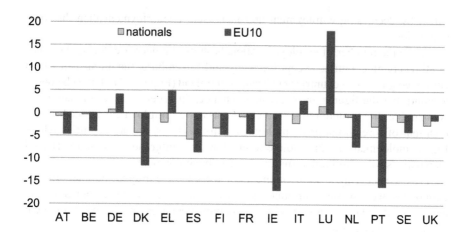

**Figure 1.6   Employment rate changes of nationals and of EU10 citizens
           on EU15 labour markets during the crisis, 2008Q2–2010Q2
           (percentage points)**

Note: Migration status defined by nationality.

Source: European Labour Force Survey.

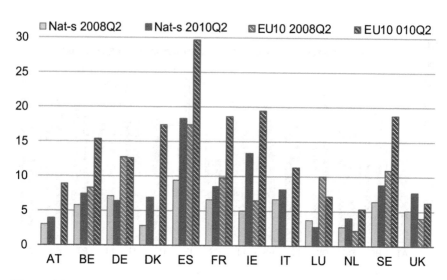

**Figure 1.7   Unemployment rate of nationals and of EU10 citizens on EU15
           labour markets during the crisis (%)**

Note: Migration status defined by nationality. Data missing for EL, FI, PT.

Source: European Labour Force Survey.

To illustrate the dynamics of employment rates during the crisis for nationals and migrants in receiving countries more clearly, Figure 1.6 shows the percentage point changes between the second quarter of 2008 and the second quarter of 2010.

In 10 out of 15 receiving countries the employment rate of EU10 citizens suffered larger decreases than that of nationals during the crisis. This is especially true of Spain, Ireland and Portugal. In the United Kingdom, however, the employment rate of EU10 workers fell less than that of locals, while in Greece and in Italy the employment rate of EU10 nationals grew while the employment rate for nationals decreased. In Germany and Luxembourg, the employment rate of EU10 citizens increased more than that of nationals during the crisis (Figure 1.6). From a comparative European perspective, the employment rates of nationals and EU10 migrants seem to move in parallel during the crisis with more pronounced changes in the latter group (with the exception of Italy and Greece).

Prior to the crisis, the unemployment rates of EU10 migrants were higher than for nationals in all receiving countries for which we have data except the United Kingdom and the Netherlands. Figure 1.7 shows how the unemployment rates of EU10 migrants changed in receiving countries during the crisis, compared to nationals. The unemployment rates of migrants increased to a greater extent than for nationals in Belgium, Ireland, Spain, France, the Netherlands and Sweden, whereas in Germany and Luxembourg, the only EU15 countries with a strong labour market performance during the crisis, unemployment was declining in line with developments among nationals. The United Kingdom showed similar increases in unemployment among nationals and migrant workers (several countries have incomplete data).

The most typical pattern, therefore, is for EU10 workers to have experienced a larger increase of unemployment, in terms of unemployment rates, from a higher initial level. The increase and levels of EU10 unemployment are particularly high in Spain and Ireland, where these rates substantially exceed the unemployment rates of nationals, themselves very high in comparison with other countries.

3.2 A Look Inside the Black Box: Labour Market Trends during the Crisis for Nationals and Migrants by Sector, Employment Type and Skill Level

In the previous section we looked at labour market developments as a whole for the EU10, comparing them with the results for nationals. This macro-analysis, which is all that is possible on the basis of the readily available LFS data, has already enabled us to draw a number of relevant conclusions. However, we would like to go further and break down the statistics along a number of relevant dimensions. To this end we obtained a special extraction of the LFS data which enables us, in this sub-section, to perform an analysis with respect to sector, employment type and skill group.

Sectoral Concentration of Migrant Workers

The sectoral distribution of employment changes to a surprisingly little extent over the crisis period (Figure 1.8). In almost all cases the sectoral shares do not change by more than 1 percentage point, although variability among the EU2 is greater, reflecting the more recent migration, but also the smaller numbers involved, and thus the greater likelihood of measurement error. A notable exception is construction. Prior to the crisis it accounted for just under 15 per cent of EU8 and more than 28 per cent of EU2 employment; by the first quarter of 2011 these figures had fallen to just over 10 per cent and 20 per cent, respectively. The share of nationals in manufacturing fell by more than 1.2 percentage points, and by 1.5 points for EU2 workers, while the share of EU8 workers employed in manufacturing actually increased slightly.

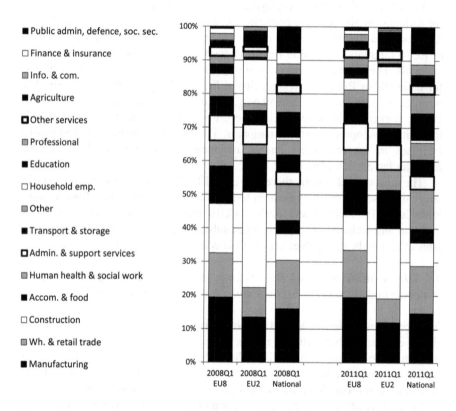

Figure 1.8   Sectoral shares of total employment by nationals, EU8 and EU2 workers, 2008Q1–2011Q1

Source: European Labour Force Survey, special extraction.

This also implies that the sectoral-share gaps between natives, EU8 and EU2 nationals in the EU15 remained broadly stable in most cases. The largest gaps are to be found as follows. In accommodation and food services both the EU8 and EU2 shares, at around 11 per cent, are about three times as high as for nationals. Working in households is completely marginal for nationals (less than 1 per cent) but important for EU8 workers and a key sector for EU2 immigrants, even growing in importance during the crisis (from 13 to 17 per cent).[8] Before the crisis, the proportion of EU8 and EU2 workers that worked in construction was around twice and almost four times respectively higher than was the case for nationals: this divergence was reduced somewhat in the crisis however (suggesting that non-national labour has served as a buffer in that hard-hit industry). Manufacturing is peculiar in that the proportion of EU8 workers is somewhat higher than that for natives whereas that for EU2 is somewhat lower. Perhaps surprisingly a similar picture emerges in agriculture: it is actually less important for EU8 workers as a source of employment than for natives, but it is more significant – although not dramatically so – for those from Bulgaria and Romania. Administrative and support services also account for a rather higher proportion of Central and Eastern European workers. In all the other sectors the sectoral shares are either broadly balanced or the concentration among natives is higher. The latter is particularly the case, unsurprisingly, in public administration, education and among the professions.

A rather different perspective is given by analysing the data in terms of the proportion that EU8 and EU2 workers represent in the total workforce of different sectors. From this perspective the size of the sector in the economy is not relevant; rather the focus is on the 'likelihood' that a worker in a given sector is a national or from either the EU8 or EU2. Putting this another way it shows an over- or underrepresentation of migrants in a particular sector compared to their share in total employment. On average across the whole economy EU8 workers accounted for 0.74 per cent of total employment in 2008, rising to 0.87 per cent in 2011 (in each case in the first quarter). The corresponding figures for EU2 workers were 0.59 per cent and 0.84 per cent, respectively.[9]

To assess sectoral concentration, the figure depicts all the sectors in which the share of either EU8 or EU2 workers exceeded 1 per cent of the sectoral total in

---

8   It should be noted that the LFS data on which this classification is based certainly underreport undeclared work in the household sector. See Section 2.1 on data limitations and definitions.

9   In other words, by the first quarter of 2011 workers from Romania and Bulgaria on EU15 labour markets were almost as numerous as from the EU8 countries. This needs to be seen against the background of the very much larger population of the EU8 (ca. 74 million) compared with the EU2 (ca. 29 million) (Eurostat data for 2010). Thus the 'migration intensity' is more than twice as high for the EU2.

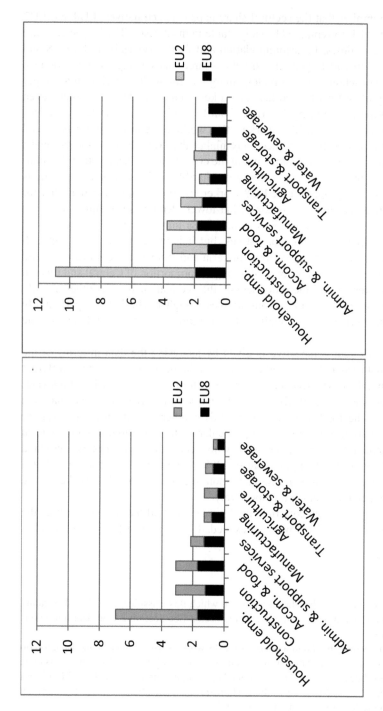

Figure 1.9   Proportion of EU8 and EU2 workers by selected sector in EU15 countries, 2008Q1 and 2011Q1

Note: No figure for water and sewage in the EU2 in 2011 due to the small case size.

Source: European Labour Force Survey, special extraction.

either period.[10] Using this (arbitrary) definition gives seven 'high concentration' sectors (Figure 1.9). By far the most prominent is employment within the household sector. This largely applies to EU2 workers and is particularly pronounced in 2011: overall, more than one in ten workers in this sector was from the EU10; given underreporting of undeclared work the figure may be even higher. Next come construction, administrative services, and accommodation and food services, where EU10 workers represent around 3 per cent of employment in 2008, rising, especially in the latter case, during the course of the crisis; here there is a broadly even balance between EU8 and EU2. Administration and support services follow close behind. Manufacturing and agriculture are, perhaps surprisingly, not particularly high concentration sectors overall, and make the list only by virtue of the imbalance in favour of EU8 in manufacturing and EU2 in agriculture. In agriculture there is, however, likely to be considerable under-coverage by the LFS. First quarter figures have been used in all these comparisons as they are the most recent. Agricultural work, however, is highly seasonal (as is also construction). Annual average figures would be higher.[11]

Similarly, concentrations in transport and storage and in water supply and sewage are skewed and only slightly above average. Overall then, only four sectors can be considered consistently high-concentration at the level of the EU15 as a whole: household employment, construction, accommodation and food, and administrative and support services.

Employment Effects of the Crisis by Sector and Nationality of Workers
In order to consider more precisely the differential effects of the crisis on native labour compared with migrant labour from the EU8 and EU2, it is instructive to look at the percentage change in their respective employment levels by sector for different nationality groups. To keep the presentation within limits we focus here on those sectors with the largest quantitative importance for EU10 migrant labour: construction, manufacturing, wholesale and retail trade, accommodation and food services, household employment, health and social work, and administrative and support services (see Figure 1.10).

It is worth bearing in mind when evaluating these figures that the total loss in employment between the first quarter of 2008 and the first quarter of 2011 was almost seven million jobs, or 1.97 per cent for all workers and sectors in the EU15. In comparing percentages it needs to recalled that the nationals group is much larger than the two migrant groups, where appropriate reference is made to the absolute changes in thousands. The figures refer to net losses or gains for each nationality groups over the period; of course the turnover was considerably

---

10   The rather special case of extra-territorial organisations and bodies (miniscule in any case) has been excluded.

11   A sense of this can be gained from the figures for 2010 which progress as follows across the four quarters (in construction: 393,000, 428,000, 451,000 and 435,000; in agriculture: 91,000, 112,000, 122,000 and 118,000.

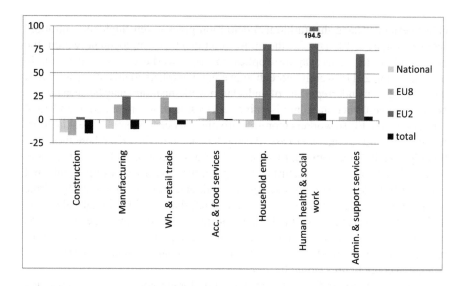

Figure 1.10 Change of employment by sector and nationality during the crisis, between 2008Q1 and 2011Q1 (%)

Source: European Labour Force Survey, special extraction.

higher, with some workers in each category leaving offset by others from that group joining the sector.

Job losses were extremely heavy in construction, which shed more than four and a quarter million jobs. In percentage terms, national and EU8 employment losses were bracketed around the sectoral average of 14.4 per cent, suggesting that they bore the brunt of the sectoral employment crisis in roughly equal proportions. However, astonishingly, EU2 employment in construction actually increased slightly, although the absolute increase – around 13,000 – is small. It is worth noting the huge employment losses among non-EU nationals (not shown), more than 600,000, more than one quarter of the pre-crisis total in construction lost their jobs.

In manufacturing we see clear signs of a substitution process during the crisis. Almost five-and-a-half million jobs were lost over the three-year period, representing 9.7 per cent of total employment in the sector. Job losses among nationals were, in percentage terms, marginally above average and among non-EU nationals (not shown) substantially higher. But the number of migrant workers from Central and Eastern Europe increased substantially, by around 15 per cent and almost 25 per cent for EU8 and EU2 workers, respectively, adding almost

140,000 EU10 jobs in this sector, in the face of massive overall job losses. The picture in wholesale and retail is fairly similar against the background of overall job losses on a substantially smaller sale, both absolutely and in percentage terms.

All the remaining four sectors saw employment gains – mostly small – over the period: in health care and social work the gains, though small in relative terms, were large in absolute terms, at 2.8 million.[12] In all these sectors there was a large jump in the number of workers from Bulgaria and Romania. In household employment the increase was a full 200,000 and it was in the vicinity of 100,000 in the three other sectors. In contrast, the total increase for all four sectors for EU8 workers fell considerably short of 150,000. To some degree, EU2 workers may well have taken the places of returning EU8 workers.

If we consider the absolute totals for all these seven sectors – which, it should be recalled, were selected not randomly but because of their importance for EU10 employment – we see an overall employment loss of around 8 million jobs. At the same time, there was a net *increase* in EU10 employment of some 820,000 jobs in these sectors combined; more than two-thirds of this (582,000) was from EU2.

A crucial conclusion from this sectoral analysis is that the greater vulnerability of EU10 workers in the crisis (greater likelihood of job losses and unemployment), partially masked by the reality of continued inflow, reflects to a considerable extent the higher concentration of such workers in construction and manufacturing which were disproportionately badly affected by the slump in output.

Self-employment as a Possible Way of Circumventing Transitional Measures
One of the most controversial issues in the EU labour mobility debate, not least in the context of transitional measures imposed by some member states, has been the possible substitution of employees by self-employed workers, making use of the freedom of service provision to circumvent restrictions imposed as transitional measures on waged employment. The special extraction of LFS data enables us to break total employment down into employees, family workers, self-employed persons with employees of their own, and those without.[13] We are primarily interested in the split between employees and the self-employed without workers of their own.

---

12   This may seem surprising. It is worth noting that the figures for the first quarter of 2011 largely exclude the large-scale public sector retrenchments, which only began to take effect in most EU countries from the start of that year.

13   Some countries also have a no response category: these are excluded from this analysis. An additional problem, especially in small countries, is that the numbers of self-employed workers from, especially, the EU2 are small. For confidentiality reasons they are not shown in the country data, although they are incorporated into the EU15 aggregates. As a result there is a discrepancy between the 15 national totals and the EU15 aggregate: for example, it amounts to about 25,000 EU2 self-employed workers in 2008 (around 144,000, compared with 169,000).

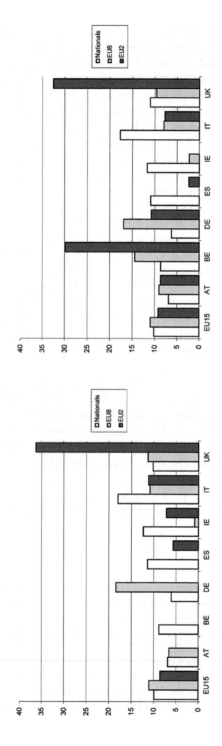

Figure 1.11   Self-employed (without employees) as share of total employment, by nationality, 2008Q1 and 2011Q1

Note: Some missing values due to small case sizes.

Source: European Labour Force Survey, special extraction.

Starting with the EU15 breakdown (which is the most reliable: see earlier footnote) Figure 1.11 shows, on the one hand, that EU10 persons in employment are considerably more likely to be employees than is the case for nationals: the figures (which change little between the second quarters of 2008 and 2011) are approximately 84 per cent for nationals but 87 per cent for EU8 and 88 per cent for EU2. At the same time, the proportions of self-employed (without own employees) are extremely similar for all three groups. They are roughly 1 percentage point higher for EU8 and 1 percentage point lower for EU2 than for nationals, for whom the figure is around 10 per cent.[14]

At the aggregate EU15 level, then, we see little evidence of widespread (ab) use of the status of self-employment (at least provided there is not substantial underreporting of self-employed vis-à-vis employed migrants).

However, the national figures show a highly differentiated picture. A case in point is Germany, where the rate of self-employment (without own workers) is around 18 per cent for EU8 and 10 per cent for EU2 (2011 figures only), compared with around 6 per cent for natives. This is highly suggestive of the use of self-employment as a means of avoiding the transitional measures imposed by that country. A similar overall pattern emerges in Austria, although the differences are much less stark. Belgium fits this pattern, with very stark differences (figures for 2008 are lacking: by 2011, Belgium had removed its transitional measures for the EU8, but some were still in place for workers from Bulgaria and Romania). The United Kingdom is also very illustrative. The proportion of self-employed amongst EU8 migrant workers – to whom no transitional measures applied – is broadly in line with the figure for natives (at a fairly high level of around 10 per cent). But among EU2 workers, who remain subject to such measures, the proportion is more than three times as high.

The picture is reversed in the southern EU15 countries for which we have robust data (and for Ireland). Here a high proportion of native workers is self-employed (many of them in agriculture), whereas the self-employed share among migrants is typically very low. An exception is Italy, where the self-employment share is very high for natives, but also rather high for EU10 migrant workers.

Finally, it should be noted that there are no systematic changes in self-employment shares between 2008 and 2011, rising in some countries while falling in others for one or both sub-groups. The crisis does not appear to have had a consistent effect on the split between employees and own account self-employed workers.

The conclusion from this analysis is that while at the aggregate level (EU15) we do not see 'excessive' recourse to (bogus) self-employment, it clearly is an adjustment strategy that is used in those countries and by those groups whose access to the labour market is prevented or restricted by transitional measures.

---

14   The discrepancy between the findings for shares of employees and self-employed without own workers is explained by the higher proportion of nationals that are self-employed while employing workers of their own.

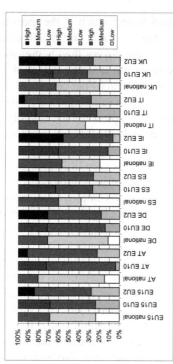

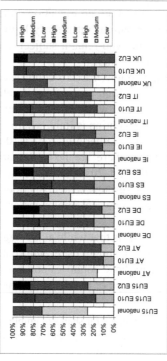

Figure 1.12   Comparison of skill levels, 2008Q1 and 2011Q1

Note: UK, EU2: No 'low' category in 2008.

Source: European Labour Force Survey, special extraction.

Skill Levels of Migrant Workers

Another controversial debate has surrounded the balance of skills levels of the migrants that different EU countries have managed to attract to their labour markets. Eurostat LFS data enable us to distinguish between three broad skill/ education categories: low, medium and high.

Starting again with the EU15[15] aggregate, Figure 1.12 shows that before the crisis EU8 workers were considerably overrepresented amongst medium-skilled (58 per cent compared with 45 per cent for natives) and correspondingly underrepresented, to approximately equal extents, amongst the low and high-skill categories. Strikingly, however, by the first quarter of 2011 the distribution among EU8 workers had shifted so as to be almost indistinguishable from that of nationals. (This partly reflects a very sharp drop in EU8 mid-level skills in the United Kingdom, which may partly be a statistical artefact (see Bettin in this volume). In contrast, the skill mix among EU2 workers remained fairly stable over the three-year crisis period; the relative size of the medium-skill level is comparable with that of EU8 at the start of the period, but the low-skilled are relatively overrepresented, with the high-skilled correspondingly underrepresented (in each case by around 5 percentage points) by the end of the period.

A number of remarks can be made about specific countries. In Germany, the skill distribution was fairly close to the composition for nationals. This does not tend to support the view that Germany predominantly attracted low-skilled migrants as an unintended result of its imposition of transitional measures. Austria experienced a contradictory development in terms of EU8 and EU2 migrants. Among EU8 workers the share of low- and of high-skilled workers declined and increased, respectively, implying an overall significant rise in skill levels, whereas the share of low-skilled workers from EU2 more than doubled over the three-year period. The success of the United Kingdom in attracting high-skilled workers emerges from these numbers, at least for 2011, although statistical concerns remain (see Bettin in this volume). Italy is characterised by a high share of medium skills amongst EU10 migrants, particularly given that among natives the low-skilled are, on these data, overrepresented. Spain has similar patterns. In Ireland, the high-skill shares increased substantially for all three population groups, which most likely reflects that the huge employment losses in that country were heavily skewed towards the low and medium skilled.

---

15   The above remarks concerning data also apply to these data: the EU15 data are more reliable. However, the number of missing cells is more limited than with regard to employment status, and greater confidence can be placed in the findings also for individual countries.

The picture on skills is rather mixed and it seems difficult to draw clear conclusions from these data. More specific studies are needed to shed light on the relevant issues (see Bettin, Hazans and Korpi in this volume).

3.4 Summary of the Main Trends of Intra-EU Labour Mobility during the Crisis

The overall stock of EU10 population in EU15 countries has continued to grow during the crisis (except in Ireland and Spain). This occurred in the face of declining overall employment in most countries (except Germany, Luxembourg and Poland) and seemingly contradicts previous expectations in the literature that deep recessions result in a setback in migration flows and the concrete forecasts that this would happen in the European post-crisis context. Against this overall trend, however, migration from EU8 and EU2 countries showed different dynamics during the crisis with temporary reductions for EU8 – and, more particularly, Polish – migrants but a growing intensity of EU2 labour mobility, particularly to Italy. To that extent there *has* been a tendency for the crisis to depress inflows, but this has been overridden by a surge of migrants from the two most recent accession countries.

Even this disaggregation conceals some important differences among individual sending countries, notably a decreasing migration intensity among Polish workers (with signs of return migration) and a partial substitution from other sending countries, especially from Romania and Bulgaria.

- Changes in receiving country composition were also observed, as receiving countries hard hit by the crisis (Spain and Ireland) saw a net decrease in EU10 migration stock, while all other receiving countries experienced further growth (especially Italy).
- This suggests that both push and pull factors were subject to dynamic changes in this turbulent period but it was stronger push factors from sending countries that seem to have been the more dominant force.

Looking at labour market outcomes of nationals, EU8 and EU2 migrants in receiving countries, the overall conclusion was that EU10 migrants were harder hit by the crisis and effectively acted as a buffer. We saw the following main trends:

- Both nationals and EU10 migrants experienced employment losses and unemployment increases in the vast majority of countries;
- While the employment rates of EU10 migrants tended to decrease more than those of nationals,
- the unemployment rates of EU10 nationals generally increased to a greater extent than those of nationals.
- The greater vulnerability of EU10 workers in the crisis reflects to a considerable extent the higher concentration of such workers in sectors

disproportionately badly affected by the slump in output; job losses were, for example, extremely heavy in construction, which shed more than four and a quarter million jobs and is a sector with a high concentration of EU10 workers.

- Another important finding is that recourse to (bogus) self-employment is an important adjustment strategy in those countries and by those groups whose access to the labour market is prevented or restricted by transitional measures.
- The picture with regard to skills is fairly mixed across countries and it is difficult to draw clear conclusions from these data.

In order to see the full picture, we also need to bear in mind that the total loss in employment between the second quarter of 2008 and the first quarter of 2011 was almost 7 million jobs, or 1.97 per cent of all workers and sectors in the EU15. In the same period, however, due to continuous inflows of EU10 workers the share of EU10 workers within EU15 total employment rose by 0.38 per cent points from 1.33 to 1.71 per cent. Thus, while EU10 workers were more affected in terms of decreasing employment and increasing unemployment than nationals, due to continuing EU10 migration inflow, in absolute terms EU10 employment on EU15 labour markets grew at a time when EU15 labour markets shrank and employment of nationals decreased.

4. Structure of the Book and Main Results of the Chapters

The first section of the book deals with different types of cross-border labour mobility, including commuting, that are important for recent intra-EU migration developments, and addresses the issue of skills–job mismatches. The individual chapters in this section highlight how skills mismatch appears among different groups of migrants, and in different economic and institutional contexts, as well as the relevant changes over time.

Chapter 2 by Giulia Bettin uses national labour force survey data to compare the socio-economic characteristics, skills composition and labour market outcomes of EU8 and EU2 migrants in Italy and the United Kingdom. One of the key findings is the striking difference between the skills composition of both immigrants and nationals between the United Kingdom and Italy, with both UK migrants and nationals having a considerably higher skills profile. However, as the majority of EU8 and EU2 immigrants in Italy have completed upper secondary education they are relatively more educated than nationals and non-EU immigrants.

Skills–jobs mismatch among migrant workers is substantial in both the United Kingdom and Italy, with disproportionate shares of migrant workers in both countries working in blue-collar jobs. Whereas similar levels of skills–jobs mismatch can be identified for migrants with medium skill-levels, the mismatch of high-skilled EU8 and EU2 migrants is significantly lower in Italy and the skills–

jobs match of high-skilled EU2 migrants is especially favourable. This might be explained by a selective migration policy in Italy with high-skilled and managerial jobs exempted for work permits for EU2 citizens and the low share of high-skilled nationals in Italy as compared to the United Kingdom.

The United Kingdom's overall stock of EU10 immigrants does not seem to have been negatively affected by the economic crisis. The stock of EU8 migrants has remained relatively constant while, despite the transitional measures, the number of EU2 migrants has increased further reflecting not least the dire economic conditions in the countries of origin (see also Heyes and Hyland in this volume). There are some indications that behind the stable EU8 stocks a redistribution of migrants might have taken place corresponding to return migration to Poland (see Fihel and Anacka in this volume) which has been compensated for by higher rates of migration from the Baltic states to the United Kingdom in line with the severe impact of the crisis in those countries (see Hazans in this volume).

Interesting differences emerge between EU8 and EU2 migrants to the United Kingdom with regard to labour market outcomes. Whereas employment rates of EU8 nationals were relatively stable between 2006 and 2010, despite the economic crisis, and unemployment remained below the national level, EU2 nationals experienced a fairly constant decrease in their employment rate and an increase in unemployment. This divergence could indeed be related to differences in return migration patterns, with Polish migrants – who make up the largest share of EU8 migrants to the United Kingdom – having some incentive to return to their home country, in contrast to EU2 and Baltic migrants, given the better economic developments in their home country.

Among EU10 migrants Romanians – with a long tradition of migration to Italy (not least because the two languages are similar) – are by far the most important group, with a share of more than 80 per cent. In fact, the number of EU2 nationals increased by about 60 per cent between 2006 and 2010 to almost 800,000, whereas the EU8 population remained relatively stable at a low level. The constantly growing stock of EU2 immigrants, despite increasing unemployment, illustrates that jobless status in Italy seems to be preferable to the present labour market (and welfare) situation in Romania and Bulgaria.

Chapter 3 by Kea Tijdens and Maarten van Klaveren uses data from *WageIndicator* – a self-administered online survey – to examine how skills and occupational characteristics of EU8 migrants compare with those of non-migrant workers within EU15 countries. An important finding is that only 65 per cent of migrant workers born in the EU10 and working in EU15 countries report a correct job–education match, which compares with 74 per cent of the whole sample and 72 per cent of all migrants. The empirical model confirms the finding that over-qualification is highest for migrants from EU10 countries working in EU15 countries. Over-education is also related to workers' vulnerability: the analysis shows that recent employment entrants – workers with poor bargaining power, such as trainees and workers with unemployment spells and women – are more likely to be over-educated. Moreover, migrant workers who arrived in the 'host country' in adulthood (>21) are considerably more likely to be over-qualified. This points to the lack of transparency of credentials but possibly also language deficiencies. The fact that not only first but also second generation migrants, as well as ethnic minorities, are more likely to be over-qualified also points to discriminatory behaviour on the part of employers.

Chapter 4 by Peter Huber makes use of data from the European Labour Force Survey 2006 and describes the extent and structure of cross-border commuting, focussing particularly on skills–job mismatch in the EU25. Cross-border commuters are compared to recent and established migrant workers and the findings show that cross-border commuting is important only in a small number of border regions with strong linguistic (for example, Belgium and France or Austria, Switzerland and Germany), historical (Czech Republic and Slovakia) or institutional (Austria–Hungary, with special arrangements) ties. Cross-border out-commuting exceeded 5 per cent of employment only in eight regions (three Slovak regions, Alsace-Lorraine in France, the Belgian Provinces of Luxemburg and Limburg, Freiburg in Germany and Vorarlberg in Austria). For the vast majority of NUTS2 regions, less than 0.5 per cent of the resident employed commute across borders. As out-commuting is higher in regions with low GDP per capita and high unemployment, it is not surprising that the share of cross-border out-commuters is higher in the EU10 than in the EU15. The majority of EU10 and EU15 commuting is concentrated in the EU15. Apart from the outlier of Luxemburg (where over one-third of the employed commute from other countries) the share of cross-border in-commuters exceeds 1 per cent of those employed in a workplace only in Belgium, Austria, the Netherlands and the Czech Republic (due to commuters from Slovakia).

Cross-border commuters are more often manufacturing workers, male and young than non-commuters and in comparison to established and recent migrants more often have medium-level, and less often high-level educational attainment. With regard to the match between education and jobs, cross-border commuters face bigger problems in utili*si*ng both their formally and informally acquired skills than established migrants, non-commuters and internal commuters. In comparison to recent migrants, however, they perform better. Problems of skill transfer among cross-border commuters and recent migrants in the EU seem to apply primarily to migrants and cross-border commuters from the EU10. While in the EU15, in all cases, mobility of cross-border commuters seems to significantly improve education–job matches, for cross-border commuters from the EU10 the opposite is true as they have significantly higher over-education risks and also significantly lower under-education risks than non-commuters. It is important to point out, however, that recent *migrants* from EU10 countries are even worse off than *commuters* from EU10 countries as regards over-qualification, which implies that cross-border commuting entails a lower degree of brain waste than migration for these countries.

Part II of this book looks at the extent and qualitative characteristics of migrant workers, with a specific focus on return migration against the background of the economic crisis.

Chapter 5 by Agnieszka Fihel and Marta Anacka estimates the scale of return migration to Poland and compares the socio-demographic structure of return migrants to the structure of non-returning emigrants. Typical returnees are middle-aged, rural dwellers with a low level of education: by contrast, younger people from cities and with higher education levels are more likely to settle down abroad.

Results from Poland's Central Statistical Office, using various data sources and looking at stocks, show that already in 2007 returns of Polish nationals started to outnumber the outflow and the phenomenon of return migration started to pick up. According to theses results returns have taken place from many destinations, regardless of geographical proximity. Large falls in stocks were evident in the United Kingdom, Ireland and Germany and smaller declines in Austria. In line with the deterioration of the economic situation, declines in the number of Polish nationals occurred much earlier in, for example, the United Kingdom and Ireland (2008) than in Germany and Austria (2009), whose labour markets were much less affected by the crisis. Countries such as Belgium, Spain and Sweden still saw the stocks of Poles somewhat increasing between the end of 2007 and 2009, emphasi*si*ng that Polish nationals remain mobile after leaving their home country and move from one destination to another, as has been shown for Polish migrants to Norway (Napierała and Trevena 2010).

Using the Labour Force Survey data, which contained a special module on migrants in the second quarter of 2008, the number of Polish returnees are estimated to have been 580,000 in the period 2004 (first quarter) to 2008 (second quarter), including 213,000 in 2007 alone. Returnees as defined in this chapter can also engage in circular mobility, however. Bettin's findings (in this volume) and newly released Polish data (Polish Statistical Office 2011) which indicate that net migration flow from Poland to the United Kingdom came to a halt, indeed, support the phenomenon of circular mobility.

Selectivity is observed with regard to level of education as more persons with a vocational education return than emigrate, whereas the share of people with university diplomas is higher among emigrants than returnees. This finding strongly suggests the importance of skills and qualifications for settling abroad but may also point to a rising demand for specific vocational skills on the Polish labour market. Whereas the share of emigrants coming from urban areas is larger than that from rural ones, with regard to returnees the opposite is true. The fact that the rural areas in question often had poor labour market characteristics indicates that improved labour market demand in the home country does not seem to be a major pull factor.

According to the authors a major motivating factor for returns is difficulty adapting to life abroad, with positive return selectivity of older and low-qualified persons with a rural return destination.

The analysis of the pooled data (covering 10 years) shows that some destination countries are rather 'settlement countries' (United States, United Kingdom and Ireland), whereas others (such as Germany) are rather characterised by temporary labour mobility. However, while returns from Germany were evenly distributed over the past decade – there is longer tradition of circular mobility between Germany and Poland, not least because of geographical proximity – outflows from the United Kingdom and Ireland started abruptly in 2007 when the economic situation worsened.

Chapter 6 by Mihails Hazans uses the Labour Force Survey data (2002–2009) for Latvia and Estonia to compare the profiles of temporary workers abroad (migrant workers) and return migrants, as well as the factors affecting mobility decisions, during the three migration waves: before EU accession, between accession and the crisis of 2008–2009 and in the crisis period. Data from Eurobarometer are used to *compare the* migration intentions of Latvian, Lithuanian and Estonian populations at the end of the 2009 (that is, after one year of recession). For Latvia, two representative surveys conducted in December 2010–February 2011 give further insight into the human capital of emigrants, as well as migration intentions and prevailing push factors after large-scale emigration during the first two years of the crisis. The primary focus of the chapter is on the skill level of movers, stayers and returnees.

Another question of specific interest for Latvia and Estonia is how the mobility behaviour of the Russian-speaking minority compares to that of the native population.

The findings demonstrate the role of pull and push factors in turbulent times both in the period of economic boom (when pull factors dominated) and during the crisis when push factors, especially unemployment in the sending country, played the main role (in Latvia also general dissatisfaction and loss of prospects).

Migrant characteristics show a differentiated response to changing conditions. Data showed that after accession economic emigrants from Estonia and Latvia featured a significantly lower proportion of tertiary educated persons, as well as ethnic minorities, especially non-citizens, in comparison with the pre-accession period. These findings reflect the lower costs and lower human capital threshold (in terms of skills, risk taking and so on) associated with labour migration, on the one hand, and the fact that Estonian and Latvian non-citizens (mostly Russians) are not covered by the legal provisions on free movement of labour within the EU on the other.

During the crisis, in comparison with the pre-crisis period, Latvian emigration intensified to a much larger extent than Estonian emigration. The author attributes this difference to the fact that the crisis in Latvia has been perceived by a majority of the population as a systemic – rather than just a financial – crisis, which was not the case in Estonia. Moreover, emigrants from Latvia were to a much larger extent than before oriented towards long-term or permanent emigration.

As regards return migration, university graduates were less likely to return than other groups of emigrants, while the low-skilled were overrepresented among returnees. Both for Latvia and Estonia, the crisis resulted in a sharp increase (or fall) of the selectivity index of returnees regarding low (or high) education level. This suggests that in the period of crisis, success or failure on foreign labour markets were the decisive factors for return (these results correspond to similar findings by Anacka and Fihel in this volume for Polish returnees).

Part III looks at policy implications of and responses to cross-border labour mobility in the EU after 2004.

Chapter 7 by Jason Heyes and Mary Hyland shows that the UK labour market showed signs of saturation from the crisis year of 2008, while Ireland experienced a radical reversal of migration trends during the crisis. The crisis in the United Kingdom meant that the previous dynamic growth of the EU8 population came to a halt in 2008 and started to decline slightly. At the same time, the inflow of EU2 migrants to the United Kingdom has grown despite restrictions and has resulted in a slight net increase of all EU10 nationals on the UK labour market. In Ireland, the number of EU10 nationals peaked in 2008 and had decreased by as much as 25 per cent by the end of 2010. The number of EU2 migrants remained at a very low level, reflecting, among other things, the effect of the transitional measures and the dramatically deteriorating labour market situation in Ireland.

The national trade union confederations of Ireland and the United Kingdom – the Irish Congress of Trade Unions (ICTU) and the Trades Union Congress (TUC), respectively – have both supported the principle of free movement of workers from the EU8 member states. They also objected to the Irish and UK governments' decision to restrict migrant workers' access to certain welfare benefits. The two union movements have, however, differed in their stances with regard to Romanian and Bulgarian migrant workers. While the TUC opposed the UK government's decision to restrict EU2 workers' access to the UK labour market, the ICTU supported the introduction of temporary transitional measures in Ireland.

The union movements in both countries have adopted an inclusive and 'rights-based' approach to immigration and have sought equal rights and entitlements for migrant workers. At the same time, they have also been concerned to ensure that migration does not lead to indigenous workers' pay and conditions being undermined. The UK and Irish trade unions differ somewhat in the way they have sought to apply policy positions, however. UK unions have focused on recruiting and organising within workplaces and communities but have had relatively little influence on government policy. Irish trade unions, by contrast, have been able to influence government policy on the introduction and implementation of legislation to protect migrant workers by way of the 'Towards 2016' social partnership agreement, reflecting the institutionalised social partnership that has characterised Irish industrial relations since 1987. However, the agreement has come under increasing pressure since the beginning of the economic downturn.

In Ireland and the United Kingdom, the rate of unionisation among migrant workers is lower than that of indigenous workers. In both countries, it has been recognised that traditional servicing approaches are insufficient to reach the majority of migrant workers or to serve their particular needs and so unions have begun to move towards a more proactive organ*is*ing approach that has, in some cases, involved creating links (or building upon established links) with community groups, NGOs and education providers. Also, a considerable amount of advice and guidance has been provided through web-based sources, in some cases in the migrants' own languages. A number of individual trade unions have established or supported advice and guidance centres and have also established their own community projects.

Chapter 8 by Line Eldring and Thorsten Schulten discusses the impact of post-enlargement migration on wages and wage setting in four destination countries which have different wage-setting models and took different approaches to the free movement of labour after 2004. In all these countries labour market and collective bargaining institutions played an important role in channelling the impact of migration on wages and wage setting.

In Germany, migrant workers are overrepresented in the low-wage sector, which is reflected in a substantial (unadjusted) wage gap with recent EU8 migrants, who earn only 75 per cent of the average native wage. This wage gap is suggestive (but not conclusive) of downward wage pressure. Given the transitional measures, any downward wage pressure has largely come via posting of workers. Along with some other factors – notably a more general decline in collective bargaining coverage – inward migration, and political concerns about its possible impact, have contributed to considerable policy and institutional changes. In particular, the German trade union movement has changed its position and is now campaigning actively for a statutory minimum wage. Also, the posted workers law (based on the EU directive) has been used to reinvigorate the use of legal extension of collective bargaining outcomes to entire sectors.

Despite transitional measures, Norway saw substantial inward migration post-2004, including by posted workers not covered by the transitional measures. Wage competition was initially strong. This led to the legal extension of collective agreements in construction, shipbuilding and agriculture, with a similar move in the cleaning sector under consideration. This marks a significant change in Norwegian industrial relations. Despite the policy measures there is considerable evidence that migrant workers and particularly posted workers have lower wages even within a given sector, implying downward wage pressure.

In Switzerland, the bilateral agreements with the EU on the free movement of labour had to be approved by a referendum, which gave left-wing parties and the trade union movement significant leverage. A number of key 'flanking measures' have subsequently been introduced. They include minimum wages and working conditions for posted workers, facilitation of the extension of collective agreements to the whole sector and the introduction of various monitoring and control instruments. These measures have contributed to a significant re-regulation of the Swiss labour market and have strengthened collective bargaining. The impact on domestic wages has therefore been fairly limited, largely avoiding additional pressure on the low-wage sector. The (unadjusted) migrant–native wage gap narrowed slightly between 2004 and 2008 although it remains significant(87.3 per cent).

The British industrial relations system had already been substantially deregulated and decentral*ised* in the 1980s. The statutory national minimum wage, introduced in 1997, was the key tool to prevent wage competition at the bottom of the labour market, given the lack of encompassing collective bargaining coverage and no provision for the legal extension of sectoral collective agreements. Despite the statutory minimum wage the (unadjusted) migrant–native wage gap is substantial, with EU8 workers earning only 67 per cent of the UK median. Migrants are also more likely to be paid (illegally) below the minimum wage.

The chapter by Eldring and Schulten illustrates that, with the opening of labour markets for EU8 and EU2 migrants, previously ignored problems related to low collective bargaining coverage rates have come to the surface, and the setting of new sectoral or national wage floors will affect all workers in national labour markets.

The recent European discussion around immigration policy has been based on the premise, implicit or explicit, that stricter selection of immigrants, primarily according to various labour market criteria, will produce a pool of skilled immigrants, simplify their economic integration and boost national economies.

Chapter 9 by Tomas Korpi seriously questions this assumption. It uses the International Adult Literacy Survey, which was conducted in the late 1990s, to look at the long-term evidence on international migration on the basis of a set of generic skills and earnings. The underlying hypothesis is that country variation in migration policies should lead to differences in the generic skills of immigrants to different countries. The results of this chapter raise questions regarding the general success of selective migration policies used by countries such as Canada and New Zealand. Despite their selective systems the skills of non-native speakers are not particularly high but roughly average. This indicates substantial difficulties in using immigration policy as a strategy to upgrade the labour force. Moreover, the indications of successful 'cherry-picking' by Canada, New Zealand (and Ireland) partly hinge on the availability of a large pool of English speakers. This in turn suggests that the possibilities for applying similar systems in other countries are limited. Indeed, the two main findings are that skills are important for the economic integration of immigrants, but there is no obvious link between national migration policies that target skilled migrants to different extents and integration success.

Korpi also presents evidence on the adjusted average native–immigrant earnings gap for the late 1990s, showing that immigrants are located on average about 5 percentage points below the median for natives. Countries vary significantly, although Canada, the United Kingdom, Ireland, New Zealand and the United States do not exhibit clear evidence of an immigrant–native earnings gap. In contrast, immigrants in Germany, Norway, Switzerland and Sweden earn markedly less than natives. The German and Norwegian earnings gaps are particularly large, at around 10 percentage points.

Taking the rich and varied finding of the various chapters of this book together, it is evident that East–West post-enlargement EU migration is a highly differentiated process with diverse implications. It includes various forms of mobility in a rapidly changing economic and regulatory environment. Since the 2004 and 2007 enlargement waves, push and pull factors affecting migrants have been subject to rapid and often contradictory changes. The economic and wage convergence between source and target countries that was characteristic of the initial period after accession has been interrupted by the crisis. However, as regards the impact of the latter, the dividing line has not been between source and target countries but between a group of European countries severely affected by the crisis (particularly the Baltic countries, Spain and Ireland) and another group (for example, Germany and Poland) that has been much less affected.

It evident that intra-EU labour mobility is much more reactive to changes in the environment than was the case with previous migration waves. The shock of the crisis was not just a general test of labour markets throughout Europe but gave us an insight into the relative position of migrants within it. Although both target and source country labour markets have performed diversely, (short-term) migrant labour has acted as a buffer in most target countries.

Over-education proved to be a clear phenomenon for EU10 migrants, with a number of explanations. EU10 migrants characteristically have higher educational attainment than non-EU migrants and often also higher than the local population in the target countries. This is a new phenomenon in migration history. The jobs–skills mismatch and thus the under-utili*sa*tion of human capital which has been highlighted in several chapters of this book points to one of the biggest challenges facing intra-EU labour mobility in recent years. Labour mobility in post-enlargement Europe is still relatively new, but it is of great concern that we see little sign that the associated waste of human resources and inefficient cross-border labour allocation rapidly declines as migration duration increases. On a more optimistic note there is some evidence that policy action by governments, but also by actors such as trade unions, can positively improve migration outcomes.

Annex 1

Data Sources and Definitions: An Overview

The most commonly used definitions of migrant workers are by country of birth and nationality: migrant workers are persons with a different nationality or place of birth than the country in which they are working. In some cases migrant status is also defined by country of birth of parents (second or third generation migrants). The place of birth definition also includes naturalised migrants. The European

Labour Force Survey contains information on both nationality and country of birth and the outcomes with regard to, for example, employment rates do not on average vary strongly between the two definitions.[16] Also, differences between the two definitions seem to be more relevant for extra-EU27 migrants than for EU27 (and EU15) nationals.

A common problem is that data sources usually do not allow us to distinguish between migrants who have been in the country for a long period and those who arrived only recently.

In our volume the definition of migrant worker is largely shaped by the available information in the respective data sources. Although it was not entirely possible to stick to one definition for the whole book, the majority of chapters define migrants in terms of country of birth.

A Note on Data Sources

There is no single perfect data source that makes it possible to capture intra-EU migration movements. This is due to administrative problems with tracking and registering cross-border labour mobility but also due to different, often incompatible definitions between countries.

As an alternative to population registers, the European Labour Force Surveys are widely used in research on cross-border labour mobility (see in addition to this introduction the chapters by Bettin, Huber, Hazans and Anacka and Fihel). Even though they have a number of limitations (see below) they make it possible to analyse population movements and the main developments on the labour market for national and migrant workers as they use comparable methodology in all EU countries and contain both detailed questions on employment experience and information on nationality and country of birth. Also, the fact that they are regularly conducted and that case numbers are comparatively large render them an attractive source for research on cross-border labour mobility. As respondents are interviewed repeatedly for several quarters (rolling panel),[17] to a limited degree the Labour Force Survey data make possible an examination of stocks of migrants at a given point in time, as well as flows. The 2008 European Labour Force Survey included a special module on migration with larger case numbers and more encompassing information on the issue. The European Labour Force Survey also allows researchers to capture commuter migration for most countries as it contains information on place of residence and place of work (see the chapter by Huber in this volume).

However, a number of problems arise when comparing cross-border labour mobility and the characteristics of migrant workers between European countries.

---

16   The special 2008 module on migrant workers also contains information on country of birth of parents.

17   The technical features (for example, sampling design) of the national surveys vary (for details, refer to Eurostat 2011).

Some migration flows are not picked up by survey data; the most obvious example is undocumented work. Also short-term migration (for example, seasonal employment) is unlikely to be picked up in survey data because migrant workers who stay for only a limited period of time are usually not captured by standard survey procedures.

Data deficiencies with regard to the migrant population are even more evident when we consider return migration which is usually recorded only when taking place by way of special programmes. Information on return migration can also be derived from population censuses but they take place very infrequently and are therefore not a suitable monitoring instrument. Anacka and Fihel in this volume use the pseudo-panel structure of the Labour Force Survey to detect return migrants. A disadvantage of this strategy, however, is that it underestimates both outward and return migration.

Other data can derive from specific administrative sources. Recent intra-EU migration flows are, for example, in some cases recorded by specific obligatory registration schemes such as the Worker Registration Scheme in the United Kingdom, which is used for monitoring purposes (see the chapter by Heyes and Hyland in this volume).

However, these schemes often lack enforcement mechanisms, which leads to underestimation of inflows, and also they do not pick up outward migration flows or return migration, which can lead to overestimation of the stock figures. The countries that are currently making use of schemes specifically geared to migrant workers will have to abolish them once the period in which transitional measures can be applied is over. Also, data from passenger registration and survey schemes (at ports and airports) has in some cases been used to analyse cross-border mobility (see, for example, Kaczmarczyk 2006; Office for National Statistics 2011).

Lately, the internet has also been exploited to collect data on, among other things, migrant workers. An example is the comparative *WageIndicator* dataset which is derived from a voluntary web survey about working conditions and wages (Tijdens and Klaveren in this volume). Because of the voluntary nature of this survey questions of representativeness emerge, however. Also, migrants with insufficient language skills – a group likely to suffer from particular disadvantages – will be either excluded from the survey or give incomplete or wrong answers. Information on migrants is also included in more specialised surveys such as the International Adult Literacy Survey used in this volume by Korpi.

To capture the characteristics of migrant workers, so-called mirror statistics – administrative records or survey data in *receiving* countries – usually have to be used as there are insufficient incentives to deregister and outward migration is thus severely underestimated in sending countries.

Smaller-scale surveys of migrant workers in specific localities can solve some of the above problems and provide more detailed information on the labour market situation of migrant workers. The downside is that the results are usually not representative: in the absence of encompassing records of migrant workers in specific localities researchers usually have to resort to the 'snowball method' (word-of-mouth) to gain access to this group. There are possibilities, however, to improve the representativeness of these studies. A good example of a smaller-scale survey using an improved version of the snowball method is the 'Polonia I Oslo' study (compare Friberg and Tyldum 2007).

The data constraints discussed in this sub-section imply that any comparative analyses on migrant workers require cautious interpretation.

Definition of Qualifications and Skills and Related Data Issues

In comparative studies the International Standard Classification of Education (ISCED), originally designed by UNESCO in the early 1970s and since then regularly revised, is commonly used. It contains seven education levels, ranging from pre-primary education (level 0) to the second stage of tertiary education (level 6). Commonly – and also in the European Labour Force Survey – the seven levels are bundled into three education levels: pre-primary, primary and lower secondary education (ISCED 0–2), upper secondary and post-secondary non-tertiary education (ISCED 3–4) and tertiary education (ISCED 5–6).[18] Clearly, this is a fairly broad classification that does not enable us to go into much depth in analysing skills levels. Moreover, particularly with regard to migrant workers it is not always evident which is their correct qualification level. When large numbers of migrant workers are found in the category 'other qualification' – as is the case for the UK labour force survey (see Bettin in this volume) – it may be a better strategy to use years of education or age when full-time education was finished instead of the ISCED classification. Years of education are also used in the chapter by Korpi who uses a specific skills measure: literacy. It is important to point out that particularly low-skilled migrants are more likely to be underrepresented in (labour force) survey data due to language competence or because they are more likely to be irregular or seasonal workers.

With regard to occupations, in comparative studies the International Standard Classification for Occupations (ISCO) conceived by the International Labour Organisation (ILO) is the most commonly used classification. ISCO was last revised in 2008. While there are very detailed ISCO categories, the least detailed categorisation, more suitable for comparative analysis and where case numbers may be limited, ranges from elementary occupations to professional, technical and related workers and contains 10 groups.[19] The most basic distinction is between blue- and white-collar workers (see Bettin in this volume). Some of the authors in this volume link the information on educational attainment (ISCED) and that on occupations (ISCO) in order to measure education–job mismatch (see particularly Huber and Tijdens and Klaveren in this volume). ILO (1987) and OECD (2007)

---

18   For more information on the ISCED methodology and typology refer to: http://www.uis.unesco.org/ev.php?ID=7433_201&ID2=DO_TOPIC.

19   For more information on the ISCO methodology and typology refer to: http://www.ilo.org/public/english/bureau/stat/isco/index.htm.

suggest different ways of linking education and occupation information (for a discussion and comparison of the two methods see Huber in this volume).

Some surveys also include a self-assessed question on skills–job matches. An example in our book is the *WageIndicator* dataset analysed by Tijdens and Klaveren which enables the authors to compare results by different definitions of skills–job matches, including subjective self-assessment, the linking of ISCED and ISCO, and a measure of over-education derived from theoretical considerations concerning the lack of transparency of credentials and lower language abilities.

Bibliography

Alvarez-Plata, P., H. Brücker, and B. Siliverstovs (2003) 'Potential migration from Central and Eastern Europe into the EU-15 – An update', Berlin: DIW.

Ahearne, A., H. Brücker, Z. Darvas and J. von Weizsäcker (2009) 'Cyclical dimensions of labour mobility after EU enlargement', WP 2009/2, Brussels: Bruegel. Available at: http://www.econ.core.hu/file/download/mtdp/MTDP0910.pdf.

Ambrosini, J.W, K. Mayr, G. Peri and D. Radu (2011) 'The selection of migrants and returnees: evidence from Romania and implications', research paper, University of California, Davis. Available at: http://www.econ.ucdavis.edu/faculty/gperi/Papers/return_ro_march_13_2011.pdf.

Barro, R., and X. Sala-i-Martin (1991) 'Convergence across states and regions', Brooking Papers on Economic Activity, 22(1), 107–82.

Borjas, G.J. (1989) 'Economic theory and international migration', *International Migration Review*, 23(3), 457–85.

Borjas, G.J. (1995) 'The economic benefits from immigration', *Journal of Economic Perspectives*, 9(2), 3–22.

Dølvik, E. and L. Eldring (2008) *Mobility of labour from new EU states to the Nordic region – Development trends and consequences*, Copenhagen: Nordic Council of Ministers. Available at: http://www.norden.org/en/publications/publications/2008-537/at_download/publicationfile.

Drinkwater, S., J. Eade and M. Garapich (2009) 'Poles apart? EU enlargement and the labour market outcomes of immigrants in the United Kingdom', *International Migration*, Vol. 47(1), 161–90.

Dustmann, C. and Y. Weiss (2007) 'Return migration. theory and empirical evidence from the UK', *British Journal of Industrial Relations*, Vol. 45(2), 236–56.

Clark, K. and S. Drinkwater (2008) 'The labour-market performance of recent migrants', *Oxford Review of Economic Policy*, Vol. 24(3), 495–516.

European Commission AMECO database.

European Commission (2011) Commission decision of 11 August 2011 authorising Spain to temporarily suspend the application of Articles 1 to 6 of Regulation (EU) No 492/2011 of the European Parliament and of the Council on freedom of movement for workers within the Union with regard to Romanian workers (2011/503/EU), Official Journal of the European Union L 207/23.

European Integration Consortium (2009) *Labour mobility within the EU in the context of enlargement and the functioning of the transitional arrangements*, Nuremberg.

Eurostat (2011 edition) Labour Force Surveys in the EU, candidate and EFTA countries: Main characteristics of national surveys, Methodologies and Working Papers. Available at: http://epp.eurostat.ec.europa.eu/cache/ITY_OFFPUB/KS-RA-11-010/EN/KS-RA-11-010-EN.PDF.

Fellmer, S. and H. Kolb (2009) 'EU labour migration: Government and social partner policies in Germany, in B. Galgóczi, J. Leschke and A. Watt (eds), *EU labour migration since enlargement: Trends, impacts and policies*, Aldershot: Ashgate.

Fihel, A., P. Kaczmarczyk, N. Wolfeil and A. Zylicz (2009) 'Brain drain, brain gain and brain waste', in European Integration Consortium, *Labour mobility within the EU in the context of enlargement and the functioning of the transitional arrangements – country studies*, Nuremberg.

Fihel, A. and M. Okólski (2009) 'Dimensions and effects of labour migration to EU countries: the case of Poland', in B. Galgóczi, J. Leschke and A. Watt (eds), *EU labour migration since enlargement: trends, impacts and policies*, Aldershot: Ashgate.

Friberg, J.H. and G. Tyldum (2007) 'Polonia i Oslo. En studie av arbeids- og levekår blant polakker i hovedstadsområdet', Fafo-rapport 27, Oslo. Available at: http://www.fafo.no/pub/rapp/20027/20027.pdf.

Galgóczi, B., J. Leschke and A. Watt (2009) *EU labour migration since enlargement: trends, impacts and policies*, Aldershot: Ashgate.

Grogger, J. and G.H. Hanson (2008) 'Income maximization and the selection and sorting of international migrants', NBER Working Paper No. W13821. Available at: http://papers.ssrn.com/sol3/papers.cfm?abstract_id=1093659.

Hardarson, O. (2006) 'The 2008 Ad hoc module of the EU-LFS: Describing and analysing migrants, opportunities and limitations'. Joint UNECE/Eurostat Work session on migration statistics organised in collaboration with UNFPA, Edinburgh, Scotland, 20–22 November 2006, Working Paper 12. Available at: http://www.unece.org/stats/documents/ece/ces/ge.10/2006/wp.12.e.pdf.

Hardy, J. (2010) 'Brain drain, brain gain or brain waste: East–west migration after enlargement', in Heinrich Böll Stiftung (2010) *Mobility and inclusion: managing labour migration in Europe*, Dossier, pp. 48–54. Available at: http://www.migration-boell.de/downloads/migration/DOSSIER_Mobility_and_Inclusion.pdf.

Hazans, M. (2008) 'Post-enlargement return migrants' earnings premium: Evidence from Latvia', Working Paper Series, University of Latvia and BICEPS. Available at: http://ssrn.com/abstract=1269728.

Huber, P. and K. Nowotny (2009) 'Regional effects of labour mobility', in European Integration Consortium (2009), *Labour mobility within the EU in the* context of enlargement and the functioning of the transitional arrangements – background reports, Nuremberg.

Ivlevs, A. (2007a) 'Country study: Denmark', in European Integration Consortium (2009), *Labour mobility within the EU in the context of enlargement and the functioning of the transitional arrangements – country studies*, Nuremberg.

Ivlevs, A. (2007b) 'Country study: Sweden', in European Integration Consortium (2009), *Labour mobility within the EU in the context of enlargement and the functioning of the transitional arrangements – country studies*, Nuremberg.

IZA (2008) *Geographic mobility in the European Union: Optimising its economic and social benefits*, Research Report No. 19: Bonn: IZA. Available at: http://www.iza.org/en/webcontent/publications/reports/report_pdfs/iza_report_19.pdf.

Kahanec, M. and F. Zimmermann (2010) *EU labour markets after post-enlargement migration*, Berlin/Heidelberg: Springer.

Kaczmarczyk, P. (2006) 'Highly skilled migration from Poland and other CEE countries – myths and reality', Reports & Analyses 17/06, Center for International Relations. Available at: http://csm.org.pl/fileadmin/files/Biblioteka_CSM/Raporty_i_analizy/2006/Pawe%C5%82%20Kaczmarczyk_Highly%20skilled%20migration%20from%20Poland%20.pdf.

Kaczmarczyk, P. and M. Okólski (2008) 'Demographic and labour-market impacts of migration on Poland', *Oxford Review of Economic Policy*, Vol. 24(3), 599–624.

Krings, T. (2009) 'A race to the bottom? Trade unions, EU enlargement and the free movement of labour', *European Journal of Industrial Relations*, Vol. 15(1), 49–69.

Layard, R., O. Blanchard, R. Dornbush and P. Krugman (1992) *East–West migration: The alternatives*, Cambridge, MA: MIT Press.

McKenzie, D. and H. Rapoport (2008) 'Network effects and the dynamics of migration: The role of migration networks', *Journal of Development Economics*.

Napierała, J. and P. Trevena (2010) 'Patterns and determinants of sub-regional migration: a case study of Polish construction workers in Norway', in R. Black, G. Engbersen, M. Okólski and C. Pantiru (eds), *A continent moving west*. Amsterdam: Amsterdam University Press, 51–71.

OECD (2007) 'Immigrant health workers in OECD countries in the broader context of highly skilled migration', *International Migration Outlook*, SOPEMI, Paris: OECD, pp. 161–228.

OECD (2009) *International Migration Outlook*, SOPEMI, Paris: OECD.

OECD (2010) *International Migration Outlook*, SOPEMI, Paris: OECD.

Office for National Statistics (2011) *Migration Statistics Quarterly Report August 2011*, Statistical Bulletin. Available at: http://www.ons.gov.uk/ons/dcp171778_223724.pdf.

Petersen, P. and M. Pytlikova (2008) 'EU enlargement: migration flows from Central and Eastern Europe into the Nordic countries – exploiting a natural experiment', Department of Economics, Working Paper 08-2. Available at: http://www.hha.dk/nat/wper/08-29_marp.pdf.

Polish Statistical Office (September 2011) *Informacja o rozmiarach i kierunkach emigracji z Polskiw latach 2004–2010.*

Rangelova, R. (2009) 'Labour migration from east to west in the context of European Union integration', *South-East Europe Review*, 1/2009, 33–56.

Wickramasekara, P. (2002) *Policy responses to skilled migration: Retention, return and circulation*, Geneva: ILO.

Data Sources

AMECO (Annual macro-economic online database): http://ec.europa.eu/economy _finance/db_indicators/ameco/index_en.htm.

European Labour Force Survey, online database: http://epp.eurostat.ec.europa.eu/ portal/page/portal/labour_market/introduction.

Web Sources

International Labour Organisation (ILO): International Standard Classification of Occupations: http://www.ilo.org/public/english/bureau/stat/isco/index.htm.

UNESCO Institute for Statistics: International Standard Classification of Education – ISCED: Comparing education systems globally: http://www.uis.unesco.org/ ev.php?ID=7433_201&ID2=DO_TOPIC.

European Commission, Employment, Social Affairs and Inclusion: Enlargement – transitional provisions: http://ec.europa.eu/social/main.jsp? catId=466&langId=en.

PART I
Different Types of Cross-border Labour Mobility and Skills–Job Mismatch

PART I

Chapter 2

Migration from the Accession Countries to the United Kingdom and Italy: Socio-economic Characteristics, Skills Composition and Labour Market Outcomes

Giulia Bettin

1. Introduction

The 2004 and 2006 enlargements represented a central point in the ongoing debate on the economic and social consequences of international migration in Europe. The number of resident citizens from the EU8 (Czech Republic, Estonia, Hungary, Latvia, Lithuania, Poland, Slovakia and Slovenia) and the EU2 (Bulgaria and Romania) in the original EU15 has increased by roughly 1.1 million: from 900,000 in 2003, it rose to about 2 million in 2007 (European Commission 2008). However, the shares of non-EU nationals and other EU15 citizens residing in the EU15 are still definitely higher.

In 2004, a few countries among the old Member States (Ireland, Sweden, United Kingdom) granted immediate free access to their labour markets to workers from the EU8, while the restrictive measures applied elsewhere cease in 2011 at the latest. When Bulgaria and Romania entered the EU in 2007, only Sweden and Finland immediately opened their labour markets; the rest of the EU15 adopted restrictions that in most cases are still operating.

If these policies resulted in legal limitations on East–West mass flows in the enlarged EU, economic incentives to migrate have been severely affected by the recent economic crisis, too, due to the rising unemployment rates in European labour markets. According to Papademetriou et al. (2010), net immigration to the EU fell by 41 per cent between 2008 and 2009. In Spain, overall EU inflows fell by two-thirds, while in Ireland immigration from the new member states dropped 60 per cent. A large decrease occurred also in all relevant indicators of illegal migration (apart from asylum applications) in the first half of 2009[1] (Frontex, 2009).

---

1   Also the US Department of Homeland Security reported that the number of apprehensions at the southern border with Mexico has fallen by almost two-fifths since

The toll imposed by economic recessions cannot simply be reduced to earnings losses due to unemployment because it often translates into long-term unemployment conditions and possibly into situations of poverty and severe deprivation. Migrants are likely to represent one of the categories most affected by the crisis. Due to low educational attainment, but also to the difficulty of transferring human capital at international level, in many host countries they account for a large share of the low-skilled workforce that is easier to replace compared to trained qualified workers. Moreover, the involvement in cyclical industries and occupations and in general their role as temporary workforce, together with possible discriminatory practices in hiring and layoffs and less secure contractual agreements, may account for a higher level of vulnerability during recessions (OECD 2009). Consequences are not limited to immigrants and households living in the host countries, but involve also relatives left in the country of origin who often rely on remittances to improve their standard of living.[2]

The purpose of this chapter is to shed light on what is currently happening to the immigrant population (and the immigrant workforce, specifically) in two countries of the EU15: United Kingdom and Italy.

The United Kingdom has traditionally been a country of immigration thanks to its high level of economic development and former colonial empire. Italy, on the other hand, had a long tradition as a country of emigration, mainly to the US, Australia, Latin America and the rest of continental Europe and started to receive the first migration inflows only at the end of the 1980s. While the United Kingdom granted immediate free access to its labour market to workers from the EU8, the Italian government instead decided to apply a transitional arrangement that was finally removed in July 2006. In both countries, transitional restrictions for EU2 employees are still in force and workers need a work permit to enter the labour market. In Italy, occupations in certain sectors or under certain conditions (agriculture, hotels and tourism, domestic work, care services, construction, engineering, managerial and high-skilled jobs, seasonal work) do not require a work permit. In the United Kingdom, the employer needs to apply for a work permit and Romanian and Bulgarian employees for an 'Accession worker card'. Restrictions based on quota schemes for low-skilled workers in the agricultural and food processing sectors still apply, whereas skilled workers can work if they qualify for a work permit, or under the Highly Skilled Migrant Programme. Self-employed immigrants are allowed to work in both countries without the need for a specific permit (see Directive 2006/123/EC on services in the internal market).

The different backgrounds in terms of migration history and the different migration policies adopted in the two countries allow for an interesting comparison. Using data from the National Labour Force Surveys, socio-economic

---

2007, showing the global dimension of the crisis (www.dhs.gov/xlibrary/assets/statistics/publications/enforcement_ar_2009.pdf).

2   Total remittance inflows towards developing countries decreased by 6 per cent between 2008 and 2009, from 336 to 316 billion US$ (Ratha et al. 2010).

characteristics of EU8 and EU2 immigrants are investigated to understand the differences between the two groups inside each country but also to highlight possible common features compared to non-EU nationals. In particular, the size of immigrant population, age, gender and skill composition, as well as labour market outcomes of immigrants will be discussed.

The second section provides a detailed description of the data and of the main variables employed in the analysis for both countries. The third and the fourth sections respectively present evidence from the United Kingdom and Italy, while in the fifth section a joint discussion of the specialisation patterns of immigrant groups across economic branches of activity is offered. The final section summarizes the results from the whole analysis, highlights the main differences between the two host countries and concludes.

2. Data Sources and Definitions

As in many other empirical analyses concerning immigration to the EU15, the data employed here come from the National Labour Force Surveys.[3] The UK Quarterly Labour Force Survey (QLFS) is conducted by the Office for National Statistics through a systematic random sample design which provides adequate coverage and sample sizes for analysing the immigrant population. The Italian Institute of Statistics (ISTAT) introduced similar strategies in 2004 to collect representative data on the foreign-born population for the Italian QLFS.[4]

Questionnaires for both surveys cover a wide range of topics, such as earnings, employment situation and socio-economic characteristics, to offer a detailed picture of the interviewees' labour market experience.

The period considered here extends from the first quarter of 2006 to the second quarter of 2010. Such a time span is useful to obtain hints about the effects of the EU's Eastern enlargement, but also about the impact of the recent economic crisis on immigrant populations in the United Kingdom and Italy.

In the following analysis, immigrants are identified on the basis of their nationality. The reference immigrant population is therefore represented by non-nationals residing in the country aged 15 and over.[5] Characteristics of nationals (British and Italians, respectively) are also reported to allow for comparison.

---

3   Both the UK and the Italian Labour Force Survey are part of the European Labour Force Survey.

4   All elaborations on the data from the ISTAT Quarterly Labour Force Survey (2006–2010) were conducted at the ISTAT 'Laboratorio per l'Analisi dei Dati ELEmentari' within the framework of the law on statistical confidentiality and personal data protection. The results and the opinions expressed in this chapter are the sole responsibility of the author and by no means represent official statistics.

5   The only exceptions are Table 2.2 and Table 2.5 where the age class from 0 to 14 years is also considered.

Based on the nationality criterion, four major immigrant groups are identified: EU15 nationals, EU8 nationals, EU2 nationals and non-EU nationals.[6]

Specific definitions concerning the labour market situation are adopted: the employment rate is calculated as the percentage of employed people in the working age population; the unemployment rate is defined as the percentage of unemployed people in the labour force; the activity or participation rate is defined as the percentage of the labour force in the working age population. The labour force is represented by people of working age who are actively employed or seeking employment, while the working age population is in turn defined as people in the 15 to 64 age bracket. Since the data sources considered here are Labour Force Surveys, the employment status of each individual is based on self-assessment.[7]

Information on immigrants' educational attainment is coded differently for the two countries. While in the Italian QLFS there is complete coverage of the immigrant population with education variables, in the United Kingdom QLFS the information on immigrants' education is not fully reliable since in many cases a generic reference to 'other qualifications'[8] is reported, without any further specification. This forced us to exploit the variable referring to the age at which individuals completed full-time education to proxy the educational level (Saleheen and Shadforth 2006). The minimum age for leaving school is 16 in the United Kingdom, and the standard age for graduating from higher education is 21. This schedule is likely to vary across countries but based on the UK experience people are divided into those who left full-time education before 16 years of age, those who left full-time education between the ages of 16 and 20 and those who left after age 21. Roughly speaking, the first category includes individuals with an incomplete schooling, the second those who completed secondary school and the third those who completed a degree. This classification is clearly far from accurate since it does not take into account the fact that individuals may continue education on a part-time basis or, for various reasons, may go through schooling levels faster or slower than usual. However, it gives more hints concerning immigrants' situation than what the recorded highest level of education would do.

In the Italian LFS the situation is much simpler and the educational level is coded using three different categories: up to lower secondary education (ISCED

6   The EU15 includes Austria, Belgium, Denmark, Finland, France, Germany, Greece, Ireland, Italy, Luxembourg, Netherlands, Portugal, Spain, Sweden and the UK. The EU8 includes the Czech Republic, Estonia, Hungary, Latvia, Lithuania, Poland, Slovakia and Slovenia. The EU2 includes Bulgaria and Romania.

7   Respondents could classify themselves as in employment, ILO unemployed or inactive. The 'unemployed' include all people that were without work, currently available for work and seeking work, in accordance with the definitions of the International Labour Organization (ILO).

8   See variable *hiqual8* from the survey. Saleheen and Shadforth (2006) show that in 2005 nearly 60 per cent of new immigrants were allocated to the 'Other qualification' category.

categories 1 and 2), upper secondary education (ISCED 3) and tertiary education (ISCED 5 and 6).

Workers are classified according to the skill contents of their job into white-collar and blue-collar: white-collar jobs include managerial, professional administrative and secretarial occupations, while blue-collar jobs essentially consist of manual occupations. Furthermore, employees are distinguished from self-employed workers.[9]

The last part of the chapter focuses on the distribution of employed immigrants across different branches of activity. For this purpose, economic sectors have been aggregated in terms of eleven major groups: 1. Agriculture, forestry and fishing; 2. Manufacturing, energy and water; 3. Construction; 4. Wholesale, retail and motor trade; 5. Hotels and restaurants; 6. Transport and communication; 7. Financial intermediation; 8. Real estate, renting and business activities; 9. Public administration; 10. Education and health; and 11. Other services.[10]

3. The UK Experience

In 2004, the United Kingdom was one of the few countries that from the outset allowed EU8 workers to move freely across national borders. This certainly had a strong effect on the inflows from the new member states, that rapidly increased after enlargement while being relatively stable before it (Boeri and Brücker 2005; Barrell et al. 2007).

Figure 2.1 shows that the total number of immigrants aged 15 and over increased by 30 per cent from almost 3 to 4 million between 2006 and 2010. There seems to be a seasonal component in the overall trend, since a drop was cyclically registered every year in the third quarter. When looking at the trend for the different groups, this cyclical component is more evident for immigrants from the new EU Member States compared to non-EU nationals.

The explanation is probably related to their geographical proximity to the United Kingdom compared to third countries, that allows for higher rates of seasonal and circular migration, and also to the fact that immigrants from these countries can move freely across European borders. The largest drop was in the second quarter of 2009 (–4 per cent with respect to the first quarter of 2009) but afterwards the trend became positive again and the size of the overall stock of immigrants does not seem to be particularly affected by the global economic crisis. Despite the common approach of Ireland and the United Kingdom to the 2004 enlargement in

---

9   The classification of white- and blue-collars is recovered respectively from the variable *sc2kmmj* in the UK QLFS and from the variable *c9* in the Italian QLFS, while employee/self-employed status refers to the variable *stat* in the UK data and to the variable *dipind* in the Italian data.

10   This classification is recovered respectively from the variable *inds07m* in the UK QLFS and from the variable *cat12* in the Italian QLFS.

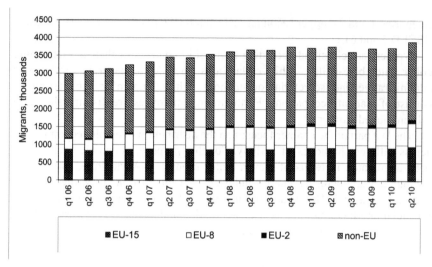

Figure 2.1   Total number of immigrants in the United Kingdom by nationality groups, 2006–2010

Source: Author's calculations based on data from the UK QLFS, 2006–2010.

terms of labour market regulation, Barrett and Kelly (2010) show that, differently from the United Kingdom, the stock of immigrants in Ireland reached a peak at the end of 2007 and then constantly declined, with a fall from the peak of almost 13 per cent at the end of 2009 due to the worsening of economic conditions in Ireland.

Non-EU nationals represent more than half of the total immigrant population. The share of EU8 citizens in the whole immigrant population rose from 10 per cent in 2006 to around 17 per cent in 2010, while the share of EU2 citizens, while representing a minor group, increased significantly from 0.7 per cent to 2.4 per cent of the total immigrant population.

When looking at individual nationalities of new EU citizens (Table 2.1), the increasing trend is far more evident. Fihel and Okólski (2009) show that, while the first destination for Polish migrants was Germany prior to EU enlargement, after 2004 the leading role as host country was assumed by the United Kingdom. Polish and Baltic immigrants (respectively 456,000 and 132,000 people in 2010) were indeed the most strongly represented groups at the beginning of 2006 and together still represent more than 75 per cent of total immigration from Eastern EU member states in the United Kingdom. However, it is interesting to notice that the largest increase in absolute terms involves the stock of Romanians, which has risen by 854 per cent in the past four years. In particular, since the onset of the crisis (q1 2008) the stock of Polish migrants has been relatively constant, while the number of Romanians and Baltic immigrants kept on increasing due to the dramatic economic conditions in the countries of origin.

Table 2.1   Total number of immigrants in the United Kingdom from the new EU member states by country of origin, aged 15+ (thousands)

	Q1 2006	Q2 2010
Baltic States	54.2	132.0
Bulgaria	15.1	29.1
Czech Republic	21.1	20.2
Hungary	8.7	32.4
Poland	189.5	456.3
Romania	6.6	62.9
Slovakia	25.6	28.5
Slovenia	0.5	1.8
	267.2	631.3

Source: Author's calculation with data from the UK QLFS, first quarter 2006 and second quarter 2010.

To get an idea of the impact of the economic crisis on the labour market experience of immigrants, it is useful to examine indicators such as employment, unemployment and activity rates. Clearly, when referring to these indicators one must keep in mind that the full picture regarding the labour market situation of immigrants might be hard to pick up due to the fact that unemployed individuals could have a higher probability of moving back to their country of origin. Within our data framework the rate of return migration cannot be quantified, and this surely affects employment statistics, particularly in the context of a global recession that hit both source and destination countries.

Employment rates for UK nationals, EU8, EU2 and non-EU citizens are reported in Figure 2.2.[11]

The impact of the economic crisis is visible: the rate for UK nationals declined by almost 3 percentage points between 2008 and 2010, from over 73 per cent to 70.5 per cent. While the rates for non-EU immigrants have been systematically lower, EU8 and EU2 immigrants showed higher rates compared to UK nationals, but with very different trends. The employment rate of EU8 nationals was fairly stable between 2006 and 2010 despite the economic crisis, ranging from 81 to 84 per cent; EU2 nationals, in contrast, experienced a rather constant decrease[12] in

---

11   Activity rates show exactly the same trends; the figure is not reported in the text for the sake of brevity.

12   The only exception is the third quarter of 2008 when the employment rate for the EU2 peaked at 91 per cent, but from the following quarter it started to diminish again.

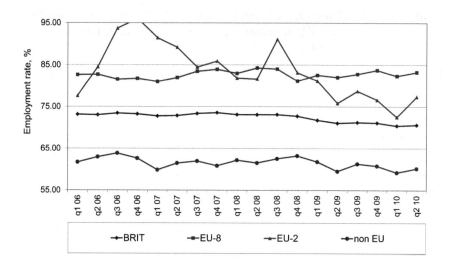

Figure 2.2   Employment rates in the United Kingdom by nationality group, 2006–2010

Source: Author's calculations based on data from the UK QLFS, 2006–2010.

their employment rate from a peak in the last quarter of 2006 (almost 96 per cent) to a minimum value of 73 per cent at the beginning of 2010.

In parallel, EU2 nationals' unemployment rate peaked at 10.8 per cent at the beginning of 2010, while EU8 citizens still showed an unemployment rate below that of natives (5.8 per cent and 7.6 per cent, respectively).[13] This divergence in unemployment rates between EU2 and EU8 citizens could indeed be related to different patterns in return migration.

A relatively good performance by Poland – which is responsible for the vast majority of EU8 inflows to the United Kingdom, as we have just seen – during the crisis[14] could have acted as a pull factor driving immigrants back home, or limiting further emigration. Bulgaria and Romania, in contrast, were severely hit by the crisis and this kept pushing people out of the country. The argument is also valid

---

13   These results are not completely in line with what emerges from the study by Dustmann et al. (2009) that finds significantly larger unemployment responses for immigrants relative to natives within the same skill group. In their analysis, however, immigrants are simply disaggregated into OECD and non-OECD countries.

14   Real GDP growth rate in Poland in 2009 was around 1.7 per cent, the only positive value in the whole EU27 (http://epp.eurostat.ec.europa.eu/portal/page/portal/eurostat/ home/). GDP per capita in Purchasing Power Standard grew from 56 in 2008 to 61 in 2009 while inflation rate was around 4 per cent.

for the Baltic immigrants, even if this trend is less visible from the data because of the predominant share of Poles in the EU8 group. Figure 2.3b shows that the size of the stock of immigrants from the EU2 registered a marked rise despite the increasing trend in the unemployment rate since the third quarter of 2008. While in the second quarter of 2010 the EU2 population in the United Kingdom increased by almost 20 per cent compared to one year earlier, the stock of EU8 citizens in the same period rose by less than 8 per cent.

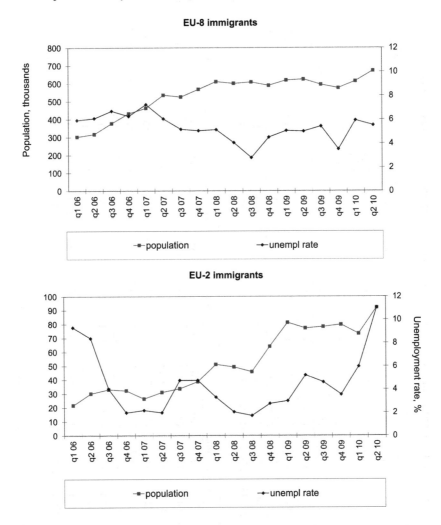

Figure 2.3   Unemployment rates and population of EU8 and EU2 citizens, 2006–2010

Source: Author's calculations based on data from the UK QLFS, 2006–2010.

Table 2.2   Population structure in the UK by age, gender and immigration status, 2006 and 2010 (%)

2006 Age class	UK nationals M	F	Tot	EU15 nationals M	F	Tot	EU8 nationals M	F	Tot	EU2 nationals M	F	Tot	Non-EU nationals M	F	Tot
0–14	19.3	17.7	18.4	12.4	9.7	11.0	9.6	11.5	10.5	4.5	12.0	7.8	15.0	13.3	14.2
15–24	13.8	12.7	13.2	8.7	8.8	8.8	25.4	27.2	26.3	14.0	17.7	15.7	14.5	15.0	14.8
25–34	12.1	11.9	12.0	21.9	20.4	21.1	46.6	44.9	45.8	52.4	46.6	49.6	33.7	32.1	32.9
35–44	15.4	15.3	15.4	18.9	17.8	18.3	9.4	7.8	8.7	19.1	16.0	17.8	20.4	20.0	20.2
45–54	13.5	13.3	13.4	10.7	12.6	11.7	4.6	5.0	4.8	7.4	3.8	5.8	9.3	9.7	9.5
55–64	12.4	12.4	12.4	12.3	10.5	11.3	1.2	1.6	1.4	2.1	3.2	2.7	3.3	5.4	4.4
65+	13.5	16.8	15.2	15.1	20.1	17.8	3.1	2.0	2.6	0.8	1.4	1.1	3.8	4.5	4.1
Total	100	100	100	100	100	100	100	100	100	100	100	100	100	100	100
Thousands	27343	28365	55708	435	496	931	212	188	399	17	14	32	1074	1104	2177

2010 Age Class	UK nationals M	F	Tot	EU15 nationals M	F	Tot	EU8 nationals M	F	Tot	EU2 nationals M	F	Tot	Non-EU nationals M	F	Tot
0–14	18.9	17.4	18.1	12.7	11.4	12.0	13.8	12.9	13.3	8.7	12.2	10.5	14.5	14.5	14.5
15–24	13.6	12.9	13.3	11.0	10.4	10.6	15.8	16.4	16.1	12.0	31.8	21.3	17.0	13.5	15.3
25–34	12.2	11.6	11.9	20.1	17.8	18.9	44.5	46.8	45.7	56.4	28.5	43.2	31.9	31.2	31.5
35–44	14.3	14.2	14.3	20.8	19.7	20.2	14.2	12.5	13.4	12.3	12.1	12.1	20.0	18.6	19.3
45–54	14.3	14.2	14.2	12.9	12.8	12.9	7.7	8.2	8.0	8.8	11.1	10.0	8.9	10.8	9.8
55–64	12.5	12.5	12.5	10.0	11.1	10.6	1.2	1.5	1.4	0.0	3.1	1.5	4.0	5.9	5.0
65+	14.2	17.2	15.7	12.5	16.9	14.8	2.7	1.8	2.2	1.8	1.2	1.5	3.8	5.5	4.7
Total	100	100	100	100	100	100	100	100	100	100	100	100	100	100	100
Thousands	27698	28518	56216	481	565	1046	377	393	770	50	44	95	1239	1242	2481

Source: Author's calculations based on data from the UK QLFS, 2006 and 2010.

The socio-economic characteristics of the immigrant population will now be examined to try to understand whether the current economic crisis had any impact on the composition of migration flows to the United Kingdom.

When looking at the composition by age and gender, Table 2.2 does not show any big change between the pre-crisis and the crisis period. The population from the EU8 and the EU2 is represented mainly by immigrants aged 25–34 (more than 40 per cent of the whole population for both EU8 and EU2 immigrants) and this is particularly evident when compared with UK nationals whose distribution by age class is more homogeneous. While the EU8 population is equilibrated in terms of gender across almost all age classes (especially considering working age bands), EU2 immigrants are predominantly male immigrants between 25 and 34, while the youngest generation (especially those aged 15–24, in other words the student population) is composed mainly of females.[15]

Educational attainment plays a fundamental role in determining immigrants' assimilation potential and, more generally, the likelihood of getting a job corresponding to their skills. The less than perfect international transferability of human capital, often associated with the lack of adequate language skills, might contribute to situations of overeducation for recently arrived immigrants that should mitigate with length of stay in the host country (Chiswick and Miller 2009).

Table 2.3 shows the educational attainment of immigrants. As already illustrated in the previous section, the results presented here need to be considered with caution since the real educational attainment of immigrants might be underestimated/overestimated because of international disparities in the length of time spent in education. The average level of human capital varies according to different nationality groups. New EU citizens seem to be more educated compared to UK nationals, EU15 and non-EU immigrants. The share of those who left school before they were 16 years of age is extremely low and became slightly higher only in 2010 for EU2 immigrants. This is likely to be related to the effects of the crisis in Romania and Bulgaria, since low-educated people might have been hit hardest during the recession and thus have more incentive to leave. The share of those who completed secondary education is above 50 per cent for both EU8 and EU2 immigrants in 2010, while four out of ten new EU citizens had a university degree, with a higher share among females compared to their male counterparts.

For both groups, gender differences among the tertiary educated are indeed significant, since female migrants seem generally more educated than males. The figure for the EU2 group for 2006 is particularly striking: almost two out of three females had completed a degree. Again, the lower figure for 2010 might be due to the downturn effects who might have increased the relative incentive to migrate for low-educated compared to well-educated EU2 citizens.

---

15   In other studies evidence was found that young females are more mobile than their male counterparts (see, for example, Kröhnert and Vollmer (2008) on migration from East to West Germany).

Table 2.3   Immigrant population in the United Kingdom by level of education, 2006 and 2010 (%)

2006 By age at which they left full-time education	UK nationals			EU15 nationals			EU8 nationals			EU2 nationals			Non-EU nationals		
	M	F	Total	M	F	Total	M	F	Total	M	F	Total	M	F	Total
<16 years	16.3	14.3	15.3	16.4	10.5	13.4	2.8	2.7	2.7	3.5	0.0	2.1	6.6	9.0	7.8
16–20 years	59.4	62.1	60.7	40.9	46.2	43.6	61.3	51.8	56.9	52.4	37.6	46.0	40.1	45.1	42.6
21+ years	24.3	23.6	23.9	42.7	43.3	43.0	35.9	45.5	40.4	45.9	62.4	52.9	53.3	45.9	49.6
Total	100	100	100	100	100	100	100	100	100	100	100	100	100	100	100

2010 By age at which they left full-time education	UK nationals			EU15 nationals			EU8 nationals			EU2 nationals			Non-EU nationals		
	M	F	Total	M	F	Total	M	F	Total	M	F	Total	M	F	Total
<16 years	15.6	16.0	15.8	13.1	12.0	12.5	1.9	2.5	2.2	5.3	5.6	5.5	6.5	8.2	7.4
16–20 years	57.9	59.0	58.5	34.3	42.4	38.6	62.0	54.1	57.9	58.0	44.7	51.3	36.6	41.3	38.9
21+ years	26.5	25.0	25.8	52.7	45.7	48.9	36.1	43.4	39.9	36.7	49.7	43.2	56.8	50.5	53.7
Total	100	100	100	100	100	100	100	100	100	100	100	100	100	100	100

Source: Author's calculations based on data from the UK QLFS, 2006 and 2010.

Table 2.4   Job qualifications of immigrants in the United Kingdom, 2006 and 2010 (%)

2006	United Kingdom	EU15	EU8	EU2	Non-EU
White-collars	54.6	59.7	16.9	27.4	55.2
Blue-collars	45.4	40.3	83.1	72.6	44.8
Total	100.0	100.0	100.0	100.0	100.0
2010					
White-collars	56.0	64.2	18.0	21.4	52.8
Blue-collars	44.0	35.8	82.0	78.6	47.2
Total	100.0	100.0	100.0	100.0	100.0

Source: Author's calculations based on data from the UK QLFS, 2006 and 2010.

Ideally, the human capital level should be reflected in the kind of job immigrants have. Table 2.4 shows that, while UK nationals and EU15 citizens are employed mainly as white-collars (56 per cent and 64 per cent, respectively, in 2010), the share of blue-collar workers is around 82 per cent for EU8 and slightly lower for EU2 nationals (79 per cent). It is interesting that overeducation seems to be far more widespread across EU8 and EU2 immigrants compared to the other groups (Table 2.5).

The situation for EU8 workers was exacerbated by the crisis, as the share of the tertiary educated performing qualified jobs fell by almost 6 per cent between 2006 and 2010. Lindley (2009) shows that the most recent cohorts of immigrants to the United Kingdom are more likely to experience overeducation, and our results are in line with these findings since the average length of stay in the United Kingdom is shorter for new EU citizens compared to non-EU and EU15 nationals. In 2010, the average length of stay was over nine years for non-EU immigrants, six years for EU8 immigrants and almost five years for EU2 immigrants.

One final interesting aspect is that every second EU2 immigrant in 2006 declared themselves self-employed, while for all other nationality groups the share was between 10 and 15 per cent. Given the presence of transitional arrangements, this could be read as evidence of a 'diversion effect', since EU2 self-employed workers do not need authorisation to work in the UK labour market.[16] The advantage of exercising such a Treaty right, however, may translate into lower social security coverage and scant protection of other work-place related rights that are usually better guaranteed through an employee's contract. The fact that the share of self-

---

16   Sriskandarajah and Cooley (2009) also explained the high numbers of self-employed Romanians and Bulgarians in the data gathered from the UK Home Office and the Department for Work and Pensions in 2007 as a diversion effect of the transitional arrangement.

Table 2.5 Job mismatch of immigrants in the United Kingdom, 2006 and 2010 (%)

2006	UK nationals		EU15 nationals		EU8 nationals		EU2 nationals		Non-EU nationals	
	White-collars	Blue-collars	White-collars	Blue-collars	White-collars	Blue-collars	White-collars	Blue-collars	White-collars	Blue-collars
By age at which they left full-time education										
<16 years	28.9	71.2	24.0	76.0	4.9	95.1	0.0	100.0	29.1	70.9
16–20 years	49.3	50.7	46.8	53.2	11.0	89.0	16.8	83.2	40.4	59.6
21+ years	79.4	20.6	82.0	18.0	32.3	67.7	38.5	61.5	71.3	28.7

2010	UK nationals		EU15 nationals		EU8 nationals		EU2 nationals		Non-EU nationals	
	White-collars	Blue-collars	White-collars	Blue-collars	White-collars	Blue-collars	White-collars	Blue-collars	White-collars	Blue-collars
By age at which they left full-time education										
<16 years	30.4	69.6	14.7	85.3	0.0	100.0	0.0	100.0	15.6	84.4
16–20 years	51.3	48.7	52.1	47.9	10.7	89.3	18.8	81.2	41.0	59.0
21+ years	78.2	21.8	81.2	18.8	35.5	64.5	46.1	53.9	65.8	34.2

Source: Author's calculations based on data from the UK QLFS, 2006 and 2010.

employed decreased between 2006 and 2010 – but was still significantly higher than the corresponding figure for EU8 citizens – might hint at a higher risk of failure and bankruptcy for businesses owned by immigrants during a recession due to restricted access to credit and limited financial assets (OECD 2007).

Table 2.6   Employees and self-employed workers by nationality group in the United Kingdom, 2006 and 2010 (%)

2006	United Kingdom	EU15	EU8	EU2	Non-EU
Employee	87.6	87.8	87.7	40.7	88.7
Self-employed	12.4	12.2	12.3	59.3	11.3
Total	100.0	100.0	100.0	100.0	100.0
2010					
Employee	86.9	86.8	89.9	55.9	89.6
Self-employed	13.1	13.2	10.1	44.1	10.4
Total	100.0	100.0	100.0	100.0	100.0

Source: Author's calculations based on data from the UK QLFS, 2010.

4. The Italian Experience

Figure 2.4 shows that also in Italy the biggest group of immigrants is non-EU nationals. However, whereas at the beginning of 2006 they accounted for more than three-quarters (76 per cent) of total foreign residents in Italy, in the second quarter of 2010 non-EU migrants decreased to 68 per cent of the overall immigrant population mainly in favour of EU2 nationals whose share rose by about 60 per cent in the same period, from less than 280,000 to almost 800,000 people.

Table 2.7 clearly shows that EU2 immigration almost completely overlaps with inflows from Romania, which in general represent about 82 per cent of the total population from eastern EU countries. The phenomenon did not start after Romania had entered EU, however, but in the early 1990s.[17]

The common origin of the Romanian and Italian languages in Latin means that there are considerable similarities between the two languages and this certainly

---

17   Di Comite and Andria (2008) report that Romanian citizens, together with Albanians, were the two nationalities that registered the biggest increase in the overall stock of foreign born population in Italy between 1992 and 2007. The incidence of Romanians rose from 1.2 per cent to more than 11 per cent. When looking at the average length of stay for Romanian immigrants in 2010, it was about seven years, longer than in the UK case.

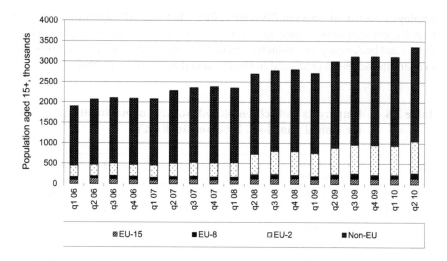

Figure 2.4   Total number of immigrants in Italy by nationality group, 2006–2010

Source: Author's calculations based on data from the Italian QLFS, 2006–2010.

Table 2.7   Total number of immigrants in Italy from the new EU Member States by country of origin, aged 15+ (thousands)

	Q1 2006	Q2 2010
Baltic States	0.9	3.5
Bulgaria	14.0	34.7
Czech Republic	10.4	5.2
Hungary	2.7	10.3
Poland	52.6	101.5
Romania	262.5	757.0
Slovak Republic	3.4	4.3
Slovenia	2.9	1.8
Total	349.3	918.3

Source: Author's calculations based on data from the Italian QLFS, first quarter 2006 and second quarter 2010.

acted as a determinant pull factor to attract Romanians to Italy.[18] Many people entered Italy on a temporary tourist visa and then overstayed: given the large size of the Italian shadow economy, it was relatively easy for them to find an irregular (usually low-paid) job and wait for one of the frequent amnesties declared by the Italian government. In this mechanism, ethnic networks played a key role, since friends and relatives that were already working in Italy could arrange jobs and accommodation for the newcomers, thus determining the rapid growth of the Romanian community in Italy. In fact, the Romania–Italy migration corridor is reported to be one of the top 10 migration corridors in 2010 in the Migration and Remittances Factbook 2011. According to the World Bank's bilateral estimates of migrant stocks in 2010, 813,037 Romanians live in Italy, representing about 30 per cent of the total stock of Romanians living abroad.

Contrary to what might be expected, the largest increase in the stock of Romanians and Bulgarians was registered after the onset of the crisis; as a matter of fact, in the first quarter of 2008 the whole EU2 population was around 350,000 and its stock more than doubled in the following two years. The role of the harsh

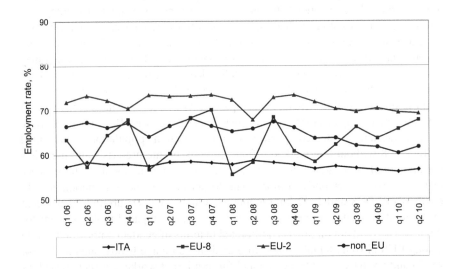

Figure 2.5   Employment rates in Italy by nationality group, 2006–2010

Note: Not seasonally adjusted.

Source: Author's calculations based on data from the Italian QLFS, 2006–2010.

_____

18   Many Romanian immigrants stated that three months are long enough to reach a decent level of proficiency in Italian (Veneto Lavoro 2007).

economic conditions in the countries of origin as push factors probably outweighed the less attractive prospects Italy could offer to immigrants due to the recession.[19]

The evolution of Polish immigration is also fairly interesting: although Italy had not represented a major destination for Polish immigrants immediately after the 2004 enlargement compared to the United Kingdom or Ireland, their absolute number arguably increased, representing in the second quarter of 2010 around 80 per cent of total immigration from the EU8. A cyclical component, however, is more evident in EU8 inflows compared to EU2 ones and the EU8 population as a whole did not undergo a marked increase and remained stable at around 4 per cent of the total immigrant population.

Employment rates (Figure 2.5) are in general higher for immigrants compared to native workers. The trend for the EU8 is extremely unstable with strong cyclical fluctuations; the lower peaks for 2008 and 2009 compared to the previous years could point to the impact of the economic crisis.

EU2 immigrants experienced a different situation, their employment rate being fairly constant (between 72 and 73 per cent) before the onset of the crisis. After the last quarter of 2008, however, it was pushed down below 70 per cent.

The same discrepancy is also reflected in Figure 2.6. As far as EU8 immigrants are concerned, the correlation between the stock of population and its unemployment rate seems to be negative: higher unemployment rates are associated with decreases (or moderate increases) in the overall stock of immigrants. This could indicate a very dynamic pattern of migration flows, with people coming from the EU8 when they have concrete job opportunities on the Italian labour market and going back when unemployed. Instead, the stock of EU2 immigrants has grown constantly in recent years despite the notable increase in unemployment rates: jobless status in Italy was in any case better compared to the serious situation in Romania and Bulgaria in the crisis.

The age and gender composition of the immigrant population is presented in Table 2.8 without any marked difference between the pre-crisis and the crisis period. Population ageing is fairly visible for Italian nationals, whose share of the elderly corresponds to more than 20 per cent of the total population. In comparison, EU8 and EU2 immigrants are much younger: around 70 per cent of the total population is between 25 and 54 years, compared to 40 per cent for Italians. The EU2 population is equilibrated in terms of gender composition, while among EU8 citizens females seem to prevail in some age bands, such as 25–34, 45–54 and 55–64 years. Strong demand for immigrant workers in sectors such as

---

19   Concerning EU2 countries, Eurostat shows that real GDP growth rates for 2009 were –7.1 per cent for Romania and –5.5 per cent for Bulgaria. Bulgaria's and Romania's GDP are the lowest in the EU27. The slowdown was only slightly milder in Italy (–5.2 per cent) but its labour market was fairly resilient during the crisis: http://epp.eurostat. ec.europa.eu/tgm/table.do?tab=table&init=1&plugin=1&language=en&pcode=tsieb020.

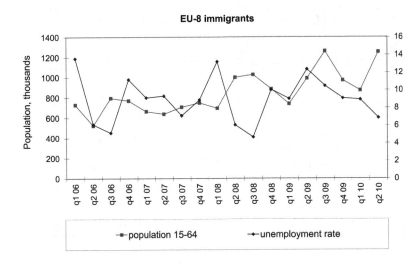

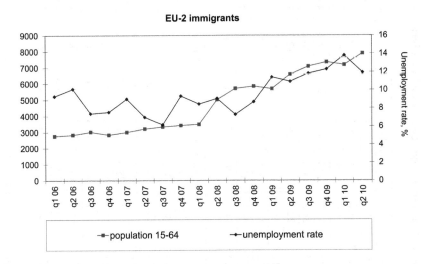

Figure 2.6   Unemployment rates and population of EU8 and EU2 citizens in Italy, 2006–2010

Note: Not seasonally adjusted.

Source: Author's calculations based on data from the Italian QLFS, 2006–2010.

Table 2.8   Population structure in Italy by age, gender and immigration status, 2006 and 2010, (%)

2006

Age class	Italian nationals			EU15 nationals			EU8 nationals			EU2 nationals			Non-EU nationals		
	M	F	Tot	M	F	Tot	M	F	Tot	M	F	Tot	M	F	Tot
0–14	14.6	13.1	13.9	11.0	7.4	8.8	27.7	10.1	13.7	18.0	15.6	16.8	23.1	21.2	22.2
15–24	10.8	9.7	10.2	3.5	3.9	3.8	13.2	7.4	8.6	11.7	15.8	13.9	12.9	13.4	13.1
25–34	14.4	13.0	13.7	12.1	24.1	19.5	21.8	48.6	43.0	40.0	37.2	38.5	21.7	27.5	24.4
35–44	16.4	15.4	15.9	26.3	30.1	28.7	27.1	16.0	18.5	17.6	19.2	18.4	27.7	23.2	25.6
45–54	13.7	13.3	13.5	22.7	16.6	18.6	7.7	12.7	11.7	11.4	10.1	10.7	11.3	9.9	10.6
55–64	12.5	12.4	12.4	9.5	9.1	9.3	2.6	5.0	4.4	1.2	1.5	1.4	2.3	3.0	2.6
65+	17.6	23.0	20.4	14.9	8.8	11.2	0.0	0.2	0.1	0.1	0.5	0.3	1.0	1.8	1.4
Total	100	100	100	100	100	100	100	100	100	100	100	100	100	100	100
Thousands	27110	28756	55866	47	79	126	18	64	82	162	183	345	1068	947	2015

2010

Age class	Italian nationals			EU15 nationals			EU8 nationals			EU2 nationals			Non-EU nationals		
	M	F	Tot	M	F	Tot	M	F	Tot	M	F	Tot	M	F	Tot
0–14	14.5	13.0	13.7	5.3	3.2	4.1	20.5	12.3	15.2	17.2	16.2	16.6	23.0	20.9	22.0
15–24	10.5	9.4	9.9	5.2	4.3	4.7	6.0	5.2	5.5	13.5	12.0	12.7	13.2	13.3	13.3
25–34	12.6	11.5	12.0	15.1	15.3	15.2	29.3	35.9	33.6	31.8	33.5	32.7	20.9	24.0	22.4
35–44	16.1	15.2	15.7	19.2	28.0	24.1	27.0	17.8	20.9	26.3	25.2	25.7	25.7	22.7	24.2
45–54	14.8	14.3	14.6	23.0	30.2	27.0	15.0	20.2	18.4	9.7	9.5	9.6	12.9	11.7	12.3
55–64	12.9	12.8	12.8	16.4	8.9	12.3	2.1	8.1	6.1	1.5	3.3	2.4	3.1	5.3	4.2
65+	18.6	23.9	21.3	15.8	10.2	12.7	0.2	0.5	0.4	0.2	0.4	0.3	1.2	2.1	1.6
Total	100	100	100	100	100	100	100	100	100	100	100	100	100	100	100
Thousands	27173	28765	55939	64	80	143	43	83	126	418	488	906	1457	1416	2872

Source: Author's calculations based on data from the Italian QLFS, 2006 and 2010.

Table 2.9   Immigrant population in Italy by level of education, 2006 and 2010 (%)

2006 Education	Italian nationals			EU15 nationals			EU8 nationals			EU2 nationals			Non-EU nationals		
	M	F	Tot	M	F	Tot	M	F	Tot	M	F	Tot	M	F	Tot
Lower second or less	56.8	59.7	58.3	13.3	17.7	16.0	47.3	35.3	37.6	32.6	31.8	32.2	63.4	57.0	60.3
Upper secondary	33.7	30.6	32.1	34.2	36.5	35.7	49.4	51.1	50.7	63.8	58.5	61.0	29.2	32.9	30.9
Tertiary	9.6	9.7	9.6	52.5	45.8	48.3	3.3	13.6	11.8	3.6	9.6	6.9	7.4	10.1	8.7
Total	100	100	100	100	100	100	100	100	100	100	100	100	100	100	100
Thousands	23146	24977	48123	42	72	115	13	57	71	133	154	287	821	746	1567

2010 Education	Italian nationals			EU15 nationals			EU8 nationals			EU2 nationals			Non-EU nationals		
	M	F	Tot	M	F	Tot	M	F	Tot	M	F	Tot	M	F	Tot
Lower second or less	54.2	57.0	55.6	15.6	16.6	16.2	29.1	24.4	26.0	37.7	31.9	34.6	60.4	55.7	58.0
Upper secondary	35.2	31.7	33.4	42.0	42.5	42.2	62.8	63.1	63.0	58.5	58.6	58.5	32.3	32.6	32.5
Tertiary	10.7	11.4	11.0	42.4	41.0	41.6	8.1	12.5	11.1	3.8	9.6	6.9	7.3	11.8	9.5
Total	100	100	100	100	100	100	100	100	100	100	100	100	100	100	100
Thousands	23237	25033	48270	60	77	138	34	73	107	346	410	756	1121	1119	2240

Source: Author's calculations based on data from the Italian QLFS, 2006 and 2010.

family and elderly care might be responsible for the fact that women are highly represented among older generations.[20]

With a rapidly ageing population and a welfare system that has not been developed enough to take care of the problem, the employment of migrant female workers (mainly from Eastern Europe and Latin America) for home-based elderly care has become a general trend in the past decade, with the implicit support of the state and institutions (Lyon 2006).

The majority of EU8 and EU2 immigrants (both males and females) have completed upper secondary education and are therefore relatively more educated than non-EU immigrants (Table 2.9). Between 2006 and 2010 the share of EU8 immigrants with at least secondary education increased from 51 per cent to 63 per cent. The EU15 population is quite different, with a share of tertiary educated above 40 per cent, which is also much higher compared to the correspondent figure for Italian nationals (10–11 per cent). Among new EU citizens, the share of tertiary educated is higher for female immigrants compared to their male counter parts, as already seen in the United Kingdom.

Table 2.10 reports the incidence of high-skilled and low-skilled jobs across immigrant groups. While Italian workers are almost equally distributed between white-collar and blue-collar jobs, the foreign-born population is fairly polarised. On the one hand, eight out of ten EU15 citizens are employed as white-collars, thus taking advantage of their higher level of human capital. On the other hand, the remaining groups are specialised in low-skilled jobs, especially EU2 and non-EU immigrants. The economic crisis apparently had no impact on this situation. What changed with the crisis, instead, is the extent of overeducation among immigrants (Table 2.11). While in 2006 only two out of ten EU8 immigrants with tertiary

Table 2.10   Job qualifications of immigrants in Italy, 2006 and 2010 (%)

2006	ITA	EU15	EU8	EU2	Non-EU
White-collars	54.4	82.1	13.8	4.9	5.2
Blue-collars	45.6	17.9	86.2	95.1	94.8
Total	100	100	100	100	100
2010					
White-collars	57.0	86.6	13.9	5.5	6.1
Blue-collars	43.0	13.4	86.1	94.5	93.9
Total	100	100	100	100	100

Source: Author's calculations based on data from the Italian QLFS, 2006 and 2010.

20   Other studies (for example, Inps, 2007) attest that immigrant women employed in the Italian care sector are on average at least 40 years old and that Romanian and Polish nationalities are among the most represented in the sector.

Table 2.11   Job mismatch of immigrants in Italy, 2006 and 2010 (%)

2006	ITA		EU15		EU8		EU2		Non-EU	
	White-collars	Blue-collars	White-collars	Blue-collars	White-collars	Blue-collars	White-collars	Blue-collars	White-collars	Blue-collars
Up to lower secondary	18.8	81.2	36.4	63.6	7.3	92.7	1.6	98.4	2.7	97.3
Upper secondary	69.7	30.3	67.1	32.9	10.9	89.1	4.3	95.7	5.3	94.7
Tertiary	97.1	2.9	97.5	2.5	80.0	20.0	24.5	75.5	21.2	78.8

2010	ITA		EU15		EU8		EU2		Non-EU	
	White-collars	Blue-collars	White-collars	Blue-collars	White-collars	Blue-collars	White-collars	Blue-collars	White-collars	Blue-collars
Up to lower secondary	19.9	80.1	13.7	86.3	6.2	93.8	1.8	98.2	2.3	97.7
Upper secondary	68.3	31.7	82.0	18.0	10.7	89.3	3.6	96.4	6.6	93.4
Tertiary	96.8	3.2	98.1	2.0	50.7	49.3	38.2	61.8	22.2	77.8

Source: Author's calculations based on data from the Italian QLFS, 2006 and 2010.

education had low-skilled jobs, the share increased to four out of ten in 2010. In contrast, the share of EU2 tertiary educated immigrants employed as white-collars rose from 25 per cent to 38 per cent: high-skilled and managerial jobs have been work permit-exempt since the beginning of 2007 for EU2 citizens. Even without disaggregating by nationality, Dell'Aringa and Pagani (2010) using data from the same source (LFS) for the period 2005–2007 show that foreign workers are much more likely to be overeducated than natives. This result is valid upon immigrants' arrival in Italy, but does not change significantly even with experience acquired on the Italian labour market.

The vast majority of immigrants in Italy work as employees and are not self-employed (Table 2.12). On the other hand, the figures for self-employed among Italians and EU15 immigrants are much higher. The situation is quite different from the United Kingdom, where the share of self-employed among EU2 immigrants is much higher, which is probably due to the different transitional arrangements applied in the two host countries. As a matter of fact, Romanians and Bulgarians in Italy can benefit from a wider set of exceptions compared to the United Kingdom: immediate access was granted from 2007 to specific sectors and occupations such as family and care services and the construction sector, which indeed are the branches EU2 immigrants are mainly employed in (see next section).

Table 2.12   **Employee and self-employed workers by nationality group in Italy, 2006 and 2010 (%)**

2006	ITA	EU15	EU8	EU2	Non-EU
Employee	72.9	60.4	87.4	90.4	85.3
Self-employed	27.1	39.6	12.6	9.6	14.7
Total	100	100	100	100	100
2010					
Employee	73.3	68.3	84.2	89.5	86.3
Self-employed	26.7	31.7	15.8	10.5	13.7
Total	100	100	100	100	100

Source: Author's calculations based on data from the Italian QLFS, 2006 and 2010.

5. Were Immigrants' Sectors of Activity Noticeably Affected by the Economic Downturn? Evidence from the United Kingdom and Italy

Between the 1990s and the 2000s Europe and OECD countries in general experienced a phase of employment growth in which immigrant labour played a determinant role. Immigrants' share in net job creation between 1997 and 2007 was at least 60 per cent in Italy and slightly more than 70 per cent in the United

Kingdom (OECD 2009). The global economic crisis caused a sudden change in this positive trend and hit the labour market conditions hard in both countries. After the onset of the crisis, the United Kingdom unemployment rate rose by 2.8 per cent to reach 7.9 per cent in March 2010, in line with the average rise for the OECD area, while in Italy the unemployment rate was around 8.7 per cent in May 2010, with a 2 per cent increase that is somewhat below the OECD average (OECD 2010). In this context, immigrant workers are likely to be among the most vulnerable categories due to the different structural factors mentioned in the Introduction.

In the previous sections evidence was found that immigrant workers from the new EU Member States are employed mainly in blue-collar jobs in both the United Kingdom and Italy. Here the distribution of immigrants across economic sectors will be analysed to highlight possible patterns associated with specific nationality groups and to verify whether the immigrant workforce is concentrated in industries severely affected by the economic downturn.

Table 2.13 shows the distribution of the main nationality groups across economic sectors both in the United Kingdom (upper panel) and in Italy (lower panel). Data from three different quarters are reported: the beginning (q1 2006) and the end (q2 2010)[21] of the time period and then the first quarter of 2008 that represented the highest peak in the GDP trend for both countries just before the onset of the crisis.

The situation in the United Kingdom appears fairly stable over time. The distribution of immigrants across economic sectors is polarised compared to UK nationals: Romanians and Bulgarians are concentrated in the construction sector, EU8 citizens are mainly employed in manufacturing and energy industries, while EU15 and non-EU nationals are not particularly different from one another, being employed in more qualified jobs in health services, education, real estate and business activities.

The construction sector continues to employ the majority of EU2 immigrants, but the share has decreased considerably, falling from 38 per cent in 2006 to 24 per cent in 2010. This is probably linked to the fact that the construction sector was one of the most adversely affected by the economic downturn. EU2 immigrants moved towards new sectors where their presence was negligible before the crisis, such as hotels and restaurants and health and education services (respectively, 16 per cent and 17 per cent in 2010), or moved back to real estate and business activities (18 per cent in 2010, compared to 13 per cent in 2008 and 20 per cent in 2006).

EU8 immigrants in 2006 were fairly widespread across manufacturing, constructions, hotels and restaurants and wholesale and retail (13–17 per cent in each sector). Over time, their tendency towards specialisation is evident: in 2008 and 2010, every fourth EU8 immigrant was working in the manufacturing sector.

---

21   A preliminary check for seasonal effects was made using q1 2010 data but there were no appreciable differences with respect to q2.

Table 2.13 Economic sectors of activity by nationality group in the United Kingdom and Italy

United Kingdom

Economic sectors	2006					2008					2010				
	UK	EU15	EU8	EU2	Non-EU	UK	EU15	EU8	EU2	Non-EU	UK	EU15	EU8	EU2	Non-EU
Agriculture and fishing	1.33	0.93	0.62	3.24	0.25	1.4	0.5	2.3	0.0	0.6	1.6	0.5	1.7	1.6	0.3
Manufacturing and energy	14.11	12.60	17.10	5.06	9.78	13.6	10.5	25.1	6.7	10.0	11.9	10.5	24.7	4.9	7.6
Construction	8.19	5.08	16.36	38.26	3.27	8.3	5.9	13.6	33.4	3.5	7.6	4.7	6.6	23.7	3.4
Wholesale, retail and motor trade	15.03	10.53	13.38	5.23	12.66	14.9	8.9	12.3	4.5	12.4	14.1	9.8	15.8	9.4	13.3
Hotels and restaurants	3.90	7.59	14.01	3.21	9.96	4.1	8.1	10.4	9.5	9.6	4.4	9.1	14.9	16.3	12.0
Transport and communication	6.81	5.69	8.89	6.83	6.81	6.7	7.2	9.0	8.8	7.0	6.3	6.8	8.3	4.6	5.4
Financial intermediation	4.47	6.43	0.42	0.00	4.43	4.3	8.5	2.0	0.0	5.9	4.1	6.5	0.8	0.0	5.1
Real estate and business activities	11.09	16.80	9.94	19.56	14.32	11.8	16.5	10.5	13.1	17.7	12.6	16.0	11.5	18.1	16.3
Public administration	7.55	4.16	0.91	0.00	4.23	7.5	2.7	0.7	1.5	4.0	7.1	2.6	1.0	0.0	4.5
Education and health	21.61	25.39	8.58	6.74	26.97	21.4	22.7	7.8	13.6	24.0	24.0	28.4	11.0	17.0	26.8
Other services	5.91	4.81	9.81	11.87	7.34	6.0	8.5	6.1	9.0	5.3	6.3	5.1	3.8	4.3	5.3
Total	100	100	100	100	100	100	100	100	100	100	100	100	100	100	100

Italy	2006					2008					2010				
Economic sectors	ITA	EU15	EU8	EU2	Non-EU	ITA	EU15	EU8	EU2	Non-EU	ITA	EU15	EU8	EU2	Non-EU
Agriculture and fishing	4.0	1.1	2.8	8.0	3.7	3.8	1.3	4.6	3.4	3.2	3.9	1.6	4.1	4.9	4.2
Manufacturing and energy	21.7	22.8	14.0	25.1	24.0	21.1	13.0	7.9	15.2	25.5	19.9	26.1	16.0	13.8	20.6
Construction	7.9	2.5	12.3	19.1	18.4	7.7	2.2	17.2	29.6	14.5	7.6	1.6	14.9	26.1	14.6
Wholesale, retail and motor trade	15.6	11.9	6.6	7.6	10.9	15.8	17.6	5.8	6.7	9.7	15.3	10.3	7.4	5.2	9.4
Hotels and restaurants	4.5	3.3	15.5	9.6	10.0	4.5	3.7	10.2	8.7	10.1	4.9	6.6	11.5	7.9	9.8
Transport and communication	5.5	3.7	2.2	2.2	4.0	5.5	8.2	0.7	7.2	4.7	5.5	3.7	1.9	4.2	4.9
Financial intermediation	4.0	2.4	0.0	0.0	0.7	3.5	5.8	3.2	0.6	0.2	3.8	2.3	1.1	0.7	1.0
Real estate and business activities	10.1	21.5	0.0	5.3	6.6	11.3	17.0	3.9	6.5	7.4	11.3	18.0	5.6	4.7	7.3
Public administration	6.7	0.4	0.0	0.1	0.1	6.7	0.0	0.0	0.0	0.2	6.7	0.1	0.0	0.0	0.1
Education and health	14.5	10.3	7.3	3.6	2.9	14.9	17.6	14.5	4.5	3.1	15.0	22.1	9.2	5.4	3.6
Other services	5.6	20.2	39.3	19.4	18.9	5.2	8.6	32.2	17.5	21.5	6.2	7.6	28.3	27.1	24.6
Total	100	100	100	100	100	100	100	100	100	100	100	100	100	100	100

Source: Author's calculations based on data from the United Kingdom and Italian QLFS, q1 2006, q1 2008 and q2 2010.

EU15 and non-EU citizens, on the other hand, did not move much between 2006 and 2010. The shares employed in health and education, as well as real estate and business activities, were relatively constant in the time span considered. Due to the crisis, however, their role in financial intermediation decreased slightly between 2008 and 2010.

This pattern of specialisation is in line with the evidence reported above. In terms of educational attainment, Table 2.3 showed that EU15 and non-EU immigrants are better educated than citizens from the new EU Member States. Furthermore, the share of workers performing white-collar jobs is higher and the mismatch between job and education is less severe among the former groups. EU8 and EU2 immigrants, respectively, are concentrated in energy and manufacturing industries and in the construction sector, while other immigrants have higher job profiles.

The situation is not entirely surprising when we consider the past history of the United Kingdom and its immense colonial empire. Immigrants from countries with a longer tradition as labour exporters to the United Kingdom, such as Commonwealth members, seem to be employed in qualified jobs, while more recent immigrants represented mainly by citizens of the new EU Member States are stuck in labour-intensive sectors that in many cases represent the typical access to the host country labour market regardless of immigrants' level of education. Moreover, non-EU immigration is partly similar to the flows coming from the EU15 since Australia, Canada and New Zealand play a non-negligible role as countries of origin.

The lower panel of Table 2.13 describes the situation in Italy. As in the United Kingdom, the share of Romanians and Bulgarians employed in the construction industry is fairly high; in 2008, just before the beginning of the crisis, almost every third EU2 immigrant was working in construction. This share somewhat decreased in 2010, probably because of the recession, and the sector absorbing the majority of EU2 immigrants became the service sector where a key role is played by family and elderly care services.[22] This is also the sector in which EU8 immigrants have specialised since 2006, although the share has decreased from almost 40 per cent to less than 30 per cent. Their presence in manufacturing, construction and hotels and restaurants is significant too, but much lower (10–17 per cent).

Non-EU nationals also were employed mainly in low-skilled jobs in the energy and manufacturing industries between 2006 and 2008 and in other services in 2010. Over time, there has been a clear tendency across immigrant groups to concentrate in the service (care) sector. While in 1991 foreign nationals represented only 16 per cent of 181,000 officially recorded domestic care workers, the most recent estimates refer to almost 1.5 million people employed in the sector, of whom 72 per cent are foreign-born (Lamura et al. 2010). A traditional cultural preference for family-centred assistance compared to residential care, together with the scarcity

---

22   Unfortunately, the data analysed here do not allow for a differentiation of the family and elderly care sector from other services.

and unequal distribution of formal care services throughout the country and an increasing activity rate among Italian females stimulated the demand for foreign-born workers that could offer long-term home-based care at affordable prices for middle-income households (Bettio et al. 2006). Domestic work is also likely to be relatively unaffected by the recession since private households often have no other alternative, especially in the case of child or elderly care. EU8, EU2 and non-EU immigrants seem likely to compete with one another for low-skilled jobs, thus confirming the results on job mismatch from Table 2.11.

The segmentation of the immigrant labour market in Italy is closely linked to the recent transition from being a country of emigrants to being a destination for immigrants from developing countries and to the fact that Italy is still not able to attract a high-skilled workforce. Pull factors such as the economic situation and job market opportunities are not appealing enough compared to other rich countries such as the United Kingdom which can recruit higher stocks of human capital.

When analysing the specialisation patterns of immigrants, however, there is some evidence of the effects of the economic downturn: a lower degree of concentration in specific industries that were heavily affected by the recession, such as the construction sector, is noticeable in both the United Kingdom and Italy.

6. Conclusions

The present chapter provides a descriptive analysis of the main socio-economic characteristics of the immigrant population in two European countries: the United Kingdom and Italy. Data from the Quarterly Labour Force Surveys have been employed to obtain information on composition by country of origin and on the employment performance of immigrants in the period between 2006 and 2010. In both countries, the immigrant population is constituted predominantly by non-EU nationals who account for at least 60 per cent of the total immigrant population. With regard to new EU Member States, the situation is quite different. In the United Kingdom, EU8 nationals (Polish and Baltic immigrants in particular) represent a significant share of the total immigrant population aged 15+ that ranges between 14 and 17 per cent, while EU2 nationals, despite a remarkable increase in recent years, still do not account for more than 2.5 per cent of the total immigrant population. The reverse holds true in the Italian case, since the EU2 share increased from 14 per cent to 23 per cent of the total immigrant population between 2006 and 2010, whereas EU8 nationals never exceeded 4 per cent.

Although immigrants' performance on the labour market is fairly difficult to assess from QLFS data without information on return migration, it seems clear that EU8 and EU2 immigrants had higher employment rates compared to UK nationals; this applies also to EU2 immigrants in Italy, while cyclicalities in the employment performance of EU8 immigrants are fairly evident. Turning to the unemployment rates of new EU citizens, it is striking how the EU2 population in

Italy kept on increasing during the recession despite the marked rise of the relative unemployment rate. To a certain extent this is valid also for the United Kingdom, showing that the harsh situation in Bulgaria and Romania definitely acted as a deterrent to those unemployed in the host country.

The age and gender composition, the level of education and the job profiles of the immigrant population before and during the crisis have been compared. In terms of educational attainment, both in Italy and in the United Kingdom the majority of EU8 and EU2 citizens have completed secondary education. While the share of tertiary educated increased in the United Kingdom, especially among EU8 immigrants (from 10 per cent in 2006 to 24 per cent in 2010), there were no significant changes in Italy. The gender gap is evident, with a higher share of tertiary educated among females from the Eastern EU compared to their male counterparts.

In both countries, low-skilled jobs are predominant across EU8 and EU2 immigrant groups and the share of tertiary educated employed as white-collars is much lower compared to the native population and EU15 immigrants. Self-employment is widespread among EU2 immigrants in the United Kingdom, this being a 'diversion effect' of the specific transitional arrangement still in force. In Italy, on the other hand, EU2 immigrants are work permit-exempt in specific economic sectors that exactly represent the occupations they are mainly employed in (for example, construction and care).

Finally, the economic sectors of activity of the different nationality groups between 2006 and 2010 have been investigated to try to understand whether the current economic crisis has had an impact on immigrants' specialisation patterns. The picture that emerges from the comparison between Italy and the United Kingdom is quite different. In the UK economy, specialisation according to geographical origin is fairly pronounced and the relatively more recent immigration history of EU8 and EU2 citizens seems to be unfavourable in terms of occupational skills. EU8 nationals are employed mainly in manufacturing and energy, EU2 nationals have specialised in the construction sector, while non-EU and EU15 nationals seem to have similar profiles, being employed mainly in better jobs such as financial intermediation, business activities, public sector, health and education. The main visible consequence of the economic crisis is represented by the decreasing share of EU2 (but also EU8) workers in the construction sector.

In Italy, EU8 nationals specialise in the service sector, and mainly in family and elderly care services where they face the increasing competition of EU2 and non-EU immigrants. Romanians and Bulgarians have partly moved out of the construction sector because of the economic crisis, even though every fourth EU2 immigrant in 2010 was still employed in the branch. Non-EU citizens instead have a totally different profile compared to their counterparts in the United Kingdom: in Italy, non-EU immigrants compete with new EU citizens for low-skilled jobs instead of with EU15 citizens for high-skilled ones, as in the United Kingdom. This situation might reflect a different composition of non-EU immigration in terms of human capital and skills between the two countries but also other factors, such as discrimination or different motivations behind migration strategies.

In general, however, diverging evidence can be read as due to the different background of the United Kingdom and Italy as countries of immigration. In a few decades the picture for Italy might become more similar to the current situation on the UK labour market.

Acknowledgements

The author is grateful to Janine Leschke, Béla Galgóczi and Andrew Watt for their invaluable support and comments, as well as Riccardo Lucchetti for precious advices. Final thanks go to the Italian Institute of Statistics, the UK Office for National Statistics and the Economic and Social Data Service for making the data from the Labour Force Surveys available. All errors are my own.

Bibliography

Barrell, R., FitzGerald, J. and Riley, R. 2007. 'EU enlargement and migration: Assessing the macroeconomic impacts'. NIESR Discussion Paper No. 292.

Barrett, A. and Kelly, E. 2010. 'The impact of Ireland's recession on the labour market outcomes of its immigrants'. IZA Discussion Paper No. 5218, Institute for the Study of Labor (IZA).

Bettio, F., Simonazzi, A. and Villa P. 2006. 'Change in care regimes and female migration: the "care drain" in the Mediterranean'. *Journal of European Social Policy*, 16(3), 271–85.

Boeri, T. and Brücker, H. 2005. ,Migration, co-ordination failure and EU enlargement'. IZA Discussion Paper No. 1600, Institute for the Study of Labor (IZA).

Chiswick, B.R. and Miller, P.W. 2009. 'The international transferability of immigrants' human capital'. *Economics of Education Review*, 28, 162–9.

Dell'Aringa, C. and Pagani, L. 2010. 'Labour market assimilation and over education: the case of immigrant workers in Italy'. DISCE Working Paper No. 58, Università Cattolica del Sacro Cuore.

Di Comite, L. and Andria, L. 2008. 'L'emigrazione albanese tra Grecia e Italia', in Moretti, E. (ed.), *Lungo le sponde dell'Adriatico. Flussi migratori e percorsi di integrazione*. Milan: FrancoAngeli.

Dustmann, C., Glitz, A. and Vogel, T. 2009. 'Employment, wages, and the economic cycle: differences between immigrants and natives'. IZA Discussion Papers No. 4432, Institute for the Study of Labor (IZA).

European Commission. 2008. 'The impact of free movement of workers in the context of EU enlargement'. Communication from the Commission to the European Parliament, the Council, the European Economic and Social Committee and the Committee of the Regions, COM/2008/0765.

Fihel, A. and Okólski, M. 2009. 'Dimensions and effects of labour migration to EU countries: the case of Poland', in Galgóczi, B., Leschke, J. and Watt, A. (eds), *EU Labour Migration Since Enlargement*, Ashgate.

Frontex. 2009. 'The impact of the global economic crisis on illegal migration to the EU'. European Agency for the Management of Operational Cooperation at the External Borders of the Member States of the European Union (Frontex), Risk Analysis Unit.

Jobson, J.D. 1992. *Applied Multivariate Data Analysis*, Vol. 2. New York: Springer Verlag.

Kröhnert, S. and Vollmer, S. 2008. 'Where have all young women gone? Gender-specific migration from East to West Germany'. Background paper for the World Development Report 2009, The World Bank, Washington D.C.

Lamura, G., Di Rosa, M., Melchiorre, M.G. and Chiatti, C. 2010. 'The interaction among migrant care workers, family carers and professional services in the Italian elder care sector'. 8th ESPAnet Conference, Budapest, 2–4 September 2010.

Lindley J. 2009. 'The over-education of UK immigrants and minority ethnic groups: evidence from the Labour Force Survey'. *Economics of Education Review*, 28, 80–89.

Lyon, D. 2006. 'The organization of care work in Italy: gender and migrant labour in the new economy'. *Indiana Journal of Global Legal Studies*, 13(1), 207–24.

Papademetriou, D.G., Sumption, M., Terrazas, A., with Burkert, C., Loyal, S. and Ferrero-Turrión, R. 2010. 'Migration and immigrants two years after the financial collapse: where do we stand?'. Washington, DC: Migration Policy Institute.

OECD. 2009. *International Migration Outlook*, Paris: OECD.

OECD. 2010. *Employment Outlook*, Paris: OECD.

Office for National Statistics. 2010. Social and Vital Statistics Division and Northern Ireland Statistics and Research Agency. Central Survey Unit, Labour Force Survey 2006–2010 Colchester, Essex: UK Data Archive [distributor].

Ratha, D., Mohapatra, S. and Silwal, A. 2010. Outlook for Remittance Flows 2010–2011. Migration and Development Brief No. 12. World Bank Development Prospects Group, Washington D.C.: The World Bank.

Saleheen, J. and Shadforth, C. 2006. 'The economic characteristics of immigrants and their impact on supply'. *Bank of England Quarterly Bulletin*, autumn, 374–85.

Sriskandarajah, D. and Cooley, L. 2009. 'Stemming the flow? The causes and consequences of the UK's "closed door" policy towards Romanians and Bulgarians', in Eade, J. and Valkanova, Y. (eds), *Accession and Migration*. Ashgate.

Veneto Lavoro. 2007. 'Gli Immigrati Rumeni in Italia e nel Veneto', Veneto Lavoro Osservatorio e Ricerca.

Venturini, A. and Villosio, C. 2008. 'Labour-market assimilation of foreign workers in Italy'. *Oxford Review of Economic Policy*, 24(3), 517–41.
World Bank. 2011. Migration and Remittances Factbook 2011, Washington D.C.: The World Bank.

Chapter 3

A Skill Mismatch for Migrant Workers? Evidence from *WageIndicator* Survey Data

Kea Tijdens and Maarten van Klaveren

1. Introduction

Are overeducation and undereducation more common among migrants compared to domestic workers? If so, are overeducation and undereducation similar across migrants from various home countries and across various host countries? This chapter is aimed at unravelling the incidence of skill mismatch, defined as the situation in which workers occupy jobs for which lower or higher skill levels are required compared to their current educational level. We focus on the skill mismatch of domestic and migrant workers employed in 13 countries of the European Union, namely Belgium, the Czech Republic, Denmark, Finland, France, Hungary, Italy, the Netherlands, Poland, Slovakia, Spain, Sweden, and the United Kingdom. Due to data limitations countries such as Austria, Germany and Ireland could not be included, although in the recent past they have attracted a substantial number of migrants. Migrants are defined as workers not born in the country where they are currently living. In the sample they originate from more than 200 countries, thereby reflecting a heterogeneous group, ranging from those who have migrated for economic reasons and refugees, to expats, intercultural married couples and others.

The academic discourse on mismatch in the labour market covers issues such as residential mismatch and hours mismatch, but this chapter focuses on skill mismatch. The literature on skill mismatch can be classified into three categories. A number of studies investigate the incidence of over- and undereducation, some of which provide breakdowns for specific groups in the labour market, such as gender and firm size. Many studies address the impact of over- and undereducation, mostly on wages. Finally, an important body of knowledge relates to the dynamics of overeducation: that is, how educational requirements and the educational composition of the workforce have changed over time.

This chapter addresses solely skills mismatch, focussing on the incidence of over- and undereducation. As pointed out by Leuven and Oosterbeek (2010) in their overview study, few studies have addressed the incidence of over- and undereducation of migrants. Our data are particularly suited to investigate differences in skill mismatch between domestic and migrant workers. We contribute to the body of knowledge on over- and undereducation in particular as we are able to provide a detailed breakdown of migrants from a wide variety of home countries. Our first research objective is to investigate whether migrants are more often over- and underqualified compared to domestic workers. The second objective is to investigate whether a range of theoretically based assumptions, including assumptions related to migrants, affect the incidence of over- or undereducation.

Given that our research objectives focus on the incidence of over- and undereducation, taking account of the effect of the crisis goes beyond the scope of this investigation. We refrain from an analysis of how the crisis has affected migrant flows, employment and the working conditions of migrants. Although we use a pooled dataset covering the years 2005–2010, this chapter does not investigate the impact of the economic crisis on skill mismatch either. Understanding the incidence of over- and undereducation is a condition of being able to hypothesise the impact of the crisis on this phenomenon.

The outline of this chapter is as follows. Section 2 goes into the theoretical and empirical literature with regard to the skill mismatch of migrant and domestic workers. In Section 3 data and methods are described. We present our results in Section 4. Section 5 discusses our findings and conclusions.

2. Review of the Literature on Migrants' Skill Mismatch and Earnings

2.1 What is Skill Mismatch?

Skill mismatch refers to the mismatch between a worker's educational attainment and the requirements of the job occupied, whereby several types of skill mismatch are distinguished (for example, McGuinness and Sloane 2011). A vertical mismatch refers to workers possessing an education that either exceeds or is below the educational level required for their jobs. Here, the terms 'overeducation' (also referred to as 'overschooling') and 'undereducation' are used. Educational level is a crude measure for indicating an individual's educational attainment or job requirements. For jobs, the skill based approach seems more adequate, as are the terms 'overskilling' and 'underskilling'. However, skills are more difficult to measure than educational attainment. The most common method is to measure an individual's generic skills, for example in cognitive tests or in OECD's IALS and PIAAC literacy surveys, whereas job-specific skill requirements are hardly used because they are far more difficult to measure. A horizontal mismatch refers to workers who are educated in another field than their job requires. Particularly in Germany, the concept of occupational mismatch is clearly distinguished from that of educational mismatch because of the country's widespread vocational training system, which provides the majority of the labour force with a generally accepted qualification for a wide range of occupations (Burkert and Seibert 2007). This chapter focuses solely on vertical skill mismatch, defined as overeducation and undereducation, because the data do not allow us to detail skills and skill requirements and thus horizontal mismatch.

Studying skill mismatch requires information about the educational attainment of individuals, as well as insight into the educational level required for jobs. The former is less subject to dispute than the latter. In country-specific surveys the educational attainment of individuals is measured mainly in terms of national educational categories. For cross-country comparisons, the ISCED classification is most often used, applying seven educational attainment levels (OECD 1999). In order to collect information about the educational requirements of jobs, the most frequently applied method is asking individual workers to indicate the educational attainment required for their job or to indicate whether they have sufficient skills to perform their job. This is called the subjective method, because it is based on surveys entailing workers' self-assessment (Van der Velden and Van Smoorenburg 1997; Groot and Maassen van den Brink 2000; Jensen et al. 2007; Leuven and Oosterbeek 2010; Piracha et al. 2010). A second method is called the objective method, because it is based on expert classification of the education and skills required by particular jobs. Here, a wide range of approaches can be noted. One approach is to classify jobs according to broad job levels: for example, the four skill levels ranging from unskilled to highly skilled, distinguished by the International Labour Organisation (ILO) in the first digit of its ISCO-08 occupational classification (ILO 2007). In many countries, national statistical agencies have adopted ISCO in their Labour Market Surveys, either by classifying occupations directly in terms of ISCO or by using crossover tables from a national occupational classification. Statistics Netherlands has attempted to classify the 1,200 occupations in its SBC classification in terms of seven job levels (CBS 1993). O*net, the occupations database in the United States, indicates skill requirements for a large range of occupations, based on desk research and company visits (O*net 2002).[1] A third method is called the empirical method, whereby the mean years of schooling of all workers in a given occupation or group of occupations are compared to the schooling of an individual in the occupation. Individuals are defined to be overeducated if their schooling level is more than one standard deviation above the mean of all individuals in that occupation (Clogg and Shockey 1984; Verdugo and Verdugo 1989; Van der Velden and Van Smoorenburg 1997).

Objections have been raised to all three methods. The first method is criticised because workers may be inclined to overstate the educational requirements of their job or simply to equate these requirements to their own level of education

---

1   For the purpose of matching job seekers to vacancies, skill requirements need to be far more detailed. This is usually done by professional job analysts, analysing skill requirements in job advertisements, studying realised job matches or undertaking company studies of required skills. However, this method typically addresses a selected set of occupations and does not cover all occupations in a national labour market, as the latter is a huge undertaking.

(Hartog and Jonker 1997). Furthermore, respondents may not always have a good insight into the level of education required for a job (Cohn and Khan 1995; Halaby 1994). The second method, the objective one, is criticised because skill requirements within a given occupation cannot vary (Halaby 1994). Based on a survey of school-leavers, Van der Velden and Van Smoorenburg (1997) conclude that job analysts systematically overestimate the level of required education, probably because they do not use the 'real' situation as the basis of their rating, but descriptions of the tasks and the nature and required level of knowledge and skills. The third method also ignores the variation in terms of educational requirements within an occupation. Additionally, the choice of one standard deviation seems rather arbitrary (Halaby, 1994). Therefore, Hartog and Jonker (1997) and Verhaest and Omey (2006) even conclude that this should be the least preferred method for determining overschooling.

2.2 The Incidence of Skill Mismatch

All studies on skill mismatch conclude the existence of overeducation. Based on their meta-analysis of more than 180 studies covering five decades and countries in Asia, Europe (predominantly the EU15), the Americas and Australia, Leuven and Oosterbeek (2010) conclude that, on average, 30 per cent of the workforce is overeducated and 26 per cent is undereducated. Overeducation is less often found in Latin America and most often in the USA/Canada. From the 1970s to the 1990s, overeducation declined, but the 2000s exhibit an increase, although the authors note that this might be due to a single 2008 study. In an earlier meta-analysis, Groot and Maassen van der Brink (2000) concluded that the overall incidence of overeducation in the labour market appears to be about 26 per cent.

The incidence of overeducation is likely to be affected by the measurement method. According to Leuven and Oosterbeek (2010) the studies based on self-assessment and job analysis methods do not reveal large differences in this respect, but the method on the mean reveals lower levels of overeducation. Groot and Maassen van der Brink (2000) find that overeducation is more frequent when self-reported rather than when objective measures are used. Leuven and Oosterbeek have found that many studies have estimated probit or similar binary models of the determinants of overeducation and undereducation, but that the specifications of these models vary widely. More or less consistent findings across studies are that young people, women and migrants are more likely to be overeducated. Remarkably few findings refer to the incidence of overeducation for specific educational categories. Mavromaras et al. (2009), analysing the Australian HILDA Survey 2001–2006, have found that overeducation occurs more often in the top half of education brackets than in the lower half, pointing to a relative lack of high-skilled jobs.

According to Leuven and Oosterbeek (2010), only a few studies have addressed the incidence of over- and undereducation among migrants. The available evidence indicates that migrants are more likely to be overeducated. In a study based on the

Labour Force Survey in the United Kingdom, Lindley and Lenton (2006) suggest that immigrants initially experience higher overeducation but that this difference is eroded with time spent in the UK. In a study based on the Longitudinal Survey of Immigrant Australians (LSIA) Green et al. (2007) conclude that migrants are more likely to be overeducated than the native population, even if the migrants entered the country in question on skill-based visas. They were better educated than the native-born population but were relatively less likely to be found in managerial and professional occupations and were overrepresented in unskilled work. The authors find that overeducation is greatest for migrants from non-English speaking backgrounds(see also Korpi in this volume). Further details on home countries are provided by Battu and Sloane (2002), using a survey of Ethnic Minorities in the UK. They conclude that different ethnic groups have varying levels of overeducation, with the highest incidence of overeducation among Indian and African-Asian groups. However, the results of a study of the US high-skilled labour market by Chiswick and Miller (2009) show that overeducation is widespread, among both migrants and native-born. In the USA, the extent of overeducation declines with duration as high-skilled migrants obtain jobs commensurate with their educational level. Using the Longitudinal Survey of Immigrants to Australia, Piracha et al. (2010) reveal that a significant part of the variation in the migrants' probability of being over- or undereducated in the Australian labour market can be explained by having been over- or undereducated in their last job in the home country. Home-country mismatch was notably large in the case of undereducation.

Turning to the dynamics of over- and undereducation over time and their methodological implications, there is a massive literature on upgrading and downgrading with regard to occupations. In the past 15 years, much of this literature has been devoted to so-called skill-biased technological change, assuming – and largely confirming – that in developed countries educational requirements for a similar job within industries have increased over time, mainly due to technological developments (Berman et al. 1998; Machin 2001; Autor et al. 2001). Upgrading entails that, with tenure, the incidence of undereducation increases, whereas downgrading works out the other way. A second dynamic process refers to the inflation of qualifications, implying that new entrants are more likely to be overeducated. Third, dynamics over time may also be caused by fluctuations in labour market conditions, with alternating periods of scarce and excess labour supply: in periods of scarce supply, new entrants are more likely to be undereducated, whereas the reverse holds for entrants in periods of excess supply. No studies have yet revealed the impact of the economic crisis on the skill structure of the labour market: whether losses have targeted high-skilled jobs more than low-skilled jobs or vice versa. Finally, in a study of skill mismatch among migrants the dynamics over time caused by national migration policies should be taken into account. Policies stimulating access for high-skilled migrants may affect the educational composition of relevant cohorts of migrants, but this also applies to more restrictive policies towards migration (see also Korpi in this volume). This study does not consider these dynamic processes.

Few empirical attempts have been made to investigate the longitudinal impact of over- and undereducation, while a legitimate question is whether job allocation frictions diminish over time. Korpi and Tahlin (2009) do not find support for the assumption that mismatch dissolves with the time individuals spent in the labour market. Using cross-sectional and panel data from the Swedish Standard of Living Surveys 1974–2000, the authors conclude that the overeducated are penalised early on by an inferior rate of return to schooling from which this group does not recover.

A final caveat must be made here. Following Piracha et al. (2010), a match or mismatch is observed only for employed individuals. Skill mismatches may be larger for the unemployed labour force, for example, if the educational level of the unemployed does not match the educational requirements of relevant job vacancies. When assuming a higher incidence of mismatch for migrants, the fact that they may constitute a self-selected sub-sample may be overlooked.

2.3 Explanations of Skill Mismatch among Migrants

In this section, we will explore the theoretical explanations of overeducation and undereducation, and the implications of such explanations for the higher incidence of over- and undereducation among migrants. Concerning overeducation, most of the literature points to explanations related to job allocation frictions. We found six explanations for overeducation, which we will treat successively here. A first explanation refers to the assumption that, to begin with, entry-level workers might occupy jobs for which they are overeducated and later on move to jobs that better match their educational attainment. In their overview studies, Leuven and Oosterbeek (2010) and Cedefop (2010) conclude that, according to many studies, younger workers are more likely to be overeducated than older workers. This supports the assumption that overeducation is part of an adaptation process in the early stages of a working career, in which it compensates for the lack of other human capital endowments, such as ability, on-the-job training, or experience. Following this explanation, we will investigate job allocation frictions in our empirical study by testing the assumption that the incidence of overeducation is higher among workers who have recently entered the labour market.

A second explanation details the assumption of job allocation frictions. This explanation refers to specific groups of workers when entering the labour market. It is assumed that, in particular, students with a job on the side; re-entering housewives for whom a job–education match does not rank high among their preferences; workers who have had unemployment spells and involuntary quits; and other workers with poor bargaining power; will occupy jobs for which they are overeducated. This assumption is supported by a range of research results. According to Groot and Maassen van den Brink (2000), workers who have experienced a career break are more likely to be found in jobs for which they are overeducated. Sloane et al. (1999) found that overeducated workers had more unemployment spells and involuntary quits than others. The evidence of Sicherman

(1991) showed that overeducated workers changed jobs more frequently, and that they had less experience, tenure and on-the-job training than correctly matched workers. In our empirical part, we will investigate this type of job allocation friction by testing the assumption that the incidence of overeducation is higher among workers who have experienced unemployment spells and quits.

A third theoretical explanation of overeducation refers to job allocation frictions that are related to career mobility. This explanation assumes that individuals accept a lower-level job if the probability of promotion is higher (Sicherman and Galor 1990). In our empirical study, we will test whether the incidence of overeducation is higher for jobs with good promotion prospects compared to jobs with average or poor promotion prospects.

A fourth theoretical explanation refers to job allocation frictions due to imperfect information on the employer's side, which is particularly associated with a lack of transparency with regard to diplomas or transferability of credentials (Cedefop 2010; OECD 2007). However, we did not encounter empirical studies which investigated this assumption. In our empirical study we assume that migrants who arrived in the host country at an adult age will be more likely to be overeducated, because this group will be confronted by this lack of transparency and transferability of their credentials.

A fifth theoretical explanation concentrates on job allocation frictions due to the poor abilities of individual workers. This assumption goes beyond the crude measurement of educational attainment and details a worker's ability as well as the skill requirements of a job. In particular, one ability has been investigated, namely the worker's mastery of the native language or lingua franca of the host country. Thus, in this approach the language ability of the worker is critical. According to a study of Australia, workers from a non-native language speaking background showed a higher and persistent incidence of overeducation than those from a native-language speaking background (Kler 2005). In our empirical study, we will test whether migrants from home countries where the native language or lingua franca does not match that of the home country are more likely to experience overeducation.

A sixth theoretical explanation refers to job allocation frictions due to labour market discrimination: employers have a preference for workers from the 'same group'. Field experiments show pervasive ethnic discrimination in many countries (OECD 2007). In our empirical study, we will assume that migrants not born in the country of survey are more likely to be overeducated compared to domestic workers. In addition, in a few additional analyses we will also investigate whether second generation migrants and individuals from ethnic minorities are more likely to be overeducated compared to domestic workers.

Concerning undereducation, fewer theoretical explanations exist. Empirical studies have focussed more often on overeducation than on undereducation. When explaining undereducation, the literature barely points to job allocation frictions. The theoretical explanations for undereducation are associated mainly with career progress. Workers with high abilities may be promoted in the corporate hierarchy and their job level therefore may increase, whereas their educational attainment will remain unchanged. This is consistent with the findings of Sloane et al. (1999), showing that promotion and supervisory experience are found least frequently among the overeducated and most frequently among the undereducated. In our empirical study, we will test whether the incidence of undereducation is higher in supervisory positions.

3. Methods and Data

3.1 Data and Definitions

This chapter builds on statistical analyses of the large *WageIndicator* dataset. The *WageIndicator* project is currently running in more than 50 countries on five continents. It consists of national websites, each receiving large numbers of visitors, primarily because the websites post a Salary Check that provides free information on occupation-specific wages. Worldwide, the national *WageIndicator* websites attract large numbers of web visitors: in 2009, more than 10 million. The websites are consulted by workers when making job mobility decisions, or for annual performance talks or wage negotiations. The sites are also consulted by school pupils, students or re-entrant women facing occupational choices, or by employers in small and medium-sized companies when recruiting staff or negotiating wages with their employees. The project website can be found at www.wageindicator.org.

The *WageIndicator* dataset is derived from a web survey on work and wages, posted on all national *WageIndicator* websites and comparable across all countries. The survey is in the national language(s) and adapted to country-specific issues, where needed. In return for the free information provided, visitors are asked to complete the survey. Thus, the survey is voluntary, continuous and multi-country.[2] The survey takes approximately 10 minutes to complete for part 1 and 10 minutes for part 2. It contains detailed questions, among others about education, occupation, skill mismatch, industry, country of birth, country of birth of mother and father and, in some countries, ethnic group. The data from the web survey are used for research and for the calculations underlying the Salary Check. The dataset is advantageous for our purpose because it has sufficient observations to distinguish detailed migrant groups. It is disadvantageous, however, because by definition a web survey will be completed only by individuals with sufficient language skills to read the survey questions. This might be particularly off-putting for migrants and will definitely lead to biased data, although the problem is not

2   Note that also web-surveys based on email invitations from a large database (panel) of respondents are volunteer surveys. Only a very few web-surveys, such as the LISS panel from Tilburg University, are randomly sampled using non-internet sampling frames. Note further that random sampled surveys may also be biased in case of substantial non-response, which nowadays in many surveys drops below 50 per cent.

as bad as it seems, because it can be assumed, first, that literacy skills are higher among employed migrants compared to unemployed migrants and second, that the size of the group of employed migrants with insufficient literacy skills is relatively small compared to the labour force as a whole.

The *WageIndicator* web survey includes several questions to identify minority groups. In the analyses, country of birth is used to identify the major migrant groups. In the web survey, respondents are asked if they are born in the country of survey; if not, they can tick a country from a list of approximately 200. In this chapter we use 'domestic workers' and 'migrant workers' to identify the two groups. The web survey does not allow the identification of return migration.

Although *WageIndicator* currently has websites and surveys established in almost all EU member states, some of them did not start until 2010 (for example, Austria and Ireland). In a few other countries, the question about skill mismatch is not asked (for example, Germany). Therefore, the analyses were performed with data from 13 EU member states. In order to have sufficient observations to distinguish migrant groups in detail, we used the pooled annual data of the years 2005–20010. Note, however, that four of the 13 countries – the Czech Republic, France, Slovakia and Sweden – joined the web survey only in 2008. Respondents with ages under 14 or over 70, unemployed, school pupils, students and those who have never had a job were excluded, and so were those with no valid values on the skill mismatch question and country of birth. Altogether, 291,699 observations were included in the analysis. The large sample size allows a breakdown of migrant groups according to country of birth in order to better capture the heterogeneity of migrants.

Although the survey is completed voluntarily, we do not use within-country weights. First, compared to the means of demographic variables known from other sources the sample variable means do not deviate to a large extent. For example, based on 180 studies Leuven and Oosterbeek (2010) found an average of 30 per cent overeducation, of which the USA revealed the highest overeducation. Our dataset reveals 22 per cent overeducation in the EU member states. The most underrepresented groups are small groups, for example, workers with a part-time job of less than 10 hours per week. Weighting to correct for these groups will scarcely affect the means of the variables under study. Second, and most important, weighting volunteer surveys to control for socio-demographic composition does not solve the small bias in wages, our targeted variable (Steinmetz et al. 2009). However, we do use country weights, using data from the European Labour Force Survey in the respective years, so that the sample reflects the relative sizes of the national labour forces.

3.2 The Model

Skill mismatch is the dependent variable in this chapter. The *WageIndicator* survey includes a question 'Do your qualifications match your job?' The three response options are 'Yes', 'No, I am overqualified for my job' and 'No, I am underqualified for my job'. Thus, we will analyse workers' self-assessed skill mismatch. We will use 'correct match', 'overeducation' and 'undereducation' to identify the three answer groups. The first model investigates whether migrant workers, categorised in groups according to their country of birth, are more or less likely to be under- or overeducated.

In a second model, skill mismatch is considered to be dependent on educational attainment and job levels. Regarding education, the web survey asks: 'What is the highest level of education you have attained (with certificate)?' The question uses a predefined list of national educational categories. An instruction to the survey question says 'If you went to school abroad, enter the equivalent level'. Thus, the measurement of migrants' attained education might cause measurement errors if they received their education in the country of origin and not in the host country. Unfortunately, this measurement error cannot be corrected. For the sake of international comparison the national educational categories have been recoded into the worldwide International Standard Classification of Education classification 1997, as designed by UNESCO.[3] The variable ranges from 1 (primary level of education) to 6.1 (6A second stage of tertiary education, leading to an advanced research qualification). For the analyses, ISCED specifications such as 2A or 2B have been recoded as 2. Note that the *WageIndicator* web survey has an additional value of 0, indicating 'no education'. The dataset has seven values for the ISCED variable, ranging from 0 to 6.

We have already considered the difficulties related to measuring job levels in Section 2. For this chapter, four job level indicators have been explored, three of which are derived from the occupation variable. The dataset holds detailed information on occupation, extending the ILO's ISCO-08 four-digit occupational classification by adding further digits to approximately 1,700 occupations (Tijdens 2010). The first job level indicator is the ISCO-08 skill level, based on the ILO's definition of the four ISCO-08 job levels, ranging from 1 = unskilled, reflecting ISCED 0-1, to 4 = highly skilled, reflecting ISCED 5a and 6 (ILO 2007). The reader should note that the ILO's skill levels are not based on global empirical investigations. Moreover, based on wage studies the skill levels are considered poor proxies (Dumont 2006). The second indicator is called 'Corporate hierarchy' which is based on a mapping of the 1,700 occupations into six corporate hierarchical levels, ranging from 0 = helper to 6 = CEO, developed by the first author. The third indicator is the well-known socio-economic status of jobs, based on the ISEI measure of Ganzeboom (2010). A fourth indicator, 'hierarchy within occupation', is not based on ISCO-08, but on self-assessed status within the occupation, ranging from 1 = assistant/trainee to 3 = supervisor/teamleader. After analysing these four variables (see the Appendix for mean scores across migrant groups), it turned out that the ISCO skill level and the ISCO socio-economic status were closely related, and therefore the ISCO socio-economic status was not included in the

---

3   For details about ISCED, see: www.unesco.org/education/information/nfsunesco/doc/isced_1997.htm.

analyses. The occupation variable had a non-negligible number of missing values, and therefore we included a dummy variable indicating the missing cases for the skill level variable. For the missing values in the variable 'corporate hierarchy' we added information from the variable on supervisory position. Thus, in our analyses three variables are used as proxies for job level. These analyses will be controlled for industry and firm size.

In a third model, three general assumptions have been derived from the theoretical considerations in Section 2.3, thus not distinguishing between migrant and domestic workers. Overeducation is expected to be applicable for:

1. workers who recently entered the labour market, here defined as five years' or less work experience;
2. workers with poor bargaining power, here defined as workers who are on sick leave, housewives or retirees with a job on the side, workers with an unemployment spell, and trainees;
3. female workers as opposed to male workers.

In a fourth model, three assumptions with regard to migrants have been derived from the theoretical considerations in Section 2.3. Overeducation is expected to be applicable for:

1. workers facing lack of transparency of credentials, here defined as migrant workers who have arrived in the host country at an adult age (age 21 or older) and thus having completed their education in a country with credentials that are most likely unknown to the employer;
2. workers facing discrimination from employers, here defined as workers who were not born in the country of survey, workers who were born in the country of survey but whose parents were not born in the country of survey and workers who are part of an ethnic minority group;
3. workers with lower language abilities, here defined as migrant workers born in a country with a native language or a lingua franca that does not match that of the host country.

Logit analyses have been used to estimate the likelihood of being overqualified compared to having a correct match or being underqualified. No estimatins have been made for underqualification. These analyses are controlled for some workplace and personal characteristics, namely aggregate industry, firm size and gender.

The analyses were carried out with data from 13 EU member states, nine countries of the so-called old EU15 member states, namely Belgium, Denmark, Finland, France, Italy, Netherlands, Spain, Sweden, and United Kingdom, and four new accession EU12 countries, namely the Czech Republic, Hungary, Poland and Slovakia. The large sample size allows a clustering into two categories of domestic and nine categories of migrant workers (see Table 3.1). The two categories of domestic workers include workers in the nine EU15 countries and in the four EU12 countries. Four categories of migrant workers are aimed at capturing migration within the European Union and include migrants living in the nine EU15 countries and born in the EU15, living in the nine EU15 countries and born in the EU12, living in the four EU12 countries and born in the EU12 and living in the four EU12 countries and born in the EU15. Five categories of migrant workers aim to capture migration from outside the European Union and currently living in either the nine EU15 or the four EU12 countries. This group includes migrants born in a European but non-EU country (predominantly Russia and CIS countries), migrants born in USA, Canada or Australia, migrants born in Africa, migrants born in Latin America, and migrants born in Asia.

4. Empirical Findings on Skill Mismatch

4.1 Descriptive Analysis of Skill Mismatch

Table 3.1 shows that the share of migrant workers in the nine EU15 countries is much higher than in the four EU12 countries (14 per cent versus 2 per cent). In the nine EU15 countries, almost half of the largest migrant group comes from other countries within the EU15 countries (40 per cent from all migrants in the EU15), whereas the second largest migrant group originates from Latin America (18 per cent). The substantial share of this second group is in part due to the migrants from Surinam and the Dutch Antilles in the Netherlands. In the four EU12 countries, the largest migrant group is born in other countries within the EU12 (52 per cent of all migrants in the EU12), followed by the group from European non-EU countries (31 per cent).

Using workers' skill match assessment, Table 3.2 shows that almost three of four respondents in the entire sample assess their job level and educational attainment to be a correct match (74 per cent). The differences between the domestic and migrant workers are minor (74 per cent, sd .44 versus 72 per cent, sd .45). When detailing the incidence of a correct match for the various groups, Table 3.2 reveals that migrants born in the EU15 and working in the EU12 most frequently report a correct match (89 per cent), followed by domestic workers in the EU12 (87 per cent). In contrast, the migrant workers born in the EU12 and working in the EU15 and the migrant workers born in Asia report it least frequently (64 per cent and 65 per cent, respectively).

One in five workers assess themselves as overqualified (20 per cent). When comparing domestic and migrant workers, overqualification occurs less often among domestic workers than among migrant workers (19 per cent, sd .39 versus 24 per cent, sd .43). When detailing overqualification, migrants of Asian origin and those of Latin American origin report being overqualified most frequently (32 per cent and 27 per cent, respectively). In contrast, the migrants born in the EU15 and working in the EU12, migrants born in non-EU Europe and domestic workers

Table 3.1   Distribution over native and immigrant groups and over immigrant groups only, breakdown by EU15 and EU12 (N_unweighted=291,699)

		Country of survey = EU15		Country of survey = EU12		N_unweighted
1	EU15 domestic	85.57%				247516
2	EU15 migrant born in EU15	5.84%	40.49%			5719
3	EU15 migrant born in EU12	1.13%	7.80%			994
4	EU12 domestic			98.18%		26295
5	EU12 migrant born in EU12			0.94%	51.77%	665
5	EU12 migrant born in EU15			0.19%	10.22%	42
6	EU27 migrant born in non-EU Europe	1.11%	7.69%	0.57%	31.41%	799
7	EU27 migrant born in USA, Canada or Australia	0.77%	5.34%	0.03%	1.84%	627
8	EU27 migrant born in Africa	1.31%	9.04%	0.03%	1.61%	1888
9	EU27 migrant born in Latin America	2.66%	18.44%	0.02%	0.92%	4436
10	EU27 migrant born in Asia	1.62%	11.20%	0.04%	2.23%	2718
		100%	100%	100%	100%	291699

Source: WageIndicator data 2005–2010, selection 13 EU member states. The data are weighted across countries and years, using European Labour Force Survey data (weighting for 2010 data is based on 2009 ELFS data, because 2010 ELFS data were not yet available at the time of writing).

in the EU12 report least frequently being overqualified (7 per cent, 8 per cent and 11 per cent). Overqualification is much more common in the labour markets of the EU15 compared to the EU12 (22 per cent versus 11 per cent), but in both areas migrants more often report being overqualified than domestic workers.

One in twenty workers assess themselves as underqualified (6 per cent). Domestic workers report being underqualified more frequently compared to migrants (7 per cent, sd .25 versus 4 per cent, sd .20). Underqualification occurs more often in the EU15 compared to the EU12 (7 per cent versus 2 per cent). In the EU15, domestic workers more often report being underqualified than migrant workers do, whereas the reverse pattern can be seen in the EU12. The most frequent incidences of overqualification are reported by domestic workers in the EU15 and by migrants born in the EU12 and working in the EU15 (9 per cent and 7 per cent, respectively). The EU12 born migrants in the EU15 frequently report both being underqualified and being overqualified.

Table 3.2   Distribution over self-assessed skill mismatch (row percentages) for EU15+12 natives and migrant groups (N_ unweighted=291,699)

Country of birth	Under-qualified	Correct match	Over-qualified	Total
EU15 domestic	8.0%	70.5%	21.5%	100%
EU15 migrant born in EU15	2.7%	73.7%	23.6%	100%
EU15 migrant born in EU12	7.4%	64.1%	28.5%	100%
EU12 domestic	2.2%	86.9%	10.9%	100%
EU12 migrant born in EU12	3.7%	70.9%	25.4%	100%
EU12 migrant born in EU15	4.5%	88.7%	6.8%	100%
EU27 migrant born in non-EU Europe	5.9%	85.8%	8.2%	100%
EU27 migrant born in USA, Canada or Australia	2.4%	80.9%	16.7%	100%
EU27 migrant born in Africa	5.8%	68.9%	25.2%	100%
EU27 migrant born in Latin America	6.2%	66.4%	27.4%	100%
EU27 migrant born in Asia	2.4%	65.5%	32.1%	100%
Total	6.5%	73.7%	19.8%	100%
Belgium – Domestic worker	12.0%	72.4%	15.6%	100%
Belgium – Migrant worker	8.9%	67.5%	23.6%	100%
Denmark – Domestic worker	3.3%	77.8%	18.9%	100%
Denmark – Migrant worker	1.0%	54.3%	44.6%	100%
Finland – Domestic worker	5.1%	68.6%	26.3%	100%
Finland – Migrant worker	3.4%	69.7%	26.9%	100%

France – Domestic worker	6.0%	80.8%	13.2%	100%
France – Migrant worker	2.1%	75.6%	22.3%	100%
Italy – Domestic worker	12.3%	68.1%	19.5%	100%
Italy – Migrant worker	5.4%	77.5%	17.1%	100%
Netherlands – Domestic worker	13.1%	68.9%	18.1%	100%
Netherlands – Migrant worker	10.3%	63.6%	26.1%	100%
Spain – Domestic worker	5.3%	64.0%	30.7%	100%
Spain – Migrant worker	4.6%	65.3%	30.1%	100%
Sweden – Domestic worker	3.1%	76.2%	20.7%	100%
Sweden – Migrant worker	3.9%	72.8%	23.3%	100%
United Kingdom – Domestic worker	6.5%	72.5%	21.0%	100%
United Kingdom – Migrant worker	4.0%	71.4%	24.6%	100%
Total – EU15 – Domestic worker	8.0%	70.5%	21.4%	100%
Total – EU15 – Migrant worker	4.2%	71.5%	24.3%	100%
Total – EU15	7.5%	70.7%	21.9%	100%
Czech Republic – Domestic worker	7.4%	67.5%	25.1%	100%
Czech Republic – Migrant worker	4.6%	68.0%	27.5%	100%
Hungary – Domestic worker	3.2%	73.2%	23.6%	100%
Hungary – Migrant worker	5.9%	69.2%	24.9%	100%
Poland – Domestic worker	1.1%	94.2%	4.7%	100%
Poland – Migrant worker	3.0%	94.8%	2.2%	100%
Slovakia – Domestic worker	5.2%	61.2%	33.6%	100%
Slovakia – Migrant worker		58.9%	41.1%	100%
Total – EU12 – Domestic worker	2.2%	86.9%	10.9%	100%
Total – EU12 – Migrant worker	4.2%	77.7%	18.2%	100%
Total – EU12	2.2%	86.8%	11.0%	100%
Total – Domestic worker	6.8%	73.9%	19.2%	100%
Total – Migrant worker	4.2%	71.7%	24.1%	100%
Total	6.5%	73.7%	19.8%	100%

Source: *WageIndicator* data 2005–2010, selection 13 EU member states. The data are weighted across countries and years, using European Labour Force Survey data (weighting for 2010 data is based on 2009 ELFS data, because 2010 ELFS data were not yet available at the time of writing).

Table 3.3 presents the means for all variables in the model, broken down for the three skill match categories. All variables reveal a significant difference across categories. Not surprisingly, the mean educational attainment for the underqualified workers is lowest and for the overqualified workers highest, whereas the mean job levels are highest for the workers with a correct match and lowest for the overqualified workers. The overqualified workers are most frequently female, most frequently have fewer than five years' experience, most frequently have poor bargaining power and least frequently are in a supervisory position. The correctly matched workers have, on average, the highest socio-economic status.

Table 3.3   Descriptive statistics (means) over the three skill match categories for all variables in the model (N_unweighted=291,699)

Descriptive statistics	Total	Under qualified	Correct match	Over qualified	Sign Chisq
EU15 domestic (0, 1)	69.6%	85.8%	66.6%	75.2%	***
EU15 migrant born in EU15 (0, 1)	4.8%	2.0%	4.8%	5.7%	***
EU15 migrant born in EU12 (0, 1)	0.9%	1.0%	0.8%	1.3%	***
EU12 domestic (0, 1)	18.2%	6.2%	21.5%	10.0%	***
EU12 migrant born in EU12 (0, 1)	0.2%	0.1%	0.2%	0.2%	***
EU12 migrant born in EU15 (0, 1)	0.0%	0.0%	0.0%	0.0%	***
EU27 migrant born in non-EU Europe (0, 1)	1.0%	0.9%	1.2%	0.4%	***
EU27 migrant born in USA, Canada, Australia (0, 1)	0.6%	0.2%	0.7%	0.5%	***
EU27 migrant born in Africa (0, 1)	1.1%	1.0%	1.0%	1.4%	***
EU27 migrant born in Latin America (0, 1)	2.2%	2.1%	2.0%	3.0%	***
EU27 migrant born in Asia (0, 1)	1.3%	0.5%	1.2%	2.1%	***
ISCED educational level (0–7)	4.16	3.55	4.19	4.28	***
Corporate hierarchy (1=helper; ... ; 6=CEO)	28.9%	45.9%	33.2%	7.4%	***
Socio-economic status (10–89)	52.07	50.76	53.46	47.29	***
Firm size 1–10 (0, 1)	22.4%	19.5%	21.4%	26.7%	***
Firm size 10–50 (0, 1)	26.6%	30.9%	26.3%	26.7%	***
Firm size 50–100 (0, 1)	12.0%	10.7%	12.6%	10.5%	***
Firm size 100–500 (0, 1)	19.5%	18.7%	19.7%	19.2%	***
Firm size 500 and over (0, 1)	19.4%	20.2%	20.1%	16.9%	***
Industry – Agriculture, manufacturing, construction (0, 1)	27.3%	26.4%	27.7%	25.9%	***
Industry – Trade, transport, hospitality (0, 1)	31.9%	36.5%	31.1%	33.4%	***
Industry – Commercial services (0, 1)	19.8%	17.6%	20.3%	18.5%	***

Industry – Public sector, health care, education (0, 1)	21.0%	19.5%	20.8%	22.2%	***
Female (0, 1)	45.1%	40.9%	44.5%	48.6%	***
Work experience <= 5 year (0, 1)	26.3%	17.7%	26.6%	27.9%	***
Poor bargaining power (0, 1)	9.7%	6.7%	9.8%	10.0%	***
Supervisory position (0, 1)	36.5%	39.8%	38.3%	29.1%	***
Good promotion prospects (0, 1)	44.2%	53.5%	44.1%	41.3%	***
Migrant speaking domestic language (0, 1)	91.3%	93.9%	91.5%	89.5%	***
Migrant including 2nd generation and ethnic group (0, 1)	13.6%	11.5%	13.3%	15.2%	***
Migrant arrived as adult (0, 1)	7.1%	3.9%	7.1%	8.4%	***

Source: *WageIndicator* data 2005–2010, selection 13 EU member states. The data are weighted across countries and years, using European Labour Force Survey data (weighting for 2010 data is based on 2009 ELFS data, because 2010 ELFS data were not yet available at the time of writing).

4.2 Does Overeducation Occur More Often among Migrant Workers?

Our first research objective is to investigate whether migrants are more often overqualified compared to domestic workers. Table 3.4 confirms that overeducation occurs more often among migrant workers. Based on Model 1a in the table the conclusion is confirmed that the odds of being overqualified increases by a factor of 1.47 for migrants compared to domestic workers. However, the table also reveals that the odds of a worker being overqualified increases substantially when working in the EU15 compared to the EU12. Thus, both the characteristics of migrants and those of national labour markets influence the incidence of overeducation. In Model 1b the heterogeneity of the migrant groups is taken into account. The model reveals large differences across these groups. Of all migrant and domestic groups, the odds of being overqualified are highest for migrants working in the EU15 and born in the EU12. In the model, the latter is the reference group. In contrast, the odds decrease most for migrants from the USA, Canada and Australia, followed by domestic workers in the EU12. These findings underline that generalisations about migrants drawn in Model 1a need to be specified for various migrant groups.

4.3 Is Overeducation Related to Labour Market Characteristics?

The second research objective concerns whether overeducation is related to national labour market characteristics, assuming that skill mismatch varies among workers' educational attainment and their job levels. Model 2 in Table 3.4 reveals, not surprisingly, that the odds of being overqualified increase with educational attainment. Overeducation is also related to job levels. We used three proxies

Table 3.4 Chance of overeducation compared to a correct skill match or undereducation (logistic regression: odds ratio, significance levels and standard errors in brackets)

	Model 1a		Model 1b		Model 2		Model 3		Model 4	
	Exp(B)	S.E.	Exp(B)	S.E.	Exp(B)	S.E.	Exp(B)	S.E.	Exp(B)	S.E.
Migrant(0,1)	1.545 ***	(0.02)								
Working in EU15 (0,1)	1.284 ***	(0.02)								
EU15 domestic			0.384 ***	(0.08)	0.453 ***	(0.08)	0.476 ***	(0.08)		
EU15 migrant born in EU15			0.493 ***	(0.09)	0.553 ***	(0.09)	0.572 ***	(0.09)		
EU12 domestic			0.298 ***	(0.08)	0.333 ***	(0.09)	0.346 ***	(0.09)		
EU12 migrant born in EU12			0.533 ***	(0.13)	0.615 ***	(0.13)	0.651 **	(0.13)		
EU27 migrant born in non-EU Europe			0.816	(0.12)	0.825	(0.13)	0.837	(0.13)		
EU27 migrant born in USA, Can., Aus.			0.297 ***	(0.15)	0.353 ***	(0.16)	0.364 ***	(0.16)		
EU27 migrant born in Africa			0.653 ***	(0.10)	0.702 ***	(0.11)	0.732 **	(0.11)		
EU27 migrant born in Latin America			0.648 ***	(0.09)	0.708 ***	(0.09)	0.735 ***	(0.09)		
EU15 migrant born in Asia			0.535 ***	(0.10)	0.592 ***	(0.10)	0.615 ***	(0.10)		

	Model 1a		Model 1b		Model 2		Model 3		Model 4	
	Exp(B)	S.E.	Exp(B)	S.E.	Exp(B)	S.E.	Exp(B)	S.E.	Exp(B)	S.E.
Educational level (ISCED 0=no edu, .., 7=tert. edu)					1.498 ***	(0.00)	1.482 ***	(0.00)	1.471 ***	(0.00)
Hierarchy within occupat. (1=trainee, .., 3=superv)					0.708 ***	(0.01)	0.743 ***	(0.01)	0.740 ***	(0.01)
Corporate hierarchy (1=help, .., 6=CEO)					0.839 ***	(0.01)	0.847 ***	(0.01)	0.843 ***	(0.01)
Occupation semi-skilled					0.522 ***	(0.03)	0.517 ***	(0.03)	0.515 ***	(0.03)
Occupation skilled					0.252 ***	(0.03)	0.254 ***	(0.03)	0.253 ***	(0.03)
Occupation highly skilled					0.147 ***	(0.03)	0.148 ***	(0.03)	0.147 ***	(0.03)
Occupation skill level missing					0.304 ***	(0.03)	0.305 ***	(0.03)	0.314 ***	(0.03)
Firm size 1–10					1.114 ***	(0.02)	1.088 ***	(0.02)	1.088 ***	(0.02)
Firm size 10–50					1.036	(0.02)	1.027	(0.02)	1.028	(0.02)
Firm size 100–500					0.929 ***	(0.02)	0.937 ***	(0.02)	0.936 ***	(0.02)
Firm size 500 and over					0.809 ***	(0.02)	0.826 ***	(0.02)	0.830 ***	(0.02)

	Model 1a		Model 1b		Model 2		Model 3		Model 4	
	Exp(B)	S.E.	Exp(B)	S.E.	Exp(B)	S.E.	Exp(B)	S.E.	Exp(B)	S.E.
Industry – Agriculture, manufacturing, construction					0.847 ***	(0.01)	0.910 ***	(0.01)	0.907 ***	(0.01)
Industry – Trade, transport, hospitality					1.213 ***	(0.01)	1.259 ***	(0.01)	1.253 ***	(0.01)
Industry – Commercial services					0.755 ***	(0.02)	0.768 ***	(0.02)	0.767 ***	(0.02)
Industry – Missing value					0.942	(0.03)	0.989	(0.03)	0.963	(0.03)
Recent labour market entrant (0,1)							1.202 ***	(0.01)	1.192 ***	(0.01)
Poor bargaining power (0,1)							1.190 ***	(0.02)	1.192 ***	(0.02)
Female (0,1)							1.216 ***	(0.01)	1.213 ***	(0.01)
Lack of transparent credentials (0,1)									1.509 ***	(0.04)
Speaks native language (0,1)									0.955	(0.03)
Migrant 1st/2nd generation or ethnic minority (0,1)									1.174 ***	(0.02)

	Model 1a		Model 1b		Model 2		Model 3		Model 4	
	Exp(B)	S.E.	Exp(B)	S.E.	Exp(B)	S.E.	Exp(B)	S.E.	Exp(B)	S.E.
Constant			0.639	*** (0.08)	0.357	*** (0.09)	0.262	*** (0.09)	0.136	*** (0.05)
−2 Log likelihood	268716.8		268598.6		252339.3		251640.2		251843.0	
Nagelkerke R Square	0.00		0.00		0.10		0.10		0.10	
Chi-square (df) sign	611.46 (2)	***	729.72 (9)	***	16989.01 (24)	***	17688.16 (27)	***	17485.27 (21)	***

Notes:

N = 271,372.

*** *p<0.001.*

** *p<0.005.*

* *p<0.010.*

Reference groups are EU15 migrants born in the EU12, occupation unskilled, firm size 50–100, industry: public sector, health care, education.

The group of EU15 migrants born in the EU12 was removed from the model because of the lack of observations.

Source: WageIndicator data 2005–2010, selection 13 EU member states.

to measure the workers' job level. Regarding the first proxy, the table reveals that the odds of being overqualified decrease with hierarchical level within an occupation. The second proxy investigates the effect of the corporate hierarchy across occupations. The odds of being overqualified decrease for each level in the hierarchy. Regarding the third proxy, the skill level of the workers' occupation, the table reveals that the odds of being overqualified decrease for workers in semi-skilled occupations compared to those in unskilled occupations. It decreases even more for workers in highly skilled occupations. In summary and not surprisingly, the higher the individual's education, the more overeducation can be expected and the higher the individual's job level, the less overeducation can be expected.

The analyses in Table 3.4, Model 2 were controlled for other labour market characteristics. The findings show that the odds of being overqualified increase for small firms of up to 10 employees compared to middle-sized firms with 50–100 employees and that the odds decrease for large firms compared to medium-sized firms. The findings reveal further that, compared to the public sector, the odds of being overqualified are higher in trade, transport and hospitality, but lower in all other industries.

4.4 Is Overeducation Related to Workers' Vulnerability?

The third research objective concerns whether a range of theoretically based assumptions affect the incidence of overeducation. In Section 3.2, based on theoretical considerations, we derived three assumptions relating overeducation to recent labour market entry and to poor bargaining power. The results in Model 3 in Table 3.4 confirm these assumptions. For recent labour market entrants, defined as those with fewer than five years' service, the odds of being overqualified increases by 20 per cent compared to workers with more years of service. Note that in case of migrants these years of service include years of service, if any, in the country of birth. For workers with poor bargaining power – here defined as workers with a job on the side (students with a small part-time job, housewives or retirees working a few hours per week), trainees and workers with an unemployment spell – the odds of being overqualified increase by 19 per cent compared to workers with more power. Finally, for female workers the odds of being overqualified increase by 22 per cent compared to male workers.

4.5 Is Overeducation Related to Migrants' Characteristics?

The fourth research objective investigates whether a range of theoretically based assumptions related to migrants affect the incidence of overeducation. Model 4 in Table 3.4 presents the findings. Note that in this model a breakdown into different migrant and domestic groups is not included because here the migrants are classified in terms of groups related to the characteristics under study.

In Section 3.2 it was assumed that workers affected by a lack of transparency with regard to their credentials were more likely to be overqualified. Here, this group is defined as migrant workers who arrived in the host country at an adult age (21 years). This group will probably have completed their education in their country of birth, thus hampering the transparency of credentials in the host country. This assumption is supported. The odds of being overqualified increase by 51 per cent for migrants who arrived at an adult age compared to workers – both migrant and domestic – who received their credentials in the country in which they are currently living.

In Section 3.2 it was also hypothesised that workers facing discrimination from employers are more likely to report overeducation. This group is defined as workers who were not born in the country of survey, workers who were born in the country of survey but whose parents were not born in the country of survey and workers who belong to an ethnic minority. Th hypothesisus it is assumed that first and second generation migrants and ethnic minorities are similar with regard to labour market discrimination and that this in turn increases the likelihood of overqualification. From Table 3.4 Model 4 it turns out that this is indeed the case. The odds of being overqualified increase by 17 per cent for first and second generation migrants and ethnic minorities compared to domestic workers.

Finally, it was also hypothesised in Section 3.2 that migrant workers with more restricted language skills with regard to the host country – here defined as migrant workers born in a country with a native language or lingua franca that does not match that of the host country – are more likely to report overeducation. This assumption is not supported by our results, although it should be added that respondents filling in the questionnaire must have had good enough language skills to read and respond to it.

5. Conclusion and Discussion

Is skill mismatch more common for migrants compared to domestic workers? If so, is the incidence similar across migrant workers from the 'old' EU15 member states and the 'new' EU12 member states, and across domestic workers from the EU15 and the EU12? This chapter uses survey data, whereby workers themselves assess whether they are qualified, overqualified or underqualified for their job. The data stem from the multi-country, continuous WageIndicator web survey, using pooled annual data for the years 2005–2010 from nine EU15 countries (Belgium, Denmark, Finland, France, Italy, the Netherlands, Spain, Sweden and the United Kingdom) and four EU12 countries (Czech Republic, Hungary, Poland and Slovakia). In this chapter, migrants have been defined as persons not born in the country of survey.

The share of migrant workers in the nine EU15 countries is much higher than in the four EU12 countries (14 per cent versus 2 per cent). The data show that 18 per cent of migrants in the EU12 are overqualified compared to 24 per cent of migrants in the EU15. Both overeducation and undereducation are much more common in the EU15 than in the EU12 (25 per cent and 9 per cent, respectively, for overeducation and 7 per cent and 2 per cent, respectively, for undereducation). Overeducation occurs more often for migrants compared to domestic workers, and it occurs more often in the EU15 compared to the EU12. Thus, the characteristics of both migrants and national labour markets influence the incidence of overeducation.

A few theoretically based assumptions are used to try to explain overeducation on the basis of educational attainments and job levels. The analyses show, not surprisingly, that the higher the individual's level of education, the more overeducation can be expected and the higher the individual's job level, the less overeducation can be expected. Controls for firm size and industry reveal that overeducation occurs more often in small firms compared to large firms and more often in trade, transport and hospitality compared to the public sector. Recent labour market entrants, workers with a job on the side and female workers are more likely to be overqualified.

A few theoretically based assumptions aim to explain why migrants are more prone to be overqualified. A lack of transparency of credentials is assumed to increase the incidence of overeducation. Migrant workers who arrived in the host country at an adult age indeed are more likely to be characterised by overeducation. Employer discrimination is assumed to increase the incidence of overeducation. Indeed, first and second generation migrants and ethnic minorities are prone to labour market discrimination and this in turn increases the likelihood of overqualification. Finally, it is hypothesised that migrant workers with poorer language abilities – here defined as migrant workers born in a country with a native language or a lingua franca that does not match that of the host country – are more likely to report overeducation. This assumption is not supported by our results.

This study in part confirms the existing literature, in particular the job allocation frictions for the entire labour market. It expands existing empirical findings with regard to the reasons why migrants are more likely to be overeducated. In addition, our analysis classifies migrants into seven groups not previously studied. This chapter calls for further investigations on the incidence of overeducation in general, because the fit of the models is not particularly high. It also asks for further theoretical underpinnings with regard to undereducation. It underlines the need for further research on cross-national differences with regard to over- and undereducation, in particular the differences between the EU15 and EU12 countries.

Our analyses also have a number of shortcomings. First, we were not able to test the impact of labour market conditions – in particular, the impact of labour shortages – due to the absence of relevant data. Second, we were not able to control for the skill composition of the annual stock of immigrants as a result of a country's immigration policies, again due to absence of data. Third, our analyses might be subject to measurement errors regarding the educational attainment of migrants who arrived the host country at an adult age because this group should be asked about its education in the home country, not its equivalent in the host country, as is the case in our data.

Bibliography

Autor, D.H., F. Levy and R.J. Murnane. 2001. *The Skill Content of Recent Technological Change: An Empirical Investigation.* Cambridge, MA: National Bureau of Economic Research (NBER), Working Paper 8377.

Battu, H., P.J. Sloane. 2002. 'To what extent are ethnic minorities in Britain overeducated?', *International Journal of Manpower*, 23(3), 192–208.

Berman, E., J. Bound and S. Machlin. 1998. 'Implications of skill-biased technological change: international evidence', *Quarterly Journal of Economics*, 113(4), 1245–79.

Burkert, C. and H. Seibert. 2007. *Labour Market Outcomes after Vocational Training in Germany: Equal Opportunities for Migrants and Natives?* Nuremberg: IAB, IAB Discussion Paper 200731.

Cedefop. 2010. *The Skill Matching Challenge. Analysing Skill Mismatch and policy Implications.* Luxembourg: Publications Office of the European Union.

Chiswick, B.R. and P.W. Miller. 2009. *Educational Mismatch: Are High-Skilled Immigrants Really Working at High-Skilled Jobs and the Price They Pay If They Aren't?* Bonn: IZA, IZA Discussion Paper No. 4280.

CBS (Centraal Bureau voor de Statistiek). 1993. *Standaard Beroepsclassificatie 1992.* Voorburg/Heerlen: CBS (Statistics Netherlands).

Clogg, C.C. and J.W. Shockey. 1984. 'Mismatch between occupation and schooling: a prevalence measure, recent trends and demographic analysis', *Demography*, 21, 235–57.

Cohn, E. and S. Khan. 1995. 'The wage effects of overschooling revisited', *Labour Economics*, 2(1), 67–76.

Dumont, M. 2006. 'The reliability – or lack thereof – of data on skills', *Economics Letters*, 93, 348–53.

Ganzeboom, H.B.G. 2010. 'A new International Socio-Economic Index [ISEI] of occupational status for the International Standard Classification of Occupation 2008 [ISCO-08] constructed with data from the ISSP 2002–2007; with an analysis of quality of occupational measurement in ISSP. Paper presented at Annual Conference of International Social Survey Programme, Lisbon, 1 May 2010'.

Green, C., P. Kler and G. Leeves. 2007. 'Immigrant overeducation: evidence from recent arrivals to Australia', *Economics of Education Review*, 26, 420–32.

Groot, W. and H. Maassen van den Brink. 2000. 'Overeducation in the labor market: a meta-analysis', *Economics of Education Review*, 19(2), 149–58.

Halaby, C. 1994. 'Overeducation and skill mismatch', *Sociology of Education*, 67(1), 47–59.

Hartog, J. and N. Jonker. 1997. 'A job to match your education: does it matter?', in H. Heijke and L. Borghans (eds), *Towards a Transparent Labour Market for Educational Decisions*. Avebury: Aldershot.

ILO. 2007. Annex 1 International Standard Classification of Occupations (ISCO-08) – Conceptual Framework. Draft for consultation through second questionnaire on updating ISCO-88. Geneva, ILO. Available at: http://www.ilo.org/public/english/bureau/stat/isco/index.htm.

Jensen, U., H. Gartner and S. Rässler. 2007. *Measuring Overeducation with Earnings Frontiers and Multiply Imputed Censored Income Data*. Nuremberg: IAB Discussion Paper No. 11/2006.

Kler, P. 2005. 'Graduate overeducation in Australia: a comparison of the mean and objective methods', *Education Economics*, 13(1), 47–72.

Korpi, T. and M. Tahlin. 2009. 'Educational mismatch, wages, and wage growth: Overeducation in Sweden, 1974–2000', *Labour Economics*, 16, 183–93.

Leuven, E. and H. Oosterbeek. 2010. *Overeducation and Mismatch in the Labor Market*. Paper. Amsterdam: University of Amsterdam.

Lindley, J. and P. Lenton. 2006. *The Over-Education of UK Immigrants: Evidence from the Labour Force Survey*. Sheffield: Sheffield Economic Research Paper Series SERP Number: 2006001.

Machin, S. 2001. 'The changing nature of labour demand in the new economy and skill-biased technological change', *Oxford Bulletin of Economics and Statistics*, 63(S1), 753–76.

Mavromaras, K., S. McGuinness and Y.K. Fok. 2009. *Overskilling Dynamics and Education Pathways*. Bonn: IZA Discussion Paper 4321.

McGuinness, S. and P.J. Sloane. 2011. 'Labour market mismatch among UK graduates: An analysis using REFLEX data', *Economics of Education Review*, 30(1), 130–45.

O*net. 2002. *Appendix D – The Development of the Occupational Information (O*NETTM) Analyst Database*.

OECD. 1999. *Classifying Educational Programmes Manual for ISCED-97 Implementation in OECD Countries*. Paris: OECD.

OECD. 2007. 'On the move. International migration'. *DELSA Newsletter*, Issue 5. Paris: OECD.

Piracha, M., M. Tani and F. Vadean. 2010. *Immigrant Over- and Under-education: The Role of Home Country Labour Market Experience*. Bonn: IZA Discussion Paper No. 5302.

Sicherman, N. 1991. '"Overeducation" in the labor market', *Journal of Labor Economics*, 9(2), 101.

Sicherman, N. and O. Galor. 1990. 'A theory of career mobility', *Journal of Political Economy*, 98(1), 169–92.

Sloane, P.J., H. Battu and P.T. Seaman. 1999. 'Overeducation, undereducation and the British labour market', *Applied Economics*, 31, 1437–53.

Steinmetz, S., K. Tijdens and P. de Pedraza. 2009. *Comparing Different Weighting Procedures for Volunteer Online Panel: Lessons to Be Learned from German and Dutch WageIndicator Data.* Amsterdam: University of Amsterdam, AIAS Working Paper 09-76.

Tijdens, K.G. 2010. *Measuring Occupations in Web-surveys: The WISCO Database of Occupations.* Amsterdam: University of Amsterdam, AIAS Working Paper 10-86.

Van der Velden, R.K.W. and M.S.M. van Smoorenburg. 1997. *The Measurement of Overeducation and Undereducation: Self-Report vs. Job-Analyst Method.* Maastricht: Maastricht University, Research Centre for Education and the Labour Market (ROA).

Verdugo, R.R. and N.T. Verdugo. 1989. 'The impact of surplus schooling on earnings', *Journal of Human Resources,* 24(4), 629–43.

Verhaest, D. and E. Omey. 2006. 'Discriminating between alternative measures of over-education', *Applied Economics*, 38(18), 2113–20.

Chapter 4

Educational Attainment and Education–Job Mismatch of Cross-border Commuters in the EU

Peter Huber[1]

1. Introduction

Increased mobility and the integration of European labour markets could have significant repercussions for the skill distribution of the workforce residing and working in a region. This has long been recognised by the migration literature, in which the determinants of the skill structure of migrants have been a central concern in both empirical and theoretical research (for example, Chiswick 1999; Hunt 2004; Borjas 1999) and experts (for example, Chiswick 2005) have argued that policy should aim to attract highly skilled migrants. A related strand of this literature also argues that migrants' skills should be measured not only by their highest completed education, but also in terms of their education–job match (OECD 2007), since even the most highly educated migrants are unlikely to contribute to the receiving regions' human capital when their skills are used inappropriately. A number of recent contributions (Chiswick and Miller 2007; Huber et al. 2008; OECD 2007) have thus attempted to measure education–job mismatch among native and foreign-born workers in the US, the EU and other countries.

However, this literature has largely ignored cross-border commuting as an alternative mode of labour mobility. To the best of our knowledge only MKW (2001 and 2009) analyse the extent, structure and motivations for cross-border commuting from a European perspective. These studies, however, focus on information from EURES officials and address neither commuters' skills nor education–job mismatch. Most of the commuting literature has analysed either commuting within a country (for example, White 1986; Hazans 2003; Rouwendahl 1999; Van Ommeren 1999) or cross-border commuting in individual border regions (for example, Van der Velde et al. 2005; Greve and Rydbjerg 2003a, 2003b; Bernotat and Snickars 2002; Mätha and Wintr 2009). These studies indicate that commuting within a country is much more dependent on distance than migration. Since this

1   I would like to thank Janine Leschke, Klaus Nowotny and participants in two ETUI Workshops on Intra-EU migration trends for helpful comments, and the Austrian National Bank (Jubiläumsfondsprojekt 13804) for financial support. The usual disclaimer applies.

is also to be expected from cross-border commuting, this implies a regionally asymmetrical impact of cross-border commuting on border regions. In addition, White (1986) and Rouwendahl (1999) show that commuters are more often male than female. Rouwendahl (1999) finds a decreasing propensity to commute with age and Van Ommeren (1999), Hazans (2003) and, again, Rouwendahl (1999) find that better educated workers are more likely to commute than less educated workers.

Some of these 'stylised facts' may also apply to cross-border commuters and recent case studies (Buch et al. 2008; Gottholmseder and Theurl 2006, 2007) suggest that they are indeed mostly male but differ from within-country commuters with regard to education and age. The lack of more general insights for the entire EU is, however, a shortcoming not only from an analytical but also from a policy perspective, since in the context of European integration, issues of labour mobility and their effects on sending and receiving regions, as well as on those who are actually moving around are becoming increasingly relevant. Influencing cross-border commuting as one component of cross-border labour mobility would, however, require a clear understanding of the motivations, structure and potential problems of cross-border commuters.

In this chapter I analyse cross-border commuting in the EU27 using data from the European Labour Force Survey (ELFS). Given the paucity of previous results the aims are primarily descriptive. I first determine how many people commute across borders and in which regions and countries cross-border commuting is most important. Second, I analyse how commuters' demographic structure differs from that of migrants, within-country (internal) commuters and persons living and working in the same region. While my emphasis is on education, I also consider other important demographic characteristics, such as age and gender. Third, I assess whether the problems of education–job mismatch often found among migrants also apply to cross-border commuters and once more compare them to migrants, internal commuters and non-commuters.

2. Data and Definitions

The data are taken from the ELFS for 2006. This representative survey conducted in all EU27 countries asks persons who had been in paid employment for at least one hour in the week preceding the interview for their place of residence as well as their place of work and a number of demographic and workplace characteristics (for example, branch of employment, age, gender, occupation and highest completed level of education). From the data the extent and structure of commuting in the EU27 can be calculated and occupations can be matched to educational attainment to allow measurement of education–job mismatch. Unfortunately, the Greek, Portuguese and Cypriot questionnaires do not pose the question of place of work. Furthermore, data for Slovenia deviate grossly from the data provided in official

EUROSTAT sources;[2] for Italy the share of non-respondents to the question on place of work exceeds 5 per cent;[3] and data are lacking on cross-border commuting for Ireland. Thus I exclude these countries from the analysis. The data also contain only a sample of the households in the EU27 and are therefore subject to sampling error. To avoid misinterpretation, I follow EUROSTAT's[4] reporting rules, putting all numbers with high standard errors in brackets and suppressing numbers where commuting levels are below the lower confidence bounds suggested by EUROSTAT.

I define cross-border commuters as persons who work in a different country from the one they live in. I do not differentiate between daily, weekly and monthly commuting and some commuters could be working abroad for several weeks or months in a row. This implies relatively distant commuting for some observations. I compare cross-border commuters to persons who live in the same NUTS2 region as they work in (referred to as 'non-commuters') and persons who work in a different NUTS2 region from the one they live in, in the same country (internal commuters). One consequence of this is that differences in size across NUTS2 regions severely limit the comparability of data across national and regional entities. Since commuting is highly distance-dependent, the extent of commuting is ceteris paribus higher in smaller regions. In addition, I compare commuters to migrants that currently live and work in a different country from the one they were born in. Since more established migrants are likely to differ from recent migrants in their education structure on account of return migration and in terms of education–job mismatch due to better labour market integration, I differentiate between 'established' (having lived abroad for 10 or more years) and 'recent' (having lived abroad for less than 10 years) migrants. Also, to ensure comparability I focus only on the employed and exclude foreign-born persons from outside the EU from the analysis.

To measure education–job mismatch I use two alternative approaches (Table 4.1).[5] The first – and my preferred one – is the link between the standard international taxonomy of educational attainment (ISCED) and the international classification of occupations (ISCO) at the 1-digit level suggested by OECD (2007) on the basis of a job analysis. The second is based on the implied skill levels suggested by the ILO (1987) when constructing the ISCO classification. According to OECD (2007) high education levels (that is, ISCED 5 and 6) are

---

2   Official EUROSTAT data suggest that in the data regional codes for Slovenia may have been confused.

3   In total, 0.1 per cent of the employed covered in the ELFS do not respond to the question on place of work. This is sizeable relative to cross-border commuting (see below) and may cause underreporting if respondents are more likely to answer questions concerning their place of work when not commuting. I thus also report non-respondents.

4   See http://circa.europa.eu/irc/dsis/employment/info/data/eu_lfs/index.htm

5   See Cohn and Khan (1995), Kiker et al. (1997) Verdugo and Verdugo (1989) as well as Hartog (2000) for discussions of alternative measures of job–skill mismatch.

required from legislators, senior officials and managers, as well as professionals and technicians and associate professionals. I refer to these occupations as high-skilled occupations. Low education levels (ISCED 0, 1 and 2) are required for elementary occupations (referred to as low-skilled occupations) and all other occupations are associated with intermediate education levels (medium-skilled occupations). According to the ILO definition only professionals have high skilled occupations (requiring an educational attainment of ISCED 6 or more), technicians and associate professionals by contrast have medium skilled education (requiring an educational attainment of ISCED 5) and all other occupations are low skilled, requiring ISCED level 3 or less. Educational attainments at the ISCED 4 level are not assigned to any occupation and thus are excluded from the sample in this method, since they can be neither over- nor under-educated.[6]

Table 4.1   Correspondence of major occupation groups (ISCO-88) and required education levels (ISCED-97)

ISCO-88 Major groups	Required education level according to OECD (2007)		Required education level according to ILO (1987)	
1: Legislators, senior officials and managers	High-skilled	ISCED 5,6	No assignment	
2: Professionals		ISCED 5,6	High-skilled	ISCED 6
3: Technicians and associate professionals		ISCED 5,6	Medium-skilled	ISCED 5
4: Clerks	Medium-skilled	ISCED 3,4	Low-skilled	ISCED 1,2,3
5: Service workers and shop and market sales workers		ISCED 3,4		ISCED 1,2,3
6: Skilled agricultural and fishery workers		ISCED 3,4		ISCED 1,2,3
7: Craft and related trades workers		ISCED 3,4		ISCED 1,2,3
8: Plant and machine operators and assemblers		ISCED 3,4		ISCED 1,2,3
9: Elementary occupations	Low-skilled	ISCED 0,1,2		ISCED 1,2,3
(0: Armed forces)	No assignment		No assignment	

Source: OECD (2007).

6   Unfortunately, in the ELFS the lowest educational attainment measured is ISCED2 or lower, so that I cannot make use of the fact that, according to the ILO (1987), elementary occupations require only an ISCED 1 education.

Based on these reference levels, education–job mismatch is measured by comparing a persons' highest completed education level to that required in their occupation according to both definitions. A person is over-educated if their educational attainment is higher and under-educated if their educational attainment is lower than required for their occupation. Over- and under-education are thus characteristics of the employee relative to their occupation: highly educated workers cannot be under-educated (as there are no occupations requiring higher educational attainment than high education) and less educated workers cannot be over-educated (since there are no occupations requiring education lower than low education). One problem with both measurement methods is that occupational categories are broad. This may induce measurement error if these broad categories encompass jobs requiring different educational attainment levels. Our approach can, however, be justified by its focus on differences in education–job mismatch between migrants, cross-border commuters, internal commuters and non-commuters, since these differences will be less affected by measurement error.

Furthermore, the two measurement methods are likely to yield different results with regard to the extent of over- and under-education. In particular, according to the ILO (1987) only persons with an educational attainment of ISCED level 5 and above can be over-educated, while according to OECD (2007) this can also be the case for persons with ISCED 3 and 4 education. Accordingly, over-education rates will tend to be higher in the latter method. Similarly, since a larger share of occupations are classified as low skill occupations and the ISCED level 4 educational attainment is excluded from the analysis according to the ILO (1987), the share of appropriately employed persons is likely to be higher in this classification than according to OECD (2007).

3. The Extent of Commuting

Table 4.2 provides information on the extent of internal and cross-border out-commuting as a percentage of the employed at the place where commuters live. In conjunction with Figure 4.1 it suggests that cross-border out-commuting is fairly rare in the EU27 and is important only in a small number of regions. In 2006, only around 0.7 per cent of the employed commuted across borders. This is low relative to the 7.4 per cent commuting across NUTS2 regions within their respective countries. Among the 220 NUTS2 regions in our sample the share of cross-border out-commuting in total employment at place of residence exceeds 5 per cent in only eight regions: three Slovak regions, Alsace-Lorraine in France, the Belgian Provinces of Luxemburg and Limburg, Freiburg in Germany and Vorarlberg in Austria. In another 31 regions it is between 1 per cent and 5 per cent. For the vast majority of NUTS2 regions, less than 0.5 per cent of the resident employed commute across borders.

Cross-border commuting is also highly dependent on geography. High rates of cross-border out-commuting occur in border regions or regions close to the

Table 4.2   Out-commuting in the EU27 by country, 2006

	Internal commuters	Cross-border commuters	Non-respondents	Internal commuters	Cross-border commuters	Non-respondents
	Absolute (thousands)			As a % of employed at workplace		
Total	13369.8	1169.5	115.7	7.5	0.7	0.1
EU15*	12580.1	792.8	113.0	9.2	0.6	0.1
Austria	397.9	39.7	–	10.1	1.0	0.0
Belgium	828.3	95.0	–	19.4	2.2	0.0
Germany	3846.5	173.2	56.1	10.3	0.5	0.2
Denmark[1]	0.0	5.5	27.0	0.0	0.2	1.0
Spain	382.7	55.6	0.0	1.9	0.3	0.0
Finland	66.9	(3.0)	0.0	2.7	(0.1)	0.0
France	1468.9	279.0	19.9	5.9	1.1	0.1
Luxemburg[1]	0.0	1.7	0.0	0.0	0.9	0.0
Netherlands	1056.2	32.4	–	12.9	0.4	0.1
Sweden	195.7	38.3	3.1	4.4	0.9	0.1
UK	4337.0	69.4	–	15.4	0.2	0.0
NMS12**	789.7	376.7	–	1.9	0.9	0.0
Bulgaria	39.2	10.3	–	1.3	0.3	0.0
Czech Republic	230.7	25.1	–	4.8	0.5	0.0
Estonia[1]	0.0	10.7	–	0.0	1.7	0.0
Hungary	147.5	24.9	0.0	3.8	0.6	0.0
Lituania[1]	0.0	26.2	–	0.0	1.7	0.0
Latvia[1]	0.0	14.3	–	0.0	1.3	0.0
Malta	0.0	–	–	0.0	0.5	0.0
Poland	216.3	71.6	–	1.5	0.5	0.0
Romania	57.9	36.9	–	0.6	0.4	0.0
Slovakia	98.1	156.8	–	4.3	6.8	0.1

Notes: Figures in brackets = unreliable data due to few observations; – = no data reported due to few observations.

* excluding Greece, Portugal, Ireland and Italy.

** excluding Cyprus and Slovenia.

[1] Country has only 1 NUTS2 region, thus no internal commuting measured.

Source: EUROSTAT-LFS, author's calculations.

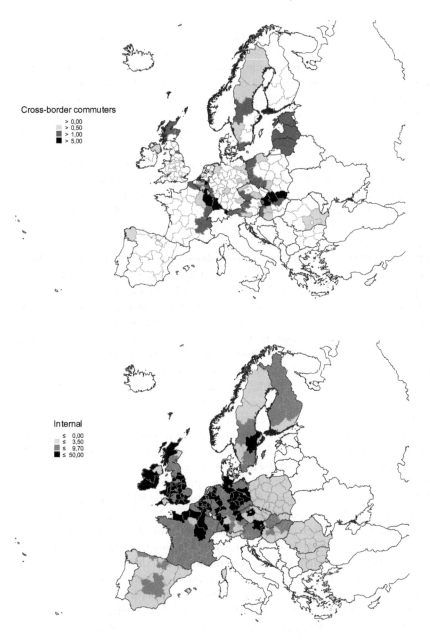

Figure 4.1   Out-commuting in the EU27 by NUTS2 regions, 2006

Note: Figure shows out-commuting as a percentage of employed persons at place of residence. Top panel = cross-border commuting, bottom panel= internal commuting.

Source: Eurostat, ELFS.

border. The major areas of cross-border commuting are located in border regions of countries which share a common language (for example, Belgium and France or Austria, Switzerland and Germany), have strong historical ties (for example, the Czech Republic and Slovakia) or where special institutional arrangements influence cross-border commuting (as in the Austro-Hungarian case, where commuting for Hungarian commuters was substantially liberalised in 1998: Bock-Schappelwein et al. 2010), as well as in small countries (such as Belgium, Austria and the Baltics), where most regions are located close to the border. In all other border regions (except those located at the German–French border), the share of cross-border out-commuters is lower than 0.5 per cent of the resident workforce. High rates of internal out-commuting, by contrast, are found primarily near large urban agglomerations (for example, London, Berlin, Vienna, Prague and Stockholm), and in smaller NUTS2 regions.

Aside from size and geography, out-commuting is also higher in regions with low GDP per capita and high unemployment (Huber and Nowotny 2008) and – although this comparison is influenced by region size, which is larger for the peripheral regions and leads to a downward bias for commuting in these regions – there seems to be a core–periphery pattern in both cross-border and internal commuting. Regions located closer to the centre of the EU (for example, in Austria, Belgium, Germany and the Netherlands) have higher internal and cross-border out-commuting rates. Regions located on the periphery (for example, Spain, Bulgaria and Romania) have low commuting rates (MKW 2009).

Finally, the share of cross-border out-commuters is higher in the NMS12 than in the EU15. I would have expected the opposite due to the shorter time span during which the NMS12 have been integrating into the EU, not to mention due to institutional barriers to cross-border commuting from the NMS12 in important receiving countries of the EU15 in 2006. Cross-border commuting rates in the NMS12 are, however, increased by the high share of cross-border commuters from Slovakia to the Czech Republic and a large number of small countries among the NMS12 as well as high income differences between the NMS and the EU15.

From the receiving region's perspective (Figure 4.2) the total share of cross-border in-commuters from the EU27 among employed persons working in a country is also low. Apart from the outlier of Luxemburg (where over one-third of the employed commute from other countries) the share of cross-border in-commuters exceeds 1 per cent of those employed in a workplace only in Belgium, Austria and the Netherlands. For the NMS12, cross-border in-commuting is of even lower importance. Among them the share of cross-border in-commuters in total employment at workplace exceeds 1 per cent only in the Czech Republic (due to commuters from Slovakia) and 0.5 per cent in Hungary.

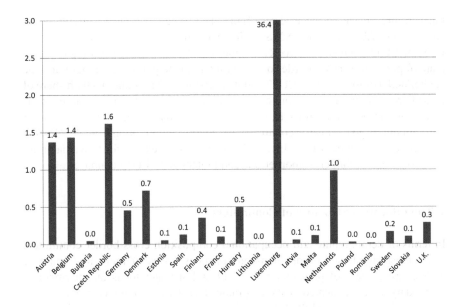

Figure 4.2   Cross-border in-commuting from the EU27 by country, 2006 (% of those employed at workplace)

Source: Eurostat LFS, author's calculations.

Table 4.3   Place to place cross-border commuting by country groups, 2006

	Receiving region			
	EU15	NMS12	Other countries	Total
Sending region	*Absolute (thousands)*			
EU15	479.7	10.6	302.5	792.8
NMS12	243.0	105.2	29.3	377.4
	Percentage share			
EU15	60.5	1.3	38.2	100.0
NMS12	64.4	27.9	7.8	100.0

Source: EUROSTAT-LFS, author's calculations.

Furthermore, place–to-place data (Table 4.3) suggest a clear differentiation between the EU15 and the NMS12. Most of the cross-border out-commuting from the EU15 countries is directed to other EU15 countries (accounting for more than 90 per cent of cross-border out-commuters in Belgium, Luxemburg and the Netherlands) or to other non-EU27 countries (which, on account of a high share of cross-border commuters to Norway and substantial long distance commuting, is particularly important for the UK, where more than 50 per cent of the cross-border out-commuters go to non-EU countries). By contrast, commuting from the NMS12 is more focused on the EU15. In all NMS12 countries, except for Slovakia, more than 70 per cent of all cross-border out-commuters go to EU15 countries.

4. The Education Structure of Commuters

In terms of demographic and occupational composition cross-border commuters differ most significantly from non-commuters in terms of their high share of males, larger share of persons aged 25–44 and stronger focus on intermediate (secondary level) educated workers (Table 4.4). Cross-border commuters also often work in medium-skilled occupations and construction or manufacturing. Relative to internal commuters, cross-border commuters are more often medium-educated, more strongly concentrated in manufacturing employment, typically work in medium-skilled occupations according to the OECD (2007) definition and have a higher share of males. This accords with previous case studies: Buch et al. (2008) find that German–Danish cross-border workers are often manufacturing workers, while Gottholmseder and Theurl (2006 and 2007) find that cross-border commuters from Vorarlberg to Switzerland are often male, medium-skilled manufacturing workers. One explanation for this is that the lower importance of language skills in these occupations and sectors makes it easier to find jobs across the border. Another explanation is provided by differences in economic structure between border regions as destinations for cross-border commuters and large cities as destinations for internal commuters, since cities are more focused on the service sector.[7] Relative to migrants (both established and recent), cross-border commuters are also more often male, more often have intermediate education as well as medium-skilled occupations (at the expense of lower shares of both high and low skilled), and compared to recent migrants are slightly older (less often aged 25–44, more often 45–60) and less often work in non-market services but substantially more often in manufacturing.

Some of these findings may, however, be due to co-linearity. For instance, the high share of medium skilled and males may be due to the high share of manufacturing and construction workers among cross-border commuters or vice

---

7 Some of these results may also be due to residential sorting. Since, for instance, more highly qualified workers may choose to live outside urban agglomerations and thus become commuters even without changing jobs.

Table 4.4 **Commuters and migrants in the EU27 by demographic and job characteristics, 2006 (%)**

	Non-commuters*	Internal commuters	Cross-border commuters	No response	Established migrants	Recent migrants
Gender						
Female	46.1	36.3	28.3	32.3	49.2	45.4
Male	53.9	63.7	71.7	67.7	50.8	54.6
Age						
Age 15–24 years	10.8	11.3	13.7	15.7	5.1	14.8
Age 24–45 years	51.3	55.0	57.0	56.3	50.4	70.4
Age 45–60 years	33.0	30.4	27.0	21.3	37.4	14.0
Age 60 years or over	5.0	3.4	2.4	6.7	7.1	0.8
Education						
Missing	0.2	0.3	–	–	0.4	0.6
Low education (ISCED 2 or less)	21.9	16.1	13.8	18.0	22.4	20.2
Medium education (ISCED 3 or 4)	51.4	47.5	60.1	48.9	45.0	52.0
Higher education (ISCED 5 or more)	26.6	36.1	25.9	33.0	32.1	27.2
Occupation						
High-skilled*	37.3	50.1	33.4	44.4	44.2	26.0
Medium-skilled*	51.9	41.4	56.2	41.5	44.8	47.6
Low-skilled*	10.0	6.1	9.3	7.8	10.1	26.1
Missing	0.8	2.4	1.1	6.3	0.8	0.3
Sector of employment						
Agriculture/ mining	6.6	1.9	5.1	–	2.7	5.9
Manufacturing/ construction	26.5	27.6	41.8	31.4	23.9	32.9
Market services	36.3	41.7	36.0	38.1	39.1	38.1
Non-market services	30.6	28.9	17.1	23.5	34.3	23.0

Notes: – = no data reported due to lack of observations; column sums for individual characteristics are 100%. * according to OECD (2007) measurement.

Source: EUROSTAT-LFS, author's calculations.

Table 4.5 Results for probability of non-, internal and cross-border commuting, and migration (marginal effects)

	Non-commuting		Internal commuting		Cross-border commuting		Established migrant		Recent migrant	
	Coeff	S.E	Coeff	S.E	Coeff	S.E	Coeff	S.E	Coeff	S.E
All										
Male	-0.0220***	0.00004	0.0204***	0.00003	0.0025***	0.00001	-0.0009***	0.00001	0.0001***	0.00001
Age 25–44[2]	-0.0072***	0.00006	0.0027***	0.00005	-0.0009***	0.00001	0.0059***	0.00003	-0.0005***	0.00001
Age 45–59[2]	0.0023***	0.00007	-0.0047***	0.00005	-0.0017***	0.00001	0.0083***	0.00004	-0.0041***	0.00001
Age 60 or more[2]	0.0087***	0.00012	-0.0200***	0.00006	-0.0021***	0.00002	0.0172***	0.00011	-0.0038***	0.00001
Low education (ISCED 2 or less)[3]	0.0246***	0.00004	-0.0241***	0.00003	-0.0019***	0.00001	0.0007***	0.00002	0.0006***	0.00001
Medium education (ISCED 3 or 4)[3]	0.0223***	0.00004	-0.0179***	0.00003	-0.0003***	0.00001	-0.0023***	0.00002	-0.0018***	0.00001
Manufacturing/construction[1]	-0.0513***	0.00016	0.0322***	0.00014	0.0020***	0.00003	0.0110***	0.00008	0.0061***	0.00003
Market services[1]	-0.0523***	0.00014	0.0332***	0.00013	0.0004***	0.00002	0.0129***	0.00007	0.0058***	0.00003
Non-market services[1]	-0.0386***	0.00015	0.0215***	0.00013	-0.0015***	0.00002	0.0137***	0.00008	0.0049***	0.00003
EU15										
Male	-0.0289***	0.00005	0.0271***	0.00004	0.0023***	0.00001	-0.0007***	0.00002	0.0002***	0.00001
Age 25–44[2]	-0.0133***	0.00008	0.0059***	0.00007	0.0002***	0.00002	0.0057***	0.00003	0.0015***	0.00002
Age 45–59[2]	-0.0030***	0.00009	-0.0034***	0.00007	-0.0002***	0.00002	0.0075***	0.00005	-0.0010***	0.00001
Age 60 or more[2]	0.0118***	0.00014	-0.0265***	0.00009	-0.0007***	0.00003	0.0163***	0.00011	-0.0010***	0.00002
Low education (ISCED 2 or less)[3]	0.0388***	0.00006	-0.0347***	0.00005	-0.0021***	0.00001	0.0005***	0.00002	-0.0025***	0.00001

	Coef.	S.E.	Coef.	S.E.	Coef.	S.E.	Coef.	S.E.	Coef.	S.E.
Medium education (ISCED 3 or 4)[3]	0.0287***	0.00005	-0.0242***	0.00005	-0.0006***	0.00001	-0.0017***	0.00002	-0.0022***	0.00001
Manufacturing/construction[1]	-0.0404***	0.0002	0.0368***	0.0002	0.0026***	0.00004	0.0009***	0.00005	0.0001***	0.00003
Market services[1]	-0.0441***	0.00019	0.0392***	0.00018	0.0010***	0.00003	0.0029***	0.00005	0.0009***	0.00003
Non-market services[1]	-0.0250***	0.00019	0.0234***	0.00018	-0.0010***	0.00003	0.0028***	0.00005	-0.0002***	0.00003
NMS12										
Male	-0.0100***	0.00005	0.0095***	0.00003	0.0026***	0.00002	-0.0016***	0.00002	-0.0004**	0.00002
Age 25–44[2]	0.0077***	0.00009	-0.0054***	0.00005	-0.0032***	0.00002	0.0057***	0.00006	-0.0048***	0.00004
Age 45–59[2]	0.0204***	0.00012	-0.0094***	0.00004	-0.0047***	0.00002	0.0094***	0.0001	-0.0157***	0.00004
Age 60 or more[2]	0.0058***	0.00029	-0.0085***	0.00005	-0.0043***	0.00002	0.0213***	0.00029	-0.0143***	0.00002
Low education (ISCED 2 or less)[3]	-0.0246***	0.00014	-0.0027***	0.00005	0.0007***	0.00004	0.0043***	0.00006	0.0223***	0.00011
Medium education (ISCED 3 or 4)[3]	0.0088***	0.00007	-0.0073***	0.00005	0.0012***	0.00002	-0.0031***	0.00003	0.0004***	0.00004
Manufacturing/construction[1]	-0.0827***	0.0003	0.0208***	0.00014	0.0016***	0.00003	0.0343***	0.00026	0.0261***	0.00011
Market services[1]	-0.0902***	0.00035	0.0199***	0.00014	-0.0004***	0.00003	0.0433***	0.00032	0.0274***	0.00012
Non-market services[1]	-0.0919***	0.00044	0.0140***	0.00014	-0.0018***	0.00003	0.0516***	0.00042	0.0280***	0.00014

Notes: Table reports marginal effects of a multinomial logit regression on the probability of outcomes listed in the first row. Results for sending country fixed effects are not reported, *** (**) (*) significant at the 1%, (5%), (10%) level respectively. S.E.= heteroscedasticity robust standard error. 1) base category = agriculture/mining, 2) base category = 15–24 years old, 3) base category = higher education (ISCED4 or more).

Source: EU-LFS.

versa. To address this issue, I run a series of multinomial logit regressions for out-commuters from all EU countries, as well as separately for commuters from the EU15 and the NMS12. Here the dependent variable takes on a value of zero for non-commuters, 1 for internal commuters, 2 for cross-border commuters, 3 for non-respondents, 4 for established and 5 for recent migrants. I include dummies for each (EU) country of residence and exclude countries that have only one NUTS2 region (the Baltic countries, Luxemburg and Malta) since they have no internal commuters. Further controls are included for sector of employment (agriculture and mining [as base category], manufacturing, construction and private or public services), dummy variables for the age of respondents (for individuals aged 25–44, 45–59, 60 and more years, with 15–24 year olds as base category), a dummy for males, and two dummies for low (ISCED2 or less) or medium (ISCED3 or 4) education, with higher education (ISCED 5 or 6) as the excluded base group.

The results provide strong evidence of a positive selection of commuters on education irrespective of the type of commuting (Table 4.5). The coefficients of the dummy variable for both low and medium education are highly significant and negative. Internal commuters are, however, more strongly positively selected than cross-border commuters: persons with a low education have a 2.4 percentage point lower probability of commuting to another location in the same country than persons with a higher education. Their probability of commuting across borders, however, is only 0.2 percentage points lower. Similarly, persons with medium education have a 1.8 percentage point lower probability of being internal commuters, but only a 0.03 percentage point lower probability of being cross-border commuters than the higher educated. Relative to (both established and recent) migrants, however, cross-border commuters are more often medium educated and less often higher educated after controlling for other characteristics. The medium educated have a 0.2 percentage point lower probability of being (established or recent) migrants. By contrast, the less educated are about 0.1 of a percentage point more likely to be recent or established migrants.

Besides positive selection on education, cross-border commuters are significantly more often male than female. By contrast, established migrants are around 0.1 percentage points less likely to be male, while for recent migrants the impact of gender is statistically significant, but numerically very small (0.01 percentage points). Highly significant marginal effects are also found for age. Here the internal commuting probability attains a maximum for the age group of 25 to 44 year olds, with marginal effects suggesting a 0.3 percentage point higher internal commuting probability than for 15 to 24 year olds. For cross-border commuters, the commuting probability is highest for 15 to 24 year olds, as is the probability of being a recent migrant. The marginal effects are small (below 0.1 percentage points), however, for both groups. More established migrants, who have lived abroad for longer, are also most likely to be older, as was to be expected.

The separate estimates for persons living or born in the EU15 and in the NMS12 suggest that cross-border commuters from the NMS12 are more strongly drawn from the medium skilled and young than in the EU15. The probability of cross-border commuting among low skilled NMS12 residents – in contrast to that of EU15 residents – is higher than for the higher educated and the highest probability is found for the medium educated. Similarly, the peak in the probability of cross-border commuting in the group of 15 to 24 year olds in the EU27 is solely due to the higher probability of 15 to 24 year old residents of the NMS12 commuting across borders. Among EU15 residents the probability of cross-border commuting peaks in the 25 to 44 age group. Similar observations apply to recent migrants. They too are younger (but also substantially more often less educated) if born in the NMS12 than if born in the EU15. This suggests that the different economic structure and substantial restructuring in the NMS12 in the past few decades, as well as the recent emigration from these countries have also impacted on the structure of cross-border commuting and migration from the NMS12.

5. Over- and Under-education

As already pointed out, however, cross-border commuters' and migrants' skills should be measured not only against their highest completed education, but also in terms of the match between their education and their jobs. Besides educational attainment, the over- or under-education of commuters should also be considered. A number of recent contributions show that the probability of over- and under-educated employment among both natives and migrants depends on age, gender and education. Females often have higher over- but lower under-education rates (which may be due to discrimination but has also been attributed to their lower geographical mobility – Kiker, Santos and Oliveira 1997; Büchel and Battu 2003). Over-education usually decreases with age, while under-education increases since the limited information of younger workers may lead to them to accept jobs below their qualification level and older workers will have obtained firm- or industry-specific human capital. However, this is countered by technological change and the depreciation of knowledge. If knowledge acquired recently is more relevant for an occupation, older workers may face higher over-education rates (Rubb 2003; Groot-Maasen and van den Brink 2000). The more educated have higher over-education rates (Sanroma, Ramos and Simon 2009), while the less educated are more often under-educated.

Previous studies also show that the probability of over-educated employment is lower among natives than among migrants and that the probability of under-educated employment is higher, but that these differences diminish with duration of stay abroad and differ substantially by migrants' country of birth (Chiswick and Miller 2007; Sanroma, Ramos and Simon 2009). Migrants' higher over-education rates are usually attributed to the difficulties (arising from language problems or differences in education systems) encountered by foreigners in utilising formal skills abroad. These typically diminish as they integrate into the host society (for example, by learning the language). Lower under-education rates, by contrast, are interpreted as an indication of problems experienced in transferring informal skills, since under-educated employment implies that workers have acquired the skills necessary for performing this job through experience or learning on the job.

I am, however, not aware of any studies analysing the over- and under-education of commuters. Tables 6 and 6b thus report the share of cross-border, internal and non-commuters, as well as (established and recent) migrants in under- and over-educated employment, stratified by some of the major correlates of the probability of over- and under-educated employment according to the two measurement concepts used in this chapter. These results are highly consistent with the literature, irrespective of the measurement method used. The share of over-educated employed is substantially – 15.5 percentage points according to the OECD (2007) definition and 6.4 percentage points according to the ILO (1987) method – higher and the share of under-educated employed substantially (10.3 percentage points and 4.6 percentage points, respectively) lower among recent migrants than among non-commuters. These differences almost disappear for more established migrants. Similarly, irrespective of the type of commuter or migrant considered, over-education is higher among females than males, which in part is due to the different sector and education structure of female cross-border commuters, since they more often than males are higher educated and also more often work in services. It also decreases with age (with the exception of over 60 year olds and recent migrants when the OECD [2007] measurement is used) and the education level required in the job, but increases with education, while under-education is lower for females than for males, increases with age after 25 and diminishes with education and skills required in the job.

Internal commuters, by contrast, have rates of over- and under-education that are about comparable to those of non-commuters. According to the OECD (2007) measurement, 30.9 per cent of both internal and non-commuters in the EU work in jobs requiring an education in excess of their actual attainment, and are thus under-educated[8] and 10.3 per cent of the non-commuters and 9.1 per cent of the internal commuters have an educational attainment higher than what is required by their job and are thus over-educated. According to the ILO (1987) measurement, the under-education rate among internal commuters is 26.0 per cent (as opposed to 22.2 per cent among non-commuters) and the over-education rate is 6.0 per cent and only 0.1 per cent higher than among non-commuters. Internal commuters thus seem to have only minor problems in utilising both formally as well as informally obtained skills.

Among cross–border commuters these problems are greater. In almost all demographic groups they have higher over- and lower under-education rates than either internal or non-commuters: 13.6 per cent of the cross-border commuters in the EU are over-educated and 24.0 per cent are under-educated according to the OECD (2007) measurement. According to the ILO (1987) measurement,

8   These under-education rates are consistent with previous studies and reflect the substantial human capital obtained among less qualified and experienced workers through 'learning by doing' or training after completed education.

under-education rates are 20.0 per cent among cross-border commuters and over-education rates amount to 6.5 per cent. These over- and under-education rates are, however, substantially lower than among recent migrants, according to both measurement concepts. Once more, this applies to almost all demographic groups. More established migrants, by contrast, have lower over-education rates in most demographic groups than cross-border commuters, while their under-education rates are higher in most groups.

To summarise, cross-border commuters are faced with greater problems in utilising both their formally and informally acquired skills than established migrants, non-commuters and internal commuters. In comparison to recent migrants, however, they perform better. One reason for this may be that cross-border commuters will be willing to commute only if they find adequate employment opportunities abroad (or will terminate inadequate employment quickly when offered a better job back home); while migrants may have a weaker bargaining position once they have moved abroad. These results as well as all the others apply to both measurement methods used, although as expected over-education rates – and to a lesser degree also under-education rates – are substantially lower when using the ILO definition than when using the OECD definition of over- and under-education. One can therefore conclude that, while measurement issues have a strong impact on results as regards the extent of over- and under-education, qualitative results with respect to differences in over- and under-education rates across groups are less strongly affected by such measurement issues.

Once more, these results may be due to composition effects and could also differ among groups of cross-border commuters. Thus, as before, I conduct multinomial logit regressions in which I use the OECD (2007) measurement concept to form a dependent variable which takes on a value of zero if a person is appropriately qualified for their job, 1 if a person is over-educated and –1 if a person is under-educated. As before, these regressions are run for the overall EU27, as well as separately for the NMS12 and the EU15. Besides the explanatory variables already included in the previous analysis the equation includes a set of dummy variables for internal commuters, cross-border commuters and individuals, whose commuting status is unknown, as well as for established and recent migrants (with non-commuters the base category). A positive and significant coefficient of these variables indicates that, after controlling for composition effects, the respective group has higher over- or under-education rates than non-commuters; a significantly negative value indicates lower over- and under-education rates.

Furthermore, because the ease of skill transfer across borders also depends on language knowledge, I include a dummy variable for cross-border commuting and migration between countries that share a common language (France–Belgium, Netherlands–Belgium and Austria–Germany), as well as for commuting between

Table 4.6a Over and under-education rates by types of commuting, demographic and job characteristics according to OECD (2007) measurement, 2006 (EU27)

	Under-education					Over-education				
	Commuters			Migrants		Commuters			Migrants	
	Non	Internal	Cross-border	Established	Recent	Non	Internal	Cross-border	Established	Recent
Total	30.9	30.9	24.0	32.6	19.6	10.3	9.1	13.6	10.5	25.8
Gender										
Female	30.0	30.1	25.3	27.4	16.6	11.0	10.1	19.9	12.3	32.2
Male	31.8	31.3	23.4	37.6	22.1	9.7	8.5	11.1	8.8	20.5
Age										
Age 15–24 years	35.3	34.0	15.0	39.1	26.3	10.9	11.3	19.8	10.4	25.9
Age 24–45 years	26.6	27.7	20.8	28.8	18.3	11.3	9.6	15.6	9.6	25.5
Age 45–60 years	34.5	34.6	32.6	35.2	18.5	8.7	7.4	7.4	9.9	28.2
Age 60 or more years	42.3	40.0	51.2	40.6	32.2	9.0	7.7	–	7.8	7.0
Education										
Low education (ISCED 2 or less)	77.1	82.5	84.6	76.0	58.9					
Medium education (ISCED 3 or 4)	27.2	37.3	20.6	34.3	14.5	8.9	6.4	11.3	9.3	29.6
Higher education (ISCED 5 or more)						21.5	16.5	26.0	19.6	37.8
Profession										
High-skilled*	44.4	40.6	42.8	41.9	34.9					
Medium-skilled*	27.2	23.7	16.8	30.7	22.0	10.1	13.2	11.1	12.8	16.8
Low-skilled*						49.9	55.2	77.6	46.9	68.1

Notes: – = no data reported due to lack of observations; * according to OECD (2007) measurement.
Source: EUROSTAT-LFS, own calculations

Table 4.6b Over and under-education rates by types of commuting, demographic and job characteristics according to ILO (1987) measurement, 2006 (EU27)

	Under-education					Over-education				
	Commuters			Migrants		Commuters			Migrants	
	Non	Internal	Cross-border	Established	Recent	Non	Internal	Cross-border	Established	Recent
Total	22.2	27.4	20.0	26.0	15.3	5.9	6.0	6.5	6.1	10.5
Gender										
Female	19.8	25.7	19.6	26.9	15.4	6.4	7.4	8.7	7.6	12.4
Male	25.0	30.5	21.0	25.2	15.2	5.5	5.5	5.4	5.5	8.8
Age										
Age 15–24 years	13.3	17.9	10.2	15.1	6.1	7.5	11.2	–	–	1.8
Age 24–45 years	23.0	28.9	21.2	25.8	16.9	6.3	7.4	8.2	7.9	11.7
Age 45–60 years	24.0	28.0	21.8	27.8	14.6	4.2	4.4	3.9	5.9	11.1
Age 60 or more years	21.5	30.0	27.1	26.0	60.2	4.3	4.7	–	–	–
Education										
Low education (ISCED 2 or less)	95.1	94.4	90.7	94.0	90.9					
Medium education (ISCED 3 or 4)	60.6	55.6	61.3	57.6	50.7	0.2	0.6	0.1	0.8	0.7
Higher education (ISCED 5 or more)						9.4	12.8	–	–	–
Profession										
High–skilled*	95.1	94.4	90.7	94.0	90.9					
Medium–skilled*	60.6	55.6	61.3	57.6	50.7	0.2	0.6	–	–	–
Low–skilled*						9.4	12.8	9.7	11.7	14.1

Notes: – = no data reported due to lack of observations, *according to ILO (1987) measurement.

Source: EUROSTAT-LFS, author's calculations.

Table 4.7 Regression results for probability of over-and under-educated employment (marginal effects)

	Low educated: P(Under-educated)		Medium educated P(Under-educated)		Medium educated P(Over-educated)		Higher educated P(Over-educated)	
	Coefficient	S.E.	Coefficient	S.E	Coefficient	S.E.	Coefficient	S.E.
Sending Region: All								
Internal commuter[3]	0.039***	0.0003	0.070***	0.0002	-0.022***	0.0001	-0.055***	0.0002
Cross-border commuter[3]	0.057***	0.0012	-0.019***	0.0007	0.039***	0.0005	0.029***	0.0009
No response[2]	-0.040***	0.0037	-0.053***	0.0018	0.001	0.0014	-0.106***	0.0013
Established migrant[3]	-0.007***	0.0007	0.048***	0.0006	0.008***	0.0004	0.017***	0.0006
Recent migrant[3]	-0.120***	0.0009	-0.070***	0.0005	0.202***	0.0005	0.175***	0.0008
Common language	0.057***	0.0014	0.065***	0.0012	-0.050***	0.0004	-0.100***	0.0007
Slovak–Czech	0.025***	0.0035	-0.085***	0.0014	-0.004***	0.0009	-0.015***	0.0037
Scandinavia	0.025***	0.0030	-0.030***	0.0017	-0.025***	0.0009	0.004*	0.0026
Male	0.061***	0.0002	0.027***	0.0001	-0.007***	0.0001	-0.058***	0.0001
Age 25–44[2]	-0.026***	0.0002	0.122***	0.0002	-0.021***	0.0001	-0.163***	0.0003
Age 45–59[2]	-0.008***	0.0002	0.172***	0.0002	-0.015***	0.0001	-0.166***	0.0002
Age 60 or more[2]	0.016***	0.0003	0.219***	0.0004	0.008***	0.0002	-0.133***	0.0002
Manufacturing[1]	-0.022***	0.0003	0.230***	0.0004	-0.030***	0.0001	-0.165***	0.0002
Construction[1]	-0.044***	0.0004	0.116***	0.0005	-0.020***	0.0001	-0.084***	0.0003
Market services[1]	-0.085***	0.0003	0.330***	0.0003	-0.020***	0.0001	-0.213***	0.0003
Non-market services[1]	-0.216***	0.0004	0.432***	0.0004	-0.007***	0.0001	-0.372***	0.0003
Sending Region: EU15								
Internal commuter[3]	0.038***	0.0003	0.076***	0.0002	-0.027***	0.0001	-0.061***	0.0002
Cross-border commuter[3]	0.095***	0.0011	0.044***	0.0009	-0.037***	0.0004	-0.013***	0.0009
No response[3]	-0.032***	0.0037	-0.052***	0.0021	-0.012***	0.0013	-0.123***	0.0013
Established migrant[3]	0.003***	0.0008	0.081***	0.0007	-0.031***	0.0003	-0.046***	0.0006
Recent migrant[3]	0.065***	0.0017	0.133***	0.0013	-0.038***	0.0005	-0.059***	0.0007
Common language	0.014***	0.0018	-0.011***	0.0012	0.022***	0.0011	-0.031***	0.0012

Scandinavia	0.010***	0.0031	−0.058***	0.0018	0.024***	0.0016	0.112***	0.0036
Male	0.072***	0.0002	0.058***	0.0001	−0.001***	0.0001	−0.066***	0.0001
Age 25–44[2]	−0.025***	0.0002	0.139***	0.0002	−0.022***	0.0001	−0.166***	0.0003
Age 45–59[2]	−0.007***	0.0002	0.188***	0.0002	−0.018***	0.0001	−0.171***	0.0002
Age 60 or more[2]	−0.016***	0.0004	0.223***	0.0004	0.004***	0.0002	−0.141***	0.0002
Manufacturing[1]	0.046***	0.0003	0.209***	0.0006	−0.033***	0.0002	−0.184***	0.0002
Construction[1]	0.041***	0.0004	0.057***	0.0006	−0.029***	0.0002	−0.090***	0.0003
Market services[1]	−0.006***	0.0003	0.317***	0.0005	−0.019***	0.0002	−0.241***	0.0003
Non-market services[1]	−0.104***	0.0004	0.380***	0.0005	−0.015***	0.0002	−0.401***	0.0004
Sending Region: NMS12								
Internal commuter[3]	0.036***	0.0014	0.023***	0.0006	0.007***	0.0005	−0.028***	0.0006
Cross-border commuter[3]	−0.027***	0.0030	−0.095***	0.0006	0.138***	0.0010	0.226***	0.0028
No response[3]	0.002***	0.0005	−0.077***	0.0065	0.013**	0.0060	0.026	0.0203
Established migrant[3]	0.030***	0.0014	−0.024***	0.0007	0.074***	0.0008	0.231***	0.0015
Recent migrant[3]	−0.085***	0.0010	−0.112***	0.0003	0.251***	0.0006	0.534***	0.0014
Slovak–Czech	0.025***	0.0038	0.006***	0.0016	−0.039***	0.0005	−0.082***	0.0007
Male	0.019***	0.0004	−0.049***	0.0002	−0.021***	0.0001	−0.017***	0.0002
Age 25–44[2]	−0.020***	0.0006	0.070***	0.0003	−0.019***	0.0002	−0.141***	0.0006
Age 45–59[2]	−0.009***	0.0006	0.111***	0.0004	−0.008**	0.0002	−0.134***	0.0003
Age 60 or more[2]	0.110***	0.0006	0.203***	0.0009	0.016***	0.0004	−0.089***	0.0002
Manufacturing[1]	−0.067***	0.0007	0.193***	0.0005	−0.023***	0.0002	−0.092***	0.0003
Construction[1]	−0.187***	0.0010	0.198***	0.0007	−0.005**	0.0002	−0.083***	0.0002
Market services[1]	−0.162***	0.0007	0.277***	0.0005	−0.031***	0.0002	−0.102***	0.0004
Non-market services[1]	−0.469***	0.0008	0.529***	0.0005	0.013***	0.0002	−0.258***	0.0006

Notes: The table reports marginal effects of multinomial logit regressions on the probability of over- and under-educated employment. Results for base category (appropriate employment) and for sending country fixed effects are not reported. (1) base category = agriculture and mining, (2) base category = aged 15–24, (3) base category = non-commuters; ***, **, and * significant at 1%, 5% and 10%, respectively. S.E. = heteroscedasticity robust standard error.

Source: EU-LFS.

Slovakia and the Czech Republic and among Scandinavian countries.[9] Since low educated workers cannot be over-educated and higher educated workers cannot be under-educated I run these regressions separately for each education group.[10]

The marginal effects of these estimates[11] (Table 4.7) in accordance with descriptive results suggest that males have lower over- but higher under-education risks than females; that the risk of over-educated employment declines, while the under-education risk increases with age (although there is some variation across education groups); and that there are more varied patterns of over- and under-education by sector of employment, which may reflect differing sectoral employment strategies with respect to education. In addition, commuting between countries that share a common language – as expected – increases under- and reduces over-education rates, with the marginal effects varying between 1.0 and 6.0 percentage points for the increase in under-education and between –2.4 and –11.7 percentage points for the reduction in over-education. Commuters between the Czech Republic and Slovakia also have higher under- and lower over-education rates. Here marginal effects suggest an increase in under-education of between 2.3 and 6.4 percentage points and a reduction of over-education between 0.5 and 8.7 percentage points. For cross-border commuters among Scandinavian countries results are more mixed. Low educated cross-border commuters between these countries have higher under-education rates, while the medium educated have a higher one. Similarly for medium skilled cross-border commuters among Scandinavian countries over-education is 2.5 percentage points lower, while for higher educated workers the results are only at the margin of significance.

In addition, in the regressions for the complete EU27 the risk of under-educated employment for cross-border out-commuters is 5.0 percentage points higher than for non-commuters among the less educated. For medium educated cross-border commuters, by contrast, the under-education risk is 3.7 percentage points lower. With regard to over-education, medium skilled cross-border commuters have a 4.2 percentage point higher risk of over-qualified employment than non-commuters, while for highly skilled cross-border commuters the risk is 3.3 percentage points higher. For all education groups, however, cross-border commuters face substantially lower over- and higher under-education rates than recent migrants.

---

9   In addition, I was concerned that commuters to Luxemburg may be an outlier on account of the high share of in-commuting to this country. I conducted a similar analysis excluding commuters to Luxemburg. These results were qualitatively similar. I also excluded the Scandinavia dummy, as well as the dummy for commuting between the Czech and Slovak Republic. Once more this leaves qualitative results unchanged.

10   The low numbers of over-educated cross-border commuters with ISCED level 6 or higher education preclude estimation of a similar model for the higher educated for the ILO (1987) definition. However, a similar analysis to the one here was conducted for low and medium skilled commuters based on the ILO definition. Again, results are qualitatively similar with respect to both measurement concepts.

11   Coefficient estimates are reported in the Appendix.

For internal commuters, by contrast, the probability of under-educated employment after controlling for other influences is actually (by 3.9 percentage points for the low skilled and 6.9 percentage points for the medium skilled) higher than for non-commuters and the risk of over-educated employment is lower (by 2.2 percentage points for the medium skilled and 5.5 percentage points for the high skilled).

The results also point to large differences between cross-border commuters from the EU15 and the NMS12. In the EU15 cross-border commuters have lower over- and higher under-education risks than non-commuters for all education groups. For workers from an EU15 country, cross-border commuting is therefore not associated with a higher risk of de-education when compared to non-commuters. Indeed, in all cases the mobility of cross-border commuters seems to significantly improve education–job matches. For cross-border commuters from the NMS12 the opposite applies. They face significantly (between 16.0 for medium to 21.9 percentage points for higher educated) higher over-education risks and also significantly (between 4.0 percentage points for low and 10.4 percentage points for medium educated) lower under-education risks than non-commuters.

Similar observations apply to both recent and established migrants from the EU15. They also have lower over- and higher under-education rates than non-commuters for all education groups. Results suggest that the probability of under-educated employment is higher among low skilled recent migrants and that the over-education risk is higher among high skilled recent migrants than for cross-border commuters from the EU15, while recent migrants from the NMS12 face substantially lower under-education as well as substantially higher over-education rates than cross-border commuters from the NMS12. Thus, problems of skill transfer among cross-border commuters and recent migrants in the EU seem to apply primarily to migrants and cross-border commuters from the NMS12, while cross-border commuters and migrants from the EU15 actually have lower risks of de-education than non-commuters. This may be due to the shorter integration time of the NMS12 and associated lower progress in the mutual recognition of skills across borders.

6. Conclusions

This chapter considers cross-border commuting in the EU27, a rarely analysed mode of international labour mobility. According to the results this is still of limited quantitative importance, with only about 0.7 per cent of employed persons commuting across borders in 2006. Results, however, also show that while in most regions cross-border commuting is low, it does attain some relevance in a small number of border regions with strong linguistic, historical or institutional ties. This suggests that, where such ties are absent, substantial barriers to cross-border commuting still exist and that policy measures directed at increasing labour mobility through commuting could be complementary to measures aimed at international migration to achieve a higher degree of labour mobility in Europe.

In addition, cross-border commuters differ from migrants in a number of ways: they are more often manufacturing workers, males and young than non-commuters and in comparison to migrants more often have medium educational attainment. Improving possibilities for cross-border commuting will thus affect different groups of the population in comparison to policies directed at removing barriers to migration. They are, in consequence, also likely to have different implications for the human capital base and the competitiveness of sending and receiving (border) regions.

I also find that cross-border commuters as well as migrants from EU15 countries do not have higher over- and lower under-education rates than workers working and living in their region of residence. By contrast, cross-border commuters from the NMS12, although having higher over- and lower under-education rates than workers working and living in their region of residence, have substantially lower over- and higher under-education rates than recent migrants from these countries. Although the available data cannot control for the duration of working abroad and also misses a number of other variables that have been found important in explaining over- and under-education among migrants (such as language knowledge) this suggests that cross-border commuting entails a lower degree of 'brain drain' than migration, at least when considering European 'East–West' migration. This may be because cross-border commuters will be willing to commute only if they find adequate employment opportunities abroad, while migrants may have a weaker bargaining position once they have moved abroad.

Furthermore, our results, in conjunction with the finding that cross-border commuters from the NMS12 are even more often medium skilled and younger than those from the EU15, also point to some interesting heterogeneity among cross-border commuters. Substantial efforts at improving the transferability of skills from the NMS12 are still needed to increase the attractiveness of cross–border commuting (and migration) for residents of these countries. Finally, in common with many previous studies, I find higher over-education risks for females and young workers. Policies focusing on these target groups may thus be needed, since they face much greater problems in skill-utilisation than others.

Bibliography

Bernotat, K. and Snickars, F. 2002. 'Regional development expectations in the Öresund region – travel patterns and cross-border mobility', Paper presented at the 42nd Congress of the European Regional Science Association, Dortmund.

Bock-Schappelwein, J. et al. 2010. Effekte der Zuwanderung im Rahmen des Grenzgängerabkommens auf die burgenländische Wirtschaft, WIFO-Monatsberichte 8/2010.

Borjas, G. 1999. 'The economic analysis of immigration', in *Handbook of Labor Economics*, Vol. 3A, edited by O. Ashenfelter and D. Card. Amsterdam: Elsevier.

Buch, T., et al. 2008. Grenzpendeln in der deutsch dänischen Grenzregion, IAB-regional, No. 4/2008.

Büchel, F., and Battu, H. 2003. 'The theory of differential overqualification: does it work?', *Scottish Journal of Political Economy*, 50, 1–16.

Chiswick, B.R. 1999.' Are immigrants positively self-selected?', *American Economic Review* 89, 181–5.

Chiswick, B.R. 2005. 'High skilled immigration in the international arena', IZA Discussion Paper No. 1782, Bonn: IZA.

Chiswick, B.R. and Miller, P.W. 2007. 'The international transferability of human capital skills', IZA Discussion Paper 2670, Bonn: IZA.

Cohn, E. and Khan, S. 1995. 'The wage effects of overschooling revisited', *Labour Economics*, 2(1), 67–76.

Greve, B. and Rydberg, M. 2003a. 'Cross-border commuting in the EU: obstacles and barriers, country report: the Sonderylland-Schlesswig region', University of Roskildens, Research Papers 10/03.

Greve, B. and Rydberg, M. 2003b. 'Cross-border commuting in the EU: obstacles and barriers, country report: the Oresund region', University of Roskildens, Research Papers 11/03.

Gottholmseder, G. and Theurl, E. 2007. 'Determinants of cross-border commuting: do cross-border commuters within the household matter?', *Journal of Borderland Studies*, 22(2), 97–112.

Gottholmseder, G. and Theurl, E. 2006. Nicht-PendlerInnen, BinnenpendlerInnen, GrenzpendlerInnen – Eine sozi-ökonomische Charakterisierung am Beispiel der Pendlerregion Bodenseeraum, *Wirtschaft und Gesellschaft*, 2/2006.

Groot, W. and van den Brink, M.H. 2000. 'Overeducation in the labour market: a meta-analysis', *Economics of Education Review*, 19(2), 158–79.

Hartog, J. 2000. 'Over-education and earnings: Where are we, where should we go?', *Economics of Education Review*, 19(2), 131–47.

Hazans, M. 2003. 'Commuting in the Baltic States: patterns, determinants and gains', Zentrum für Europäische Integrationsforschung, Working Paper B02/2003, Bonn.

Huber, P., Nowotny, K. and Bock-Schappelwein J. 2009. 'Qualification structure, over- and underqualification of the foreign born in Austria and the EU', FIW Research Reports 2009/2010 N° 08, Vienna.

Huber, P. and Nowotny, K. 2008. 'Regional effects of labour mobility', in European integration consortium, *Labour mobility in the EU in the context of enlargement and functioning of the transitional arrangements*, European Commission, Brussels: DG Employment.

Hunt, J. 2004. 'Are migrants more skilled than non-migrants? Repeat, return and same employer migrants', *Canadian Journal of Economics*, 37(4), 830–49.

ILO. 1987. ISCO-88: International Standard Classification of Occupations. Geneva: International Labour Office.

Kiker, B.F., Santos, M.C. and de Oliveira, M.M. 1997. 'Overeducation and undereducation: evidence for Portugal', *Economics of Education Review*, 16(2), 111–25.

Mätha, T. and Wintr, L. 2009. 'Commuting flows across bordering regions: a note', *Applied Economics Letters*, 16, 735–8.

MKW. 2001. Scientific report on the mobility of cross-border workers within the EEA, Report for the European Commission, DG Employment and Social Affairs, MKW, Munich.

MKW. 2009. Scientific report on the mobility of cross-border workers within the EU-27/EEA/EFTA countries, FINAL REPORT, Report for the European Commission, DG Employment and Social Affairs, MKW, Munich.

OECD. 2007. SOPEMI Report – International Migration Outlook 2007, Paris: OECD.

Rouwendal, J. 1999. 'Spatial job search and commuting distances', *Regional Science and Urban Economics*, 29(4), 491–517.

Rubb, S. 2003. 'Overeducation: a short or long run phenomenon for individuals?', *Economics of Education Review*, 22(4), 389–94.

Sanromá, E., Ramos, R. and Simón, H. 2009. 'Immigrant wages in the Spanish labour market: does the origin of human capital matter?', IZA Discussion Papers 4157, Institute for the Study of Labour (IZA).

Van der Velde M., Janssen, M, van Houtum H. 2005., Job mobility in the Dutch-German regional labour market: The threshold of indifference', manuscript,

Van Ommeren, J., Rietveld, P. and Nijkamp, P. 1999. 'Job moving, residential moving, and commuting: a search perspective', *Journal of Urban Economics*, 46(2), 230–53.

Verdugo, R. and Verdugo, N. 1989. 'The impact of surplus schooling on earnings: some additional findings', *Economics of Education Review*, 22(4), 690–95.

White, M. 1986. 'Sex differences in urban commuting patterns', *American Economic Review* 76(2), 368–72.

Appendix A: Regression results

Table 4.A1 Results for probability of non-, internal and cross-border commuting, and migration (coefficients)

	Internal (Commuters)		Cross-border		Migrants: Established		Recent	
	Coeff.	S.E.	Coeff.	S.E.	Coeff.	S.E.	Coeff.	S.E.
Sending Region: All								
Male	0.42***	0.001	0.60***	0.002	−0.08***	0.002	0.04***	0.002
Age 25–44[2]	0.06***	0.001	−0.20***	0.003	0.70***	0.004	−0.12***	0.002
Age 45–59[2]	−0.09***	0.001	−0.44***	0.003	0.82***	0.004	−1.22***	0.003
Age 60 or more[2]	−0.48***	0.002	−0.66***	0.007	1.14***	0.005	−2.12***	0.010
Low education (ISCED 2 or less)[3]	−0.56***	0.001	−0.52***	0.003	0.06***	0.002	0.11***	0.003
Medium education (ISCED 3 or 4)[3]	−0.37***	0.001	−0.09***	0.002	−0.29***	0.002	−0.47***	0.002
Manufacturing/construction[1]	0.60***	0.002	0.48***	0.005	1.05***	0.005	1.19***	0.004
Market services[1]	0.64***	0.002	0.14***	0.005	1.28***	0.005	1.25***	0.004
Non-market services[1]	0.42***	0.002	−0.33***	0.005	1.25***	0.006	1.03***	0.004
Log likelihood					−64628163			
Observations					174081589			
Sending Region: EU15								
Male	0.40***	0.001	0.60***	0.003	−0.05***	0.002	0.13***	0.003
Age 25–44[2]	0.09***	0.001	0.07***	0.004	0.68***	0.004	0.59***	0.006
Age 45–59[2]	−0.04***	0.001	−0.04***	0.004	0.77***	0.004	−0.40***	0.007
Age 60 or more[2]	−0.44***	0.002	−0.20***	0.007	1.10***	0.005	−0.48***	0.011
Low education (ISCED 2 or less)[3]	−0.57***	0.001	−0.63***	0.004	0.01***	0.002	−1.32***	0.005
Medium education (ISCED 3 or 4)[3]	−0.36***	0.001	−0.17***	0.003	−0.24***	0.002	−0.88***	0.003
Manufacturing/construction[1]	0.49***	0.002	0.59***	0.007	0.15***	0.006	0.07***	0.011

Market services[1]	0.54***	0.002	0.29***	0.007	0.38***	0.006	0.40***	0.011
Non-market services[1]	0.33***	0.002	−0.21***	0.008	0.34***	0.006	−0.05***	0.011
Log likelihood	−53110260.00							
Observations	134617782							
Sending Region: NMS12								
Male	0.75***	0.003	0.61***	0.004	−0.20***	0.003	−0.02***	0.002
Age 25–44[2]	−0.41***	0.004	−0.71***	0.005	0.77***	0.009	−0.39***	0.003
Age 45–59[2]	−0.83***	0.004	−1.31***	0.006	1.00***	0.009	−1.55***	0.004
Age 60 or more[2]	−0.99***	0.008	−2.26***	0.022	1.40***	0.011	−3.87***	0.023
Low education (ISCED 2 or less)[3]	−0.20***	0.005	0.18***	0.009	0.51***	0.006	1.16***	0.004
Medium education (ISCED 3 or 4)[3]	−0.51***	0.003	0.29***	0.006	−0.40***	0.004	0.03***	0.003
Manufacturing/construction[1]	1.30***	0.007	0.43***	0.007	2.48***	0.012	1.58***	0.004
Market services[1]	1.26***	0.007	0.01***	0.007	2.74***	0.012	1.61***	0.004
Non-market services[1]	0.94***	0.007	−0.37***	0.009	2.72***	0.012	1.53***	0.005
Log likelihood	−11284412.00							
Observations	39463807							

Notes: Table reports coefficients of a multinomial logit regression on the probability of outcomes defined in first row relative to non-commuting. See Table 4.5 for notes.

Source: EU-LFS.

Table 4.A2 Regression results for probability of over- and under-educated employment

	Low educated: P(Under-educated)		Medium educated: P(Under-educated)		P(Over-educated)		Higher educated: P(Over-educated)	
	Coefficient	S.E.	Coefficient	S.E.	Coefficient	S.E.	Coefficient	S.E.
Sending Region: All								
Internal commuter[3]	0.245 ***	0.002	0.317 ***	0.001	-0.212 ***	0.002	-0.400 ***	0.001
Cross-border commuter[3]	0.379 ***	0.009	-0.048 ***	0.004	0.396 ***	0.005	0.180 ***	0.005
No response[3]	-0.221 ***	0.020	-0.306 ***	0.011	-0.079 ***	0.018	-0.955 ***	0.017
Established migrant[3]	-0.043 ***	0.004	0.261 ***	0.003	0.181 ***	0.004	0.108 ***	0.004
Recent migrants[3]	-0.611 ***	0.004	-0.087 ***	0.003	1.432 ***	0.003	0.903 ***	0.004
Same language	0.375 ***	0.011	0.246 ***	0.006	-0.834 ***	0.011	-0.874 ***	0.008
Czech Republic-Slovakia	0.158 ***	0.023	-0.523 ***	0.010	-0.168 ***	0.011	-0.105 *	0.026
Scandinavia	0.154 ***	0.019	-0.207 ***	0.010	-0.427 ***	0.016	0.029 *	0.016
Male	0.357 ***	0.001	0.138 ***	0.001	-0.043 ***	0.001	-0.378 ***	0.001
Age 25–44[2]	-0.150 ***	0.001	0.631 ***	0.001	-0.088 ***	0.001	-1.003 ***	0.002
Age 45–59[2]	-0.048 ***	0.001	0.850 ***	0.001	0.073 ***	0.001	-1.264 ***	0.002
Age 60 or more[2]	0.098 ***	0.002	1.046 ***	0.002	0.504 ***	0.002	-1.283 ***	0.002
Manufacturing[1]	-0.129 ***	0.002	1.065 ***	0.002	-0.048 ***	0.002	-1.542 ***	0.003
Construction[1]	-0.245 ***	0.002	0.537 ***	0.002	-0.099 ***	0.002	-0.678 ***	0.003
Market services[1]	-0.486 ***	0.002	1.663 ***	0.002	0.275 ***	0.002	-1.619 ***	0.002
Non-market service[1]	-1.099 ***	0.002	2.093 ***	0.002	0.759 ***	0.002	-2.537 ***	0.002
Log likelihood	-19164699		-71561501				-22141060	
Sending Region: EU15								
Internal commuter[3]	0.245 ***	0.002	0.313 ***	0.001	-0.268 ***	0.002	-0.411 ***	0.001
Cross-border commuter[3]	0.706 ***	0.011	0.149 ***	0.004	-0.535 ***	0.009	-0.080 ***	0.006
No response[3]	-0.184 ***	0.020	-0.291 ***	0.011	-0.246 ***	0.019	-1.059 ***	0.017
Established migrant[3]	0.019 ***	0.005	0.327 ***	0.003	-0.345 ***	0.006	-0.310 ***	0.004
Recent migrants[3]	0.444 ***	0.013	0.536 ***	0.005	-0.397 ***	0.011	-0.411 ***	0.006
Same language	0.089 ***	0.011	-0.018 ***	0.006	0.246 ***	0.012	-0.203 ***	0.008

	(1) Coef.		SE	(2) Coef.		SE	(3) Coef.		SE	(4) Coef.		SE
Scandinavia	0.064	***	0.020	−0.269	***	0.010	0.188	***	0.017	0.589	***	0.016
Male	0.427	***	0.001	0.290	***	0.001	0.083	***	0.001	−0.402	***	0.001
Age 25–44[2]	−0.151	***	0.001	0.665	***	0.001	−0.059	***	0.001	−0.966	***	0.002
Age 45–59[2]	−0.042	***	0.001	0.868	***	0.001	0.082	***	0.001	−1.208	***	0.002
Age 60 or more[2]	−0.096	***	0.002	1.025	***	0.002	0.503	***	0.002	−1.242	***	0.003
Manufacturing[1]	0.291	***	0.002	0.903	***	0.002	−0.119	***	0.002	−1.614	***	0.003
Construction[1]	0.258	***	0.002	0.224	***	0.002	−0.348	***	0.003	−0.669	***	0.003
Market services[1]	−0.034	***	0.002	1.525	***	0.002	0.300	***	0.002	−1.726	***	0.003
Non-market services[1]	−0.573	***	0.002	1.766	***	0.002	0.541	***	0.002	−2.598	***	0.003
Log likelihood	−16301228			−52333308			−19406556					
Sending Region: NMS 12												
Internal commuter[3]	0.219	***	0.009	0.163	***	0.004	0.121	***	0.006	−0.327	***	0.008
Cross-border commuter[3]	−0.146	***	0.016	−0.715	***	0.008	1.046	***	0.006	1.426	***	0.013
No response[3]	0.036	***	0.008	−0.659	***	0.074	0.067	***	0.069	0.249		0.174
Established migrant[3]	0.181	***	0.009	−0.078	***	0.006	0.711	***	0.006	1.457	***	0.007
Recent migrants[3]	−0.438	***	0.005	−0.775	***	0.005	1.634	***	0.003	2.732	***	0.006
Slovakia – Czech Republic	0.151	***	0.023	−0.009		0.011	−0.676	***	0.011	−1.496		0.027
Male	0.111	***	0.002	−0.369	***	0.001	−0.347	***	0.002	−0.180	***	0.002
Age 25–44[2]	−0.139	***	0.003	0.475	***	0.002	−0.153	***	0.002	−1.278	***	0.005
Age 45–59[2]	−0.050	***	0.004	0.712	***	0.002	0.041	***	0.003	−1.707	***	0.005
Age 60 or more[2]	0.724	***	0.005	1.125	***	0.004	0.527	***	0.005	−1.586	***	0.007
Manufacturing[1]	−0.359	***	0.003	1.140	***	0.003	−0.054	***	0.002	−1.384	***	0.005
Construction[1]	−0.897	***	0.004	1.092	***	0.003	0.235	***	0.003	−1.386	***	0.007
Market services[1]	−0.806	***	0.003	1.616	***	0.003	−0.051	***	0.002	−1.222	***	0.005
Non-market services[1]	−2.110	***	0.004	2.807	***	0.003	1.280	***	0.003	−2.559	***	0.005
Log likelihood	−2735656.6			−1862931			−1862931			−1862931		

Notes: Table reports coefficients of a multinomial logit regression on the probability of over-, under-educated employment relative to appropriate employment. See Table 4.7 for notes.

Source: EU-LFS.

PART II
The Extent and Qualitative Characteristics of Migration and Return against the Background of Crisis and Recovery

Chapter 5

Return Migration to Poland in the Post-accession Period

Marta Anacka and Agnieszka Fihel

1. Introduction

Return migrants (or 'returns') exhibit a specific type of mobility which – to a greater or lesser extent – accompanies every outflow. According to the regularities observed in the nineteenth century by Ravenstein (1885: 199), 'each main current of migration produces a compensating counter current' consisting of persons who, for various reasons, decided to move back to the place of their own or their ancestors' origin. Although there are a large number of studies devoted to return migration, in fact the determinants of coming back, as well as the order and course of subsequent stages of backward mobility are analogous to traditionally-defined emigration.

In recent years, return migration has become a subject of intensive public debate, government policy and scientific research in Poland. This is not by chance. After exceptionally large outflows that occurred in the wake of Polish accession to the European Union in 2004 (Fihel and Okólski 2009; Grabowska-Lusińska and Okólski 2009), return flows started to take place on a massive scale. A similar mechanism was also observed in Ireland, Italy and Spain, where accession to the European Union provoked an elevated outflow and – a couple of years later – a wave of returns (see, for example, Duszczyk 2007).

What is the scale and socio-demographic composition of post-accession return migration to Poland? What is the pattern of this kind of mobility? Is it short- or long-term? What are the determinants of 'coming back', both in the country of emigration and in the place of origin? How are the recent changes in the economic situation affecting people's propensity to come back to Poland, a country that has largely proved resistant to the worst effects of financial crisis? Finally, with regard to mismatches between migrants' level of education and occupations pursued abroad, who is the most prone to come back: persons with or persons without qualifications?

First, we present previous waves of returns, in the first and second halves of the twentieth century. Second, we quote various estimates of the scale of post-accession return migration and present its selectivity with regard to age, skills, region of origin and destination as compared to post-accession emigration. Third, we test the statistical significance of this selectivity and point out the main factors underlying the recent wave of returns to Poland. Finally, we turn to recent developments in the international economic situation, mainly the financial crisis of 2007, and discuss its impact on the propensity to return of various groups of migrants.

2. Returns to Poland in a Historical Perspective

In light of Ravenstein's theorem on the coexistence of emigration and return migration it is apparent that in contemporary Poland – a typical emigration country – waves of returns have been observed repeatedly. In the twentieth century the first return flow resulted from the Great Depression of 1929, which put an end to the freedom of international mobility that had existed hitherto. In the aftermath of reductions in production and increasing unemployment, countries that had been drawing in migrant workers, including Polish nationals, introduced policies to protect the domestic labour force (Bade 2000). The United States limited the number of entrance visas; countries in Latin America increased the sum of money migrants were required to have as a condition of residence; and France even implemented some compulsory deportations to countries of origin (Kołodziej 1998). Those actions, together with increases in unemployment and poverty in the host countries, provoked a wave of returns to Poland. Seasonal workers excluded, in the period 1926–1930 the absolute number of Polish nationals returning to the country of origin averaged 21,600 annually and in 1931–1935, the figure was 31,100 (Janowska 1981, 1984). Interestingly, returns involved mostly labour migrants resident in Belgium and France,[1] destinations relatively close to Poland. In 1931–1936, more than 160,000 Polish migrants returned from France, 63 per cent of the whole return flow: the percentage of emigrants choosing this destination was only 40 per cent. Returns were far less numerous – also compared to the scale of previous emigration – from the countries drawing settlement migration: Argentine, Canada, Palestine and the United States.

The next wave of returns – the repatriation of Polish nationals – took place after the Second World War and in the first post-war decades. It involved more than 3 million persons who had fled from armed conflicts, had been displaced or, due to the changes in Polish frontiers, had found themselves residents of a foreign country (Gawryszewski 2005). But as the displacement of population during the war had not been voluntary, the repatriation proceeded strictly according to the rules laid down by the administrative and governmental authorities. In the period 1950–1954 the organisation of returns from the Soviet Union was suspended due to political reasons, and it was restored only in 1956 thanks to the Polish–Soviet intergovernmental agreement. Thus, this flow of returns was not shaped spontaneously and the social and economic determinants remained utterly secondary to political circumstances. Return migration also took place, but

---

1   For political reasons Germany was not at that time a destination for Polish migrants.

on a relatively small scale, during the communist period. Data quoted by Slany and Malek (2002: 83) on the registered inflow to Poland in the years 1961–1989 indicates 55,000 persons, a marginal figure compared to the registered (754,000) or estimated (more than 1 million in the 1980s alone) outflow (Okólski 1994). Due to the communist regime and the country's economic backwardness 'potential return migrants had no (except for sentimental or retirement-related) motivations for coming back' to Poland (Slany and Malek 2002: 83).

Interestingly, the change of political and economic system in 1989 released in the 1990s – thus with a certain time lag – a wave of returns that included not only post-war Polish emigrants but also their descendants, representing a so-called second generation of emigrants. The Population Census conducted in 2002 provided information on the return migration of the 1990s. In the period 1989–2002, 70,000 Polish citizens returned to Poland on a permanent basis,[2] including as many as 20,000 (29 per cent) who came back, had emigrated once again before 2002 and at the critical moment of the Population Census were abroad (Fihel, Górny and Matejko 2006). It is worth noting that 27 per cent of the 50,000 Polish residents who did not re-emigrate had double – Polish and other – citizenship, indicating either naturalisation in the country of emigration or that they had been born abroad and had returned to the country of their parents. The migrants returned from the most important destinations for Polish emigration: Germany, the United States, Canada, Italy, the United Kingdom and France.

A significant feature of the return migration of the 1990s is the relatively high share of young (40 per cent below 30 years of age) and well-educated persons (as many as 69 per cent aged 20 and over had at least a secondary level of education, and half had a university degree). Among the return migrants who stayed in Poland until 2002 and undertook employment 70 per cent were employed in the private sector, the most popular occupations being experts, technicians, functionaries, middle management, personal services and sales. Thus, the return migration of the 1990s constituted an inflow of persons who were economically active and possessed high-quality human capital: they knew foreign languages, were educated and trained in the Western environment and had Western professional experience, all rare and important things in a country undergoing post-communist transition (see also Klagge and Klein-Hitpaβ 2007, 2010).

The fact that 20,000 persons (29 per cent) who had returned in the 1990s had emigrated again by the time of the Population Census indicates difficulties in adapting to the social and economic conditions in Poland. As compared to those who stayed in Poland, persons choosing re-emigration more frequently held double citizenship, were living alone, had no children or were lone-parents and on average had a lower level of education (mostly secondary and vocational). While those who stayed in Poland occupied high professional positions in the labour

---

2   That is, registered in Poland for a permanent stay. The Population Census caught only registered migration, so the above-quoted number excludes unregistered and temporary migration (Fihel, Górny and Matejko 2006).

market, those who re-emigrated and took employment abroad were mostly middle range employees, workers engaged in personal services, salespersons, workers, machine operators and performers of simple jobs. Thus, high skills on the part of return migrants enhanced economic integration, whereas the high unemployment level in Poland 'pushed out' less educated migrants. In the 1990s, the stagnation of Polish industry and construction and a slow increase in the wage level were markedly unfavourable factors for persons with a secondary, vocational or primary education.

Qualitative studies on return migration in the 1990s clearly indicate problems of adaptation in Poland, affecting subsequent international mobility. It should be emphasised, however, that those difficulties of economic and social integration existed both in the country of emigration and in Poland, the country of re-emigration. For instant, the disapproval of German society with regard to Polish migrants was repeatedly mentioned as a factor impeding adaptation to the host society and encouraging people to come back to Poland (Heffner and Sołdra-Gwiżdż 1997; Koryś 2002). In turn, the migration experiences of the second-generation Poles living in the United Kingdom proved that, for many of them, return to Poland meant only commuting, often on a weekly basis, between the workplace in Warsaw and the place of residence of the rest of a family in London (Górny and Osipovič 2006). The impossibility of leading a life – especially a personal life – on this basis over a long period favoured the abandonment of this mobility and, most often, a decision to settle down in the United Kingdom.

The return migration of the transition period, just like in the post-accession period, should then be placed in the middle of a broad spectrum of different forms of mobility, between, at one end, settlement and at the other, a short temporary stay. Decisions regarding settlement in a destination country/ return to the country of origin/ re-emigration were not definitive and underwent modifications in the rapidly changing economic and social circumstances. A relatively high share of re-emigrants registered in the Population Census and the above-quoted histories of return migrants show a certain fluidity with regard to this kind of migration and also indicate serious difficulties with integration in the social and economic environment in Poland. However, the relatively stable situation on the Polish labour market and the financial crisis in most destinations might have reinforced this fluidity of mobility and favoured the development of a 'try-it-and-see' strategy. The data presented below to a certain extent support this hypothesis.

3. Estimates of the Scale of Post-accession Return Migration

Post-accession return migration has been taking place on a massive scale. Several data sources justify this statement, although none of them provide the exact number of returns. In fact, reliable data on this phenomenon will not be available before the results of the 2011 Population Census are published.[3] This is due to the lack of registers that systematically encompass the widely-defined category of return migrants and also due to methodological problems with representative quantitative surveys of international migration.

Nevertheless, the Central Statistical Office (CSO) of Poland does attempt to calculate the stock of Polish emigrants and returnees. Since the estimates are based on various data sources – the 2002 Population Census, the Labour Force Survey and statistics from destination countries – they seem to be very reliable. Table 5.1 presents the CSO's estimates of stocks of Polish nationals remaining abroad for at least two or three months. It shows that the number of Polish nationals resident abroad evidently diminished from 2,270,000 at the peak of the outflow (end of 2007) to 2,210,000 at the end of 2008 and 1,870,000 at the end of 2009 (CSO 2010). Those figures show clearly that in 2007 returns of Polish nationals started to outnumber the outflow and the phenomenon of return migration started to intensify. It should be stressed here that the difference between those estimates does not give the number of returnees (the latter being in fact much higher) as the quoted numbers refer to stocks of Polish nationals being abroad and not to migration flows (inflow and outflow).

Returns started to take place from almost all destinations, regardless of geographic proximity or recent developments related to the financial crisis in each country. The decrease in the number of Polish nationals was registered not only in countries that in 'troubled times' experienced serious economic problems, such as the United Kingdom, Ireland and the United States, but in other destinations as well: Austria, France, Germany, Italy and the Netherlands. At three main destinations the stock of Polish nationals decreased between the end of 2007 and the end of 2009: by 135,000 in the United Kingdom, by 75,000 in Germany and by 60,000 in Ireland. Interestingly, while the beginning of the declines in Ireland and the United Kingdom – 2008 – overlapped with the deterioration in the economic situation in those countries, the decrease in Germany was registered in 2009 when no influence of the financial crisis or any change in policy towards the Polish labour force was observed. At other destinations the decrease was observed only in 2009 and it was much lower: Austria and Italy registered a drop of 2,000, France 9,000 and the Netherlands 24,000. Also, Belgium, Spain and Sweden experienced an increase, albeit not exceeding 4,000 in each country (in the period end of 2007 – end of 2009). This increase shows that Polish nationals remain highly mobile and move from one destination to another, if the latter is 'more attractive in terms of remuneration conditions or broader access to welfare benefits' (CSO 2010: 2). As CSO suggests, one may assume that the observed increase in the number of Polish nationals residing in Norway is linked to the outflow from the United Kingdom. The study on Polish construction workers living in Oslo showed that a large proportion of them (87 per cent) had previously worked in another destination country (Napierała and Trevena 2010). Thus, several years after EU enlargement

---

3   First results will be published by the end of 2012.

the international mobility of Polish nationals remains high and exhibits the features of transmigration: migration from one country of destination to another.

Table 5.1   Number of Polish citizens staying abroad for longer than 2 or 3 months[4] by destination country (estimates; thousands)

Destination	2002 (May)	2004*	2007*	2008*	2009*
Total	786	1,000	2,270	2,210	1,870
European Union	451	750	1,860	1,820	1,570
Austria	11	15	39	40	38
Belgium	14	13	31	33	34
France	21	30	55	56	47
Germany	294	385	490	490	415
Ireland	2	15	200	180	140
Italy	39	59	87	88	85
Netherlands	10	23	98	108	84
Spain	14	26	80	83	84
Sweden	6	11	27	29	31
United Kingdom	24	150	690	650	555

Notes: * End of the year.
Source: Central Statistical Office, 2010.

The number of Polish returnees can be approximated on the basis of the Labour Force Survey (LFS) which in the second quarter of 2008 included an additional module dedicated to migration and migrants.[5] On the basis of a large sample (almost 25,000 households) the scale of return migration was estimated at 580,000 in the period January 2004–June 2008, with 213,000 in 2007 alone.[6] As already mentioned, in 2007 the phenomenon of returns only *started* to intensify, so the current scale of returns (that is, as of 2011) must be significantly higher. The figure of 580,000 encompasses not only long-term, but also short-term emigrants (staying abroad less than one year) who might be involved in circular mobility. Nevertheless, the scale of flow in the recurrent direction involves hundreds of thousands of Polish nationals.

---

4   Since 2007, 3 months.

5   The research 'Labour market situation of migrants and their immediate descendants' was conducted in all EU member states, EC Regulation 102/2007, 2 February 2007.

6   A return migrant was defined as a person aged 15 or over who had remained abroad for at least two or three months and at the time of the survey (second quarter 2008) was resident in his or her household.

4. Labour Force Survey Data

In the following sections the LFS data on the international mobility of Polish nationals are used to present the features of return migration. The dataset employed in this analysis was extracted from quarterly LFS surveys conducted in the period 1999–2009 and it differs from the data presented above: the CSO's estimates *based* on the LFS and the results of a special LFS module conducted in 2008. Thus, results referring to the scale of returns and their geographic pattern are not fully comparable. The quarterly LFS provides information on sex, age, level of education, place of origin (emigrants)/residence (returnees) in Poland[7] (type of locality and region) and country of emigration. On this basis it is possible to define socio-demographic profiles of emigrants and return migrants, as well as to identify the most important directions of international mobility.

The rules for conducting the LFS assume rotation of households in the sample. A household is tracked for two subsequent quarters of a year, then skipped for the next two quarters, and then tracked for another two subsequent quarters (Table 5.2). Thus, each household is surveyed four times over the span of six subsequent quarters, and then it is excluded from the sample and replaced by a newly sampled household. For this rotation rule, according to which in each quarter 25 per cent of the sample is exchanged, the LFS is a so-called pseudo-panel. In the survey an emigrant is detected when his household's members report – in any one of four surveys the fact of his departure abroad. In turn, a return migrant is detected if he is abroad during (at least) any of the first three surveys and present during the subsequent survey.

Table 5.2   Rotation rule of the Polish Labour Force Survey

Year 1				Year 2				Year 3			
Q1	Q2	Q3	Q4	Q1	Q2	Q3	Q4	Q1	Q2	Q3	Q4
X	X	–	–	X	X						
	X	X	–	–	X	X					
		X	X	–	–	X	X				
			X	X	–	–	X	X			
				X	X	–	–	X	X		
					X	X	–	–	X	X	
						X	X	–	–	X	X

Source: Author's elaboration.

---

7   The place of origin for emigrants is equivalent to the place of residence in Poland for returnees because the LFS sample includes households, not individuals (see discussion below).

On the basis of the quarterly LFS two datasets were compiled:

1. **Emigrants Database**. This includes information on 9,912 persons aged 15 and over who migrated in the period 1999–2009, for at least two or three months. Characteristics of emigrants analysed in the further section refer to the three months (quarter) of their absence. It should be mentioned, however, that in some – albeit rare – cases such characteristics as country of residence changed because migrants moved to other destinations.
2. **Return Migrants Database**. This includes information on 902 persons that have been identified as emigrants (see definition under point 1) in one of the first three surveys and were present in Poland in the subsequent survey. Only 9 per cent of emigrants appear as return migrants.

The LFS study is oriented primarily towards labour market developments and its methodology has not been adjusted to track international mobility. First, it ignores migrants who left Poland with their entire families and thus underestimates the scale of outflow.[8] This is simply due to the fact that if all members of a household emigrate, there remains nobody to report this fact to a pollster. This effect also distorts our reasoning about returns because migrants who left with their families are less prone to come back than other groups of migrants. Second, it includes circular migrants: that is, persons who stayed abroad for a period between two to three months and one year, and excludes seasonal workers who – by definition – are supposed to work less than three months. It also includes returnees who came back for a short period and were incidentally present at their place of residence in Poland at the time the survey was conducted. Third, the LFS sample refers to households and not to individuals. Consequently, if a return migrants sets up a new household (at a new address) after coming back to Poland, he disappears from the LFS sample and is not registered as a returnee. Despite all these shortcomings, the LFS remains the only exhaustive, up-to-date and nationally representative study on international migration from and back to Poland. It will not be possible to overcome those defects in the future without a thorough revision of LFS methodology. Nor is it possible, once the data are gathered, to estimate the scale of underreporting of emigration and overreporting of circular migration.

5. Method of Analysis with Regard to Selectivity

Two groups of migrants, emigrants and returnees, were compared using the so-called 'selectivity index'. This measure is used in demography and other social sciences to compare the distribution of certain features (variables) in two

---

8   The authors wanted to analyse the documentation of surveys that failed to be conducted in order to calculate how many households disappeared from the sample due to emigration. Such an analysis turned out to be impossible because of technical impediments.

populations (Ostasiewicz 1984). It is calculated on the basis of the following formula:

$$SI_{V=i} = \frac{\dfrac{Q_{V=i}}{Q} - \dfrac{P_{V=i}}{P}}{\dfrac{P_{V=i}}{P}} \qquad (1)$$

where $SI_{V=i}$ is the index of selectivity for category i of variable V; $Q_{V=i}$ and $P_{V=i}$ stand for the number of persons in two populations having the i category/ value of variable V, and Q and P stand for overall number of persons in both populations. In this case, the Q population is compared to the P population and the latter serves as a reference group.

The selectivity index was used in the studies presenting the selectivity of the post-accession outflow from Poland with regard to the main socio-demographic variables (Kaczmarczyk, Mioduszewska and Żylicz 2009; Mioduszewska 2008). In those analyses the group of emigrants was compared to the whole adult population of the sending country. In this chapter we propose to set the group of returnees and the group of emigrants alongside one another, according to the following formula:

$$SI_{V=i} = \frac{\dfrac{RM_{V=i}}{RM} - \dfrac{E_{V=i}}{E}}{\dfrac{E_{V=i}}{E}} \qquad (2)$$

where $RM_{V=i}$ and $E_{V=i}$ stand for the number of return migrants and emigrants, respectively, having the i category/value of variable V, and RM and E stand for the overall number of return migrants and emigrants, respectively, in the general population.

According to formula (2), the selectivity index has values ranging from -1 to plus infinity. The positive values indicate that return migration involves relatively more persons with the i category/value of variable V than emigration; the zero value indicates the lack of selectivity with regard to i category/value of variable V (both groups of migrants are the same); the negative values indicate that return migration involves fewer persons with the i category/value of variable V than emigration. It is possible to compare the values of the selectivity index calculated for different categories of the same variable (for instance, various age categories) and to compare the index for different variables (for instance, for age and level of education), so we can indicate the variable that best determines return migration.

6. Selectivity of Returns

The selectivity index of returns was calculated with regard to sex, age and level of education, type of settlement (rural/ urban), region of origin in Poland and country of emigration. Sex seems to be an insignificant selective factor in the return migration process. Despite a certain overrepresentation of men in the return flow as compared to emigration (64 per cent in return migration and 61.1 per cent in emigration), the value of the selectivity index for returns is fairly small: 0.05 for men and –0.07 for women (Table 5.3). The age structure of the returnees is also only slightly different from that of the emigrants: in return migration there is a certain overrepresentation of persons aged 35 and over (40.5 per cent versus 35.8 per cent – see Figure 5.1) but the mean age is the same for both groups (34 years) and the median age differs marginally (30 for the emigrants and 31 for the returnees). Thus, selectivity of returns with regard to sex and age is fairly weak.

Table 5.3   Emigrants and return migrants by sex (in percentage terms) and the selectivity index

Sex	Emigrants (%)	Return migrants (%)	Selectivity index
Male	61.1	64.0	0.05
Female	38.9	36.0	–0.07
Total	100.0	100.0	–

Source: Authors' elaboration based on the LFS.

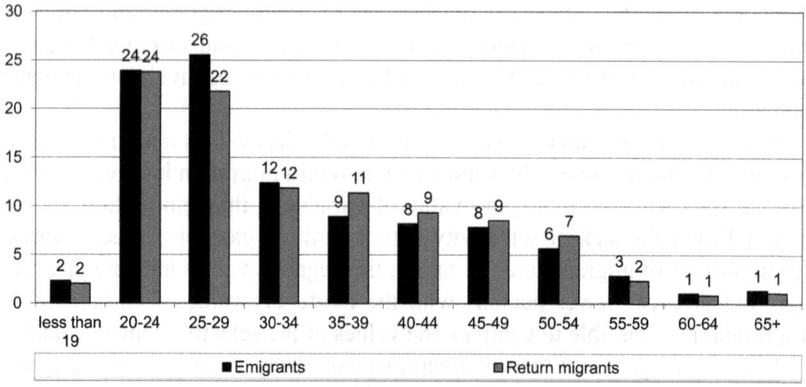

Figure 5.1   Emigrants and return migrants by age (%)

Source: Authors' elaboration based on the LFS.

Stronger selectivity of returns is observed as far as level of education is concerned. The percentage of those with a vocational education is distinctly higher among return migrants than among emigrants (38.6 per cent versus 33.4 per cent, respectively), whereas the share of those with a university degree and a secondary education is higher among emigrants (14.1 per cent for both levels of education) than among returnees (10.2 per cent and 12.9 per cent, respectively – see Table 5.4). This proves the importance of skills and qualifications, in particular knowledge of foreign languages, for people's success in settling abroad. Also, it might suggest rising demand for certain vocational skills on the Polish labour market, especially in the construction sector.

Table 5.4   **Emigrants and return migrants by level of education[1] (in percentage terms) and the selectivity index**

Level of education*	Emigrants (%)	Return migrants (%)	Selectivity index
University degree	14.1	10.2	−0.28
Secondary	14.1	12.9	−0.09
Secondary vocational	30.0	29.7	−0.01
Vocational	33.4	38.6	0.16
Primary	8.4	8.5	0.01
Total	100.0	100.0	–

Note: * The classification of levels of education may be translated to widely used ISCED categories, as follows: university degree – level 5 and 6; secondary – level 3 and 4; secondary vocational – level 3; vocational – level 3; primary – levels 1 and 2. Vocational education does not enable access to tertiary education, in contrast to secondary education.

Source: Authors' elaboration based on the LFS.

In Poland, type of settlement most determines the propensity to return. In the LFS, this variable is defined for emigrants as the last place of residence before emigration and for returnees as the current (at the moment of the survey) place of residence after coming back to Poland. The share of persons living in rural areas is 56.8 per cent among returnees and 42.9 per cent among emigrants (the selectivity index for rural areas is 0.33 – see Table 5.5). Consequently, the share of urban dwellers is higher in the outflow than in the return flow and the larger the settlement, the higher the difference between the proportions of the two categories of migrants.

According to previous statistical analyses (Kaczmarczyk and Okólski 2008; Grabowska-Lusińska and Okólski 2009), persons aged 18–44 living on very small farms were the most prone to emigrate from Poland. In this study rural inhabitants turned out to be the most determined to return, which is paradoxical because, according to the 2002 Population Census, as many as 38 per cent of Polish nationals live in the countryside. Why does residence in rural areas – regions with relatively low demand for labour – enhance return, in contrast to urban areas where local labour markets are more absorptive? It seems that this is due to a set of economic benefits derived from the fact of owning agricultural land in Poland. Farmers and their families have weakly restricted and much less expensive access to the social security system, including the retirement scheme, than employees and self-employed persons in other sectors. Moreover, the agricultural subsidy system of the European Union provides a significant disincentive to dispose of arable land. These privileges constitute the main reason for very low out-migration, whether to urban areas in Poland or abroad. With regard to seasonal mobility,[9] it was proven that the possibility of short-term employment in Germany, combined with maintaining the status of a farmer in Poland, restrained unemployed rural dwellers from looking for a permanent job elsewhere and/or from emigrating on a permanent basis (Fihel 2004). The LFS data exclude seasonal migrants but suggest that this repeated mobility might apply to longer migration as well. Indeed, a large part of post-accession emigrants did not leave the country forever and probably never intended to do so, and the mechanism of circular mobility persisted after Polish accession to the European Union.

Table 5.5   Emigrants and return migrants by type of settlement in Poland (in percentage terms) and the selectivity index

Place of origin/ residence	Emigrants (%)	Return migrants (%)	Selectivity index
Urban	57.1	43.2	−0.24
Rural	42.9	56.8	0.33
Total	100.0	100.0	-

Source: Authors' elaboration based on the LFS.

The phenomenon of selectivity of returns is also observed in the regional dimension (Table 5.6, Figure 5.2). There are regions in Poland where the share of returnees is higher than that of emigrants; those regions, to some extent, enhance coming back ('pull the returnees'). In contrast, there are regions which 'push away' migrants, where the percentage of returnees is lower than that of emigrants. Those two types of regions are so diverse with regard to the situation on regional labour markets that interpretation of the spatial pattern of returns is ambiguous. On the one hand, regions enhancing return are: *Dolnośląskie* and *Łódzkie* with a relatively

---

9   In the pre-accession period, every year hundreds of thousands of Polish nationals undertook seasonal employment in the German construction and agriculture sectors. This was regular labour mobility based on intergovernmental agreement (see Jaźwińska and Okólski 2001).

high degree of urbanisation and industrialisation and with important academic centres; *Wielkopolskie*, with one of the largest Polish cities, Poznań; and finally *Świętokrzyskie* and *Lubelskie*, rural and underdeveloped provinces with high rates of unemployment. On the other hand, regions 'pushing away' returnees are: *Śląskie*, *Mazowieckie* and *Pomorskie*, which include important cities – Warsaw, Katowice and Gdańsk – and have unemployment levels below the national average, and *Warmińsko-Mazurskie* with the highest rate of unemployment in Poland and persisting problems arising from the post-communist structure of collective agriculture. Furthermore, the geographical pattern of returns does not correspond to local emigration traditions from Poland: in the past, *Małopolskie*, *Opolskie* and *Podkarpackie* were assumed to be the most important sending regions, whereas in this analysis their role in attracting or discouraging returnees is not relevant. In the post-accession period the outflow from Poland was recorded mostly from eastern and southern Poland (Fihel and Okólski 2009), but this does not match the map of returns (Figure 5.2), which is rather fragmented.

Table 5.6   Emigrants by region of origin and return migrants by region of residence (in percentage terms) and the selectivity index

Region	Emigrants (%)	Return migrants (%)	Selectivity Index
Dolnośląskie	7.9	9.0	0.14
Kujawsko-Pomorskie	4.8	5.2	0.08
Lubelskie	8.0	11.7	0.46
Lubuskie	2.9	2.6	−0.10
Łódzkie	4.1	4.8	0.18
Małopolskie	12.5	11.0	−0.12
Mazowieckie	4.9	2.9	−0.40
Opolskie	6.0	4.8	−0.20
Podkarpackie	13.6	14.8	0.09
Podlaskie	6.3	5.6	−0.10
Pomorskie	4.3	3.0	−0.31
Śląskie	5.8	2.7	−0.54
Świętokrzyskie	5.9	8.6	0.47
Warmińsko-Mazurskie	3.7	2.7	−0.29
Wielkopolskie	4.9	6.9	0.39
Zachodniopomorskie	4.4	3.7	−0.15
Total	100.0	100.0	−

Source: Authors' elaboration based on the LFS.

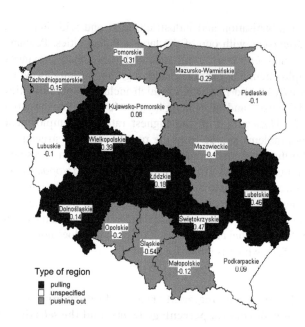

Figure 5.2   Selectivity index for returnees by regions of Poland

Note: Regions have been divided into three groups based on the value of the selectivity index: regions enhancing return migration ('pulling') SI>0.1, regions unspecified –0.1<SI<0.1, regions restraining return migration ('pushing out') SI<–0.1.

Source: Authors' elaboration based on the LFS.

Last, but not least, there is selectivity of returns with regard to countries of destination. It has already been shown that after 2007 stocks of Polish migrants declined in most receiving countries but according to the analysis of selectivity which covers a period of 10 years some destinations are able to 'keep' Polish migrants to a greater extent than others. Indeed, over this period for Austria, Ireland, the United Kingdom and the United States the percentage of emigrants is higher than that of returnees (Table 5.7), which would suggest that incentives to stay in those countries are fairly strong. The opposite appears to be true for – above all – Germany. However, this interpretation raises serious doubts because the LFS data refer to returns that took place over 1999–2009: that is, in dynamically changing economic circumstances and changing legislation as regards free movement of labour. The LFS database provides distributions of returns over this decade. It proves that, for each destination, the pattern of returns has been different: while returns from Germany were evenly distributed over the past decade, the outflow from the United Kingdom and Ireland started abruptly in 2007, that is, when the economic situation worsened.[10] Thus, if the period of analysis of selectivity was limited to 2007–2009, the results would be different with regard to countries of destination. However, narrowing the LFS sample to two years is not possible due to its small size. Nevertheless, the analysis shows the division of destination countries into those of settlement emigration (the United States, the United Kingdom, Ireland) and those of temporary labour mobility (Germany). In the case of the latter, the temporary character obviously refers also to returns that constitute only a phase of mobility. In fact, Germany is a special case as a destination country, with intensive labour migration 'traditions' from Poland, combined with long-term restrictions on labour market access.

Table 5.7   Emigrants and return migrants by country of destination (most important; in percentage terms) and the selectivity index

Country of destination	Emigrants (%)	Return migrants (%)	Selectivity index
EU15	80.8	82.6	0.02
Austria	2.0	1.4	−0.30
Belgium	2.4	2.0	−0.18
France	3.4	3.8	0.12
Germany	23.3	30.9	0.33
Greece	1.3	1.3	−0.01
Ireland	6.6	3.7	−0.43
Italy	8.9	9.8	0.10
Netherlands	4.8	5.5	0.13
Spain	2.9	3.1	0.10
Sweden	1.4	1.7	0.20
United Kingdom	22.8	18.0	−0.21
Other			
Norway	1.8	2.0	0.09
United States	11.8	8.0	−0.33

Source: Authors' elaboration based on the LFS.

7. An Econometric Model of Selectivity of Returns

The analysis of selectivity presented in Sections 5 and 6 provides a simple and intuitive description of the phenomenon of returns. However, this approach may suffer from the problem of deriving conclusions about the presence of selectivity in two or more

---

10   This result is not necessarily in accordance with Table 5.1 because the latter indicates stocks of migrants at particular moments in time, whereas the LFS database refers to flows of migrants.

dimensions (for example, age and level of education) that in fact might not take place. For instance, since younger cohorts are usually better educated than older ones we could combine the selectivity of returns with regard to age with selectivity with regard to education. The econometric model allows for controlling and separating combined effects of different variables (age and education, or any other group of variables) and proves their statistical significance (or insignificance) for return migration. In our analysis the *logistic* regression model was applied with the Boolean dependent variable equal to one if the migrant returned and zero in other cases:

$$P\left(y=1\mid x\right)=f\left(xb\right)=LOGIT\left(xb\right)$$

(3)

To estimate β coefficients the data from the Emigrants Database and Return Migrants Database were combined. By estimation procedures it was verified which socio-demographic variables (age, sex, level of education, type of settlement or region of origin[11]) significantly increase or decrease the probability of returning to Poland and which of them have the strongest influence on it. While an interpretation of β coefficients alone is not informative, their exponentials described as *odds ratios*, were calculated (Greene 2003). On the basis of the F-statistics the hypothesis that all the $\dot{x}\beta$ are insignificant ($\alpha=0.01$) was rejected, however, some of them turned out to be insignificant (Table 5.8).

In general, the econometric model yielded results similar to the previous descriptive analysis of selectivity (Section 6). Sex turned out to be insignificant, which means that it does not affect the return migration propensity (Table 5.8). However, age does, albeit slightly: the odds ratio for migrants older than 29 (the reference group was 25–29) is significantly higher than one, at 1.19. This means that the probability of return for Polish nationals aged 30 and over is almost 20 per cent higher than for younger persons. There is also a relatively strong pull effect with regard to rural areas: the probability of return to urban areas is 26 per cent lower than in the case of rural areas. As for level of education, only vocational education turned out to be significantly different from tertiary education, which constituted the reference level. In a way, both vocational and tertiary levels of education denote valuable skills but a different effect can be observed for each of them. From the Polish perspective highly skilled migrants appear to be rather 'pushed-out' abroad, whereas those with vocational skills are rather 'pulled back' (probability of return is 30 per cent higher for them than for university graduates). These results were obtained even when statistical interactions between different categories of variables were controlled for. For instance, in order to eliminate a combined effect of education and place of residence in Poland – existing if the demand for different skills was different in rural and urban labour markets –

---

11   The destination country of migrants was not included in the model as a variable: see explanation below.

Table 5.8   Logit model of return migration estimates

Variable	Return migration logit model			
	$\dot{x}\beta$	$exp(\dot{x}\beta)$	*p-value*	Significance level[1]
Age				
Age category: 'up to 24'	0.08	1.08	0.48	
Age category: '30–39'	0.17	1.19	0.12	
Age category: '40 and over'	0.17	1.19	0.10	*
Sex				
Sex: 'male'	0.11	1.12	0.15	
Education				
Education: 'primary'	0.02	1.02	0.87	
Education: 'vocational'	0.26	1.30	0.05	*
Education: 'secondary, post-secondary'	0.19	1.21	0.13	
Type of settlement				
Type of settlement: 'urban area'	−0.30	0.74	0.00	***
Region				
Dolnośląskie	−0.05	0.95	0.80	
Kujawsko-Pomorskie	0.22	1.25	0.19	
Lubelskie	−0.25	0.78	0.29	
Lubuskie	0.07	1.07	0.77	
Łódzkie	−0.38	0.68	0.03	**
Małopolskie	−0.54	0.58	0.05	**
Mazowieckie	−0.65	0.52	0.00	***
Opolskie	−0.17	0.84	0.29	
Podkarpackie	−0.24	0.79	0.21	
Podlaskie	−0.50	0.61	0.04	**
Pomorskie	−0.94	0.39	0.00	***
Śląskie	0.28	1.32	0.10	*
Świętokrzyskie	−0.52	0.59	0.03	**
Warmińsko-Mazurskie	0.16	1.17	0.42	
Wielkopolskie	−0.32	0.73	0.16	
Type of country of destination				
'New countries of emigration'[2]	−0.26	0.77	0.00	***
'Other'	0.22	1.25	0.06	**
Intercept	−2.13	0.12	0.00	***

Notes: [1] Significance level for p-value: * α=0.1; ** α=0.05; *** α=0.01. [2] New countries of emigration are United Kingdom, Ireland, Netherlands, Spain, Belgium, Norway, Sweden, Denmark, Czech Republic and Iceland. Germany, the United States, Italy, France, Austria, Greece, Canada and Australia are assumed to be the 'old' ones.

Source: Authors' elaboration based on the LFS.

additional variables combining education and place of origin were introduced but none of them turned out to be statistically significant.

In order to assess the influence of region of origin on propensity to return 16 *logistic* regression models were calculated, with each of the 16 Polish regions as the reference category[12] (Table 5.9). The results of the econometric models turned out to be almost identical to those of descriptive analysis, with some regions attracting returnees (*Dolnośląskie, Kujawsko-Pomorskie, Lubuskie, Świętokrzyskie* and *Wielkopolskie*) and some pushing them away (*Mazowieckie, Pomorskie, Śląskie, Warmińsko-Mazurskie*). Again, this spatial pattern does not reveal any equivocal relationship to the economic situation at local level: it is not bound to regional income, rate of unemployment or level of urbanisation. It does not reflect local emigration traditions, such as intensity of mobility or the most popular directions chosen by migrants from different regions either in the pre- or post-EU enlargement period. We suppose that each region of Poland constitutes a separate case of different local mobility traditions and of different economic push and pull factors and, therefore, no single explanation for spatial pattern of return migration can be provided.

Finally, our results confirmed what has been said about the selective effect of different destination countries. Coming back from one of the 'new countries of emigration' (Belgium, Czech Republic, Denmark, Iceland, Ireland, the Netherlands, Norway, Spain, Sweden and the United Kingdom) is much less probable (by 23 per cent) than from one of the 'old/traditional countries of emigration' (that is, Australia, Austria, Canada, France, Germany, Greece, Italy or the United States – see Table 5.8).[13] In addition, two separate models of selectivity were used, referring to migrants going to two main destinations: Germany and the United Kingdom. Previous research on emigration from Poland (Fihel and Okólski 2009) proved that the latter attracts mainly young and relatively well-educated Polish nationals, whereas the former seems to be the most popular among middle-aged, poorly educated persons originating from rural areas. Econometric models applied to these two outflows separately should reveal this kind of structural inconsistency, if it is statistically significant. Unfortunately, due to too-small samples of migrants coming back from particular countries the dataset did not provide such conclusions: hardly any variable turned out to be significant with regard to the model for the United Kingdom. In the case of Germany, the model revealed a negative selectivity for return to urban areas ($\beta = -0.40$) – similar to the general model – and a positive selectivity for men ($\beta = 0.28$) – as opposed to the general model, in which sex turned out to be insignificant.

---

12   This is because it is not clear which region chosen as the reference category gives the most informative result.

13   Although it would be very interesting to look at these countries separately, due to the sample size it was necessary to divide them into three groups: 'old countries of emigration', 'new countries of emigration' and 'other'.

Table 5.9 **Odds ratio** for the region of origin (compared category) in 16 logistic regression models, with each region as the reference category[*]

Reference category (region of origin)	Dolnośląskie	Kujawsko-pomorskie	Lubelskie	Lubuskie	Łódzkie	Małopolskie	Mazowieckie	Opolskie	Podkarpackie	Podlaskie	Pomorskie	Śląskie	Świętokrzyskie	Warmińsko-mazurskie	Wielkopolskie	Zachodniopomorskie	Average
Dolnośląskie	1.00	1.00	1.00	1.00	1.00	0.72	0.61	0.55	1.00	1.00	0.64	0.41	1.40	0.63	1.00	1.00	0.86
Kujawsko-pomorskie	1.00		1.00	0.62	1.00	0.55	0.47	0.42	0.68	0.63	0.48	0.31	1.00	0.48	1.00	0.58	0.68
Lubelskie	1.00	1.00		1.61	1.00	1.00	1.00	1.00	1.00	1.00	1.00	0.50	1.71	1.00	1.51	1.00	1.09
Lubuskie	1.00	1.00	1.00		1.00	0.64	0.55	0.49	1.00	1.00	0.57	0.36	1.00	0.56	1.00	1.00	0.81
Łódzkie	1.46	1.38	1.82	1.00		1.55	1.00	1.00	1.00	1.00	1.00	0.57	1.93	1.00	1.71	1.00	1.23
Małopolskie	1.72	1.63	2.14	1.00	1.83		1.00	1.00	1.00	1.00	1.00	1.00	2.28	1.00	2.02	1.00	1.37
Mazowieckie	1.91	1.81	2.38	1.00	2.04	1.00		1.00	1.61	1.50	1.00	1.00	2.53	1.00	2.24	1.00	1.54
Opolskie	1.00	1.00	1.48	1.00	1.00	1.00	1.00		0.62	1.00	1.00	0.46	1.57	1.00	1.39	1.00	1.03
Podkarpackie	1.00	1.00	1.59	1.00	1.00	1.00	1.00	0.67		1.00	1.00	0.49	1.69	1.00	1.49	1.00	1.06
Podlaskie	1.00	1.00	1.59	1.00	1.00	1.00	1.00	0.67	1.00		1.00	0.49	1.69	1.00	1.49	1.00	1.06
Pomorskie	1.65	1.57	2.06	1.00	1.76	1.00	1.00	1.00	1.00	1.00		1.00	2.19	1.00	1.94	1.00	1.35
Śląskie	2.57	2.44	3.21	2.00	2.74	1.77	1.00	1.00	2.17	2.02	1.00		3.41	1.00	3.02	1.87	2.08
Świętokrzyskie	1.00	0.72	1.00	0.59	1.00	0.52	0.44	0.39	0.64	0.59	0.46	0.29		0.45	1.00	0.55	0.64
Warmińsko-mazurskie	1.68	1.59	2.10	1.00	1.79	1.00	1.00	1.00	1.00	1.00	1.00	1.00	2.23		1.97	1.00	1.36
Wielkopolskie	1.00	1.00	1.00	0.66	1.00	0.58	0.50	0.45	0.72	0.67	0.52	0.33	1.00	0.51		0.62	0.70
Zachodniopomorskie	1.00	1.00	1.72	1.00	1.00	1.00	1.00	1.00	1.00	1.00	1.00	0.53	1.83	1.00	1.62		1.11

Odds ratio for variable 'region of origin' (compared category) in 16 logit regression model estimations where each region of origin is reference category

Note: [*]Significance level for βx is 0.1, insignificant values of βx (that is, equal to one) are coloured grey.

Source: Authors' elaboration based on the LFS.

8. Propensity to Emigrate, Propensity to Return

Similar to the model presented in Section 7, Mioduszewska (2008) analysed the selectivity of emigration from Poland in the pre-accession (1999–2004) and post-accession (2004–2006) periods. In that study the group of emigrants was compared to the general population of Poland and the dependent variable referred to propensity to stay or leave the country. Data were also derived from the LFS and included the main socio-demographic characteristics of migrants. Table 5.10 presents the results of two econometric models devoted to selectivity: selectivity of emigration (based on Mioduszewska 2008) and return migration (based on the analysis in Section 7).

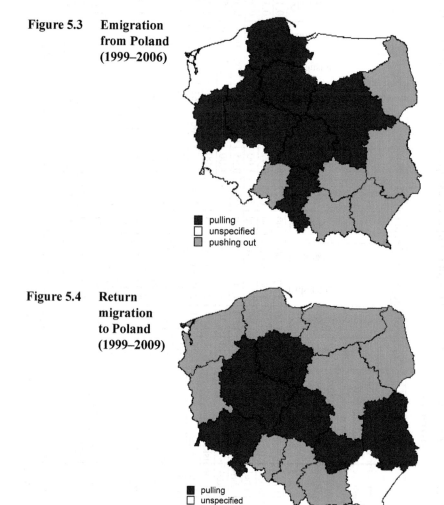

Figure 5.3   Emigration from Poland (1999–2006)

Figure 5.4   Return migration to Poland (1999–2009)

Table 5.10   Effect of the main socio-demographic characteristics on propensity to emigrate and return

Socio-demographic characteristics	Emigration from Poland (1999–2006)	Return migration to Poland (1999–2009)
Age	Influence of age is not unidirectional. Being older – up to some critical point – improves the likelihood of emigration (βx for *age* variable significantly higher than 0). However, from some point, being older decreases the propensity to emigrate (βx for *the square of age* variable significantly lower than zero).	Age categories over the median age are overrepresented in case of return inflow (*odds ratios* higher than one). Thus, being older improves likelihood of return to Poland as opposed to remaining abroad.
Sex	Being male significantly improves likelihood of emigration (*odds ratio* between 1.36 and 1.93).	Proportion of males and females is similar in the population of migrants and return migrants and the variable is not statistically significant.
Level of education	Polish nationals with university degrees and those with a vocational education were strongly prone to emigrate from Poland. However, in the case of the latter the propensity to migrate was lower (*odds ratio* 5.27–5.37 compared to 2.89–3.82).	Polish nationals with a vocational education are much more likely to return than those with a university degree (*odds ratio* 1.30). Being a university graduate increases likelihood of remaining abroad.
Type of settlement	Originating in rural areas was typical for emigrants (*odds ratio* for urban settlement of migrants was equal to 0.75) in the first period (before EU enlargement) and insignificant thereafter.	Rural areas attract ('pull') returnees, whereas originating in cities lowers the probability of coming back to Poland.
Region of origin	'Pushing-out' regions indicate areas that enhance emigration; 'pulling' areas, those that enhance likelihood of staying.	'Pulling' regions indicate areas that enhance likelihood of coming back; 'pushing' areas, those that discourage people from returning.

Source: Authors' elaboration based on the LFS, Mioduszewska (2008).

9. Conclusions: Migration or Mobility?

Poland has experienced several waves of return migration over the course of its history. One of the most sizeable took place very recently and included emigrants who left after Polish accession to the European Union. In 2007, three years after EU enlargement, return migration started to outnumber the outflow from Poland and to take place on a massive scale. The most reliable estimate of returnees is as high as 580,000 persons in the period first quarter 2004–second quarter 2008 (in 2007 alone it totalled 213,000 persons).

Previous studies have proved that post-accession emigration was selective with regard to socio-demographic characteristics. In this study, selective patterns were analysed in relation to the return flow to Poland. It turned out that being older, having a vocational education and originating in a rural area and/or particular regions in Poland significantly increase the likelihood of coming back. A typical returnee profile is that of a middle-aged rural dweller with a low level of education. In contrast, younger persons originating in cities with a higher education level are more prone to settle down abroad. Polish emigrants are relatively well educated but abroad they tend to perform low-paid, simple jobs (Fihel and Okólski 2009). Nevertheless, highly-skilled persons are not prone to come back, which means that either they make progress in terms of social and economic integration or, at least, they are better off abroad than in Poland.

Since the end of 2007 the stock of Polish migrants has decreased in almost all destinations, regardless of geographical proximity or economic situation in the country in question. However, return to the country of origin was not the only reason for this decrease: Polish nationals 'transmigrate' between different destinations in search of better working or social conditions: for instance, they may move from the United Kingdom to Norway. But it is certain that, due to cultural or family reasons, not all post-accession migrants are able to settle down abroad and that the recent economic developments – financial crisis in Ireland and the United Kingdom compared to a relatively good economic situation in Poland – also constitute a relevant incentive to return. Unfortunately, the dataset used in this analysis refers to the period 1999–2009 and one cannot distinguish the volume of return flow from different countries before the financial crisis and afterwards. It might be said that the return migration from Ireland and the United Kingdom started abruptly in 2007 – that is, when the economic situation seriously deteriorated – whereas the counter flow from Germany was registered during the whole period of analysis. The integration of Polish nationals in Ireland and the United Kingdom seems to occur more easily, maybe because of specific characteristics of migrants (younger, higher level of education) and familiarity with the English language, which in recent years has become the most prevalent foreign language in Poland (CBOS 2009). At the same time, Polish nationals in Ireland and the United Kingdom are more exposed to economic changes in the global economy, such as stagnation in the construction sector or falling investment in other domains.

In this context it is rather Germany with its 'pushing out' effect that constitutes an exception than Ireland and the United Kingdom. Despite very long traditions of migration from Poland to Germany, integration (probably both social and economic) in this destination is fairly difficult to accomplish. At the same time, almost every second post-accession emigrant heading for Germany originated in a rural area (Fihel and Okólski 2009) and rural origin turned out to most determine the propensity to return to Poland. This might suggest that Polish migrants are – in general – unwilling to settle down in Germany and that they are involved in short-term, back-and-forth mobility. This type of migration from Poland to Germany was observed throughout the 1990s and it has persisted thereafter, despite EU enlargement. This raises an important question about the utility of the term 'migration' with regard to the outflow from Poland to Germany: is it not rather mobility between relatively close or even neighbouring regions that for decades have been linked together by a circulating labour force? Since thousands of Polish nationals are already involved in this type of mobility to Germany, it seems that the opening up of the German labour market in 2011 will not increase the scale of migration, nor change its temporary character.

The most surprising result of this analysis refers to the very strong impact of rural origin on return propensity. In rural areas, labour markets cannot provide employment to all inhabitants, so local labour demand cannot be a relevant pull factor for returnees. At the same time, the Polish social welfare system and European agriculture subsidy system create incentives to maintain the status of farmer. Intuitively, the phenomenon of outflow from rural areas seems to be more complex: perhaps the younger generations have a propensity to emigrate from rural areas and settle down abroad, whereas middle-aged persons are less eager to leave their homes. All in all, in recent years the international mobility of Polish nationals has become more fluid, flexible and varied. Despite the financial crisis, Ireland and the United Kingdom still remain important destinations for Polish nationals and these countries benefited the most from the opening up of their labour markets right after EU enlargement. At the same time, the post-accession outflow from Poland 'spilled over' to the entire European Union and the return wave is now growing. It is too early to guess how permanent this return migration is going to be.

Bibliography

Bade, K. 2000. *Europa in Bewegung. Migration vom späten 18. Jahrhundert bis zur Gegenwart*. Munich.

CBOS. 2009. *Polacy o swoich wyjazdach zagranicznych i znajomości języków obcych*, press release BS/111/2009. Warsaw: CBOS.

CSO. 2010. *Informacja o rozmiarach i kierunkach emigracji z Polski w latach 2004–2009*, press release 24.09.2010. Warsaw: GUS.

Duszczyk, M. 2007. 'Doświadczenie wybranych państw członkowskich Unii Europejskiej w zakresie migracji powrotnych', CMR Working Papers/Seria Prace Migracyjne, No. 21/79, OBM UW, Warsaw.

Fihel A. 2004. 'Aktywność ekonomiczna migrantow sezonowych na polskim rynku pracy', in: P. Kaczmarczyk and W. Łukowski (eds), *Polscy pracownicy na rynku Unii Europejskiej*. Warsaw: Wydawnictwo Naukowe Scholar, 115–28.

Fihel, A., Górny, A. and Matejko, E. 2006. 'Remigracja a transfer kapitału ludzkiego do Polski w okresie transformacji', in: E. Jaźwińska (ed.), *Imigracja do Polski w świetle wyników Narodowego Spisu Powszechnego 2002*, CMR Working Papers/Seria Prace Migracyjne, No. 13/71. Warsaw: OBM UW, 29–41.

Fihel, A. and Okólski, M. 2009. 'Dimensions and effects of labour migration to EU countries: The case of Poland', in: B. Galgóczi, J. Leschke and A. Watt (eds), *EU Labour Migration since Enlargement. Trends, Impacts and Policies.* Aldershot: Ashgate, 185–210.

Gawryszewski, A. 2005. *Ludność Polski w XX wieku.* Warsaw: IGiPZ PAN.

Górny, A., and Osipovič, D. 2006. 'Return migration of second-generation British Poles', CMR Working Papers/Seria Prace Migracyjne, No. 6/64. Warsaw: OBM UW.

Grabowska-Lusińska, I., and Okólski, M. 2009. *Emigracja ostatnia.* Warsaw: Wydawnictwo Naukowe Scholar.

Greene, W.H. 2003. *Econometric Analysis.* 6th edition. New Jersey: Prentice Hall.

Heffner, K. and Sołdra-Gwiżdż, T. 1997. 'Migracje powrotne na Górny Śląsk z socjologicznej perspektywy', CMR Working Papers/Seria Prace Migracyjne, No. 9. Warsaw: OBM UW.

Janowska, H. 1981. *Emigracja zarobkowa z Polski, 1918–1939.* Warsaw.

Janowska, H. 1984. 'Emigracja z Polski w latach 1918–1939', in: A. Pilch (ed.), *Emigracja z ziem polskich w czasach nowożytnych i najnowszych (XVIII–XX w.),* Warsaw.

Jaźwińska, E., and Okólski, M. (eds). 2001. *Ludzie na huśtawce. Migracje między peryferiami Polski i Zachodu.* Warsaw: Scholar.

Kaczmarczyk, P., Mioduszewska, M. and Żylicz, A. 2009. 'Impact of post-accession migration on the Polish labour market', in: M. Kahanec and K.F. Zimmerman (eds), *EU Labor Markets after Post-Enlargement Migration.* Berlin: Springer, 219–53.

Kaczmarczyk, P. and Okólski, M. 2008. 'Demographic and labour-market impacts of migration on Poland', *Oxford Review of Economic Policy*, 24(3).

Klagge, B. and Klein-Hitpaß, K. 2007. 'High-skilled return migration and knowledge-based economic development in regional perspective'. Conceptual Considerations and the Example of Poland', CMR Working Papers/Seria Prace Migracyjne, No. 19/77. Warsaw: OBM UW.

Klagge, B. and Klein-Hitpaß, K. 2010. 'High-skilled return migration and knowledge-based development in Poland', *European Planning Studies*, 18(10), 1631–51.

Kołodziej, E. 1998. 'Emigracja z ziem polskich od końca XIX wieku do czasów współczesnych i tworzenie się skupisk polonijnych', in: A. Koseski (ed.), *Emigracja z ziem polskich w XX wieku. Drogi awansu emigrantów*. Pułtusk.

Koryś, I. 2002. 'W pół drogi' – specyfika migracji powrotnych z Niemiec', in: K. Iglicka (ed.), *Migracje powrotne Polaków. Powroty sukcesu czy rozczarowania?* Warsaw: Instytut Spraw Publicznych, 161–83.

Mioduszewska, M. 2008. 'Najnowsze migracje z Polski w świetle danych Badania Aktywności Ekonomicznej Ludności', CMR Working Papers/Seria Prace Migracyjne, No. 36/94. Warsaw: OBM UW.

Napierała, J. and Trevena, P. 2010. 'Patterns and determinants of sub-regional migration: A case study of Polish construction workers in Norway', in: R. Black, G. Engbersen, M. Okólski and C. Pantiru (eds), *A Continent Moving West*. Amsterdam: Amsterdam University Press, 51–71.

Okólski, M. 1994. 'Migracje zagraniczne w Polsce w latach 1980–1989', *Studia Demograficzne* 3, 3–59.

Ostasiewicz, S. 1984. 'Migracje', in: M. Cieślak (ed.), *Demografia. Metody analizy i prognozowania*. Warsaw: PWN, 193–214.

Ravenstein, E. 1885. 'The laws of migration', *Journal of the Statistical Society,* 46, 167–235.

Slany, K. and Małek, A. 2002. 'Reemigracje z USA do Polski w okresie transformacji ustrojowej', in: K. Iglicka (ed.), *Migracje powrotne Polaków. Powroty sukcesów czy porażki?* Warsaw: Instytut Spraw Publicznych, 78–120.

Chapter 6

Selectivity of Migrants from Baltic Countries Before and After Enlargement and Responses to the Crisis

Mihails Hazans

1. Introduction

In a historical perspective, a decade is very brief. However, the patterns of selection of Baltic emigrants have changed several times during the first decade of the twenty-first century. These changes concern the main reasons for emigration, the most popular destinations and the profile of emigrants and their plans. In this chapter, we focus on two of the three Baltic countries: Estonia and Latvia. The two countries share a similar history, after enjoying independence for slightly more than two decades before the Second World War, they were annexed by the Soviet Union in 1940, occupied by the Nazis in 1941–1944 and then were reannexed by the Soviet Union (now also classified as an occupation) until 1990, when the independent states were restored. In 2004, Estonia and Latvia, along with six other Central and Eastern European countries, as well as Cyprus and Malta, entered the EU.

Subsequently, the Baltic countries exhibited the most rapid economic growth among EU member states (see, for example, Hazans and Philips 2010, Section 7 for details). However, in the second part of 2008 both countries entered a deep recession. In 2009, both GDP and employment (full-time equivalents) were about 20 per cent below 2007 levels, while unemployment reached 14 per cent in Estonia and 17.5 per cent in Latvia (and further increased in 2010 to 17.3 per cent and 19 per cent, respectively). Despite this apparent similarity, Latvia was forced to apply for emergency financial assistance from the EU and the IMF, while Estonia, which created a stabilisation fund during the growth years, managed without external help and experienced much more modest wage cuts than Latvia (European Commission 2011: Figure I.3.1). Moreover, the crisis in Latvia is perceived by the majority of the population as a systemic, rather than just a financial crisis, which is not the case in Estonia. Table 6.1 illustrates these differences which, as we shall see, are well reflected in emigration patterns.

The demographic backgrounds of the two countries also have much in common. About two-fifths of the Latvian population and one-third of the Estonian population belong to minority groups (mostly Russian speaking; see, for example, Hazans et al. 2008 for details). Out of the minority population in Latvia and Estonia in the group of particular interest to us in this chapter – the economically active aged 18–64 – about one-half did not hold citizenship at the time of EU accession (most had so-called non-citizen passports, while a small proportion held Russian or other citizenship).

Table 6.1   Indicators of popular sentiment during the economic crisis

	Estonia (2008/11–2009/02)	Latvia (2009/04–2009/08)
Satisfaction with the state of economy	3.53	1.81
Satisfaction with the national government	3.53	1.80
Satisfaction with the state of education	5.86	4.62
Satisfaction with the state of health services	5.07	3.53
Satisfaction with the way democracy is working	4.52	3.27
Trust in parliament	3.88	1.95
Sample size	1661	1980

Notes: Satisfaction and trust are measured on a scale of 0–10. The table reports mean values (excluding non-response). Standard errors in all cases are between 0.04 and 0.06.

Source: Author's calculations based on the European Social Survey (2008–2009).

From an emigration perspective, geography and language are important differences between the two countries: in the case of Estonia, Finland, with its high living standards and a language very similar to Estonian, lies about 50 kilometres away across the sea, but Latvia does not have such a natural emigration target.

In this chapter, we focus on two aspects of selectivity on the part of migrants. First, we show how changes in the legal framework and economic conditions have influenced the relative skill levels of emigrants and potential emigrants. Second, we look at the ethnic dimension of Baltic migration flows. Two considerations motivate our interest in this issue. First, the disadvantaged position of ethnic minorities, especially non-citizens, in the Estonian and Latvian labour markets (see Figure 6.1, as well as Kahanec and Zaiceva 2009; Hazans 2010, 2011a) and the immigrant background of part of the minority population (see Hazans at al. 2008) suggest a higher propensity to emigrate among minorities. Second, both EU accession in 2004 and the start of the economic crisis in 2008 have affected migration patterns in general but have also changed the dynamics of ethnic employment and unemployment gaps (see Figure 6.1; see also Hazans 2010; 2011a). Our findings suggest that the free movement of labour introduced partially in 2004 (and enhanced in 2006, 2007 and 2009) for EU citizens, while excluding Baltic non-citizens, brought about significant changes in the way ethnicity, citizenship and country of birth affect workers' mobility. Furthermore, the crisis hit minorities more than native workers (see Figure 6.1), and both emigration rates and intentions once again changed differently depending on ethnic background and citizenship.

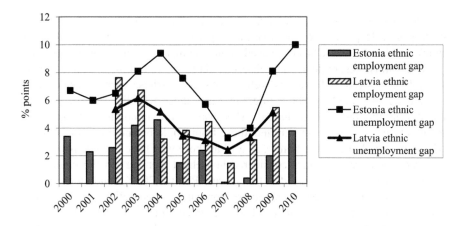

Figure 6.1 Ethnic gap in employment and unemployment rates, Estonia and Latvia, 2000–2010

Note: The gaps are defined as the differences between employment (or unemployment) rates of native and minority (or minority and native) population aged 15–64.

Source: Statistics Estonia online database; calculation with Latvian LFS data.

The chapter is structured as follows. Section 2 describes data sources and the approaches used to identify emigrants and returnees. Section 3 sets up the conceptual framework and presents the story of the three emigration waves originating in the Baltics in 2000–2010. Next, we look at the evolution of emigrants' selectivity with regard to human capital (Section 4), as well as ethnic background and citizenship (Section 5). Section 6 describes the geography of Estonian and Latvian emigration and how it responded to changes in legal and economic conditions in potential host countries. Section 7 compares the migration intentions of the Latvian, Lithuanian and Estonian populations during the crisis, looking in more detail at Latvia. Section 8 concludes.

2. Data and Identification Strategy

Our analysis is based on several complementary data sources. First, we use Latvian Labour Force Survey (LFS) data from 2002–2009 and Estonian LFS data from 2001–2009. The rotating sampling scheme of the LFS ensures that each household is observed several times. With *t* denoting the quarter in which the first observation was made, the rotation scheme for the Latvian LFS in 2002–2006 was *t, t+2, t+4* (in each quarter one-third of the households participate in the survey for the first time), but starting from 2007 it changed to the 2–(2)–2 rotation plan – namely *t, t+1, t+4, t+5* – in which a household is surveyed for two consecutive quarters,

172 *EU Labour Migration in Troubled Times*

then left out for two quarters, and again included for two quarters a year later (in each quarter 25 per cent of the households participate in the survey for the first time). The latter scheme has been used in the Estonian LFS for the whole period.

Thus, most respondents are observed three or four times. Those whose workplace is located abroad, as well as jobseekers whose current residence is abroad, are identified as labour migrants (only those who lived in the sending country in the past are included). This way, some important categories of emigrants are systematically omitted: those from single-person households, those who moved with the whole family, as well as those who have become permanent emigrants and are no longer considered household members in the country of origin.[1] Nevertheless, as argued in Hazans and Philips (2010), sending countries' LFS data are suitable for cross-country comparisons as well as for analysing accession-induced and crisis-induced changes in emigrants' characteristics.

In order to increase sample sizes when analysing the dynamics of human capital and emigrants' demographic characteristics, we use the quarterly panel structure of the LFS, as well as the retrospective questions about the situation one year before the survey to identify all respondents with some economic activity abroad either during the survey or within the last 12 months (for return migrants, the reference period is extended to 24 months). In total, we have 1,698 observations on emigrants and 238 observations on return migrants in the Estonian LFS, and 1,041 observations on emigrants and 422 observations on return migrants in the Latvian LFS.

Second, we use a survey of the Latvian population on close relatives who emigrated between 2000 and 2010 and lived abroad during the survey period (conducted in December 2010–January 2011); this gives us a sample of 471 emigrants with information on their gender, age, educational attainment, year of emigration, host country, main activity, living arrangements and plans to return within five years or within six months. Among employed emigrants we distinguish those who to a large extent use their education and/or qualifications in their job from those who do not.

Third, for Latvia we use data from representative population surveys conducted in 2006–2008 and 2010–2011 on respondents' foreign work experience. This provides three cross-sections of return migrants.

Finally, we use data on the migration intentions of the Latvian and Estonian population from several representative surveys conducted in 2005–2011.

---

1   From this perspective, receiving countries' LFS would, in theory, be more suitable for studying emigrants. However, as far as small sending countries are concerned, sample sizes are usually too small for this purpose.

3. Baltic Migration Trends: The Story of Three Waves in a Decade

According to the human capital model of migration decisions (Sjaastad 1962; Borjas 1987, 1999), an individual (or a family) decides to move if expected (over the planning period) utility in the host country (net of total cost of migration) exceeds utility in the home country. The 'calculation' should account for all factors that can affect the quality of life, including job finding and job losing probabilities, expected earnings, legal status, career prospects, working and living conditions, generosity of social security system, social and cultural norms, perceived life prospects for children and so on. The costs of migration, in turn, include monetary and effort costs related to acquiring the necessary information, job search and transportation, as well as maintaining contact with the country of origin and psychological costs related to missing people and the environment one has left behind, uncertainty associated with life in the new country and adaptation to the new reality. This framework will help us to understand the emigrants' patterns of selectivity and how these patterns change over time in response to economic, political and social developments in the source countries and in the potential host countries.

One Decade, Three Emigration Waves

The recent history of emigration from the Baltic countries can be divided into three episodes: (i) the pre-accession period (which we loosely denote as 2000–2003, although it also includes the first four months of 2004); (ii) the post-accession period of economic growth in 2004–2008 (although growth slowed down in the second half of 2008, and in the last quarter of 2008 the crisis hit both countries, although its effect on emigration appears only in the data for 2009–2010); and (iii) the crisis period, 2009–2010.

The Pre-accession Wave: Personal Initiative and Effort

Between 2000 and 2003, both Estonia and Latvia featured double-digit unemployment, while GDP per capita (at PPP) was between 40 per cent and 50 per cent of the EU15 average in Estonia and between 32 per cent and 41 per cent in Latvia. Thus, both push and pull factors were strong. No wonder emigration potential was substantial: according to a survey conducted in 2000 (see Rose 2000: 34), 16 per cent of ethnic Estonians and 18 per cent of their minority counterparts said that they (or some family member) would go abroad for (at least) a number of years when their country entered the EU. In Latvia, this opinion was expressed by 8 per cent of Latvians and 21 per cent of non-Latvians. When those who planned to remain abroad for less than a year and those who answered 'maybe' (rather than 'yes') are accounted for, it appears that 64 per cent of Estonian families and 60 per cent of Latvian families had temporary or permanent emigration intentions (see Figure 6.2 for details). Neighbouring Finland, as a migration magnet, is a likely explanation for the fact that firmly stated long-term migration intentions

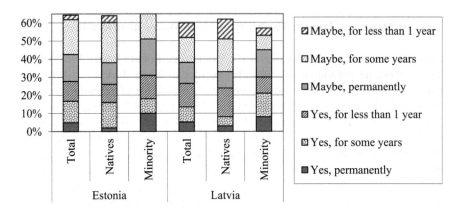

Figure 6.2   Intention to work abroad after EU accession, Estonia and Latvia, 2000

Notes: Population aged 15–74. Intentions refer to at least one family member.
Source: Rose (2000), p. 34.

were more widespread in Estonia than in Latvia (17 per cent versus 13 per cent), despite the lower level of economic development in the latter country.

Actual emigration rates were of course much lower, especially in the pre-accession period. During the four-year period before accession (2000–2003), net outflow from Estonia was about 1 per cent of the population, while from Latvia it was about 1.5 per cent (Table 6.2).

Plausibly, high migration costs and high own-initiative thresholds accounted for the relatively low emigration rates before accession. Both residence and work permits were necessary unless one was ready to take on the risk of illegal immigration and/or employment.[2] However, there were no convenient wide-coverage sources of information on living and working conditions abroad (such as the EURES portal developed after 2004); the internet was slow, expensive and limited-access; and international phone calls and flights were fairly expensive. The services of private recruitment firms were expensive and often associated with high risk of fraud. In an online survey conducted in Latvia in 2003, among 2,100 respondents who said that after EU accession they would be ready to work in another EU country, 89 per cent would move only with a work contract in hand, and only 20 per cent considered a contract with a licensed Latvian recruitment firm as a sufficient guarantee (Hazans 2003: Tables A2.12, A2.13).

In such a situation, relatively lower emigration costs were associated with a high level of initiative, professional or at least private contacts in potential host

---

2   Latvian and Estonian non-citizens, in addition, needed visas to enter most EU member states.

Table 6.2   Net emigration from Estonia and Latvia, 2000–2010 (sending and receiving country estimates)

	Estonia								Latvia							
	Persons ('000)			Net emigration rate (%)					Persons ('000)			Net emigration rate (%)				
				Annual average		Period total (vs. initial population)						Annual average		Period total (vs. initial population)		
	[1]	[2]	[3]	[2]	[3]	[2]	[3]		[1]	[2]	[3]	[2]	[3]	[2]	[3]	
2000–2003	7.3	12.2	15.0	0.22	0.27	0.9	1.1		13.3	30.6	40.0	0.33	0.43	1.3	1.7	
2004–2008	9.7	35.1	44.0	0.54	0.65	2.6	3.2		7.2	68.3	80.0	0.61	0.72	3.0	3.5	
2009–2010	3.3	18.5	25.0	0.72	0.94	1.4	1.9		12.6	70.2	80.0	1.64	1.89	3.2	3.7	
2000–2010	20.2	65.8	84.0	0.46	0.56	4.8	5.9		33.1	169.2	200.0	0.69	0.83	7.1	8.4	

Notes: [1] – official sending country estimates. [2] – conservative documented estimates based on receiving countries' and OECD population and/or migration statistics by citizenship and/or country of birth; for 2010, a conservative extrapolation has been used when data were missing. Inflows into Ireland and the United Kingdom are estimated using data on allocation of social security numbers, while data on outflows from the United Kingdom and Ireland have been corrected using Latvian and Estonian LFS data; net emigration from Latvia to countries outside the EU and the OECD is reported as in the Statistics Latvia online database. [3] realistic expert estimates based on [2] and accounting for the gaps in receiving countries' statistics (Estonian and Latvian non-citizens are likely not to be fully captured by the statistics 'by citizenship'; emigrants who are Estonian or Latvian citizens or non-citizens but were born outside these countries, typically in the former Soviet Union, are not captured by the statistics 'by country of birth'; emigrants who have not officially registered in the host country are not covered).

Sources: Eurostat, OECD, Statistics Latvia, Statistics Estonia, other national statistical offices, Department of Work and Pensions (the United Kingdom), Department of Social Protection (Ireland), author's compilation.

countries, good foreign language and IT skills, and opportunities to use the internet for private purposes at the workplace. Clearly, all these attributes are more often found among university graduates.

Emigrants' choice of host country was also probably affected by cost considerations: while some tried to minimise information and adaptation costs by using migrant networks associated with previous emigration and immigration waves to/from the United States, Canada, Australia, Sweden and Germany, as well Russia, Ukraine and Belarus, others were oriented towards relatively new directions, mainly the United Kingdom and Ireland, which combined lower language barriers than other EU countries with being much closer than other English-speaking countries.

To sum up, the following expectations emerge about the pre-accession emigration wave:

> (H1) Theoretical considerations suggest that in 2000–2003, economic emigrants from Estonia and Latvia featured:
>   (a) a higher than average proportion of tertiary educated persons;
>   (b) a higher than average proportion of ethnic minorities;
>   (c) a high degree of geographical diversification.

The Post-Accession Wave: Institutional and Market Factors

During the first five years in the EU (before the effect of the crisis on migration patterns became apparent) unemployment rates in the Baltic countries fell falling while real wages were growing (see, for example, Hazans and Philips 2010: Figure 12). As a result, migration flows were shaped mainly and increasingly by pull factors, in other words, higher income and better working conditions abroad (mentioned, respectively, by 60 to 70 per cent and about 50 per cent of potential movers in 2005, see Table 6.3), as well as family- or friend-related factors (13 per cent to 14 per cent). Together, these three factors covered about 80 per cent of potential emigrants in both Estonia and Latvia (Table 6.3).

Table 6.3   Factors encouraging emigration mentioned by those planning to move to another country within the next five years, Estonia and Latvia, September–October 2005

	Higher income	Better working conditions	Family/friends abroad	At least one of these
Estonia	68.3%	50.9%	13.6%	79.6%
Latvia	59.5%	48.4%	13.1%	83.4%

Notes: Population aged 18 to 65 years is included.
Source: Author's calculations based on Eurobarometer 64.1 data.

During this period, Estonia and Latvia lost 2.6 to 3.2 per cent and 3 to 3.5 per cent of their population, respectively, due to migration (Table 6.2). Migrant flows were shaped by gradual implementation of the free movement of labour within the EU (see Brucker et al. 2009, Table 2.1) on the one hand, and by labour market developments both in the home and in the host countries, on the other.

Migration-friendly institutional changes substantially lowered both the monetary and the non-monetary costs of job search abroad and migration, as well as the human capital threshold (in terms of skills, initiative and risk taking) for labour migration. Together with high and growing demand for migrant labour in the EU15, this triggered a sharp permanent increase in emigration rates (see Table 6.2 for Estonia and Latvia), which further lowered migration costs via migrant networks and the scale effect (the latter caused air and land transportation costs, as well as international phone call tariffs to fall; communication costs were also reduced by increased coverage and speed of internet connections). These developments mainly affected migration to the United Kingdom, Ireland and Sweden (as of 1 May 2004), and migration to Finland (and, to a smaller extent in the case of Estonia and Latvia, to Greece, Italy, Portugal and Spain) as of 1 May 2006.[3]

Hence, in 2004–2008 emigrants' self-selection in terms of human capital was driven not so much by individuals' comparative advantage in terms of falling migration costs, but mainly by expected gains in terms of income and working conditions. These gains were, on average, greater for persons with secondary or lower education. For instance, in 2005 tertiary educated employees in Latvia earned 54 per cent (76 per cent) more than otherwise similar workers with secondary (below secondary) education (Hazans, 2007: 18 and Figure 2.1). On the other hand, 40 to 60 per cent of tertiary educated Estonian and Latvian migrant workers abroad in 2004–2007 held jobs which did not require a higher education (Hazans and Philips 2010: Figure 7) and hence could not earn much more than other emigrants from Estonia and Latvia.[4]

The effect of ethnicity and citizenship on the propensity to emigrate has also changed. Due to strong economic growth and labour shortages caused by emigration (see, for example, Hazans and Philips 2010: Section 7 and Figure 12), as well as gradual improvements in language skills among minorities (Hazans 2010: Figure 3; Hazans 2011a: Tables 8.8 and 8.9), the labour market position of ethnic minorities in 2004–2007 steadily improved in both Estonia and Latvia (see Figure 6.1). On the other hand, a substantial part of the minority population – those without Estonian or Latvian citizenship – was not covered by the legal provisions on free movement of labour from the new member states to the United

---

3   When these countries abolished transitional measures with regard to EU8 countries.

4   Brucker et al. (2009, Tables 6.7 and 6.8) show that in 2004–2007 returns to schooling for post-accession immigrants from new member states in the United Kingdom were quite low: just 2 per cent per year of schooling and 82 per cent of tertiary educated representatives of this group worked in medium- or low-skilled jobs.

Kingdom, Ireland and Sweden (as of 1 May 2004) and Finland (as of 1 May 2006). Indirectly – via spouses who held Estonian or Latvian citizenship, as well as via migrant networks – new migration possibilities emerged also for non-citizens. Nevertheless, their relative position in comparison to citizens worsened.

To sum up, the following expectations emerge about the post-accession emigration wave:

> (H2) Between 2004 and 2008, in comparison with the pre-accession period, economic emigrants from Estonia and Latvia feature:
> (a) a significantly lower proportion of tertiary educated persons;
> (b) a significantly lower proportion of ethnic minorities, especially non-citizens;
> (c) re-direction of migration flows towards the United Kingdom and Ireland since 2004, and as far as Estonian emigrants are concerned, towards Finland since 2006.

The Crisis-Driven Wave: Lost Jobs and Lost Prospects

During the crisis years 2009–2010, push factors – mainly joblessness and wage cuts, but also implied inability to pay back loans – were at work again. Estonian net emigration rates increased only slightly compared to the previous period, resulting in a loss of 1.4 to 1.9 per cent of the population. By contrast, in Latvia, where the crisis was much deeper (see Table 6.1 above), net emigration rates increased by a factor of 2.7, and in two years Latvia lost more people than in the five previous years: 3.2 to 3.7 per cent of the population (see Table 6.2 for details).

Both in Estonia and Latvia the extent of crisis-triggered layoffs was inversely related to completed education level (Figure 6.3).

Hence, based on economic factors alone, one should expect a significant increase in the proportion of low-skilled workers among emigrants, whereas there is no reason to believe that the brain drain will intensify. However, given that in Latvia the crisis was perceived as systemic, and that university graduates are more forward-looking than those without a higher education, one can expect among Latvian emigrants an increased proportion of high-skilled, as well as a stronger orientation towards long-term or permanent emigration.

The latter point is supported by Table 6.4 which presents an interesting account of the changes in the profile of potential emigrants from Latvia (EURES clients) based on the daily records of EURES consultants summarised by the EURES manager in Latvia, Zanna Ribakova (2009).

Recall also from Figure 6.1 that the relative labour market position of ethnic minorities deteriorated during the crisis; in Latvia, it was accompanied by a strengthening of the state language proficiency requirements in the private sector (Hazans 2010: 151; 2011a: 187).

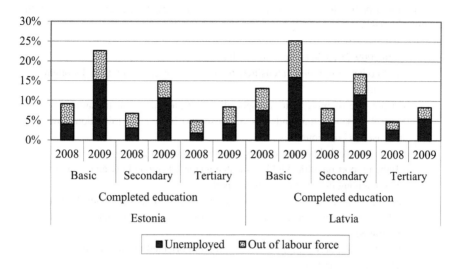

Figure 6.3　**Incidence of joblessness among persons aged 18–64 employed one year previously, by completed education, Estonia and Latvia, 2008–2009**

Source: Author's calculations based on Estonian and Latvian LFS data.

Table 6.4　**Changes in the profile of EURES clients in Latvia, 2004–2010**

2004–2007	2008–2010
Planning to move alone	Planning to move with family
Looking for temporary, low-skilled job	Looking for permanent, skilled job
Minimal knowledge of foreign languages	Better knowledge of foreign languages, higher qualifications
Planning to return	
	Interested in legal employment and social security

Source: Ribakova (2009).

To sum up, the following expectations emerge about emigration during the economic crisis:

>   (H3) In 2009–2010, in comparison with the pre-crisis period:
>   (a) Latvian emigration intensified to a much larger extent than Estonian emigration;
>   (b) the role of push factors (especially unemployment, but in Latvia also general dissatisfaction and loss of prospects) in shaping migration flows increased in both countries;
>   (c) the low-skilled became overrepresented among emigrants;
>   (d) the proportion of the highly educated increased among Latvian emigrants, but not among their Estonian counterparts;
>   (e) the proportion of ethnic minorities increased among both Latvian and Estonian emigrants; in Latvia, minorities are overrepresented among emigrants;
>   (f) at least in Latvia, migrants are much more oriented towards long-term or permanent emigration.

4. Human Capital of Emigrants: 2000–2010

Skills Selectivity of Migrants and Returnees

We start the analysis of emigrants' human capital with the data on Latvian emigrants obtained from a representative survey of the Latvian population conducted in December 2010–January 2011. The respondents were asked about close relatives who emigrated between 2000 and 2010 and were living abroad at the time of the survey. The findings are presented in Table 6.5.

To facilitate comparisons across time, we use *selectivity index* $SI = \ln (G_M /G_S)$, where G_M and G_S are shares of university graduates among movers (that is, emigrants) and stayers, respectively; thus, SI is positive (negative) if tertiary educated persons are overrepresented (underrepresented) among movers.[5]

In general, the results in Table 6.5 support hypotheses *H1(a)*, *H2(a)* and *H3(d)* about emigrants' patterns of selectivity. During both the pre-accession wave and the crisis-driven wave, university graduates were overrepresented among emigrants (when compared to stayers either at the time of departure or at the end of 2010). Emigrants who left Latvia during the boom years 2004–2008 feature a substantially lower prevalence of completed tertiary education; they were not positively selected on this attribute. A similar picture emerges also when only emigrants who were above 21 years of age at the time of the survey are considered

---

5   Kaczmarczyk et al. (2010) and Anacka and Fihel (in this volume) use $SI = G_M/G_S - 1$ with similar properties; our measure has the advantage of symmetric values for $G_M/G_S = k$ and $G_M/G_S = 1/k$.

(all but two tertiary educated emigrants in our sample belong to this group): among the pre-accession emigrants, 31 per cent had a higher education by the end of 2010; this proportion falls to 24 per cent among the boom-period emigrants, but rises again to 32 per cent (this increase is statistically significant) among those who left Latvia in 2009–2010 (Figure 6.4).

Table 6.5   Latvian emigrants, 2000–2010 (as of January 2011)

	Emigrants[a] by year of departure				Return migrants		
	2000–2003	2004–2008	2009–2010	2000–2010	2006q4–2007q1[b]	2008 July[c]	2011 January[d]
Level of education	% Distribution						
Tertiary	32.0	21.5	27.0	24.2	28.2	18.5	18.1
Secondary	53.8	70.6	59.9	61.8	58.3	64.6	70.2
Below secondary	5.3	5.4	4.6	6.0	13.2	16.9	11.6
Unknown	8.9	2.5	8.6	8.0	0.0	0.0	0.0
Total	100	100	100	100	100	100	100
N obs	55	183	117	406	469	119	89
Selectivity index of tertiary educated							
vs. stayers in January 2011, assuming the same age distribution as for movers							
	0.33	−0.06	0.16	0.06	0.21	−0.21	−0.24
vs. stayers aged 18–60 at departing time				vs. emigrants of that time[e]			
	0.36	0.03	0.14		0.26	−0.16	−0.18

Notes: [a] All emigrants aged 18 and over who in 2011 have some close relatives (but are not necessarily considered household members) in Latvia are included. Exact year of moving is missing for 12 per cent of the emigrants; they are included in the column '2000–2010' but not shown separately. [b] Those who worked abroad in 2004–2006. [c] Those who worked abroad between July 2006 and July 2008. [d] Those who between 2000 and 2010 spent three months or more abroad at a time. [e] See [b, c, d] Emigrants here also include returnees (such as in Anacka and Fihel in this volume).

Sources: Author's calculations based on survey data: [a, d] Population survey (N=1009) 'National Identity: Place, Mobility and Capability, 2010/2011' conducted by SKDS for the Faculty of Social Sciences, University of Latvia. [c] Population survey (N=4500) on alcohol and drug use conducted by SPI. [e] Population survey 'Specific problems of the labour market of Latvia and its regions', conducted by GfK Baltic for the Latvian University of Agriculture.

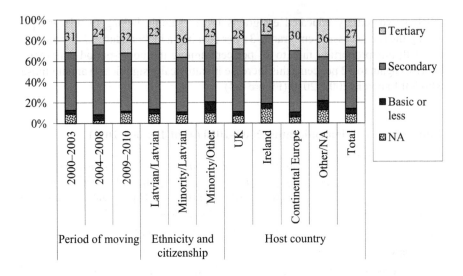

**Figure 6.4   Emigrants from Latvia (aged 22+) by completed education
at the end of 2010, depending on time of moving, ethnicity,
citizenship and host country**

Notes: Ethnicity and citizenship are proxied by attributes of the relative who provided the
information about the emigrant.

Source: Author's calculations based on data from survey on close relatives who emigrated
between 2000 and 2010 and were living abroad at the time of the population survey
'National Identity: Place, Mobility and Capability, 2010/2011' conducted in December
2010–January 2011 for the Faculty of Social Sciences, University of Latvia.

Taken together, about one-quarter of the emigrants who left Latvia between
2000 and 2010 had a higher education by the end of 2010;[6] among stayers this
proportion was slightly lower. Table 6.5 also provides, for three time periods, the
skill distribution of return migrants and their selectivity index with regard to the
prevalence of higher education vs. emigrants in the respective period. Like Anacka
and Fihel (in this volume), we account for the fact that returnees were part of the
emigrants, hence $SI = \ln (G_R/G_{M+R})$, where R are returnees and M are emigrants
who left Latvia during the period when the returnees worked abroad (and stayed
abroad at the end of 2010). In the fourth quarter of 2006 and the first quarter of
2007, return migrants who worked abroad in 2004–2006 were positively selected
from all emigrants of this period with regard to the prevalence of higher education.
However, this pattern was reversed later on. Both in mid-2008 and in December

---

6   Plausibly, those 8 per cent of emigrants whose exact level of education was not
reported by their relatives are not university graduates.

2010–January 2011, university graduates are found to be underrepresented among return migrants who worked abroad in 2006–2008 (or in 2000–2010[7]) in comparison to all emigrants in the respective period. Put differently, high-skilled emigrants were, on average, more likely to return in 2004–2006, but in 2006–2008, as well as in the whole period between 2000 and 2010, they were less likely to return.

Figure 6.4 allows for a comparison of Latvian emigrants' educational attainment also across ethnic groups and host countries. The highest proportion of university graduates is found among emigrants whose relatives – survey respondents – were non-Latvians holding Latvian citizenship. This is in line with the assertion that the ethnic employment gap is especially wide among the tertiary educated (Hazans 2010, 2011a), as well as with the fact that Latvian non-citizens are not covered by the EU's free movement of labour rules.

When different host countries are compared, one finds a striking difference between Ireland (with just 15 per cent of emigrants there holding university degrees) on the one hand and other host countries (where this proportion is varies around 30 per cent), on the other.

Table 6.6 presents the skill distributions of Latvian and Estonian stayers, emigrants and recent return migrants during the pre-accession, post-accession and economic crisis periods, along with selectivity indices, based on LFS data.

In line with expectations (see *II3(d)* above), the time profile of the proportion of university graduates among the emigrants is U-shaped for Latvia but L-shaped for Estonia. The post-accession decline in this proportion (manifesting a lower human capital threshold for emigrants due to the opening up of labour markets in 'old Europe') is striking: from 30 per cent to 17 per cent for Latvia and from 27 per cent to 20 per cent for Estonia. The selectivity index of Latvian (or Estonian) emigrants with regard to higher education fell from 0.46 to –0.27 (or from –0.10 to –0.51)[8] (see Figure 6.5).

---

7   See Note [d] to Table 6.5 for an exact definition of this group of returnees; note that at least 83 per cent of this group were economically active during their last stay abroad.

8   Note that before accession in Latvia this index was positive (in line with both our expectations and the results from Table 6.5), while in Estonia it was slightly (not significantly) negative, plausibly because the Finland factor contributed to lowering the mobility threshold even before accession.

Table 6.6[9]   Estonian and Latvian emigrants and return migrants, selectivity by educational attainment

Level of education	Distribution (%)			Selectivity index		
	Stayers	Emigrants	Recent return migrants	Emigrants vs. stayers	Returnees vs. emigrants	Returnees vs. stayers
			Estonia			
		Before EU accession (2001q1–2004q1)				
Tertiary	30.2	27.2	20.4	–0.10	–0.29	–0.39
Secondary	58.8	64.7	73.7	0.10	0.13	0.23
Below secondary	11	8.1	5.9	–0.31	–0.32	–0.62
Total	100.0	100.0	100.0			
N	30,931	201	18			
		Within EU during the growth period (2004q2–2008q3)				
Tertiary	33.2	19.9	25.2	–0.51	0.24	–0.28
Secondary	56.3	68.0	64.2	0.19	–0.06	0.13
Below secondary	10.5	12.0	10.5	0.13	–0.13	0.00
Total	100.0	100.0	100.0			
N	45,611	1,048	140			
		Within EU during the crisis (2008q4–2009q4)				
Tertiary	35.6	21.2	21.5	–0.52	0.01	–0.50
Secondary	54	65.3	61.9	0.19	–0.05	0.14
Below secondary	10.5	13.5	16.7	0.25	0.21	0.46
Total	100.0	100.0	100.0			
N	12,760	449	80			
			Latvia			
		Before EU accession (2002q1–2004q1)				
Tertiary	18.7	29.6	21.2	0.46	–0.33	0.13
Secondary	65.7	64.0	69.3	–0.03	0.08	0.05
Below secondary	15.6	6.4	9.5	–0.89	0.39	–0.50
Total	100.0	100.0	100.0			
N	26,952	262	71			

9   Note that the concept of 'emigrant' here is narrower than in Table 6.5: only those who are still considered household members in the home country are included. Those who moved as a whole family cannot appear in Table 6.6, while they could be covered in Table 6.5 if they have some close relatives in Latvia. Also, Table 6.6 does not include information on those who emigrated in 2010, so the data on the crisis-driven emigration from Latvia in Tables 6.5 and 6.6 are not directly comparable.

	Within EU during the growth period (2004q2–2008q3)					
Tertiary	22.8	17.4	15.7	−0.27	−0.10	−0.37
Secondary	63.6	69.5	68.9	0.09	−0.01	0.08
Below secondary	13.7	13.1	15.3	−0.04	0.16	0.11
Total	100.0	100.0	100.0			
N	60,341	606	233			
	Within EU during the crisis (2008q4–2009q4)					
Tertiary	26.2	21.4	13.8	−0.20	−0.44	−0.64
Secondary	61.1	60	63.2	−0.02	0.05	0.03
Below secondary	12.7	18.6	23.1	0.38	0.22	0.60
Total	100.0	100.0	100.0			
N	24,774	173	118			

Notes: Population aged 18–64. Only emigrants economically active abroad while still considered household members in Estonia (Latvia) are accounted for.

Source: Author's calculations based on Estonian and Latvian LFS data.

For the same reason (lower skill threshold), the selectivity index of emigrants regarding lower-than-secondary education levels went up from significantly negative before accession (0.89 for Latvia, −0.31 for Estonia) to nearly zero during the boom years (−0.04 for Latvia, 0.13 for Estonia). This is in line with hypothesis *H3(c)*. Figure 6.5 illustrates.

During the crisis, the low-skilled suffered the biggest job losses (see Figure 6.3), hence this group became overrepresented among both Latvian and Estonian post-crisis emigrants, with the selectivity index rising to 0.38 and 0.25, respectively. By contrast, emigrants' selectivity index regarding higher education increased only in Latvia, where the crisis was deeper and more systemic (as already discussed). However, unlike what was found in Table 6.5, this selectivity index is negative also in the crisis year 2009 (see Figure 6.5). There are two likely reasons for this apparent inconsistency. First, the higher-than-average propensity to emigrate among university graduates developed in 2010 (this can be seen when the Table 6.5 data are disaggregated by year), whereas Table 6.6 only includes the 2009 data. Second, due to the LFS design, Table 6.6 does not cover emigrants who have left no other household members behind, while Table 6.5 covers them if they have some close relatives (not necessarily household members) in Latvia. If during the crisis university graduates were more likely than other emigrants to move with the whole family (an assumption supported by data), they are underrepresented in Table 6.6.

The selectivity pattern of Latvian return migrants found in Table 6.6 suggests that throughout the whole period of 2000–2009, but especially during the pre-accession period and during the crisis, university graduates were less likely to return than other groups of emigrants, whereas the low-skilled were overrepresented

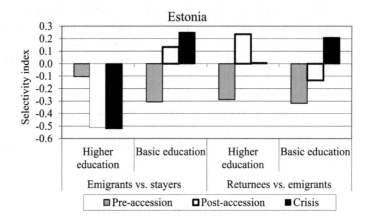

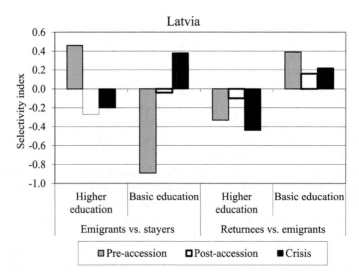

Figure 6.5   Selectivity indices of emigrants vs. stayers and return migrants vs. emigrants regarding higher and basic education, 2001–2009 (top: Estonia; bottom: Latvia)

Notes: Selectivity index of group 2 vs. group 1 regarding category X is defined as $SI = \ln (X_2/X_1)$, where X_i is the share of X in group i. See Table 6.8 for exact definitions of the pre-accession, post-accession and crisis periods. See Notes to Table 6.8 for other details.

Source: Author's calculations based on Estonian and Latvian LFS data.

among returnees. This is fully consistent with the findings from Table 6.5. Both for Latvia and Estonia, the crisis resulted in a sharp increase (or fall) of the selectivity index of returnees with regard to a low (or high) education level. This suggest that in periods when it was more difficult to find a job abroad, the higher the educational level of emigrants, the more successful they were.

Incidence of Overeducation

But to what extent were high-skilled emigrants able to use their qualifications abroad? According to the OECD definition, a tertiary educated worker is overeducated unless he or she works as a senior official, manager, professional, associated professional or technician. See Tijdens and van Klaveren (in this volume) for an analysis of self-assessed overeducation among EU8 migrants in the EU15.

Table 6.7, based on the LFS data, compares the incidence of overeducation among emigrants and stayers with a higher education. In the pre-accession period, this incidence was 27 per cent among Estonian emigrants and stayers alike, 20 per cent among Latvian stayers and 30 per cent among Latvian emigrants (the difference between the latter two is not statistically significant, however). After accession, over half of Estonian emigrants with higher education and slightly less than a half of their Latvian counterparts were overeducated. Thus, the incidence of 'brain waste' was substantial (and, based on Estonian data, increased during the crisis). The Estonian LFS also includes a direct question about (self-assessed) overeducation. By this measure, brain waste is also more common among post-accession emigrants than among stayers, although the levels are much lower, and during the crisis the gap has shrunk rather than widened (Table 6.7).

For Latvia, we also have an alternative measure of the overqualification of emigrants, but it is not directly comparable to the Estonian one, due to the different wording (see Notes to Table 6.7) and because the information was obtained via a survey of relatives. According to this measure, over half of post-accession emigrants with a higher education were overeducated at the end of 2010, and this proportion was higher among those who arrived recently (during the crisis years).

Figure 6.6 provides a more detailed breakdown of Latvian emigrants by main activity abroad (depending on educational attainment, host country and time of leaving Latvia). On average, only 26 per cent of emigrants hold a paid job in which they to a large extent use their qualifications (education), even if in a different profession. This proportion is higher (and the incidence of brain waste smaller) in the continental EU15 than in other host countries. Notably, tertiary educated emigrants feature a lower incidence of self-assessed overeducation than those with a secondary education. The incidence of self-employment is not negligible only among low-educated emigrants, and it has increased during the crisis. The proportion of jobseekers is extremely small among all groups of emigrants.

Table 6.7   Overeducation among tertiary educated Estonian and Latvian employees in the home country and abroad, 2001–2010

Definition of overeducation		Estonia			Latvia		
		Period of observation					
		2001q1–2004q1	2004q2–2008q3	2008q4–2009q4	2002q1–2004q1	2004q2–2008q3	2008q4–2009q4
Occupation-based [a]	Stayers	26.5	26.6	25.6	20.6	17.9	17.7
	Emigrants	26.9	53.5	60.5	30.5	45.9	(..)
Self-assessed [b]	Stayers	13.5	13.5	15.0	NA	NA	NA
	Emigrants	4.6	26.8	21.7	Year of moving		
	Emigrants				2002q1–2004q1	2004q2–2008q3	2008q4–2009q4
					NA	NA	NA
					2004–2008 [c]	2009–2010 [c]	
					53.8 [c]	61.1 [c]	

Notes: [a] According to the OECD definition, a tertiary educated worker is overeducated unless his or her job belongs to the first three major ISCO groups (1 – Senior officials and managers; 2 – Professionals; 3 – Associated professionals and technicians). [b] Estonia: 'The job presupposes a lower level of education'; Latvia: 'Holds a paid job in which he or she does not use or uses only to a small extent his or her qualifications (education)'. [c] Observed in 2010/12–2011/01.

Source: Author's calculations based on Estonian and Latvian LFS data; [c] Author's calculations based on the data of the population survey 'National Identity: Place, Mobility and Capability, 2010/2011'.

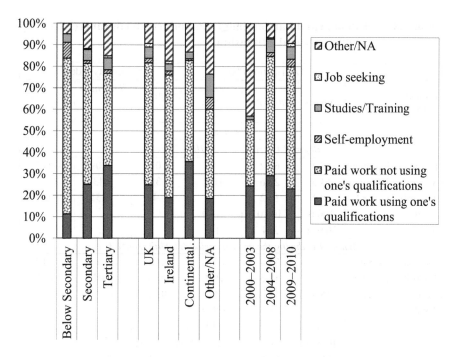

Figure 6.6   Emigrants' main activity abroad at the end of 2010, by educational attainment, host country and time of leaving Latvia

Note: 'Continental Europe' refers to the EU15 (without the United Kingdom and Ireland), Norway and Switzerland.

Source: Author's calculations based on the data of the population survey 'National Identity: Place, Mobility and Capability, 2010/2011'.

5. Ethnicity and Citizenship

Table 6.8, based on the LFS data, breaks down Estonian and Latvian stayers, emigrants and recent return migrants (separately for the pre-accession, post-accession and economic crisis periods) into three categories: (i) ethnic Estonians (or Latvians); (ii) representatives of ethnic minorities (mostly with a Slavic background) holding Estonian (or Latvian) citizenship; (iii) representatives of ethnic minorities without Estonian (or Latvian) citizenship (that is, Estonian and Latvian non-citizens,[10] as well as citizens of other countries). The table also provides selectivity indices of emigrants (vs. stayers) and return migrants (vs.

---

10   Also known as 'grey passport holders' in Estonia and 'violet passport holders' in Latvia.

Table 6.8   Estonian and Latvian emigrants and return migrants (selectivity by ethnicity and citizenship)

Ethnicity/ citizenship	Distribution (%)			Selectivity index		
	Stayers	*Emigrants*	*Recent return migrants*	*Emigrants vs. stayers*	*Returnees vs. emigrants*	*Returnees vs. stayers*
Estonia						
Before EU accession (2001q1–2004q1)						
Estonian / Estonian	65.4	66.2	60.8	0.01	−0.09	−0.07
Minority / Estonian	14.5	20.6	31.6	0.35	0.43	0.78
Minority / Other [a]	20.1	13.2	7.6	−0.42	−0.55	−0.97
Total	100.0	100.0	100.0			
N	30,931	201	18			
Within EU during the growth period (2004q2–2008q3)						
Estonian / Estonian	65.9	72.9	62.6	0.10	−0.15	−0.05
Minority / Estonian	15.7	15.5	16.2	−0.01	0.04	0.03
Minority / Other [a]	18.4	11.7	21.2	−0.45	0.59	0.14
Total	100.0	100.0	100.0			
N	45,611	1,048	140			
Within EU during the crisis (2008q4–2009q4)						
Estonian / Estonian	65.6	65.6	73.3	0.00	0.11	0.11
Minority / Estonian	16.1	14.6	2.7	−0.10	−1.69	−1.79
Minority / Other [a]	18.3	19.8	24	0.08	0.19	0.27
Total	100.0	100.0	100.0			
N	12,760	449	80			
Latvia						
Before EU accession (2002q1–2004q1)						
Latvian / Latvian	58.7	45.5	59.39	−0.25	0.27	0.01
Minority / Latvian	19.2	22.4	16.12	0.15	−0.33	−0.17
Minority / Other [a]	22.0	32.1	24.49	0.38	−0.27	0.11
Total	100.0	100.0	100.0			
N	26,952	262	71			
Within EU during the growth period (2004q2–2008q3)						
Latvian / Latvian	60.9	57.8	61.8	−0.05	0.07	0.01
Minority / Latvian	28.7	33.2	25.2	0.15	−0.28	−0.13
Minority / Other [a]	10.4	9.0	12.1	−0.14	0.30	0.15
Total	100.0	100.0	100.0			
N	60,341	606	233			

Within EU during the crisis (2008q4–2009q4)						
Latvian / Latvian	58.6	55.9	57	–0.05	0.02	–0.03
Minority / Latvian	25.4	26.3	28.5	0.03	0.08	0.12
Minority / Other [a]	16.0	17.8	14.5	0.11	–0.21	–0.10
Total	100.0	100.0	100.0			
N	24,774	173	118			

Notes: Population aged 18–64. Only those emigrants economically active abroad while still considered household members in Estonia (Latvia) are accounted for. [a] 'Other' refers to Estonian and Latvian non-citizens, as well as citizens of other countries.

Source: Author's calculations based on Estonian and Latvian LFS data.

emigrants) with regard to ethnic background and citizenship. For convenience, the dynamics of these indices is summarised in Figure 6.7.

In the pre-accession period, Latvian minorities, especially non-citizens, as well as Estonian minority citizens, were overrepresented among emigrants. After accession, the proportion of Russian-speakers among emigrants dropped sharply (at the expense of the minority group which was overrepresented: minority citizens in Estonia and minority non-citizens in Latvia), with the selectivity index falling from 0.35 to –0.01 and from 0.38 to –0.14, respectively (Figure 6.7). During the crisis, the proportion of non-citizens among emigrants increased in both countries; the corresponding selectivity index went up from –0.45 to 0.08 in Estonia and from –0.14 to 0.11 in Latvia (Figure 6.7), suggesting that non-citizens were hit harder by the crisis than other groups. Furthermore, during the crisis relative likelihood of return among emigrants/non-citizens (in Estonia – among all Russian-speaking emigrants) was much lower than before.

These findings are largely in line with our expectations (see *H1(b)*, *H2(b)*, *H3(e)* above), except for the fact that during the crisis we do not find an increase in emigration rates among minority citizens; this latter discrepancy is, however, consistent with the plausible assumption that many emigrants in this category during the crisis moved with families and therefore could not be found in Latvian LFS data.

Ethnicity and Human Capital-related Determinants of Work Abroad

Table 6.9 presents the results of an econometric analysis of determinants of working abroad, focusing on the effects of ethnicity, citizenship and place of birth, as well as educational attainment (the estimated logit models control also for other demographic variables and include time and region fixed effects). Our interest is in the change in patterns over time; this is why we present logit coefficients rather than marginal effects. The results should be interpreted with care, as they are based on sending countries' LFS data, which do not cover permanent emigrants, as well as those without household members left behind.

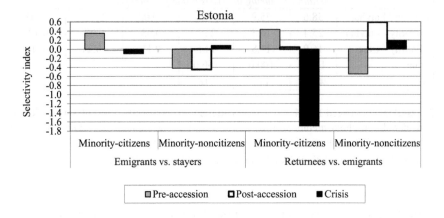

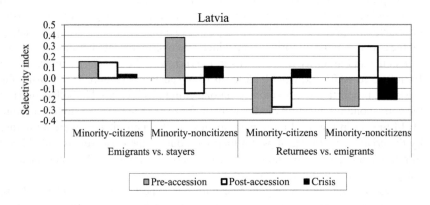

Figure 6.7   Selectivity indices of emigrants vs. stayers and return migrants vs. emigrants regarding ethnicity and citizenship, 2001–2009 (top: Estonia; bottom: Latvia)

Notes: Selectivity index of group 2 vs. group 1 regarding category X is defined as $SI = \ln (X_2 / X_1)$, where X_i is the share of X in group i. See Table 6.8 for exact definitions of the pre-accession, post-accession and crisis periods. See Notes to Table 6.8 for other details.

Source: Author's calculations based on Estonian and Latvian LFS data.

Table 6.9 Determinants of work abroad (logit coefficients), Estonia and Latvia, 2001–2009

	Estonia			Latvia		
	2001q1–2004q1	2004q2–2008q3	2008q4–2009q4	2002q1–2004q1	2004q2–2008q3	2008q4–2009q4
Ethnicity / citizenship / country of birth (vs. native/ native/native)						
Minority/native/ native	1.237***	0.001	0.259	0.371*	0.162	–0.106
Minority/native/ foreign	0.010	0.690***	0.764**	1.669***	0.428**	0.939***
Minority/other [a]/ native	–1.082	–1.159***	–0.110	0.518**	–0.200	–0.567
Minority/other [a] / foreign	0.231	0.445**	0.803***	1.067***	0.470*	0.572
Native/native/ foreign [b]	0.316	–0.518	–1.082	–11.56***	–0.176	–0.099
Education (vs. upper secondary)						
Below upper secondary	–0.283	–0.119	–0.058	–1.052***	–0.411***	0.288
Tertiary	–0.324	–0.424***	–0.466***	0.610***	–0.203(')	–0.115
Other controls	Gender, family status, age, type of settlement, region, year, quarter dummies					
N obs	24092	46519	13159	27214	60947	24947
N emigrants	169	1048	449	262	606	173
Pseudo R–squared	0.0909	0.1044	0.1088	0.1049	0.0746	0.0945

Notes: Population aged 18–64. Only emigrants economically active abroad while still considered household members in the country of origin are accounted for. The dependent variable = 1 for those who were working abroad or living and seeking a job abroad for some time during the last 12 months before the survey. [a] 'Other' citizenship includes Estonian and Latvian non-citizens. [b] In both countries, the share of foreign-born natives does not exceed 1%. ***, **, *, (') – estimates significantly different from zero at 0.01, 0.05, 0.10, 0.13, respectively (based on robust standard errors).

Sources: Calculations with Estonian and Latvian LFS data.

In Estonia and Latvia alike, both in the post-accession period and (to an even larger extent) during the crisis, *foreign-born Russian-speakers* were significantly more likely to work abroad than similar local born natives or Russian-speakers. In Latvia, this effect was observed also before accession. By contrast, among *local-born Russian-speakers*, both with and without native citizenship, propensity to work abroad does not exceed that of natives. In Estonia, being foreign-born remains a highly significant driver of emigration also if Estonian language skills are controlled for.[11]

Regarding the educational attainment effect, the results in Table 6.9 support our expectations and the findings based on descriptive statistics. In comparison with the medium-educated, propensity to work abroad among university graduates (or among the low-skilled) decreased (or increased) after EU accession in both Estonia and Latvia. During the first year of the crisis, the differences between the skill groups in terms of propensity to work abroad disappeared in Latvia (supporting the idea of the systemic nature of the crisis there), while in Estonia these differences have hardly changed since the pre-crisis period.

6. Geography

Figure 6.8, based on administrative data, presents the geographical composition of the outflows of Estonian and Latvian population before and after accession, as well as during the economic crisis.

Pre-accession emigration flows were quite diverse. More than two-thirds of Estonian emigrants went (in roughly equal proportions) to the Nordic countries and to continental Western Europe, while almost two-thirds of Latvian emigrants chose other destinations, mainly North America, Australia and Eastern Europe. Among EU countries, Finland, with its geographical and linguistic proximity to Estonia, and Ireland, with its attractive combination of English language and readily available simple agricultural jobs, played a prominent role by hosting, respectively, 26 per cent of Estonian and 22 per cent of Latvian emigrants.

After accession, emigration flows changed direction towards newly opened labour markets in the United Kingdom and Ireland; these two destinations accounted for half of Estonian emigration in 2004–2005 and for two-thirds of Latvian emigration in 2004–2008 (Figure 6.8). Following the opening up of Finland's labour market in 2006, its share in Estonian emigration increased from one-fifth in 2004–2005 to one-third in 2006–2008; the share of other Nordic countries has also increased, while the total share of Ireland and the United Kingdom fell from one-half to less than one-third. By contrast, the composition of Latvian emigration flows hardly changed (this is why the Latvian panel in Figure 6.8 shows the period 2004–2008 only as a whole).

---

11   These results are available on request. The Latvian LFS does not provide information on language skills.

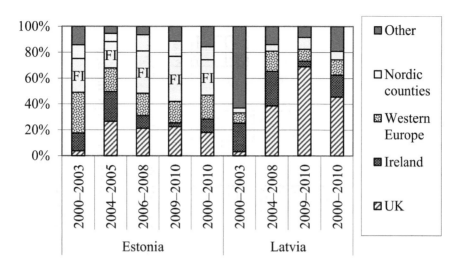

Figure 6.8   Composition of Estonian and Latvian (net) emigration flows by host country and time of departure, 2000–2010

Notes: The segments labelled 'FI' in the Estonian panel refer to Finland.

Sources: Eurostat, OECD, Statistics Latvia, Statistics Estonia, other national statistical offices, Department of Work and Pensions (the UK), Department of Social Protection (Ireland), own compilation (see Notes to Table 6.2 for details).

During the crisis, Ireland was hit by high unemployment and its share in Estonian and especially Latvian emigration further declined. Finland, other Nordic countries, Western Europe and the United Kingdom maintained their shares (plausibly, migration networks played an important role), while the share of other destinations increased from 6 per cent to 11 per cent. Latvian emigration became even more oriented towards the United Kingdom, whose share exceeded two-thirds (while the total share of the United Kingdom and Ireland reached almost three-quarters); the share of the Nordic countries increased from 5 per cent to 9 per cent (Norway alone received 3,000 Latvian expats in two years), while the shares of Western Europe and other destinations declined. To sum up, emigration flows from Estonia and Latvia were fairly responsive to changes in both legal and economic conditions in potential host countries, but the main destinations remained relatively stable over time. These findings are in line with our expectations (see *H1(c)*, *H2(c)*).

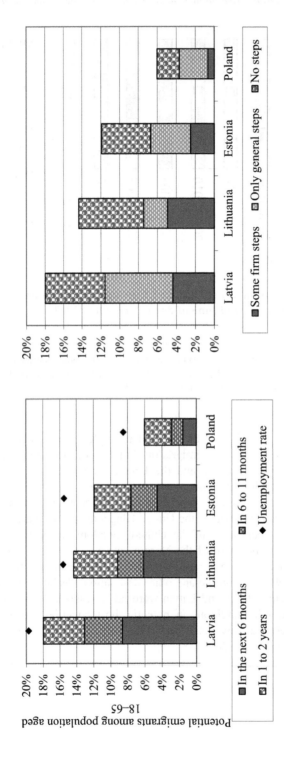

Figure 6.9 Intention to work abroad within two years, by planned time of departure and preparation steps, the Baltic countries and Poland, November–December 2009

Source: Author's calculations based on Eurobarometer 72.5. Unemployment rate (2009q4): *Eurostat* (EU LFS).

7. Migration Intentions during the Crisis

The previous sections described the development of emigration from Estonia and Latvia between 2000 and 2010. Here we try to look into the future (but also to reinforce our findings so far) by comparing the migration intentions of Latvians, Lithuanians and Estonians at the end of 2009 (that is, one year into the crisis); in the Latvian case, we also provide a more detailed analysis using data from two surveys conducted a year later. Intention data have an obvious weakness in that they present only intentions rather than actual behaviour. However, they come from representative population surveys and do not have the various sample selection and registration problems common in data on real migrants.

Intensity of Emigration Plans across Countries and Human Capital Groups

Figure 6.9 presents, for the three Baltic countries and Poland, the proportion of the population (aged 18–65) who, at the end of 2009, envisaged working abroad within two years, with a breakdown by planned time of departure, as well as by preparations made.

Total labour emigration potential within two years (18 per cent in Latvia, 14 per cent in Lithuania, 12 per cent in Estonia and 6 per cent in Poland) is exactly 2 percentage points below the unemployment rate at the time of the survey for three out of four countries; for Estonia it is 4 points below (Figure 6.9, left panel). This supports the idea of unemployment being the main driving force of emigration during the first stage of the crisis. Moreover, the proportion of those who plan to move within 6 months or a year displays a similar pattern. Furthermore, while 4 to 5 per cent of the population aged 18 to 65 in Latvia and Lithuania report having taken firm steps to prepare for moving abroad, this proportion is half as much in Estonia and less than 1 per cent in Poland (Figure 6.9, right panel). Likewise, some preparation steps (firm or general) were reported by 12 per cent of Latvian respondents, 6 to 8 per cent of their counterparts in Estonia and Lithuania, and just 4 per cent in Poland. This supports the idea that, apart from the unemployment level, the perception of the depth of the crisis also matters (recall from Table 6.1 that population sentiments were much more negative in Latvia than in Estonia).

Figure 6.10 presents, for the three Baltic countries, information on emigration potential within two years and preparation steps taken for moving abroad separately for respondents with low, medium and high education levels, as well as for those still studying.

For Latvia and Lithuania alike, the brain drain risk is apparent: one out of three students plan to work abroad within two years; in Estonia, this proportion is half as much. Moreover, firm steps have been taken by 10 per cent of Latvian students and 12 per cent of their Lithuanian colleagues, while in Estonia this figure is below 2 per cent.

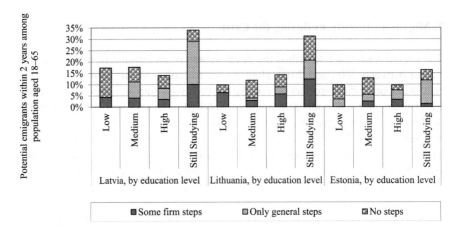

Figure 6.10   Intention to work abroad within two years and preparation steps takcn, by educational attainment, the Baltic countries, November–December 2009

Note: Respondents are classified as low educated if they left the education system before 16 years of age (intermediate, between 16 and 19 years of age and highly educated, at least 20 years of age).

Source: Author's calculations based on Eurobarometer 72.5.

    Students aside, the proportion of potential emigrants in Latvia (or Estonia) was around 15 per cent (or 10 per cent) in all the three skill groups, with the high-skilled featuring a lower-than-average propensity to move. By contrast, in Lithuania it increased with education level (from 10 per cent among the low-skilled to 15 per cent among the high-skilled). However, both in Lithuania and in Estonia, the highest proportion of potential emigrants who have made some preparations is found among the best educated, while in Latvia this group is second, slightly behind the medium-skilled. Finally, if only potential emigrants who have taken some firm steps towards moving are accounted for, in Latvia about 5 per cent of each skill group were 'decided movers', while in Lithuania this proportion was 6 per cent among the high-skilled and the low-skilled but just 3 per cent among the medium-skilled; in Estonia, 2 per cent to 3 per cent of medium- and high-skilled but none of the low-skilled were 'decided movers'.

    To sum up, even by a very conservative estimate, by the end of 2009, the high-skilled in the Baltic countries did not feature a lower-than-average propensity to emigrate, and the brain drain risk was especially high in Lithuania and Latvia.

Emigration Potential and Reasons for Emigration after Two Years of the Crisis

Figure 6.11 presents the emigration intentions of the Latvian population aged 18 to 65, at the end of 2010 and early 2011, after more than two years of recession, accompanied by a powerful emigration wave. The results are broken down by respondents' completed education, as well as by occupation.

The right panel displays respondents' answers to the question 'Do you plan to move from Latvia in the near future to improve your/your family's material well-being?'. Those who answered 'Yes' or 'I do not exclude such a possibility' are categorised as potential emigrants; the former group is further referred to as having concrete plans. The highest propensity to emigrate *in the near future* is found among the population with a secondary education: 28 per cent of them are potential movers, including 10 per cent with concrete plans. The other two groups are not far behind, however: 25 per cent of those with less than secondary education and 22 per cent of the highly-educated are potential emigrants, in both cases including 7 per cent with concrete plans (Figure 6.11, right panel).

Larger differences between the skill groups are observed with respect to *reasons for emigration* (Figure 6.11, left). We divide the reasons into two categories: *economic reasons* (no jobs available in Latvia; no possibility to earn a living in Latvia; elsewhere one can earn much more; better social protection abroad) and *non-economic reasons* (possibility to see the world, to get new impressions, to meet new friends; education and career possibilities; no future in Latvia; does not like what is going on in Latvia; does not like the political environment; wants to live in a stable country; influence of other people). Respondents could indicate more than one several reason. Note that total emigration potential is somewhat larger according to the left panel of Figure 6.11 than is found in the right panel. This is because the survey question used in the left panel is not restricted to economic emigration and refers to plans in general rather than to plans regarding the near future.

The proportion of those who plan to move abroad for economic (and maybe other) reasons decreases with education level: from 29 per cent among respondents with a basic education to 13 per cent among university graduates. By contrast, the proportion of those who plan emigration only for non-economic reasons increases from 8 per cent among the low-educated to 14 per cent among respondents with a tertiary education.

From an occupational perspective, the highest propensity to emigrate in the near future is found among students: more than a half of them are potential emigrants, including 18 per cent with concrete plans (Figure 6.11, right panel). A smaller yet significant propensity to emigrate is found among the unemployed, manual workers and non-manual workers, with between 23 and 30 per cent potential emigrants, including between 7 and 12 per cent with concrete plans (Figure 6.11, right panel). On average, one-third of potential movers mention only non-economic reasons for emigration; the only occupational group in which most

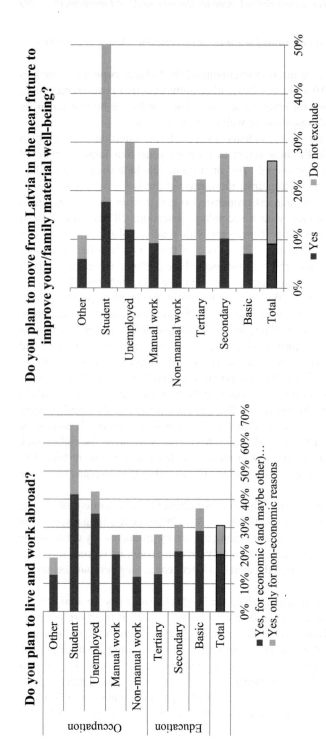

Figure 6.11 Emigration intentions of Latvian residents, by education and main occupation, 2010/12–2011/02, population aged 18–65

Source: Author's calculations based on data from population surveys 'DNB NORD Latvia's Barometer No. 35. February 2011' (left) and 'National Identity: Place, Capability, Migration. 2010/2011' (right).

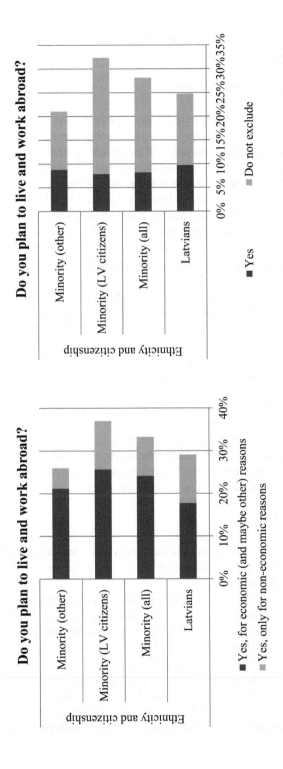

Figure 6.12 Migration intentions of Latvian residents, by ethnicity and citizenship, 2010/12–2011/01, population aged 18–65

Source: Author's calculations based on data from population surveys 'DNB NORD Latvia's Barometer No. 35. February 2011' (left panel) and 'National Identity: Place, Capability, Migration. 2010/2011' (right panel).

potential movers do not mention any economic reasons for their plans, is that of non-manual workers (Figure 6.11, left panel).

Emigration Plans by Ethnicity and Citizenship

When the population is broken down by ethnicity and citizenship, the highest propensity to emigrate in the near future is found among non-Latvians with Latvian citizenship: one-third of them are potential emigrants, compared with one-quarter among ethnic Latvians and one-fifth among non-Latvians without Latvian citizenship (Figure 6.12, right panel). Recall that the latter group is not covered by the legal provisions on free movement of labour within the EU, which reduces expected gains from migration. The same pattern is found when emigration plans regarding either the near or distant future (and for any reason) are considered (Figure 6.12, left panel): 37 per cent of non-Latvians with Latvian citizenship are potential emigrants in this wider sense, followed by ethnic Latvians with 29 per cent and minority non-citizens with 26 per cent.

In comparison with the results based on surveys conducted in 2005–2007 (see Hazans and Philips, 2010: Table 2, cols [6–10]), these findings support the above stated hypothesis *H3 (e)* about the increase of the proportion of Russian-speakers among emigrants during the crisis.

It is worth noting, however, that the proportions of potential emigrants with concrete plans differ very little across the ethnic groups, and this time the highest rate (10 per cent) is found among ethnic Latvians, followed by minority non-citizens (9 per cent) and minority-citizens (8 per cent) (see Figure 6.12, right panel). One explanation for this might be more the intensive emigration of minorities during the first stage of the crisis (see Figure 6.7 and Table 6.9).

Furthermore (see Figure 6.12, left panel), the share of potential emigrants who mention *only non-economic reasons* for emigration is much higher among Latvians (39 per cent) than among non-Latvians (28 per cent).

Emigrants' Intentions to Return

Figure 6.13 summarises information on Latvian emigrants' plans to return, as reported by their family members or close relatives during the survey conducted in December 2010–January 2011.

On average, 8 per cent of emigrants plan (or rather plan than not) to return within six months. In a longer perspective (within five years) about 20 per cent of emigrants assume the possibility of returning. These findings are in striking contrast with the situation observed five years earlier, when two-thirds of emigrants who left Latvia in 2004–2005 were planning to return within two years, most of them (almost half of all emigrants) even within one year (Hazans and Philips 2010: Figure 9). In fact, in 2002–2007, more than half of Latvian guest-workers returned home within a year, according to the Latvian LFS (Hazans and Philips 2010: Figure 10). This comparison supports hypothesis *H3 (f)* that during the crisis

Latvian emigrants are now oriented towards long-term or permanent emigration to a much larger extent.

From the ethnicity and citizenship perspective, non-Latvians without Latvian citizenship feature the smallest propensity to return: 4 per cent within six months and another 4 per cent within five years. This is in line with the findings from Table 6.8 and Figure 6.7 above. The difference between ethnic Latvians and minority-citizens is not significant. On the whole, however, minority emigrants are much

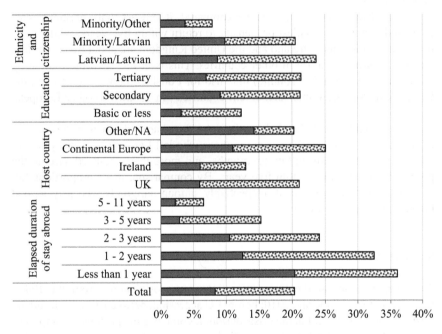

■ Plans to return within the next 6 months
☒ Plans to return within 5 years (but not within 6 months)

Figure 6.13   Return plans of Latvian emigrants, by ethnicity and citizenship, educational attainment, host country and duration of stay abroad, 2010/12–2011/01

Notes: Emigrants' characteristics and return plans as reported by their close relatives surveyed in Latvia. 'Continental Europe' refers to the EU15 (without the United Kingdom and Ireland), Norway and Switzerland.

Answers 'Yes' and 'Rather yes than no' are accounted for.

Source: Author's calculations based on data from survey on close relatives who emigrated between 2000 and 2010 and lived abroad during the population survey 'National Identity: Place, Capability, Migration. 2010/2011' conducted for the Faculty of Social Sciences, University of Latvia.

less likely to return than ethnic Latvians, once again supporting the hypothesis *H3 (e)* on the over-representation of minorities among post-recession emigrants from Latvia.

While low-educated emigrants show the lowest *intention* to return, recall from Tables 6.5 and 6.6 and Figure 6.5 that in fact they were most likely to return (especially during the crisis). On the other hand, tertiary educated Latvian emigrants are less likely to return than their counterparts with a secondary education, who constitute the majority of emigrants (see Table 6.5). This once again highlights the brain drain risk.

When different host countries are compared, it appears that Latvian ex-pats in Ireland feature the smallest propensity to return within five years, while in the near future emigrants in Ireland and the United Kingdom are about two times less likely to return than those in other countries. This is in line with the finding by Anacka and Fihel (in this volume) that also for Polish emigrants Ireland and the United Kingdom are rather 'settlement countries', in contrast to other European destinations.

As one might expect, the likelihood of returning sharply declines as the duration of stay abroad increases. Thus, among those who left Latvia less than a year ago one-fifth plan to return within six months, and more than one-third assume the possibility of returning within five years. By comparison, these proportions fall to 3 per cent and 15 per cent, respectively, among emigrants who stay abroad between three and five years.

8. Conclusions

This chapter looks at the three migration waves originating from the Baltic countries between 2000 and 2010: before EU accession, between accession and the crisis of 2008–2009, and in the crisis period. It compares the profiles of temporary workers abroad (migrant workers), settled emigrants and return migrants with that of stayers, and explores the factors affecting mobility decisions, and intentions to emigrate and to return.

The key data used for these purposes come from several sources: the Labour Force Survey data (2002–2009) for Latvia and Estonia; representative population surveys conducted in the Baltic countries in 2000 (the New Baltic Barometer, see Rose 2000) and in the late 2009 (Eurobarometer 72.5, also known as Special Eurobarometer 337, see Papacostas 2011; TNS Opinion and Social 2010); a representative survey of the Latvian population 'National Identity: Place, Capability, Migration. 2010/2011' (see Hazans 2011b: 77), with a module on close relatives who emigrated between 2000 and 2010 and were living abroad at the beginning of 2011; and a representative survey of the Latvian population 'DnB NORD Latvia's Barometer No. 35. February 2011'. In all these cases, the results are based on our own calculations with survey microdata.

The primary focus of the chapter is the skill level of movers, stayers and returnees. Another question of specific interest for Latvia and Estonia is how the mobility behaviour of the Russian-speaking minority compares to that of the native population.

We find that after the accession, in comparison with the pre-accession period, economic emigrants from Estonia and Latvia featured a significantly lower proportion of tertiary educated persons, as well as ethnic minorities, especially non-citizens. These findings reflect the lower costs and lower human capital threshold (in terms of skills, risk taking and so on) associated with labour migration, on the one hand, and the fact that Estonian and Latvian non-citizens are not covered by the legal provisions for free movement of labour within the EU, on the other.

During the crisis, in comparison with the pre-crisis period, Latvian emigration intensified to a much larger extent than Estonian emigration. We link this difference to the fact that the crisis in Latvia has been perceived by a majority of the population as a systemic (rather than just a financial) crisis, which was not the case in Estonia. Moreover, emigrants from Latvia are to a much larger extent than before oriented towards long-term or permanent emigration.

Both in Estonia and Latvia, the role of push factors (especially unemployment, but in Latvia also general dissatisfaction and loss of prospects) in shaping migration flows increased during the crisis. The low-skilled, who suffered disproportionately from the recession-triggered lay-offs, became overrepresented among emigrants. The proportion of university graduates increased among Latvian emigrants (exceeding this proportion among stayers), but not among their Estonian counterparts. The migration intentions documented after one or two years of the crisis also indicate a substantial risk of brain drain for Lithuania and Latvia.

Throughout the whole period 2000–2010, but especially during the pre-accession period and during the crisis, university graduates were less likely to return than other groups of emigrants, while the low-skilled were overrepresented among returnees. Both for Latvia and Estonia, the crisis resulted in a sharp increase (or fall) of the selectivity index of returnees regarding low (or high) education level. This suggest that in periods when it was more difficult to find a job abroad, the higher the education level of emigrants, the more successful they were.

Both by the formal (OECD) definition, and according to emigrants' self-assessment, at least half of Estonian and Latvian emigrants with a tertiary education hold jobs for which they are overeducated.

In line with findings by Anacka and Fihel (in this volume) for Poland, our results suggest that Ireland and the United Kingdom are 'settlement countries' for Latvian emigrants to a much larger extent than other European destinations.

During the crisis, the proportion of Russian-speakers (especially non-citizens) increased among both Latvian and Estonian emigrants, reflecting a deterioration of the labour market position of minorities. On the other hand, both in the post-accession period and during the crisis, foreign-born Russian-speakers were significantly more likely to work abroad than otherwise similar local born natives or Russian-speakers. In Latvia, this effect was in place also before accession.

By contrast, among local-born Russian-speakers both with and without native citizenship, the propensity to work abroad does not exceed that of natives. To determine the extent to which this effect should be attributed to slow acculturation and adaptation of the foreign born or to the role of inherent mobility, further research is required (note that in Estonia, being foreign-born remains a highly significant driver of emigration also when Estonian language skills are controlled for).

Acknowledgements

The author is grateful to Janine Leschke, Béla Galgóczi and Andrew Watt for their support and comments. This chapter includes some material from Hazans 2011b. I thank DNB Bank and the SKDS research centre for the dataset of the survey 'DNB NORD Latvia's Barometer No. 35. February 2011'. The population survey 'National Identity: Place, Capability, Migration. 2010/2011' was funded by the Latvian National Research Programme 'National Identity'. All remaining errors are my own.

Bibliography

Anacka, M. and A. Fihel. 2012. 'Return migration to Poland in the post-accession period' (in this volume).

Borjas, G.J. 1987. 'Self-selection and the earnings of immigrants', *American Economic Review*, 77(4): 531–53.

Borjas, G.J. 1999. 'Immigration and welfare magnets', *Journal of Labour Economics*, 17(4): 607–37.

Brucker, H., T. Baas, S. Bertoli, T. Boeri et al. 2009. *Labour mobility within the EU in the context of enlargement and the functioning of the transitional arrangements*. Nuremberg: European Integration Consortium (IAB, CMR, fRDB, GEP, WIFO, wiiw).

European Commission. 2008. *Employment in Europe 2008*. Luxembourg: Publications Office of the European Union. <http://ec.europa.eu/social/BlobS ervlet?docId=681&langId=en>.

European Commission. 2010. *Employment in Europe 2010*. Luxembourg: Publications Office of the European Union. <http://ec.europa.eu/social/main.js p?catId=738&langId=en&pubId=593>.

European Commission. 2011. *Labour Market Developments in Europe 2011*. <http://ec.europa.eu/economy_finance/publications/publication_summary-20110809_en.htm>.

European Social Survey. 2008–2009. Round 4 (edition 4.0) data files. *Norwegian Social Science Data Services.*

Fic, T., D. Holland, P. Paluchowski, A. Rincon-Aznar and L. Stokes. 2011. 'Labour mobility within the EU – The impact of enlargement and transitional arrangements'. NIESR Discussion Paper No. 379 (revised August 2011).

Hazans, M. 2003. *Potential emigration of Latvian labour force after joining the EU and its impact on Latvian labour market.* Available at SSRN: <http://ssrn. com/abstract=739305>.

Hazans, M. 2007. *Coping with growth and emigration: Latvian labour market before and after EU accession.* Available at SSRN: <http://ssrn.com/ abstract=971198>.

Hazans, M. 2008. 'Post-enlargement return migrants' earnings premium: Evidence from Latvia'. EALE 2008 paper No. 541. Available at SSRN: <http://ssrn.com/ abstract=1269728>

Hazans, M. 2010. 'Ethnic minorities in Latvian labour market, 1997–2009: Outcomes, integration drivers and barriers', in Nils Mužnieks (ed.), *How integrated is Latvian Society?* Riga, Latvia: University of Latvia Press, 125–58.

Hazans, M. 2011a. 'Labour market integration of ethnic minorities in Latvia', in Martin Kahanec and Klaus F. Zimmermann (eds), *Ethnic diversity in European labor markets: Challenges and solutions*, Cheltenham, UK–Northampton, MA, USA: Edward Elgar, 163–97.

Hazans, M. 2011b. 'The changing face of Latvian emigration, 2000–2010', in: B. Zepa and E. Kļave (eds), *Latvia Human Development Report 2010/2011: National Identity, Mobility and Capability.* Riga: Advanced Social and Political Research Institute of the University of Latvia, 77–101.

Hazans, M. and K. Philips. 2010. 'The post-enlargement migration experience in the Baltic labour markets', in Martin Kahanec and Klaus F. Zimmermann (eds), *EU labour markets after post-enlargement migration*, Berlin–Heidelberg: Springer, 255–304. (Also available as IZA Discussion Paper No. 5878, <http:// ftp.iza.org/dp5878.pdf>).

Kaczmarczyk, P., M. Mioduszewska and A. Żylicz. 2010. 'Impact of the post-accession migration on the Polish labour market', in Martin Kahanec and Klaus F. Zimmermann (eds), *EU labour markets after post-enlargement migration*, Berlin–Heidelberg: Springer, 219–53.

Kahanec, M. and A. Zaiceva. 2009. 'Labor market outcomes of immigrants and non-citizens in the EU: An east–west comparison', *International Journal of Manpower*, 30 (1/2): 97–115.

Lee, E.S. 1966. 'A theory of migration'. *Demography*, 3 (1): 47–57.

Papacostas, A. 2011. Eurobarometer 72.5: November–December 2009. Study Documentation.

Rose, R. 2000. New Baltic Barometer IV: A survey study. Centre for the Study of Public Policy, University of Strathclyde, Glasgow.

Sjaastad, L.A. 1962. 'The costs and returns of human migration', *Journal of Political Economy*, 70(5): 80–93.

Tijdens, K. and M. van Klaveren. 2012. 'A skill mismatch for migrant workers?', Evidence from WageIndicator survey data. (In this volume.)

TNS Opinion and Social. 2010. Special Eurobarometer 337. Geographical and labour market mobility. Report.

PART III
Policy Implications of, and Responses to, Cross-border Labour Mobility in the EU after 2004

PART III

Chapter 7

Supporting, Recruiting and Organising Migrant Workers in Ireland and the United Kingdom: A Review of Trade Union Practices

Jason Heyes and Mary Hyland

1. Introduction

Ireland and the United Kingdom were, along with Sweden, the only EU15 member states to grant full labour market access from the outset to citizens of the eight Central and Eastern European countries (the so-called EU8) that joined the European Union in May 2004. Both Ireland and the United Kingdom subsequently experienced a substantial inflow of migrant workers, many of whom took up relatively low-paid jobs in the agricultural, construction, hospitality and manufacturing sectors. However, as the number of migrants increased, so too did reports of ill-treatment of migrant workers by employers and employment agencies. Trade unions openly supported the decision to grant workers from the new EU member states the freedom to work in the United Kingdom and Ireland and have since been active in calling for improved rights for migrant workers and more effective enforcement mechanisms. Many unions have also made considerable efforts to support, recruit and organise migrant workers. These efforts have reflected traditional concerns relating to the representation and protection of workers, including a concern that employers should not use migrant workers in ways that result in the pay, conditions and employment opportunities of 'native' workers being undermined.

The aim of this chapter is to examine the various ways in which trade unions in Ireland and the United Kingdom have sought to support migrant workers. The chapter explores trade unions' national policies and specific initiatives that have been taken at the regional and local levels to support migrant workers and encourage them to become union members. The chapter draws on four sources of information: first, secondary sources, including published research, government reports, trade union policy documents and web-based materials; second, a survey of Irish trade unions' policies and practices in respect of migrant workers; third, interviews with representatives of the Trades Union Congress (TUC) and a number of individual UK trade unions (the GMB, UNITE, USDAW, Unison and UCATT); and fourth, interviews with representatives of the Irish Congress of Trade Unions

(ICTU), individual Irish trade unions (SIPTU, INMO, MANDATE), and an NGO (Migrant Rights Centre Ireland, MRCI).

2. Migration Trends and Policy Frameworks

Ireland and the United Kingdom have very different histories of immigration. While the United Kingdom has long been a destination for migrant workers, Ireland's experience was one of outward migration throughout the nineteenth, and most of the twentieth, century. With no history of immigration, little consideration was given by the Irish state to the development of a formal immigration policy until the 1990s. The country's first employment permit scheme was introduced in 1994 in response to demands from employers and employer organisations and a large majority of workers who came to Ireland between 1994 and 2004 did so under this scheme. The Irish Government's decision in 2004 to allow EU8 citizens unrestricted access to the Irish labour market was made largely at the behest of the business community (Doyle et al. 2006; Begg 2007: 182). However, in an attempt to address public concerns about 'welfare tourism' the government introduced a 'Habitual Residence Condition', which meant that EU8 citizens would not be entitled to claim social welfare for at least two years from the date of their arrival in Ireland. The government also decided to restrict the labour market access of Romanian and Bulgarian citizens following the further expansion of the EU in 2007. These restrictions are scheduled to remain in place until the end of 2013.

The Habitual Residence Condition was amended in 2007, in line with judgments of the European Court of Justice (ECJ) on the matter of habitual residence, which involved establishing criteria for determining whether a person is habitually resident and how those criteria should be applied to EEA citizens and to non-EEA citizens. While the Department of Social Protection has issued comprehensive guidelines to help deciding officers determine whether a person is 'habitually resident', there continues to be some inconsistency in how the condition is applied.

The number of EU8 migrant workers who migrated to Ireland after 2004 far exceeded official expectations. EU8 nationals occupied approximately half of the jobs created in Ireland between the May 2004 accession and the end of 2005 and the number of EU8 citizens employed in Ireland more than trebled (from 19,500 to 61,600) during this short period. The majority of EU8 workers were employed in the construction and manufacturing sectors, which together accounted for more than half of all new EU citizens working in Ireland (Doyle et al. 2006). However, the economic crisis that erupted in 2008 has been associated with a reversal of the upward trend in migrant numbers and a reduction in the proportion of non-Irish nationals in the labour force. In the second quarter of 1996, there were only 4,000 non-Irish nationals in the entire Irish labour force. By 2006, this figure had risen to 283,000 (over 13 per cent of total employment), 121,000 of whom were from EU8 countries. As can be seen from Figure 7.1, the number peaked in 2008

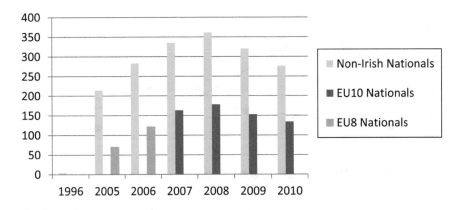

Figure 7.1   Non-Irish, EU10 and EU8 nationals in the labour force, 2005–2010 (in '000s)

Source: QNHS, Quarter 2, 2006–2010.

when 361,000 non-Irish nationals were present in the labour force (16 per cent of all those in employment), 178,000 of whom were EU10 citizens. A decline in employment and a concomitant decrease in migration began in 2009, with 36,000 non-Irish nationals leaving the labour force between the second quarter of 2008 and the second quarter of 2009 (a majority of these – 25,200 – being EU10 nationals). This decrease continued and by the second quarter of 2010 a further 49,000 non-Irish nationals had left the labour force, 18,600 of whom were EU10 nationals.[1]

As can be seen from Figure 7.2, the decline in immigration began in the second quarter of 2007 and proceeded rapidly, so that by the second quarter of 2009 emigration once again substantially exceeded immigration for the first time in over 20 years.

The United Kingdom, like Ireland, decided against implementing temporary restrictions on migration by workers from EU8 member states. The number of EU8 migrant workers who entered the United Kingdom following the 2004 expansion of the EU far exceeded official expectations and gave rise to criticism of the then Labour government's stance on migration. In response, the UK government decided to maintain restrictions on workers from Romania and Bulgaria. The issue of migration has, however, continued to be politically contested and the current Conservative–Liberal Democrat coalition government, which came to power in May 2010, has announced new restrictions on migration from non-EU countries.

---

1   It is important to note that UK and EU15 citizens accounted for more than half of all other non-Irish nationals in the labour force.

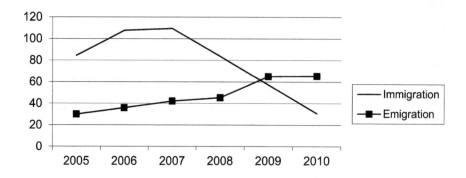

Figure 7.2   Irelands experience of immigration and emigration, 2005–2010 (in '000s)

Source: CSO, Population and Migration Estimates, 2010.

While workers from the EU8 member states were ostensibly free to work in the United Kingdom following the expansion of the EU, the government required that they apply to a 'Workers Registration Scheme' (WRS) within one month of taking up a job (for a discussion, see Heyes 2009a). As in the case of Ireland's Habitual Residence Condition, the UK government introduced the WRS because of concerns that it would be accused by the media and political opposition of allowing migrants to engage in 'benefit tourism'. Migrant workers from the EU8 countries were entitled to access child benefit, housing benefit and tax credits once they started work in the United Kingdom, but only if they registered with the WRS. However, the WRS and the associated restrictions to benefit entitlements came to an end in April 2011, as required by European law (although the government will be able to retain the restrictions on Bulgarian and Romanian workers until the end of 2013).

Ireland's changing experiences of migration prior to and following the start of the economic crisis have been mirrored in the United Kingdom. As can be seen from Figure 7.3, the United Kingdom experienced substantial net migration by EU8 citizens after May 2004. Since the start of the economic crisis, however, immigration by EU8 nationals has declined substantially, while emigration has increased. Between September 2008 and September 2009 the experience was, for the first time since 2004, one of net *emigration* by EU8 citizens.

_____

2 International Passenger Survey data.

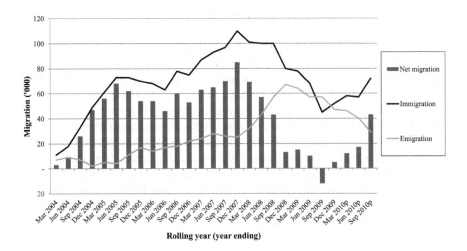

Figure 7.3 **IPS long-term international migration estimates of EU8 citizens, United Kingdom, 2004–2010**

Source: Reproduced from ONS (2010).

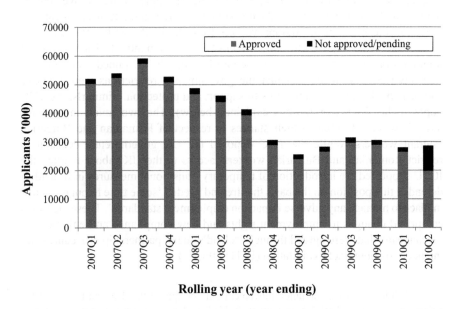

Figure 7.4 **Applicants to the Worker Registration Scheme, by rolling year of application, 2005–2010**

Source: Reproduced from ONS (2010).

The reduction in the flow of migrant workers entering the United Kingdom has been reflected in falls in applications to the WRS, as Figure 7.4 shows. According to the Office for National Statistics (ONS 2010), 105,000 successful applications were made to the WRS in the year to June 2010, representing a decrease of 12 per cent on the number during the year to June 2009 and a reduction of 47 per cent on the number made in the year to June 2008. Eight out of ten of the WRS applications approved during the year to June 2010 were made by citizens of Poland, Lithuania and Latvia (see also Bettin, this volume). Participation by workers from these countries in the UK labour market has differed, however, for while the number of applications made by Polish workers decreased over the 2009–2010 period, the number of successful applications received from citizens of Lithuania and Latvia increased (ONS 2010). It seems likely that the extremely high rates of unemployment witnessed in Latvia and Lithuania provide at least a partial explanation of the differences.

3. The Trade Union Response to Intra-European Labour Migration

The national trade union confederations of Ireland and the United Kingdom – the Irish Congress of Trade Unions (ICTU) and the Trades Union Congress (TUC), respectively – have expressed support for the principle of free movement of workers and largely agreed with the decision of the Irish and UK governments not to restrict the freedom of migrant workers from the EU8 member states to seek work.[3] They also objected to the Irish and UK governments' decision to restrict migrant workers' access to certain welfare benefits. ICTU joined with much of Irish civil society in arguing that the government's restrictions were punitive and denied EU citizens their rights to support and protection. Similarly, the TUC opposed the WRS (for reasons explained below). The two union movements have, however, differed in their stances in respect of Romanian and Bulgarian migrant workers. While the TUC opposed the UK government's decision to restrict Romanian and Bulgarian workers' access to the UK labour market, the ICTU supported the introduction of temporary transitional measures in Ireland. It defended this position on the basis that Ireland needed 'some time to put measures in place to manage any adverse impact on employment standards'. These measures comprised changes to employment rights and new compliance and enforcement mechanisms that were agreed through Ireland's social partnership procedures and intended to counteract exploitation (ICTU 2006: 3).

---

3   While the Irish trade union movement did not oppose the decision to allow EU8 citizens access to the Irish labour market, ICTU has claimed that it was not consulted to any great extent and that the decision was largely prompted by employer demands (Begg 2007). The situation differed in 2006 in relation to the accession of Romania and Bulgaria, with ICTU making a comprehensive submission to government setting out its views (ICTU 2006).

The union movements in both countries have adopted an inclusive and 'rights-based' approach to immigration and sought equal rights and entitlements for migrant workers. This position is grounded in fundamental trade union principles, as articulated in an ICTU policy document (2005), which states that 'the philosophy of trade unionism is that all people are born equal, are endowed with certain fundamental rights and that their labour cannot be treated as a mere commodity in the market system'. However, in pressing for equal rights and entitlements, trade unions have also been concerned to ensure that migration does not lead to indigenous workers' pay and conditions being undermined.

In both Ireland and the United Kingdom, the large increase in migrant workers has led to an increased trade union concern with the needs of 'vulnerable' workers and efforts to improve the support and protection available to them. Interventions have been made via various policy channels and opportunities for social dialogue. From 1987, the Irish trade union movement operated within a corporatist political model, based in part on the German example and characterised by social partnership involving the government, unions and employers and, to a lesser extent, other interest groups.[4] This arrangement provided trade unions with substantial influence over legislative and policymaking processes and allowed the unions to push for policies to help vulnerable workers, including migrant workers.[5] In 2006, following two high profile cases of exploitation of migrant workers, substantial legislative provision was made to improve protection for migrant workers. This occurred under the *Towards 2016* social partnership agreement and was seen by the trade union movement as a groundbreaking development in their effectiveness within social partnership,[6] incorporating government commitments to a robust legislative framework, higher standards of employment protection and a new designated enforcement agency, the National Employment Rights Authority (NERA).

Similarly, the increased presence of migrant workers in the United Kingdom has encouraged the TUC and its affiliated trade unions to press for greater protection for vulnerable workers. Following the deaths of 18 Chinese migrant workers in 2004, the government introduced a new body – the Gangmasters Licensing Authority (GLA) – to regulate labour suppliers in the shellfish, agriculture and food processing sectors. While ostensibly a government measure, the proposal to establish a regulatory body had already been put forward by a

---

4   Social partnership was initiated by the Fianna Fail government in 1987 with the Programme for National Recovery, an initiative that was intended to help Ireland escape from recession.

5   The position of the trade union movement in the power structure has changed somewhat in recent times with the failure of the social partners to reach agreement in 2009, followed by the cutting of public sector wages. Social partnership has now been all but formally abandoned as a decision-making model.

6   David Begg of the Irish Congress of Trade Unions (ICTU) described it as 'the single biggest leap forward in social policy initiated in Ireland' (2007).

Labour MP[7] sponsored by the Transport & General Workers' Union. Trade unions are represented on the GLA's board and are also represented on the government's Illegal Working Group (IWG), a consultative forum established by the Home Office. The TUC has used its presence on the IWG as an opportunity to voice its concerns with a number of the government's policies. According to the TUC, the WRS's registration fee and the bureaucracy associated with the WRS created disincentives for workers to register and drove many into the informal economy. It has been alleged that the ongoing restrictions relating to EU2 workers have had a similar effect. While Romanian and Bulgarian workers are free to enter the United Kingdom to work on a self-employed basis, it is likely that many of those who enter the United Kingdom as 'self-employed' are in fact employees working for 'rogue employers' (TUC 2008: 53), a problem that is particularly evident in the construction sector (see Bettin in this volume, Table 2.3).

Further criticisms of the WRS were made by the TUC's Commission on Vulnerable Employment (CoVE), which was launched in May 2007 with a remit to collect evidence and make policy recommendations in respect of vulnerable workers, including migrant workers (TUC 2008: 53). The CoVE report called for the WRS to be abolished and for Bulgarian and Romanian workers to receive the same treatment as other EU workers 'unless a strong case can be made for differential treatment' (TUC 2008: 54). It also called upon the government to extend employment rights protection to undocumented workers and highlighted the weak and fragmented nature of the United Kingdom's labour inspection system.[8] In response to the last issue, the government established a Fair Employment Enforcement Board (FEEB) to promote collaboration between the various bodies with responsibilities relating to labour inspection.

4. Recruiting and Organising Migrant Workers

Difficulties Encountered by Trade Unions

Migrant workers are among the most vulnerable workers in the labour market and studies have drawn attention to a variety of abuses by firms and employment agencies. These have included inadequate, unsafe and over-crowded accommodation, underpayment (for example, paying less than the minimum wage), unlawful deductions from wages (charges for safety equipment, over-charging for

---

7   Jim Sheridan, MP.

8   In contrast to many other countries within and outside Europe, the UK lacks a unified labour inspectorate. Responsibilities for labour inspection are divided between the Gangmasters' Licensing Authority (which issues licences to labour suppliers in the agriculture, horticulture, shellfish gathering and food processing sectors), the Employment Agencies Standards Inspectorate, the Health and Safety Executive and HM Revenue and Customs, which is responsible for enforcing the national minimum wage.

accommodation), non-payment of holiday pay, excessively long hours of work, failures on the part of employers to provide wage slips, contracts of employment or information about employment rights, and even violent treatment of migrant workers (Anderson et al. 2007; Dench et al. 2006: 63–4; Fitzgerald 2006).

While abuses such as these suggest that migrant workers have a particularly pressing need for the protection that trade unions might provide, they are less likely than non-migrants to be trade union members. In Ireland, the rate of unionisation among migrant workers in 2005 was 14 per cent, compared to a density rate for Irish workers of 37 per cent (Barrett et al. 2005: 5). As can be seen from Figure 7.5, with the exception of a fall in 2007, the unionisation rate has remained stable. Irish nationals are more than twice as likely as their non-Irish counterparts to be union members, although it is necessary to bear in mind that migrants generally work in the least unionised sectors of the economy and that the most highly unionised sector is the public service sector, where few migrant workers are employed. Two studies carried out in 2006 and 2007 (Turner et al. 2008a and 2008b) found that the sector in which workers were employed was a more important determinant of union membership than workers' nationality (availability or access to unions being the fundamental determining factors).

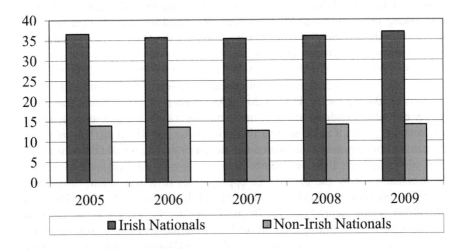

Figure 7.5   Irish trade union density, 2005–2009 (as a percentage of the labour force)

Source: CSO QNHS, Quarter 2, 2006; 2010.

While Ireland's Central Statistics Office (CSO) collects information on trade union membership levels among non-Irish nationals , the majority of individual trade unions do not. A survey of Irish trade unions by Hyland in 2010 found that 29 per cent of Irish unions   collect information.[9] SIPTU (Services, Industrial and Professional Trade Union), the largest Irish trade union and a generalist one representing both public and private sector workers, has been collecting such information for some time. In 2007, approximately 10 per cent of SIPTU's membership was composed of non-Irish nationals, who at that time comprised 15 per cent of the total workforce (CSO 2010; EIW 2007). By 2010, SIPTU's non-Irish national membership had dropped to 8 per cent, but the proportion of migrants in the workforce had also dropped (to 12.8 per cent). Among the other unions that collect information, the Irish Medical Organization (IMO) has a non-Irish national membership of 20 per cent; Mandate has levels between 11 and 15 per cent; the Irish Nurses and Midwives Organization (INMO) has 10 per cent; and Unison and the Guinness Staff Union have levels below 5 per cent. These figures provide an indication of the level of unionisation of non-Irish nationals in the Irish workforce but it is not possible to disaggregate them so as to establish the level of unionisation among EU10 citizens specifically.

Mirroring the situation in Ireland, employees of UK nationality are more likely than non-UK nationals to be members of a trade union. In 2008, the union density rate among the former was 28.2 per cent, compared to 21.1 per cent for non-nationals (although the difference becomes smaller the longer non-UK nationals have been in employment) (Barratt 2009: 3). There is evidence that migrant workers who have been trade union members in their country of origin do not tend to join UK unions once they have migrated. A survey of Polish and Lithuanian workers conducted for the TUC in 2007 (Anderson et al. 2007) found that while 13 per cent of respondents had been union members in their home country, only 3 per cent had joined a union since arriving in the United Kingdom. Nevertheless, 54 per cent of respondents indicated an interest in joining a trade union (op. cit. 22), which suggests that low membership among migrant workers may in part be accounted for by the absence of opportunities to join a union. Supporting evidence has been provided by a study of Polish workers in Ireland (Turner et al. 2008a), which contradicted the frequently posited theory that a major reason for low unionisation among migrant workers from former Eastern Bloc countries is a perception that unions are an arm of the state (Donaghey and Teague 2006). Turner et al. found that a majority of immigrants believed that unions are good for workers, can improve wages and conditions and can protect workers from being exploited (2008a).

Migrant workers are often employed in precarious jobs on the fringes of the labour market (TUC 2008) and according to one UK study (Anderson et al. 2006: 74) Central and Eastern European migrant workers employed in the agricultural,

---

9   It is important to note that many of the unions surveyed have insignificant numbers of migrant workers within their membership.

food processing and hospitality sectors are more likely than indigenous workers to work for temporary work agencies. The experiences and circumstances of migrant workers may lead them to be disinclined to join a union even where unions are present. Migrant workers may be particularly fearful of being victimized by employers or employment agencies, be suspicious of unions or simply view their period of employment as being too short to warrant joining a trade union (McKay 2006). Other potential obstacles include language barriers (Freeman 1978; Holgate 2005) and concerns relating to immigration status. However, evidence tends to suggest that it is industrial relations institutions and union attitudes and practices, rather than subjective factors related to migrant workers, that are the most important factors in the determination of union-migrant relations (Wrench 1992; Geary 2007).

Advice and Guidance

Trade unions have adopted a number of tactics in their efforts to support, recruit and organise migrant workers. Of the Irish trade unions who responded to the 2010 survey on Migrant Worker Membership, 50 per cent campaign regularly on migrant issues, while 40 per cent engage in a range of practices to encourage involvement, such as publishing materials in languages other than English, organising recruitment campaigns targeted at migrant workers and developing links with NGOs and community organisations that work with migrants. Twenty-five per cent of unions in Ireland now employ staff with special responsibility for migrant worker organisation and representation and 33 per cent have made links with unions in migrant workers' countries of origin. SIPTU, the largest and most diverse of the Irish trade unions, has led the way in policy development and support for migrant workers. It has also engaged in a process of transformation in recent times by adopting an organising approach in respect of migrant workers. It recently established a standalone strategic organising department which employs 20 full-time staff. It also translates its information leaflets on employment rights, union membership and related subjects into 14 different languages.

A common step has been to establish union-provided sources of advice and guidance. For a variety of reasons, including language difficulties, lack of information from employers and lack of knowledge about alternative sources of information, migrant workers are frequently poorly informed about their employment rights. Trade unions have sought to fill the knowledge gap and have also provided advice and guidance relating to issues that are not directly linked to workers' employment situation. A considerable amount of advice and guidance has been provided through web-based sources. In 2007 the TUC, in partnership with Citizens Advice and Solidarność, launched a website designed specifically for Polish workers. The website provides information (in Polish) about employment rights, as well as information concerning social issues such as housing and health. A further TUC website, 'Worksmart' provides a range of employment rights-related advice and includes information specifically aimed at migrant workers (although it is in English). SIPTU has a Polish language website, while the INMO nursing union supports a Filipino language section on its website. A number of other Irish unions provide targeted online information.

Several trade unions have established, or provided support to, advice and guidance centres. The Unite union, for example, has supported the South Tyrone Empowerment Project (STEP) in Northern Ireland. STEP is a community development organisation, which since 2001 has run a project designed to meet the needs of migrants and has encouraged them to become union members. Trade unions have also established their own community projects. Utilising funding from the Welsh Assembly, Unite has established advice centres in a number of Welsh towns, providing advice and guidance on a 'drop-in' basis and also providing migrant workers with opportunities to join English conversation classes. In addition to providing advice and guidance, the centres publicise the role of the union, make membership application forms available and provide migrant workers with opportunities to meet a union organiser. By building contacts with migrant workers, unions have uncovered instances of abuse that they have subsequently been able to challenge (for example, by taking an employer to court). They have also challenged boundaries that have hindered investigations of abuses by appropriate authorities. Unite, for instance, discovered that migrant workers who were working in Wales but living in England had reported a variety of concerns, such as withheld passports, to the police in England and that action had not subsequently been taken because of the geographical limit of the English police force's jurisdiction. Unite subsequently arranged a meeting with representatives of the police forces in England and Wales to raise awareness and encourage cross-border information flows and cooperation.

Recruiting through Language Tuition

In the United Kingdom, education and training have featured prominently among union strategies for engaging with migrant workers from the accession countries and a notable area of support in this context has been tuition in English for Speakers of Other Languages (ESOL). A number of UK unions have facilitated access to English classes and some have also attempted to link ESOL provision to their recruitment and organising activities, although these attempts are recent in origin and are at an embryonic stage of development (Heyes 2009b.). There has been significantly less emphasis on language training as a strategy for engagement within Irish trade unions, although lack of language proficiency has been identified as a barrier to employment and a contributing cause of vulnerability to exploitation. Provision was negotiated under *Towards 2016* for a very substantial increase in the numbers of language support teachers in the education system as a general integration measure.[10] However, only three Irish unions (SIPTU,

---

10   The recession has impacted on the implementation of this provision and the number of language support teachers is now being reduced.

MANDATE and the Bakers, Food and Allied Workers Union) have engaged in language training as a measure to increase the involvement of migrant workers. Of these unions, SIPTU, the largest of Ireland's trade unions, has an active English Literacy Scheme, which is available to SIPTU members and is operated from its head office in Dublin. This programme began in 1990 as a literacy scheme for Irish members but now primarily provides English language training to members whose first language is not English. This course has been of considerable value as ESOL training is otherwise available only at a cost through state schools or private English language schools. As a spin-off from the Basic English Scheme, the Irish Trade Union Trust (SIPTU's social solidarity service) has devised a workplace literacy programme, which has been successfully rolled out in two hospitals with a view to developing similar schemes in other places. SIPTU also assists with sourcing interpreters and translators where required (SIPTU 2003) and organises diversity training and awareness-raising for its wider membership. While the Head Office scheme has been running for ten years, the others are at a very embryonic stage of development.

Similar projects developed by UK unions have frequently been government-funded via the Regional Development Agencies, (which are due to be abolished as a consequence of cuts in government spending) or the Union Learning Fund and have often involved the creation of learning centres, either at workplaces or within communal facilities. In practice, learning centres have tended to function as advice and guidance centres (and vice versa) and have provided trade unions with opportunities to recruit migrant workers. Union Learning Representatives (ULR) have played an important role in this regard in that they have helped to organise courses for migrant workers and encouraged them to become union members. Furthermore, learning centres have provided unions with opportunities to encourage migrant workers to become ULRs and thus become more involved in their union.

Many of these initiatives have met with considerable success. Following the creation of a learning centre at a branch of the supermarket retailer ASDA in the south of England, the shop workers' union USDAW experienced an increase in union membership from 35 per cent to 95 per cent of the relevant bargaining unit. All of the Polish migrant workers employed at the branch joined the union and three subsequently became ULRs. ESOL classes organised by the GMB union's southern region also met with success in recruitment terms. While access to ESOL classes was not conditional on workers joining the GMB, more than 500 of the 600–700 migrant workers who had taken ESOL classes organised by the union in Southampton up until March 2008 had joined the GMB. Similarly, ESOL provision organised by the Community union in the South West of England resulted in the recruitment of a substantial number of migrant workers (for a full discussion, see Heyes 2009b).

ESOL classes have provided opportunities for union officers to talk with migrant workers, discuss their concerns with them and explain the functions of trade unions, the areas in which they can provide support and the benefits of union membership. Unions have encouraged tutors to run ESOL classes devoted to discussions on trade unions and have also developed learning materials that contain a union learning emphasis. The Community union's South West region, for example, has developed a DVD explaining its activities, with the intention of using this resource during class sessions devoted to trade unionism. The construction workers' union, UCATT, has developed a migrant workers' induction pack, which has been translated into Polish and is designed to encourage workers to engage in ESOL, while providing a work-based context for learning. Thus, numeracy activities are linked to understanding pay slips, while literacy encompasses being able to understand statements of employment particulars (that is, written statements that set out the principal terms of employment) and employment contracts. The inductions, which are conducted by ULRs, have been delivered on a modular basis during lunchtimes or weekends, and also as formal courses:

> It's just a useful tool that provides them [migrant workers] with, we would hope, the facility to be able to legitimately challenge from an informed perspective anything that they are unnerved about in terms of an employer's activity. (UCATT representative)

Many of the advice and guidance and learning projects developed by trade unions have involved project workers, who have typically been migrant workers themselves. The first point of contact for migrant workers seeking advice and support has therefore often been someone with whom they have something important in common and who may also share the same nationality and first language. This has proved important in terms of establishing trust and the credibility of trade unions in the eyes of the migrant workers.

Partnership and Community Links

In Ireland, the ICTU and many of its constituent unions have undertaken successful initiatives with partnership bodies and NGOs to support migrant workers. ICTU was a partner in the Anti-Racist Workplace initiative, a social partnership public awareness raising initiative which ran from 2000 to 2007[11] and which also involved the Irish Business and Employers' Confederation (IBEC), the Construction Industry Federation (CIF), Chambers Ireland, the Small Firms Association, the Department of Justice, Equality and Law Reform and the Equality Authority. Participants in the initiative committed themselves to working in partnership 'to promote anti-racist workplaces ... and within their own sphere of influence to promote a positive approach to diversity and interculturalism' (EEA, 2005). ICTU also has a North-South Anti-Racist Taskforce and a trade union advisory group on immigration (ICTU 2005; Fulton 2003) and has engaged with employer

---

11   In 2008, it was replaced by a government-sponsored Action Strategy for Integrated Workplaces.

organisations to draw up guidelines for the employment of migrant workers. SIPTU, the largest affiliated union, has worked with MRCI in seeking protection for domestic workers. This joint activity resulted in the introduction in 2007 of a Department of Enterprise, Trade and Employment Code of Practice, which sets out minimum standards for the employment of domestic workers and is supported by ICTU and IBEC. More recently a number of ICTU unions and non-governmental bodies have come together under the leadership of SIPTU to campaign for better pay and conditions and organising rights in both the hotel and catering and the contract cleaning sectors.

Trade unions in the United Kingdom have found that good relationships with NGOs and local community organisations can help them to establish trust and credibility. By engaging with community organisations, unions have also been able to contact workers who would otherwise have been difficult to reach. In its efforts to support migrant workers, the Community union's South West of England region forged links with the Polish Federation in London and locally with Polski Bristol, a Polish community association with links to the church. In addition to working in factories, many migrants in the region work in the agricultural sector and are geographically dispersed.

> I couldn't see all the cauliflower pickers and cherry pickers, but what I could do was connect to the associations like Polski Bristol. *They* would bring the people in; it didn't matter where they worked. And that was the one key thing that I found was successful. (Regional education officer, Community union)

With the support of the TUC, Community was then able to run various advice and guidance sessions, which were held in local churches.

Similarly, UCATT officials have identified links with community groups as an important prerequisite for maintaining contact with migrant workers in the construction sector. In addition to moving frequently between construction sites, many migrant workers also change their place of residence (for example, because the building site is in a different part of the country) and may even lose their accommodation altogether if they lose their job. Maintaining links with community organisations has helped the union to maintain its connection with a largely transient workforce.

Organising

While access to advice and guidance and ESOL provision facilitated by trade unions is often not conditional on migrant workers joining a trade union, recruitment is clearly an important objective for trade unions. Moreover, many unions are keen to ensure that migrant workers are able to develop self-sustaining workplace organisations, which is a particular concern where workplaces have not previously been unionised. While some unions, such as UCATT, regard both community and workplace engagement as essential to their organising activities, others have preferred to focus on the latter in the belief that this is where unions can have the most impact. USDAW, for example, has concentrated its efforts on organising migrants in workplaces that are already organised. In addition to recruiting migrant workers as members, it has sought to negotiate agreements with employers in relation to matters such as induction procedures. Other unions have similarly sought to encourage employers to take heed of the needs of migrant workers, particularly those who are supplied through an employment agency. Unite has developed a strong presence in meat factories and has attempted to force major supermarkets to clamp down on unfair treatment of migrant workers by their suppliers. In July 2009, Unite tabled a resolution at the AGM of Tesco, claiming that the supermarket chain had failed to meet its own ethical standards[12] by failing to prevent unfair treatment of migrant workers being supplied to meat factories by employment agencies.

An important element in unions' organising campaigns has been the recruitment of migrant workers as activists. In 2005, SIPTU appointed its first two non-Irish specialist organisers, who had command of a number of languages , including Polish, Russian and Lithuanian. These appointments were considered crucial in building contacts with migrant workers through social networks, as well as through workplaces. Other unions, such as the GMB's Midlands region, have trained migrant workers to act as specialist organisers who are able to visit workplaces and discuss migrant workers' concerns with them. A typical 'next step' is to encourage migrant workers to become union activists.

SIPTU has been active in recruiting and organising migrant workers in a number of industries. In 2006 it formed a special group of full-time organisers to coordinate the union's efforts to improve pay and working conditions in the mushroom industry, which was notorious for exploitative practices (Turner et al. 2008a). Subsequently, the union embarked on a collaborative project with the MRCI and ran a very successful information, recruitment and lobbying campaign in the sector. During the early stages of the campaign some claimed that it would not result in substantially increased membership because (a) SIPTU did not devote sufficient resources to support meaningful recruitment and organising at local level and (b) it continued to focus primarily on effecting change and improving conditions through negotiation and lobbying of state agencies, government and employers' organisations (Allen 2009; Arqueros-Fernandez 2009). In fact, the joint campaign was ultimately very successful. It attracted the support of the Irish

---

12   Tesco is a member of the Ethical Trade Initiative (ETI), a campaigning group composed of employers, trade unions and voluntary groups. The ETI has developed a base code of minimum labour standards and firms who are ETI members are expected to insist that their suppliers respect the base code. Unite's resolution, which required the backing of 75 per cent of shareholders in order to be accepted, was not carried. However, 11 per cent of shareholders backed the resolution, while a further 7 per cent abstained (http://www. guardian.co.uk/business/2009/jul/03/tesco-trade-unions-workers-rights?INTCMP=SRCH. Accessed 8 March 2011).

Farmers' Association (IFA) which was unhappy at the damage being done to the industry through the exploitative practices of some firms. The campaign resulted in the creation of a Joint Labour Committee (JLC) for the mushroom industry, SIPTU and MRCI being given access to workers in mushroom farms all over the country, the recruitment by SIPTU of 1,700 mushroom farm workers and the almost total eradication of employment rights abuses in the sector.

The Mushroom industry campaign has been used by SIPTU as a model of good practice and has formed the basis of an approach to be rolled out more widely. In June 2007 it launched its 'Justice for Agency Workers' campaign to fight for regulation of the area. It is also currently engaged in a campaign similar to the Mushroom industry campaign in the contract cleaning and in the hotel and catering sector, both of which have a majority non-Irish workforce. While these campaigns are SIPTU initiatives, they are based on a community unionism model, with the SIPTU organisers working closely with migrant workers on the ground and identifying and developing leaders at local level.

The Irish Nurses and Midwives Organizations (INMO) has also been proactive in its approach to this section of its membership. In 2002, it established the Overseas Nurses Section in an effort to address a number of challenges experienced by migrant nurses, including language difficulties, lack of access to promotion and tension between newly qualified Irish graduates and migrant nurses.[13] It has a full-time non-Irish organiser and one migrant executive member. Its mission is 'to support the integration of overseas nurses into the Irish health service, thus facilitating social, cultural and political integration and to ensure equality of treatment and industrial harmony'. It has four elected officers. The INMO overseas nurses section won a prestigious MAMA Award (Metro Eireann Media and Multicultural Award) in 2006 in recognition of the work which it had done to successfully integrate overseas nurses and midwives into the Irish health care system. The majority of migrant workers in the sector are drawn from outside Europe, primarily the Philippines.

A small number of UK trade unions have attempted to build self-sufficient organisations of migrant workers by establishing separate migrant workers' branches. Perhaps the most notable example to date is that of the GMB South-West region, which has established a separate migrant workers' branch with the aim of facilitating the integration of migrant workers into the union. The aim was to develop the self-confidence, knowledge, skills and collective identity of the union's migrant worker members, many of whom had had little direct experience of trade unionism prior to working in the United Kingdom. The branch was regarded by union officers as a key step in a transitional process that would lead to migrant workers forging links with indigenous union members and activists and becoming fully integrated into the union. The GMB's example encouraged

---

13   There was also an issue around the dynamic of 'high density employment areas'. For example, in 2008, 80 per cent of the nurses working at the Mater hospital in Dublin were migrant workers (Doran 2008).

Community to develop its own organising strategy, which similarly included the creation of a migrant workers' branch. The decision to create a separate branch was also seen as a means of accessing national union resources and sustaining the regional union's engagement with migrant workers in the longer term. Its activities up until that point had been supported by the Union Learning Fund, which had provided finance to support ESOL classes for migrant workers. The ESOL project's liaison officer became the branch secretary, a move that was regarded as helping to further strengthen the link between the regional union's education and organising activities.

International Links

Cross-border migration has provided a context for the development of new links between UK and European trade unions. The TUC and national trade unions in the United Kingdom have attempted to build support for migrants by cooperating with trade unions in 'sending countries', especially Poland. The TUC facilitated the involvement of a Polish organiser from Solidarność, who worked with TUC affiliates in the North-West of England and helped them to recruit Polish migrant workers. By working with the organiser, USDAW discovered that its literature was translated into an insufficient number of CEE languages. In response, USDAW translated its literature into 35 languages. The construction sector union UCATT has similarly worked with a national organiser from Solidarność and this has been an important element in the success of its recruitment efforts in the North-East of England (Fitzgerald 2006). In addition, in 2008 the TUC, Solidarność and the All Polish Trade Unions Alliance union federation signed a protocol that committed them to encouraging UK and Polish workers to join a union in whichever country they worked (Fitzgerald and Hardy 2010: 144). Some TUC affiliates have also experimented with, or considered experimenting with, international links involving trade unions in EU accession countries (particularly Poland), although views about the potential benefits have been mixed. While the Bakers, Food and Allied Workers Union (BFAWU), for example, has cooperated with Solidarność in respect of information dissemination, the GMB has remained sceptical about Solidarność's influence over young Polish workers and the benefits of joint membership agreements (op cit.: 144).

In Ireland, ICTU has forged links with confederations across Europe and has been represented on the ETUC Migration Working Group since 2007. ICTU and SIPTU have also been participants in the ETUC Workplace Europe Project which commenced in 2009 with the aim of developing methods to inform and train trade union representatives to support and organise transnational 'mobile' workers. The project concluded in September 2010 with the publication of a report (forthcoming).

SIPTU has also developed contacts with trade union movements in Poland, Latvia and Lithuania, with the aim of raising awareness about employment rights and trade unions among nationals from those countries who are considering moving to Ireland. In December 2005, SIPTU entered into a partnership agreement with the Wielkopolski Region of Solidarność to establish a project to inform Polish workers of their rights when working in Ireland or other EU states. Subsequently, the two unions signed a formal agreement in which they committed themselves to persuading and facilitating workers from each country to become trade union members when at work in the other country (this to include mutual recognition of union membership cards, provision of pro-union information and so on) and to provide mutual support in dealing with governments, employer organisations and other trade unions (Krings 2009). They also agreed to 'cooperate to ensure that they effectively counteract attempts to use competition between workers to drive down levels of pay and working conditions' (SIPTU 2007).

Economic Crisis and Emerging Tensions

While a number of unions have been successful in recruiting and organising migrant workers, they have also had to address tensions between migrant workers and indigenous workers. The underlying source of these tensions is the potential for employers to create divisions in the workforce by employing migrant workers over indigenous workers or hiring them on inferior pay and conditions. Allegations that some employers have hired migrant workers in preference to indigenous workers, whether well-founded or not, have led to social unrest and have been exploited by groups on the far-right of the political spectrum (the British National Party and the English Defence League in the case of the United Kingdom). The tensions intensified after the start of the economic crisis in 2008 and became particularly apparent in the United Kingdom's engineering construction industry in 2009. At the start of the year, wildcat strikes occurred in response to a decision by Total to hire Italian and Portuguese contractors at its Lindsey refinery. This action was perceived by local UK workers to be a deliberate instance of an employer substituting migrant workers for native workers. In February 2009, it was revealed that the power firm Alstom was paying some of its Polish construction workers £4.50 an hour less than British workers (Guardian, 4 September 2009). In May, unofficial strike action took place against Hertel UK, a construction contractor that was alleged to have employed 40 Polish construction workers in contravention of a local agreement that required them to seek to hire workers from the local labour market (Financial Times, 21 May 2009). The company eventually agreed to replace the migrant workers with British workers. In an attempt to address the wider issue of alleged undercutting of pay agreements, national officers of the Unite trade union sought a national agreement that would allow the union to 'audit' workers on construction sites so as to ensure that agreed rates of pay were being paid. Matters came to a head in September 2009, when energy sector workers voted for industrial action in support of a number of demands, including an agreement that contractors pay agreed rates and the creation of a register of unemployed workers that employers would turn to when filling vacancies. The dispute was settled in November 2009, following a number of concessions by the employers.

5. Conclusion

The policies and practices adopted by the TUC, ICTU and their constituent trade unions in respect of migrant workers have had much in common. The Irish and UK trade union movements have adopted an inclusive and rights based approach to immigration and have sought equal rights and entitlements for migrant workers under the law, regardless of their immigration status or the legality of their employment. However, the Irish trade union movement has had greater success than the UK movement in pressing for government policies that support migrant workers. UK unions have focused on recruiting and organising within workplaces and communities but have had relatively little influence on government policy. Irish trade unions, by contrast, have been able to influence government policy on the introduction and implementation of legislation to protect migrant workers. Their ability to do so reflects the institutionalised social partnership that characterised Irish industrial relations since 1987. This arrangement provided Irish trade unions with substantial influence over legislative and policymaking processes and thus enabled the trade union movement to push for legislative provisions to support migrant workers. However, social partnership has come under increasing pressure since the beginning of the economic downturn, with employers' organisations, political parties and economic commentators opposing its continuation.

In both countries, there has been a recognition that traditional servicing approaches are insufficient to reach the majority of migrant workers or to serve their particular needs. The fact that large numbers of migrant workers are engaged in atypical employment, recruited through employment agencies, subcontracted or treated by employers as 'self-employed' has encouraged a reconsideration of the traditional workplace-based, egalitarian service model. There is a growing awareness that no one measure in itself is sufficient to ensure that migrant workers are accorded their employment entitlements and that a combination of active unionisation, regulation and enforcement offer the best prospect for ensuring that migrant workers are protected from abuses (Donaghey and Teague 2006; Turner et al. 2008b). Many unions in Ireland and the United Kingdom have thus begun to move towards a more proactive organising approach that has, in some cases, involved creating links (or building upon established links) with community groups, NGOs and education providers. The attention given to migrant workers has also encouraged a greater concern with other groups of vulnerable workers, as reflected in the TUC's creation of a Commission on Vulnerable Employment (CoVE).

Though much has been achieved, questions remain concerning the sustainability and longer-term implications of some of the initiatives that have been taken. Many of the projects that have been established to assist migrant workers have been highly resource-intensive and reliant on funding, much of which has come directly or indirectly from the government. Some projects have placed considerable emphasis on organising as a means of sustaining migrant union membership and activism beyond project funding periods. In the case of ICTU and its constituent unions, funding for migrant worker integration and organisational projects has already fallen victim to austerity measures with cuts in funding from both the government department with responsibility for integration and from the Employment Equality Authority. It is less clear what the future situation is likely to be in the United Kingdom. While the government has decided that the Union Learning Fund will be retained for the time being, Regional Development Agencies, which have also acted as providers of support, are due to be abolished by 2012 as a result of the government's austerity measures.

There is also an unresolved issue concerning how best to manage the inevitable tensions within trade unions. Not all union members are happy with what they may perceive to be an unwarranted prioritisation of the needs of migrant workers and it has been suggested that the TUC's shift in focus from migrant workers to vulnerable workers was partly inspired by a concern to address this perception (Fitzgerald and Hardy 2010: 137). There are also questions about how best to represent the interests of migrant workers within union branches. Experimentation with migrant worker branches has occurred in some unions. These branches have been regarded as confidence-building exercises and a prelude to integration of migrant workers into ordinary branch structures. The hope is that migrant workers' branches will provide migrant workers with an opportunity to acquire experience, develop self-confidence and shape their own agendas without having to contend with established interests and structures that may serve to marginalise them. On the other hand, there is a risk that the creation of separate migrant workers' branches will encourage real or perceived separatism, thereby reinforcing divisions between union members. Furthermore, unions will also have to confront the question of how the agendas developed within migrant workers' branches should best be pursued and linked to the concerns of the wider membership.

Finally, there are limits to what trade unions can achieve in the absence of a supportive regulatory environment. Trade unions have been highly vocal in raising concerns about the weakness of labour inspection arrangements, the inadequate enforcement of employment rights and the ways in which these deficiencies have exacerbated the problems experienced by migrant workers and other vulnerable groups in the labour market. While labour inspection and the regulation of labour suppliers have been strengthened in both Ireland and the United Kingdom, unions have thus far been unsuccessful in persuading the Irish and UK governments to embrace a 'rights-based' policy that would decouple the issue of employment rights from the legality of a worker's employment. In both countries, government policy continues to militate against efforts to address the vulnerability of many migrant workers.

Bibliography

Allen, K. (2007) 'Neo-liberalism and Immigration', in Fanning, B. (ed.), *Immigration and Social Change in Ireland*, Manchester: Manchester University Press.

Anderson, B., B. Ruhs and S. Spencer (2006) *Fair Enough? Central and East European Migrants in Low-Wage Employment in the UK*. Oxford: Centre on Migration, Policy and Society, University of Oxford.

Anderson, B., N. Clark and V. Parutis (2007) *New EU Members? Migrant Workers' Challenges and Opportunities to UK Trade Unions: a Polish and Lithuanian Case Study*. London: TUC.

Arqueros-Fernández, F. (2009) 'Contrasts and Contradictions in Union Organizing: The Irish Mushroom Industry', in Gall, G. (ed.), *The Future of Union Organizing: Building for Tomorrow*, Basingstoke: Palgrave Macmillan.

Barratt, C. (2009) *Trade Union Membership 2008*. London: Department for Business, Enterprise and Regulatory Reform. Available at: < http://stats.berr. gov.uk/UKSA/tu/tum2008.pdf>

Barrett, A., A. Bergin and D. Duffy (2005) *The Labour Market Characteristics and Labour Market Impacts of Immigrants in Ireland*, Discussion Paper No. 1553, Institute for the Study of Labour (IZA).

Barrett, A. and D. Duffy (2007) *Are Ireland's Immigrants Integrating into its Labour Market?* Discussion Paper No. 2838, Institute for the Study of Labour (IZA).

Barrett, A. and E. Kelly (2008) *The Economic and Social Review*, 39, 3: 191–205.

Begg, D. (2007) 'Immigration, Integration and Cultural Identity', *Translocations*, 2, 1: 181–9. Available at: www.translocations.ie.

CSO (2006) *Quarterly National Household Survey*, Quarter 2 2005, Central Statistics Office.

CSO (2008) *Quarterly National Household Survey*, Quarter 2 2007, Central Statistics Office.

CSO (2008) *Quarterly National Household Survey*, Union Membership, Quarter 2 2007, Central Statistics Office.

CSO (2009) *Quarterly National Household Survey*, Quarter 2 2008, Central Statistics Office.

CSO (2010) *Quarterly National Household Survey*, Union Membership, Q2 2009, Central Statistics Office.

Dench, S., J. Hurtsfield, D. Hill and K. Akroyd (2006) *Employers' Use of Migrant Labour: Main Report*. London: Home Office.

Department of Social Protection (2010) Habitual Residence Condition – Guidelines for Deciding Officers on the determination of Habitual Residence. Available at: www.welfare.ie/EN/OperationalGuidelines/pages/habres.aspx#leg.

Donaghey, J. and P. Teague (2006) 'The Free Movement of Workers and Social Europe: Maintaining the European Ideal', *Industrial Relations Journal*, 37, 6: 652–66.

Doran, L. (2008) 'The INO and Integration', in *The Challenges of Integration in Post-Celtic Tiger Ireland*, October 2008, Dublin: Immigrant Council of Ireland.

Doyle, N., G. Hughes and E. Wadensjö (2006) *Freedom of Movement for Workers from Central and Eastern Europe: Experiences in Ireland and Sweden*, Stockholm: Swedish Institute for European Policy Studies.

Employment Equality Authority (2005) *Anti-Racism in the Workplace Resource Pack*, Dublin: EEA.

European Intercultural Workplace (EIW) (2007*) National Report for Ireland.* Available at: www.dcu.ie/eiw/.

ETUC (forthcoming) *Workplace Europe: Trade Unions Supporting Mobile and Migrant Workers* Brussels: ETUC.

Fitzgerald, I. (2006) *Organising Migrant Workers in Construction: Evidence from the North East of England.* London: TUC.

Fitzgerald, I. (2007) *A Moving Target: The Informational Needs of Polish Migrant Workers in Yorkshire and the Humber.* Northumbria University.

Fitzgerald, I. and J. Hardy (2010) '"Thinking outside the Box?" Trade Union Organizing Strategies and Polish Migrant Workers in the United Kingdom', *British Journal of Industrial Relations*, 48, 1: 131–50.

Freeman, G. (1978) 'Immigrant Labour and Working Class Politics: The French and British Experience', *Comparative Politics*, 11, 1: 25 41, reproduced in M. Messina and G. Lahav (eds), *The Migration Reader: Exploring Politics and Policies.* London: Lynne Rienner.

Fulton, L. (2003) *Migrant and Ethnic Minority Workers: Challenging Trade Unions.* ETUC.

Geary, J. (2007) 'Employee Voice in the Irish Workplace: Status and Prospect', in Freeman, R. Boxall, P. and Haynes, P. (eds), *What Workers Say: Employee Voice in the Anglo-American Workplace*, New York: ILR Press.

Hardy, J. and C. Clark (2005), 'EU Enlargement, Workers and Migration: Implications for Trade Unions in the UK and Poland'. Paper given at the Global Unions Research Network International Workshop *'Trade Unions, Globalization and Development – Strengthening Rights and Capabilities of Workers'*, Novo Hamborgo, Brazil, January 2005. Available at: http://www.tuc.org.uk/international/tuc-9472-f0.pdf. Accessed 18th April 2008.

Heyes, J. (2009a) 'EU Labour Migration: Government and Social Partner Policies in the UK', in Galgóczi, B., Leschke, J. and Watt, A. (eds), *EU Labour Mobility Since Enlargement: Trends, Impacts and Policies.* Aldershot: Ashgate.

Heyes, J. (2009b) 'Recruiting and Organising Migrant Workers Through Education and Training: A Comparison of Community and the GMB', *Industrial Relations Journal.* 40, 3: 182–97.

ICTU (2005) *Migration Policy and the Rights of Workers*, Dublin: ICTU.

ICTU (2006) *Observations and Recommendations on the Application of Transitional Measures on the Accession of Bulgaria and Romania to the EU on 1st January 2007*, Dublin: ICTU.

IOM (2006) (International Organisation for Migration) *Managing Migration in Ireland: a Social and Economic Analysis,* Dublin: National Economic and Social Council.

Krings, T. (2009) A Race to the Bottom? Trade Unions, EU Enlargement and the Free Movement of Labour, *European Journal of Industrial Relations*, 15, 1: 49–69.

McKay, S. (2006), 'Unions and Migrants', Union Ideas Network. Available at: http://uin.org.uk/index.php?option=com_content&task=view&id=81).

Mac Éinrí, P. (2005) 'Ireland: Country Report', in Niessen, J., Schibel, Y. and Thompson, C. (eds), *Current Immigration Debates in Europe*. Brussels: Migration Policy Group.

Mac Éinrí, P. (2008) *Responding to the Challenges of Migration in Ireland*, Policy Paper, Migration Studies Unit, UCC, Cork.

Milkman, R. (2006) *L.A. Story: Immigrant Workers and the Future of the U.S. Labour Movement*, New York: Russell Sage Foundation.

MRCI (2004) *Private Homes: A Public Concern, the Experience of Twenty Migrant Women Employed in the Private Home in Ireland*: Migrant Rights Centre Ireland.

Office for National Statistics (ONS) (2010) *Migration Statistics Quarterly Report.* No 6: 26 August 2010. Available at: http://www.statistics.gov.uk/pdfdir/mig0810.pdf.

Ruhs, M. (2005) *Managing the Immigration and Employment of Non-EU Nationals in Ireland,* Dublin: The Policy Institute, Trinity College.

SIPTU (2003) *Representing Immigrant Workers – A Guide for Union Representatives,* Dublin.

SIPTU (2007) *SIPTU and Solidarność co-operation agreement.* Available at: www.siptu.ie/campaigns/EXPLOITATIONandDISPLACEMENT/Name,9457,en.html.

SIPTU (2007) *Justice for Agency Workers*. Available at: www.siptu.ie/agency/JusticeforAgencyWorkers/FileDownload,10079,en.pdf.

TUC (2008) *Hard Work, Hidden Lives.* London: TUC.

Turner, T., D. D'Art and C. Cross (2008a) 'Polish Workers in Ireland: A Contented Proletariat?', *Labour Studies Journal*, 34, 1: 112–16.

Turner, T., D. D'Art and M. O'Sullivan (2008b) 'Union Availability, Union Membership and Immigrant Workers', *Employee Relations*, 30, 5: 479–93.

Wrench, J. (2004) 'Trade Union Responses to Immigrants and Ethnic Inequality in Denmark and the UK: The Context of Consensus and Conflict', *European Journal of Industrial Relations*, 10, 1: 7–30.

Chapter 8

Migrant Workers and Wage-setting Institutions: Experiences from Germany, Norway, Switzerland and the United Kingdom

Line Eldring and Thorsten Schulten

1. Introduction

Are minimal restrictions on cross-border labour mobility and maximum security of workers' rights incompatible? Since the EU enlargement in 2004, there have been widespread fears that increasing East–West migration would put wages and labour standards in the receiving countries under massive pressure. Against the background of persistently high wage differences between Western and Eastern Europe, there might be a strong incentive for companies to use migrant workers who are willing to work under inferior conditions (Schulten 2011a). Moreover, in recent years national regulatory systems have been challenged by the European Court of Justice (ECJ) rulings in cases such as *Laval*, *Viking Line*, *Rüffert* and *Luxembourg*, tending to declare strong national wage regulation as contradicting the fundamental economic freedoms of services and establishment laid down in the EU Treaty (Cremers 2010; Dølvik and Visser 2009; Woolfson et al. 2010).

What has been the impact of migration on wages in the target countries, especially since EU enlargement? In what follows we will discuss this question in two steps. First, we will critically evaluate the existing empirical literature on the issue. Here our hypothesis is that most of the literature which is dominated by econometric studies at macro-level tends to underestimate the negative wage effects of migration which are very much concentrated in certain sectors and professions. Moreover, most of the econometric studies completely ignore the institutional and regulatory factors of wage formation.

However, the latter seem to be crucial in order to understand the political dynamics of migration and its impact on wages. Here the main question concerns the extent to which national systems of wage formation are able to protect existing wage standards for both native and migrant workers. It is exactly the interrelation between wage-setting institutions and migration which are at the core of our interest.

In the second and main part of this chapter we will therefore discuss this interrelation by analysing recent developments in four European countries: Germany, Norway, Switzerland and the United Kingdom. Although Norway and Switzerland are not members of the EU, they have taken over large parts of EU legislation, including the principle of freedom of movement. Therefore, all countries have been affected by new waves of migration due to EU enlargement, although to somewhat different degrees as a result of different strategies regarding the opening up of their labour markets. The latter ranged from the United Kingdom, which opted for open borders from May 2004, to Germany, which did not lift its transitional restrictions until May 2011. On the other hand, the countries differ when it comes to national labour regulations and the extent to which wages are set by law and/or collective agreements. In all countries the experience of wage dumping through the exploitation of migrant workers has led to widespread debates on whether or not or to what extent national systems of wage formation have to be further developed.

2. The Impact of Migration on Wages – An Overview

At first glance, economic theory seems to confirm the widespread public opinion that labour migration would put significant pressure on both wages and employment in the target countries. Following standard neoclassical textbook models, an increase in the labour supply would lead either to falling wages or – if wage levels cannot be changed as a result of 'rigid' wage-setting institutions – to an increase in unemployment. Although from a different perspective, Marxist economic theory came to similar results as migrant workers are seen primarily as an 'industrial reserve army' which is used by capital to weaken trade union bargaining power in order to bring down wages.

However, taking a more differentiated approach the theoretical implications of migration on wages are far from clear (Brücker 2010). First of all, an increase in the labour supply through migrant workers implies that there is also an increase in demand, as migrant workers have to spend at least part of their salaries in the target countries, while some of the money they send to their home countries might contribute to increasing exports from the target countries. In any case, there will be some adjustments of capital to the increased labour supply in the form of new investments. Moreover, there seems to be strong evidence that at least in the long run the ratio between labour supply and capital stocks is relatively stable (ibid.). This would mean that if there is a negative impact on wages at all, it is only short-term, while in a long-term perspective an adjustment of capital stock would absorb the increased labour supply, implying higher than initial employment, at or close to the original wage level.

The impact of migration on wages also very much depends on the business cycle, as in a boom period the increase in the labour supply might be easily absorbed by the overall growth of economic activities. The latter has been the case, for example, in many western European countries since the EU Enlargement in 2004, at least until the recent economic crisis. Finally, there is also the question of whether migrant and native workers are substitutes or whether they are more complementary to the native workforce. If the latter is the case, the impact on wages is again rather uncertain, as the wages of some groups of workers might fall while the real incomes of others might rise.

As from a theoretical point of view there is no clear answer to the question concerning the wage effects of migration, it becomes very much an empirical question. The empirical literature on this issue is dominated by econometric studies which try to estimate the impact of migration on wages at the macroeconomic level. Despite some important methodological differences in the econometric modelling,[1] most empirical studies found that there is either no or only a minor wage effect of migration. According to Friedberg and Hunt (1995: 43) many older studies suggest 'that a 10 percent increase in the fraction of immigrants in the population reduced native wages by at most 1 percent'. This rule of a thumb has been confirmed by Longhi et al. (2008) and Brücker (2010) who evaluated the more recent literature (cf. also Galgóczi et al. 2009: 19ff.).

Some studies claim a somewhat more significant impact of migration on wages. One of the most prominent examples is the study by Borjas (2003) who found a much stronger negative wage effect according to which a 10 per cent increase in migrant workers would lead to a reduction of wages of between 3 and 4 per cent. However, as emphasised by Ottaviano and Peri (2011), studies with larger wage effects often treat migrant and native workers as perfect substitutes and do not take into account capital adjustments. If these assumptions were abandoned the wage effects would be much smaller (ibid., see also: Brücker 2010).

Regarding the new wave of migration caused by the EU enlargement in 2004 the wage effects seemed also to be fairly small. On behalf of the European Commission an international research consortium has analysed the impact of migration from the eight new East European member states (EU8) in the old EU member states (EU15) on various macroeconomic variables (Brücker et al. 2009: 70ff.). For the period 2004–2007 the study estimates that, on the EU15 average, wages declined slightly, by 0.09 per cent (Table 8.1). The wage effect has been somewhat higher in those countries which opened up their labour markets right after the EU enlargement in 2004. The strongest wage decline has been estimated for Ireland, at 1.61 per cent, followed by the United Kingdom, at 0.29 per cent and Sweden, at 0.06 per cent. In Germany, which restricted its labour market for migrant workers from the EU8 until May 2011, wages have been reduced by only 0.03 per cent. For all countries the study assumes that wage declines were short-term phenomena while in the long run there would be almost no wage effect due to adjustments of the capital stock.

---

1   For an overview on different methodological approaches see: Brückner (2010)

Table 8.1   Estimation of the impact of migration from EU8 countries on wages after EU enlargement, 2004–2007 (%)

	EU15	Ireland	United Kingdom	Sweden	Germany
Low-skilled					
Short-run	−0.10	−1.72	−0.35	−0.05	−0.03
Long-run	−0.01	−0.19	−0.07	0.01	0.00
Medium-skilled					
Short-run	−0.09	−1.84	−0.35	−0.05	−0.03
Long-run	−0.01	−0.23	−0.06	0.01	0.00
High-skilled					
Short-run	−0.07	−1.34	−0.19	−0.03	−0.03
Long-run	0.02	0.30	0.11	0.00	0.00
All					
Short-run	**−0.09**	**−1.61**	**−0.29**	**−0.08**	**−0.03**
Long-run	**0.00**	**0.00**	**0.00**	**0.02**	**0.00**
Change	0.36	4.87	1.28	0.38	0.10

Source: Brücker et al. (2009: 73).

Although from a macroeconomic perspective the wage effects of migration seem to be fairly limited, the picture might change if one looks from a more sectoral perspective. Migrant workers are usually concentrated in a few branches, such as construction and related trades, agriculture, cleaning services, hotels and restaurants, the care sector and some more labour-intensive and low-skilled manufacturing (Brücker et al. 2009: 152f.). There is a lot of anecdotal evidence from press reports or more qualitative studies that companies in these sectors exploit migrant workers to undermine existing wage standards (Hardy et al. 2010). However, there is still a lack of quantitative studies which systematically analyse the impact of migration on wages at sectoral level. There are only a few exceptions, for example, the study by Bratsberg and Raaum (2010) for the Norwegian construction industry. They found that if the proportion of migrant workers in construction increases by 10 per cent the wages of native workers fall by about 0.6 per cent, which is still fairly small.

The study by Bratsberg and Raaum (2010: 35) also figured out that the largest effects on wages have been among low- and semi-skilled workers. The latter has also been confirmed by other studies, such as Dustmann et al. (2008), who showed that for the United Kingdom a negative effect on wages of native workers can be found mainly in the lowest twentieth percentile of the wage scale. Moreover, the study on behalf of the European Commission on the impact of EU enlargement confirmed that in most EU15 countries, the negative wage impact is more pronounced for low-skilled workers (Brücker et al. 2009, see also Table 8.1).

A general problem with most studies on the impact of migration on wages is that they do not capture the effects of the posting of migrant workers, as this group tends not to be included in databases in the receiving countries. Posted workers constitute a large, and probably more or less permanent labour force in some sectors (construction), but there is a lack of data on both their numbers and their wage levels (Cremers 2011).

Finally, there are several studies which have identified a significant migrant/ native wage gap, underlining the strong overrepresentation of migrant workers in the low-wage sector (see also Tijdens and van Klaveren in this volume). Adsera and Chiswick (2007) analysed the differences between native and migrant workers' wages in the EU15 countries on the basis of the European Community Household Panel for the period 1994–2000. As an overall result the study states that on EU15 average a migrant worker at the time of arrival earns about 40 per cent less than a native worker. The wage gap becomes closer with length of stay, but migrants need on average between 18 and 19 years to get the same average salary as native workers (ibid: 514).

There is still a significant gap with regard to more comprehensive and updated figures on the migrant/native wage, since most countries do not monitor these data on a regular basis, as they do the gender wage gap. The OECD (2008) has collected some national data for nine OECD countries for the years 2005/2006 suggesting that – with the exception of Australia – migrant workers earn between 5 and 20 per cent less than natives (Table 8.2). In most countries the immigrant/ native wage gap is even larger for women than for men. Furthermore, there are significant wage differentials between the different groups of migrants, depending on their country of origin (ibid. 82).

Table 8.2   **Migrant/native wage gap, 2005/2006 (Migrant workers' median wage as a percentage of native workers' wages)**

	All	Men	Women
Australia	107	108	106
Canada	95	94	94
Portugal	94	100	96
Germany	93	100	87
Sweden	93	91	95
France	90	92	90
Switzerland	89	85	91
Netherlands	85	82	89
United States	79	73	84

Source: OECD (2008: 81).

Considering the distribution of wages among of migrant workers, there is strong evidence that a large proportion of them work in the low wage sector. Although the skill levels of migrant workers are usually the same or even higher than those of native workers, they often tend to accept jobs below their formal qualifications (see Bettin in this volume). The latter has been the case, in particular, for migrant workers from the EU8 countries since EU enlargement (Brücker et al. 2009: 153ff.).

Because econometric studies tend to research wage effects at macroeconomic level, the impact of migration seems to be systematically underestimated. Although the existing migrant/native wage gap does not automatically indicate a downward effect on native wages, it shows that pressure is most likely in the low paid sector. Moreover, there is little research which considers regulations and institutions on the labour market, such as the power of trade unions, collective bargaining, statutory minimum wages and so on (for an exception, see Lundborg 2006).

At first glance, the influence of wage-setting institutions seems to be rather obvious: More encompassing systems of wage formation tend to make it more difficult for companies to use migrant workers for the undermining of existing wage standards. Stronger unions with a more offensive strategy to organise migrant workers are better able to regulate migrant worker's wages. However, a strong inflow of migrant workers might also weaken trade unions' bargaining power and undermining the scope of traditional wage-setting institutions (Blanchflower and Shadforth 2009: 178f.). In the following we will focus on the role of wage-setting institutions in the regulation of migrant workers' wages by discussing the examples of Germany, Norway, Switzerland and the United Kingdom.

3. National Systems of Wage Regulation and Their Impact on Migrant Workers

3.1 Germany

Germany is one of the largest 'countries of immigration' with more than 16 million people (19 per cent of the population) having a migrant background and more than 7 million people (9 per cent of the population) having a foreign nationality (Statistisches Bundesamt 2010). The largest waves of migration into Germany took place during the late 1960s/early 1970s, as well as during the late 1980s/early 1990s. During the past decade, however, net migration into Germany was rather modest, reflecting a tightening of regulations on labour migration and asylum-seekers (Schneider 2009).

After the EU enlargement in 2004 Germany and Austria were the only countries that made use of the full transitional period and prolonged the restrictions on the freedom of movement for workers from EU8 countries until May 2011. Moreover, in a few sectors – such as construction, industrial cleaning and similar branches – the restrictions were even kept for posted workers. Since other countries – such as Ireland and the United Kingdom – had opened their labour markets right from the beginning, there was a significant re-composition of the preferred target countries. While in 2000 nearly 60 per cent of all migrants from EU8 countries lived in Germany, in 2010 only about 25 per cent did so (Baas and Brücker 2011).

The use of the transitional measures has been supported by almost all major political parties in Germany, as well as by the German trade unions (Fellmer and Kolb 2009; Krings 2009; Schulten 2011a). The prolongation of restrictions was justified on the grounds of the economic difficulties and comparatively high unemployment which existed in Germany at that time. Furthermore, there was a great fear that, because of the geographical proximity of and significant wage gap with the EU8 countries, Germany would continue to be the major target country for the new EU8 migrant workers. Finally, as emphasised by the trade unions, the liberalisation and deregulation of the German labour market had led to some key regulatory shortcomings that would have made it fairly easy for companies to use migrant workers to implement a strategy of wage dumping. The unions complained, in particular, about the lack of a general wage floor (Schulten 2011a).

While there has never been a national statutory minimum wage in Germany, the traditional form of wage formation through collective agreements has become much weaker in recent decades. On average, bargaining coverage has shown a continuous decline from about 80 per cent in the mid-1990s to about 60 per cent in 2010 (Bispinck et al. 2010). The decline has been even more pronounced in many private services sectors which account for the bulk of low paid workers. As a result, Germany has one of the fastest-growing low-wage sectors in Europe. In 2009, more than one-fifth of all workers received wages below the low-wage threshold of two-thirds of the median wage (Schulten 2011b).

As immigrant workers in Germany entered an increasingly deregulated labour market, there were widespread fears that existing wage standards would be undermined even further. Research has not confirmed these fears, however. At least in macroeconomic studies, migrants from EU8 countries are found to have had only a very small and fairly short-term negative impact on wages and employment, while in the long run there are no effects at all (Brücker 2010; Brücker and Jahn 2011). Although it is likely that the proportion of immigrants from EU8 countries will increase again after Germany finally opens its labour market in 2011, no dramatic wage effects are expected for the future (Baas and Brücker 2011).

In contrast to the macroeconomic analysis, there is at least anecdotal evidence at lower aggregation levels that migrant workers have been used to undermine wages and working standards (Hardy et al. 2010). Wage dumping strategies have been found in particular in sectors with a high concentration of migrant workers, such as construction, the meat industry and the care sector. As a result of Germany's decision to maintain its labour market restrictions for EU8 workers until 2011, the use of migrants to undermine wage standards has been reported in particular by posted workers (Cremers 2011: 70ff.) as well as by solo self-employed (Gross 2009). Self-employment can often be bogus, with workers continuing to do what they did before for a company but being given this employment status to enable the company to circumvent labour market regulations (see also Fellmer and Kolb 2009).

Finally, the possible negative effects seem to be most evident in the low wage sector, in which migrant workers are clearly overrepresented. In 2009, about 20 per cent of German workers received remuneration below the low wage threshold compared to more than 30 per cent of workers of foreign nationality (Schulten 2001b). There is a strong migrant/native wage gap in Germany that is particularly pronounced for workers from EU8 countries (Brenke et al. 2009, Figure 8.1). In 2006, a worker from an EU8 country who had immigrated after EU enlargement in 2004 earned on average only 75 per cent of the average wage of a German worker. For workers from EU8 countries who immigrated before EU enlargement the average wage was 83 per cent, although that was still much lower than the average wage of migrants from non-EU countries (90 per cent) and from EU15 countries (98 per cent).

Most studies suggest that the wages of workers with poor qualifications were disproportionately affected by the inflow of migrant workers. Especially for services workers – for example, in cleaning or retail – studies found a relatively strong negative effect on wages due to migration (Steinhardt 2009).

Against the background of declining collective bargaining coverage and a rapidly growing low wage sector, during the past decade German trade unions have undergone a fundamental shift in their position towards statutory wage regulation and are campaigning for the introduction of a national statutory minimum wage of 8.50 euros per hour. Originally, this demand was in response to negative trends

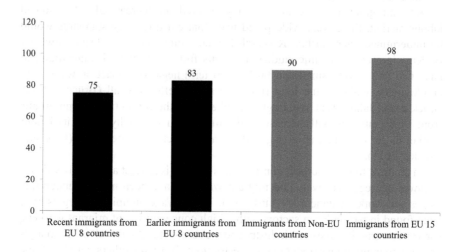

Figure 8.1   Migrant/native wage gap in Germany in 2006 (migrant average hourly wages as a percentage of native average wages)

Source: Brenke et al. (2009).

on the German labour market and not linked to the question of migration. More recently, however, the abolition of the labour market restrictions on EU8 workers became a major additional argument that further increased support for a statutory minimum wage.

The same holds true for a second instrument of labour market regulation, namely the extension of collectively agreed minimum wages on the basis of the German Posted Workers Act. When the latter was introduced in 1996, it was valid only for the construction industry and some related trades. In recent years, however, the Posted Workers Act has been extended to such sectors as cleaning, security services, waste management and the care sector. There are now 11 branches with extended sectoral minimum wages. Most recently, a change in the Law on Temporary Agency Workers created the possibility that a collectively agreed minimum wage in that sector can be made generally binding. The expected negative effects of the final opening up of the labour market for EU8 workers in May 2011 have been the major driving force behind these new sectoral minimum wages which also convinced some employers in these sectors to support new wage regulations.

3.2 Norway

Norway is not a member of the European Union but, like the other EFTA countries Iceland and Liechtenstein, it is part of the European Economic Area (EEA). As a consequence, since 1994 the country has been subject to most EU legislation and is included in the Single Market. Until 2004, EU migration to Norway was very modest and the country had – and still has – a very restrictive policy towards labour migration from third countries. In 2004, there was some fear that EU enlargement would lead to increased low wage competition and social dumping. As a result, Norway, like many other 'old' member states, introduced temporary restrictions on labour market access for individual job seekers from the accession states. According to the transitional arrangements work permits would be granted only if the applicants could document that their wage levels were in accordance with 'normal' Norwegian standards, and that they had close to full-time jobs.

However, these restrictions did not seem to hamper the inflow of migrants. In the period from May 2004 to May 2009 more than 150,000 first-time work permits and around 135,000 renewals were issued.[2] This was more than twice as many as in all the other Nordic countries combined. Most of the permits were granted to workers from Poland and the Baltic states, with construction being the dominant recruiting sector. The majority of the male migrants took up construction work, while most of the women were recruited into the cleaning/domestic sector (Friberg and Tyldum 2007; Friberg and Eldring 2011). In addition to registered individual labour migrants, a huge number of posted workers, service providers and migrants without permits entered the labour market through subcontracting, temporary

---

2   Norwegian Directorate of Immigration (UDI), various monthly statistics 2004–2009.

staffing agencies and self-employment (Andersen et al. 2009; Dølvik and Eldring 2008). Posted workers were not affected by the transitional restrictions (which only restricted the free movement of persons, not services). In 2009, the transitional restrictions were repealed, except for citizens from Bulgaria and Romania, for whom the restrictions will be continued until 2012.

In general, the Nordic model involves a high level of unionisation and collective agreement coverage. Although all the Nordic countries have unionisation rates that are far higher than the European average, Norway ranks significantly lower than its neighbours, with an average union density of 53 per cent, and only 38 per cent in the private sector. However, both trade union density and agreement coverage have been fairly stable over recent decades. There has been a small downward tendency since the early 1990s, but less than in the other Nordic countries (Nergaard and Stokke 2010). Collective agreement coverage in Norway is also lower than in many other Western European countries: in the private sector, only 58 per cent of employees are covered by collective agreements. Furthermore, there is no statutory minimum wage in Norway, and until 2004 the *erga omnes* mechanism for making collective agreements generally binding had never been applied.

Very soon it became apparent that the opening of the labour market situation had created a window of opportunity for low wage competition, and represented a huge challenge for the trade unions when it came to upholding established standards. The inflow of posted workers from the accession countries exposed existing weaknesses in the regulatory system, with a large section of the labour market being left more or less open for low wage competition and 'social dumping' (Alsos and Eldring 2008).

In construction, trade union density is 37 per cent, and 60 per cent of the workers are covered by collective agreements (Nergaard and Stokke 2010). However, the minimum wage provisions in the sector's collective agreement have traditionally had a normative effect for wage-setting even in companies without collective agreements (Stokke et al. 2003). The massive recruitment of migrant labour into the sector – especially through posting and subcontracting – characterised by a willingness to work under inferior conditions, changed this situation. Norwegian companies with collective agreements faced fierce competition from companies with low-paid workers, and there were numerous examples of migrant workers earning far less than what would be considered a living wage in the Norwegian context. After some consideration and internal debates the Norwegian Confederation of Trade Unions (LO) decided to apply for an extension of the collective agreement in construction through the long dormant Act relating to the general application of collective agreements. Employees in enterprises and posted workers from foreign firms are all covered by the generally applicable provisions. The criteria for enforcing an extension is that it is probable that foreign workers are performing work under conditions generally inferior to the norms stipulated by nationwide collective agreements for the relevant occupation or industry, or inferior to the general conditions prevailing in the relevant location or trade. Since

2004, several agreements have been made generally applicable: today, this is the case for construction, ship building, business cleaning and the agricultural sector. The legal extension of collective agreements represents a major shift in the regulatory regime in the Norwegian labour market. Traditionally, wage-setting and monitoring has been left to the bargaining parties, and there is considerable scepticism among both employers and unions with regard to this new practice. However, the construction workers' union (*Fellesforbundet*) has experienced that minimum wage-setting in the sector has not hampered the unionisation of migrant workers, but rather the opposite. The union has actually been fairly successful in organising Eastern European workers, and ascribes this partly to the new regulations, which make it possible for the union also to help members not covered by the ordinary agreement to get decent wages (Eldring et al. 2011).

On the employers' side, the resistance to generally binding collective agreements has been massive in the export-oriented shipbuilding industry, while construction employers tend to be in favour of the extension (Eldring 2010). Some of the employers' associations have declared that Norway should rather introduce a statutory national minimum wage, but this has been met with fierce opposition from the trade unions who fear downward pressure on wages in general, as well as a weakening of the collective bargaining system. As already mentioned, a substantial proportion of female migrants work in the domestic sector, which is unorganised and totally unregulated when it comes to wages. Regulating this sector by the use of collective agreements seems difficult and domestic workers could probably have benefitted from a national minimum wage regulation (Alsos and Eldring 2010). The results from a survey among Polish workers in Oslo in 2010 showed that 88 per cent of the cleaners (including both domestic work and business cleaning) earned less than the standard wage rate in the relevant collective agreement (Friberg and Eldring 2011).

In general, there is a tendency for migrants to be paid less than average in Norway. Adjusted for years of work experience in Norway, the differences are less significant (Galloway 2008), but according to a government green paper, the share of East European labour migrants living in households with a permanent low income in the period from 2006 to 2008 was 31 per cent, compared to 7 per cent of the general population. Among the East Europeans that had lived 10 years or more in Norway, their share of low income was reduced to 22 per cent (NOU 2011: 214–15). An analysis of hourly wage distribution in 2006 (see Figure 8.2) shows that migrant workers are overrepresented in the intervals below the median and underrepresented at the higher levels. It should be noted that many of the newly arrived East European workers probably were not captured in the official statistics at this time.

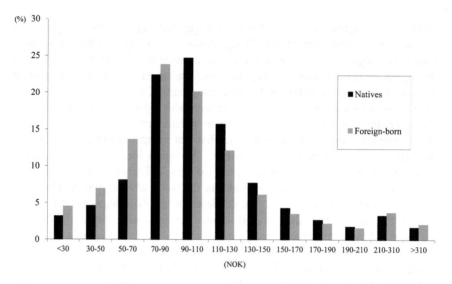

Figure 8.2　Migrant/native wage gap in Norway (distribution of hourly wages for natives and foreign born in percentage terms, 2006) (median hourly wage of the total employed population=100)

Source: Statistics Norway (OECD 2009).

Although new regulations have been put in place in the wake of EU enlargement to protect vulnerable workers in certain sectors, possible effects are so far scarcely documented.

It is well known that labour market regulations have little effect if not followed up by enforcement and monitoring. In its annual report in 2008, the Labour Inspectorate stated that their checks within construction documented an improved situation in labour migrants' wage and working conditions compared to the first years after EU enlargement. More workers than earlier had legal conditions, but there was still a higher risk of social dumping among posted workers. However, in the 2009 report, the Labour Inspectorate expressed concerns about worsening conditions among migrants in the construction sector, probably as a result of the financial crisis. The survey among Polish workers in Oslo in 2010 documented that while all Polish construction workers employed in Norwegian companies earned at least the lowest rate in the extended agreement, 38 per cent of the posted construction workers earned less than the stipulated minimum wage at that point in time. Compared to the general pay level in the sector then, the Polish construction workers lagged far behind, earning only 75 per cent of the average hourly wage (Friberg and Eldring 2011). Therefore, although the strengthened regulation of wage conditions undoubtedly had some effects, a considerable share of migrants earned less than the rates in the legally binding collective agreement, and definitely far less than the average in the sector.

When it comes to effects of the recent labour migration for the overall wage formation, there is evidence pointing to migration having subdued wage growth in some sectors. In the period from 2004 to 2008, the Norwegian economy was booming, and there was a high demand for labour. Analyses made by Statistics Norway indicated that labour immigration in this period resulted in a slower wage growth than what could otherwise have been expected in a tight labour market (Bjørnstad/SSB 2007).

3.3 Switzerland

Until the 1990s Switzerland strictly regulated labour migration based on quotas with temporary and often fairly short-term work permits (Gross 2006). Migrant workers were seen mainly as a buffer for the business cycle, recruited in boom periods and sent back home in economic downturns. During the past two decades, however, Switzerland had gradually changed towards a more liberal migration regime. These changes were closely linked to the growing convergence with EU policy, including acceptance of the principle of freedom of movement for workers (Fischer et al. 2002).

A first attempt at such a policy took place with the foundation of the European Economic Area (EEA) between the EFTA and the EU countries in 1992. For the EFTA countries the EEA created an opportunity to become part of the European single market without being an EU member. For Switzerland, however, the whole project failed after EEA membership was rejected by a bare majority of Swiss voters in a binding referendum. Hereby, the assumed negative impact of the freedom of movement played a major role in the arguments of the EEA opponents (Fischer 2003).

In the late 1990s Switzerland made another attempt and signed so-called bilateral agreements with the EU, including one agreement on the free movement of persons which came into force in 2002. This agreement foresaw a gradual opening of the Swiss labour market for EU citizens which after a transitional period have the full right to work in Switzerland. Later on, the agreement was also extended to new EU member states in Eastern Europe. The transitional period, which still allowed for restrictions on migrants, ended in 2007 for the old EU15 countries (plus Cyprus and Malta) and in 2011 for the EU8 countries of Eastern Europe, while it will continue for Romania and Bulgaria until 2016.

The strong element of direct democracy in the Swiss political system means that all bilateral agreements with the EU have to be submitted to referenda. At the beginning, the outcome of these referenda was rather uncertain, since there has always been a strong conservative/nationalistic block in Switzerland which is predisposed to vote against the free movement of workers. As the more liberal parties and the business community had a strong interest in adopting the EU agreements, however, the outcome of the referenda depended very much on the positions of the left parties and the trade unions, de facto giving the latter a veto on this issue (Fischer 2003).

During the 1990s, industrial relations in Switzerland were faced by a significant decentralisation of collective bargaining, diminishing bargaining coverage and an overall weakening of the trade unions (Oesch 2007, 2011). Against this background the trade unions were very much afraid that an increased inflow of migrants from EU countries would undermine Swiss wage standards. Therefore, the unions made clear that they would support the bilateral agreements with the EU only if the Swiss government at the same time introduced measures to strengthen wage regulation in order to protect workers against wage dumping. Since the position of the trade unions was decisive for the outcome of the referenda, the government finally agreed on the parallel introduction of so-called 'accompanying measures' (*flankierende Maßnahmen*), which, basically, addressed four issues.

The *first* was the introduction of a posted workers act which provides that posted workers should receive the same minimum wages and working conditions as native workers. *Second*, possibilities for extending collective agreements to the whole sector were facilitated. Originally, an extension was possible only if the collective agreement already covers 50 per cent of both employees *and* employers. In contrast, with the 'accompanying measures', in sectors experiencing a significant undermining of established wage standards, an extension is also possible if only a majority of the employees is covered. *Third*, in sectors which have no generally binding collective agreement the state acquired authorisation to lay down so-called 'standard work contracts' (*Normalarbeitsverträge*) which define statutory minimum wages for the respective sectors. *Fourth and finally*, the 'accompanying measures' foresaw the introduction of various instruments for monitoring and control. While formerly, monitoring of the working conditions of migrant workers was carried out by the immigration authorities it is now in the hands of the trade unions and employers' associations. In sectors with generally binding collective agreements so-called 'parity commissions' have been established to monitor compliance with agreements. In sectors with no generally binding collective agreements monitoring has been taken over by tripartite commissions (including public authorities) which focus on compliance with standard work contracts. Every year, the State Secretariat for Economic Affairs publishes a report on the implementation of the 'accompanying measures' which contains detailed documentation of the number of checks and offences against existing wage standards.[3] According to the most recent report, in 2010 checks were carried out in more than 36,000 establishments and covering around 143,000 persons (SECO 2011: 18).

The 'accompanying measures' have contributed to a significant re-regulation of the Swiss labour market and a strengthening of collective bargaining (Alfonso

---

3   The reports can be downloaded under: http://www.seco.admin.ch/dokumentation/publikation/00008/00022/04563/index.html?lang=de.

2010; Oesch 2011). The most obvious sign of this is the fact that the previously observed erosion of the collective bargaining system was reversed (Oesch 2007). After bargaining coverage reached its nadir at the end of the 1990s, at about 40 per cent, it is now back at around 50 per cent. One major cause of this development was a significant increase in the extension of collective agreements. While in 2003 only 36 agreements covering around 360,000 workers were declared generally binding, in 2007 there were 62 agreements covering nearly 590,000 workers (Bundesamt für Statistik 2011).

Despite its rising trend Swiss bargaining coverage is still fairly low, since almost half the workers are not covered by a collective agreement. With the 'accompanying measures', a new possibility has been created so that the state can now determine statutory minimum wages within the framework of standard work contracts. In practice, however, use of this instrument has been fairly limited (SGB 2011a). So far, only three cantons have introduced minimum wages, in sectors such as domestic work, beauty parlours, call centres and repair services at regional level. Moreover, from 2011 there is a first nationwide standard work contract for the domestic economy. As a significant part of the economy is not regulated by collective either agreement or standard work contract the Swiss trade unions are campaigning for the introduction of a nationwide statutory minimum wage which they hope to introduce by referendum (SGB 2011b).

There is a widespread perception that the 'accompanying measures' have made a major contribution to preventing wage dumping due to the new wave of migrant workers after the agreement on the free movement of persons. While a few studies have found that recent migration has had a dampening effect on overall wage development in Switzerland (Stadler 2008), most economic analysis concludes that the impact on wages has been fairly limited. Some studies indicate that there have been some dampening effects on wages for some high-skilled occupations (Favre 2011; Gerfin and Kaiser 2010). For those at the bottom of the wage scale, however, the same studies found no wage effects. Moreover, the State Secretariat for Economic Affairs has argued that the 'accompanying measures' have been particularly effective in avoiding additional pressure on the low wage sector (SECO 2010: 69).

Although there is still a significant migrant/native wage gap in Switzerland, it has been reduced slightly over the past decade, rising from 85 per cent in 2004 to 87.3 per cent of the native average wage in 2008 (Table 8.3). With the exception of the horticultural sector the migrant/native wage gap has become narrower in almost all other traditional low wage sectors, which suggests – although it does not prove – that migrants have not had a major negative impact on wages at the bottom of the wage scale.

Table 8.3   Migrant/native wage gap in Switzerland (average migrant wages as a percentage of average native wages)

	2004	2006	2008
Banking/insurance	104.4	108.8	109.0
Construction	92.7	94.5	94.5
Social and health services	92.9	94.0	93.4
Retail trade and repair services	91.4	92.9	93.3
Hotels and restaurants	91.5	91.8	92.4
Manufacturing	85.8	87.1	88.5
Transport and communication	84.9	85.0	85.3
Services	81.2	82.9	83.5
Horticulture	88.2	84.7	83.1
Total	85.0	86.4	87.3

Source: Swiss Statistics, Swiss Earnings Structure Survey; authors' calculations.

In contrast to economic analysis, however, official reports on the implementation of the 'accompanying measures' indicate that a significant proportion of companies are contravening Swiss wage standards. In 2010, the report found violations in about 39 per cent of all inspected establishments and by 35 per cent of all inspected persons (SECO 2011: 28). The proportion was significantly higher than in previous years, which might be explained by the higher pressure on wages in times of economic crisis. In any case, the Swiss example seems to confirm that the impact of migration on wages is strongly influenced by the existing institutions and regulations of wage formation, as well as by its effective implementation.

3.4 United Kingdom

Soon after the 2004 enlargement, it became apparent that the United Kingdom was one of the most popular destinations for labour migrants moving westwards. Like Ireland and Sweden, the United Kingdom opened its labour market for migrants from the accession states in May 2004, a strategy that was endorsed by the trade unions (Clark and Hardy 2011; Eldring et al. 2011; Heyes 2009). No transitional restrictions were introduced, except that until April 2011 nationals from the new member states who wished to take up employment in the United Kingdom for at least one month were required to register under the Worker Registration Scheme (WRS).[4] The registration requirement was linked to restrictions on certain benefits,

---

4   In conjunction with the 2007 enlargement, labour market access was restricted for Bulgarian and Romanian citizens. Work permits would be granted for skilled workers only under certain conditions, in addition to quotas for less-skilled workers in some sectors (agriculture, food processing).

such as unemployment benefits and public housing, which would be granted only 12 months after registration. In total, more than 1,200,000 applications had been registered (a figure which includes repeat registrations) when the scheme closed down after the first quarter of 2011. The number of registrations declined rapidly from 2008 (see Heyes and Hyland in this volume). Two-thirds of the registered migrants came from Poland, followed by Slovakia, Lithuania and Latvia (Home Office 2009, 2011).

The top recruiting sectors during the first five years were recruitment agencies, hospitality and caring, agriculture, manufacturing and food processing (Home Office 2011). Although many immigrants have a high level of education, they are typically to be found in low-skilled jobs (Drinkwater et al. 2010). In the early days of the financial crisis it was predicted that there would be a huge wave of return migration from the United Kingdom, but the indications are that this effect was overestimated, and that fairly large numbers are likely to settle permanently in the United Kingdom (Clark and Hardy 2011; Drinkwater et al. 2010; see also Anacka and Fihel and Heyes and Hyland in this volume).

Since the late 1970s, British trade unions have lost much of their power. While 57 per cent of workers were union members in 1979, the figure was only 28 per cent in 2007. There are a number of reasons for this development, related to economic, political, legal and social changes in British society and the labour market. Over the same period, collective bargaining coverage has declined. In 1980, about 75 per cent of all workers were covered by agreements, compared to only 35 per cent in 2007 (Brown 2011; Grimshaw 2011). Despite economic growth from the mid-1990s to 2007, there was a steady increase in the share of employees in low paid jobs, rising from around 12 per cent in 1977 to more than 20 per cent in 2001 (Grimshaw and Rubery 2010). One factor leading to pressure for the introduction of a statutory national minimum wage was that an increasing number of low paid workers lacked protection through collective bargaining. When 'New' Labour came into power in 1997, the establishment of a statutory minimum wage became a core element in the government's policy to reverse the increasing poverty in the lower segments of the labour market (Colling and Terry 2010). In 1997, a tripartite body, the Low Pay Commission (LPC), was set up to oversee the introduction, uprating and monitoring of the National Minimum Wage (Brown 2009). Following recommendations by the Commission, in 1999 the government introduced statutory minimum wage rates for workers aged 18 years and above. The National Minimum Wage is binding for all employers, regardless of which sector they are based in. In each year since its inception, the minimum rate has been raised, mostly in line with or above inflation. The first minimum adult hourly rate in 1999 was set at £3.60; as of October 2011 it will be £6.08.

The United Kingdom has taken a minimalist approach to implementation of the Posted Workers Directive (PWD). No specific legislation was introduced, implying that the existing national minimum wage should be sufficient. Although the trade unions have taken an inclusive approach to labour migrants (see Heyes and Hyland in this volume), the scale and composition of the post-2004 migration have posed a significant challenge. Trade unions fear social dumping and low wage competition, especially through posting of workers, and there have been a number of unofficial stoppages, with union members campaigning against the use of foreign posted workers on lower pay. At one point, the UK unions in engineering and construction wanted the government to declare their national agreement applicable for the purposes of the PWD, but without success. Otherwise, the unions have based their strategies mainly on a variety of measures to organise and support migrant workers (Clark and Hardy 2011; Eldring et al. 2011; Heyes 2009).

The statutory minimum wage requirements cover all workers in the United Kingdom, including labour migrants and posted workers, and have probably played an important role in securing minimum wages for recent labour immigrants. However, since migrants are overrepresented in sectors where wages below the legal minimum are found more often, they are probably at higher risk of lower pay (Clark and Hardy 2011; McKay 2009). According to the Low Pay Commission's latest annual report, migrants are more likely to be low paid than the general population (LPC 2011). A review of various data sources concludes that there is widespread evidence of migrant workers getting paid less than the minimum wage in both national and regional data sets. The likelihood of getting paid less is higher for younger workers, for migrants from the accession countries and for persons working in hospitality, agriculture and construction (Jayaweera and Anderson 2008). Several other sources point in the same direction, as well as to the fact that the minimum wage rate tends to be the maximum wage level for labour migrants in elementary occupations (McKay 2009). In addition, all the studies mentioned underline the particular vulnerability of agency workers.

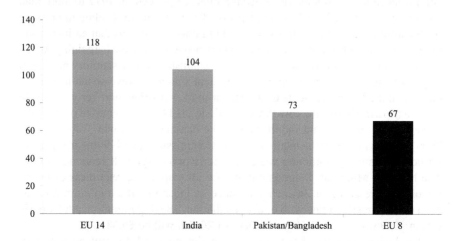

**Figure 8.3   Migrant/native wage gap in the United Kingdom, 2009
(median weekly wage of UK workers = 100)**

Source: Clancy (2009); authors' calculations.

An analysis of labour force survey wage data 2001–2005 clearly indicates that the most recent migrants are overrepresented in the lowest income group (see Bettin in this volume). While 10.9 per cent of the native employees had an hourly wage below the 10th percentile of the total population, this was the case for 16.92 per cent of recent immigrants (Dustmann 2007). A comparison of the median weekly earnings of UK and foreign workers in 2009 (not adjusted for worker or job characteristics) clearly indicates that East European workers earn far less than the average UK worker and also have lower median earnings than other migrant groups (see Figure 8.3).

4. Summary and Conclusion

From a theoretical standpoint, there are no clear answers concerning the general effects of migration on wages, but according to most empirical studies– at least at the macroeconomic level – there have been no or only minor negative effects. So far, the empirical evidence on migrant wages and their impact on native wages in the post-enlargement EU is still patchy. One reason for this is that, due to data limitations, most of the published research still captures only the early phases of the new migration waves and to a large extent only settled migrants, leaving the potentially large groups of posted and unregistered workers out of the analysis. There are, however, a number of sources that give some insight, although due to differences in the composition of national data it is not possible to draw firm comparative conclusions on, for instance, the extent of 'wage dumping', in other words, the exploitation of migrant workers to undermine existing wage standards.

In the four countries analysed here, we found that in general migrants earn less than native workers. The migrant/native wage gap seems to be particularly high for workers from the EU8 countries, who are clearly overrepresented in low wage sectors and so may induce downward pressure on native wages in these sectors. Moreover, a number of local and regional studies have documented obvious cases of wage dumping. This may seem to contradict the findings of various macro-level econometric studies. However, we argue that these studies may well underestimate the effects, partly because of data limitations, but partly also because they do not pay sufficient attention to institutional factors and national systems of wage formation, although they are obviously relevant. To close the gap, in this chapter we have emphasised the analysis of wage-setting institutions and practises, and their potential when it comes to securing migrants and native workers a decent wage.

There are significant differences between the wage-setting institutions of the countries considered, as well as in their responses to the new waves of migration after EU enlargement. Switzerland, Germany and Norway have a collective agreement coverage rate ranging from approximately 50 to 70 per cent, while the United Kingdom stands out with a rate of only around 35 per cent. The numbers reflect national differences in trade union strength and density, as well as the unions' historically developed institutional power. With regard to statutory wage mechanisms and provisions, the countries have both contrasting and similar practices. Germany's and Switzerland's ordinary extension mechanisms had over the years more or less lost their significance, but due to the opening of the labour market for workers from Eastern Europe extension practices have experienced a revival. In Norway, which long followed the Scandinavian model of free collective bargaining without state interference, the extension of collective agreements was introduced as a new practice after EU enlargement and its importance is now increasing. The United Kingdom, on the other hand, since 1999 has had a national minimum wage that sets a wage floor for all workers, and although the unions have voiced considerable concern over increased low wage competition, no new regulatory measures related to wages have been introduced.

In recent years, the German trade unions have been campaigning for the introduction of a similar system in Germany, not as an alternative to the extension of agreements but as a complementary mechanism. In Switzerland, the state can now determine statutory minimum wages in sectors without generally binding collective agreements. However, as this instrument is not much used in practice, the Swiss trade unions are also campaigning for the introduction of a national statutory minimum wage. In both cases the exploitation of migrants by wage dumping strategies are one of the main justifications for demands for a minimum wage. In contrast, the Norwegian unions still strongly opposed to such measures.

National wage-setting institutions have had an important influence on the wages of migrant workers since they determine the (legal) options open to companies seeking to undermine existing wage standards. Given the high proportion of migrants working in the low wage sector the prevention of wage dumping is first of all a question of implementing an effective wage floor. In the United Kingdom the existence of a national statutory minimum wage has proved to be an effective instrument in securing the wages of migrant workers at the bottom of the scale. In the other three countries of our sample, wage floors exist only at sectoral level on the basis of extended collective agreements. They include sectors with a high proportion of migrant workers, such as construction. However, some of the most extreme examples of wage dumping involving migrants have been found in sectors with no wage floor, such as the meat industry in Germany and the cleaning sector in Norway (Hardy et al. 2010; Alsos and Eldring 2010).

Furthermore, there is strong evidence that more encompassing collective bargaining systems make it much more difficult for companies to misuse migrants for a strategy of wage dumping. In all countries considered here a relatively large part of the economy is not directly covered by collective agreements. In principle, there are two ways to compel employers to accept collective agreements. The first is to build up trade union strength at the workplace. This strategy was followed in particular in the United Kingdom where the unions focused almost exclusively on the organising of migrant workers. Although organising strategies could be found to a greater or lesser extent in Germany, Norway and Switzerland, in these three countries the unions put much more emphasis on strengthening collective bargaining coverage through the introduction of extension mechanisms. In those sectors where collective agreements became generally binding the potential for wage dumping could be diminished significantly as employers became legally obliged to pay the same wage rate for migrants and natives.

Overall, with the exception of the United Kingdom, the opening of the borders towards Central and Eastern Europe has triggered re-regulation in wage-setting institutions, as well as pushing forward ongoing national debates on further regulation. In Germany, Norway and Switzerland the experiences of wage dumping and low wage competition in the wake of EU enlargement have led to a re-regulation – or demands for it – of national labour market regimes. Although the re-regulatory measures were triggered by the inflow of labour migrants, their potential effects are of a far more general character. Previously ignored problems related to low collective bargaining coverage rates have come to the surface,

Table 8.4   National systems of wage regulation and the impact of migration

	Germany	Norway	Switzerland	United Kingdom
Union density	19%	53%	18%	28%
Bargaining coverage	–62%	–73%	–50%	–35%
Extension of collective agreements	In a few sectors (mainly limited to minimum wages)	In a few sectors – of growing importance	Of growing importance	No extension
Statutory minimum wage	No	No	No	Yes
Re-regulation of wage formation after EU enlargement	Yes Increasing number of sectors with an extended collectively agreed minimum wage; strong demand for the introduction of a national statutory minimum wage	Yes Extension of collective agreements has become an accepted instrument of labour market regulation	Yes Preconditions for extension have been relaxed More extended collective agreements Advanced inspection system Unions demand introduction of national statutory minimum wage	No Statutory minimum wage is the core instrument for regulating wages of migrant workers

Source: Author's composition.

and the setting of new sectoral or national wage floors will affect all workers in national labour markets. Even when the extension mechanisms are linked directly to the aim of protecting workers, if enforced, they will have positive effects also for the native low wage workers.

We started this chapter by asking whether minimum restrictions on cross-border labour mobility and maximum security of workers' rights are incompatible. The simple answer is that they are not. If the host countries have comprehensive wage-setting institutions there is no reason why migrant workers should not enjoy the same rights as native workers. The country cases demonstrate that there is considerable room for action within national labour market regimes, and that development since EU enlargement has motivated a number of changes and the strengthening of wage-setting institutions. Significantly, re-regulation has had a wider impact and, directly or indirectly, also addresses problems related to low collective bargaining coverage and lack of statutory regulations which previously had been neglected. Nevertheless, it is important to distinguish between regulations and their effective implementation. New and ambitious regulations are of little value if it they are not followed by efficient enforcement and sanctions.

Bibliography

Adsera, A. and B. Chiswick. 2007. 'Are there gender and country of origin differences in immigrant labor market outcomes across European destinations?', *Journal of Population Economics* 20 (3): 495–526.

Brown, W. 2009. 'The process of fixing the British National Minimum Wage, 1997–2007'. *British Journal of Industrial Relations* 47(2):429–43.

Afonso, A. 2010. 'Europeanisation, new political cleavages and policy concertation in Switzerland', *European Journal of Industrial Relations* 16 (1): 57–72.

Alsos, K. and L. Eldring. 2008. 'Labour mobility and wage dumping: The case of Norway'. *European Journal of Industrial Relations* 14 (4): 441–59.

Alsos, K. and L. Eldring. 2010. 'Husarbeid uten grenser?' *Tidsskrift for kjønnsforskning,* 4/2010: 377–93.

Andersen, R.K., M. Bråten, L. Eldring, J.H. Friberg and A,M. Ødegård. 2009. *Norske bedrifters bruk av østeuropeisk arbeidskraft.* Fafo-rapport 2009: 46. Oslo: Fafo.

Baas, T. and H. Brücker. 2011. Arbeitnehmerfreizügigkeit zum 1. Mai 2011: Mehr Chancen als Risiken für Deutschland, *IAB-Kurzbericht* No. 10.

Bispinck, R., H. Dribbusch and T. Schulten. 2010. 'German collective bargaining in a European perspective. Continuous erosion or re-stabilisation of multi-employer agreements?' *WSI-Discussion Paper* No. 171, Düsseldorf (http://www.boeckler.de/pdf/p_wsi_diskp_171.pdf).

Blanchflower, David G. and C. Shadforth. 2009. 'Fear, unemployment and migration' *The Economic Journal* No. 119: 136–82.

Bjørnstad, R. 2007. Hva har polakkene betydd for norsk økonomi. Foredrag på Fafo Østforums årskonferanse, 5 June 2007. http://www.fafo.no/Oestforum/050607/ bjoernstad.pdf.

Borjas, G.J. 2003. 'The labour demand curve is downward-sloping: re-examining the impact of immigration on the labour market' *Quarterly Journal of Economics* 118(4): 1335–74.

Bratsberg, B. and O. Raaum. 2010. Immigration and wages: evidence from construction, *CReAM Discussion Paper* No. 06/10.

Brenke, K., M. Yuksel and K.F. Zimmermann. 2010. 'EU enlargement under mobility restrictions: consequences for Germany', in M. Kahanec and K.F. Zimmermann (eds), *EU Labour Markets after Post-Enlargement Migration* Heidelberg: Springer, 111–29.

Brücker, H. 2010. 'Neue Erkenntnisse zu den Arbeitsmarktwirkungen internationaler Migration – Ein kritischer Überblick über vorliegende Befunde', *WSI-Mitteilungen* 63(10): 499–507.

Brücker, H. and E. Jahn. 2011. 'Migration and wage-setting: reassessing the labor market effects of migration', *Scandinavian Journal of Economics*, forthcoming.

Brücker, H. et al. 2009. Labour mobility within the EU in the context of enlargement and the functioning of the transitional arrangements. Final Report of a study on behalf of the Employment, Social Affairs and Equal Opportunities Directorate General of the European Commission (http://doku.iab.de/grauepap/2009/LM_ finalreport.pdf).

Bundesamt für Statistik. 2011. Gesamtarbeitsverträge nach Typ, Grösse und Wirtschaftssektor (http://www.bfs.admin.ch/bfs/portal/de/index/themen/03/05/ blank/data/00.html).

Clancy, G. 2009. *Migration: Insights from the Labour Force Survey*, Presentation to the ESDS Government Labour Force Survey User Meeting. 15 December 2009 (http://www.ccsr.ac.uk/esds/events/2009-12-15/clancy.ppt).

Clark, N. and J. Hardy. 2011. *Free movement in the EU. The case of Great Britain.* Berlin: Friedrich Ebert Stiftung.

Colling, T. and M. Terry. 2010. 'Work, the employment relationship and the field of industrial relations', in T. Colling and M. Terry (eds), *Industrial Relations. Theory and Practice.* Chichester: John Wiley & Sons.

Cremers, J. 2010. 'Rules on working conditions in Europe: Subordinated to freedom or services? *European Journal of Industrial Relations* 16(3): 293–306.

Cremers, J. 2011. *In search of cheap labour in Europe. Working and living conditions of posted workers* CLR Studies 6. Brussels: International Books.

Deakin, S. and F. Green. 2009. 'One hundred years of British minimum legislation'. *British Journal of Industrial Relations* 47(2): 205–213.

Dølvik, J.E. and L. Eldring. 2008. *Labour mobility from the new EU member states to the Nordic countries – development, trends and consequences.* TemaNord 2008: 502. Copenhagen: Nordic Council of Ministers.

Dølvik, J.E. and J. Visser 'Free movement, equal treatment and workers' rights: can the European Union solve its trilemma of fundamental principles?' *Industrial Relations Journal* 40(6): 491–509.

Drinkwater, S., J. Eade and M. Garapich. 2010. 'What's behind the figures? An investigation into recent Polish migration to the UK'. In: Black, R., G. Engbersen, M. Okólski and C. Pantiru (eds). *A Continent Moving West? EU Enlargement and Labour Migration from Central and Eastern Europe.* Amsterdam: Amsterdam University Press.

Dustmann, C., T. Frattini and I. Preston, I. 2007. *A study of migrant workers and the National Minimum Wage and enforcement issues that arise.* Report commissioned by the Low Pay Commission (http://www.lowpay.gov.uk/lowpay/research/pdf/t0Z96GJX.pdf).

Dustmann, C., T. Frattini and I. Preston. 2008. 'The effect of immigration along the distribution of wages' *CReAM Discussion Paper* No 03/08.

Eldring, L., I. Fitzgerald, J. Arnholtz. 2012. 'Post accession migration in construction and trade union responses in Denmark, Norway and the UK.' *European Journal of Industrial Relations* 18(1): 20-35.

Eldring, L. 2010. 'Norske erfaringer med allmenngjøring', in T. Aa. Stokke (ed.), *Allmenngjøring i EU og Norge.* Fafo-report 2010: 14: 59–68. Oslo: Fafo.

Favre, S. 2011. The impact of immigration on the wage distribution in Switzerland, MS (http://www.econ.uzh.ch/faculty/favre/Liz_Arbeit.pdf).

Fellmer, S. and H. Kolb. 2009. 'EU labour migration: government and social partner policies in Germany', in B. Galgóczi, J. Leschke and A. Watt (eds), *EU Labour Migration since Enlargement.* Surrey: Ashgate, 127–48.

Fischer, A. 2003. 'Vetospieler und Durchsetzbarkeit von Side-Payments. Der schweizerische innenpolitische Entscheidungsprozess um flankierende Massnahmen zur Personenfreizügigkeit mit der Europäischen Union', *Swiss Political Science Review* 9 (2): 27–58.

Fischer, A., S. Nicolet and P. Sciarini. 2002. 'Europeanisation of a Non-EU country: the case of Swiss immigration policy' *West European Politics* 25 (4), 143–70.

Friberg, J.H. and L. Eldring. 2011. *Polonia i Oslo 2010.* Fafo Report 2011. Oslo: Fafo.

Friberg, J.H. and G. Tyldum (ed.). 2007. *Polonia i Oslo – en studie av arbeids- og levekår blant polakker i hovedstadsområdet.* Fafo Report 2007: 27. Oslo: Fafo.

Friedberg, R. and J. Hunt. 1995. 'The impact of immigrants on host country wages, employment and growth', *Journal of Economic Perspectives* 9(2), 23–44.

Galgóczi, B., J. Leschke and A. Watt (eds). 2009. *EU Labour Migration since Enlargement.* Surrey: Ashgate.

Galloway, T.A. 2008. Re-examining the earnings assimilation of immigrants. Discussion Paper 570. Oslo: Statistics Norway.

Gerfin, M. and B. Kaiser. 2010. 'The effects of immigration on wages: an application of the structural skill-cell approach', *Swiss Journal of Economics and Statistics* 146 (4), 709–39.

Grimshaw, D. and J. Rubery. 2010. 'Pay and working time: Shifting contours', in T. Colling and M. Terry (eds), *Industrial Relations. Theory and Practice.* Chichester: John Wiley & Sons.

Grimshaw, D. 2011. 'United Kingdom: Developing a progressive minimum wage in a liberal market economy', in D. Vaughan-Whitehead (ed.), *The Minimum Wage Revisited in the Enlarged EU.* Cheltenham/Geneva: Edward Elgar/ILO.

Gross, D.M. 2006. 'Immigration policy and foreign population in Switzerland', *World Bank Policy Research Working Paper* No. 3853.

Gross, E. 2009. Self-employment and bogus self-employment in the Construction Sector – Report Germany, Bremen (http://www.efbww.org/pdfs/Annex%20 12%20-%20Final%20report%20Germany.pdf).

Hardy, J., L. Eldring and T. Schulten. 2010. 'Sub-national trade union responses to A8 migrant workers: a three sector comparison in the UK, Germany and Norway, European labour: Strategic responses to globalisation and European integration', Paper presented at the World Congress of Sociology, 11–17 July 2010, Gothenburg, Sweden.

Home Office – UK Border Agency. 2009. *Accession Monitoring Report May 2004–March 2009.*

Home Office. 2011. *Control of Immigration: Quarterly Statistical Summary, United Kingdom, Quarter 1 2011.*

Jayaweera, H. and B. Anderson. 2008. *Migrant workers and vulnerable employment: A review of existing data.* Oxford: Centre on Migration, Policy and Society (COMPAS), University of Oxford.

Krings, T. 2009. 'A race to the bottom? Trade unions, EU enlargement and the free movement of labour', *European Industrial Relations Journal* 15(1), 49–69

Longh, S., P. Nijkamp and J. Poot. 2008. 'Meta-analysis of empirical evidence on the labour market impacts of immigration', *Région et Développement* No. 27, 161–90

Low Pay Commission. 2011. *National Minimum Wage. Report 2011.*

Lundborg, P. 2006. 'EU enlargement, migration and labour market institutions' *Zeitschrift für Arbeitsmarktforschung* 39(1), 24–34.

McKay, S. 2009. 'The dimensions and effects of EU labour migration in the UK', in B. Galgóczi, J. Leschke and A. Watt (eds), *EU Labour Migration since Enlargement.* Surrey: Ashgate.

Nergaard, K. and T.Aa. Stokke. 2010. *Organisasjonsgrader og tariffavtaledekning i norsk arbeidsliv 2008.* Fafo-notat 2010:07. Oslo: Fafo.

NOU. 2011. *Velferd og migrasjon.* Official Norwegian Report/Green Paper. Oslo: Ministry of Children, Equality and Social Inclusion.

OECD. 2008. *International Migration Outlook 2008*, Paris: OECD.

OECD. 2009. *Jobs for immigrants. Labour market integration in Norway.* Paris: OECD.

Oesch, D. 2007. 'Weniger Koordination, mehr Markt? Kollektive Arbeitsbeziehungen und Neokorporatismus in der Schweiz seit 1990', *Swiss Political Science Review* 13(3), 337–68.

Oesch, D. 2011. 'Trade unions and industrial relations in Switzerland', in: C. Trampusch and A. Mach (eds), *Switzerland in Europe. Continuity and Change in the Swiss Political Economy*, London: Routledge, 82–102.

Ottaviano, G. and G. Peri. 2011. 'Rethinking the effects of immigration on wages', *Journal of the European Economic Association* 10, forthcoming.

SECO. 2010. Auswirkungen der Personenfreizügigkeit auf den Schweizer Arbeitsmarkt. 6. Bericht des Observatoriums zum Freizügigkeitsabkommen Schweiz-EU, Bern.

SECO. 2011. FlaM-Bericht vom 03. Mai 2011: *Umsetzung der flankierenden Massnahmen zum freien Personenverkehr Schweiz – Europäische Union 1. Januar – 31. Dezember 2010*, Bern.

SGB (Schweizerischer Gewerkschaftsbund). 2011a. *Erlass von Mindestlöhnen aufgrund der flankierenden Massnahmen*. Eine Praxisübersicht, SGB-Dossier Nr. 75.

SGB. 2011b. Dokumentation Mindestlohninitiative des Schweizerischen Gewerkschaftsbundes', Paper for the Press Conference on 25 January 2011 (http://mindestlohn-initiative.ch/wp-content/uploads/2011/01/110125_Pressedok_mlohn.pdf).

Schneider, J. 2009. The organisation of asylum and migration policies in Germany, Bundesamt für Migration und Flüchtlinge (eds), Working Paper No. 25, Nürnberg.

Schulten, T. 2011a. Zwischen offenen Arbeitsmärkten und transnationalem Lohngefälle, Gewerkschaften und Migration im Zuge der EU-Osterweiterung, in: G. Hentges and H.-W. Platzer (eds), *Europa - quo vadis? Ausgewählte Problemfelder der europäischen Integrationspolitik, Wiesbaden*: VS, 127–50.

Schulten, T. 2011b. Niedriglöhne in Deutschland. Ursachen, soziale Folgen und Alternativen, in: G. Wallraff, F. Bsirske and F.-J. Möllenberg (eds), *Leben ohne Mindestlohn- Arm wegen Arbeit,* Hamburg: VSA, 68–81.

Simms, M. and A. Charlwood. 2010. 'Trade unions: power and influence in a changed context'. In: Colling, T. and M. Terry (eds), *Industrial Relations. Theory and Practice*. Chichester: John Wiley & Sons.

Stadler, P. 2008. Personenfreizügigkeit: Auswirkungen auf den Arbeitsmarkt und das Wirtschaftswachstum' *Die Volkswirtschaft* No. 11, 7–11

Statistisches Bundesamt. 2010. Bevölkerung mit Migrationshintergrund – Ergebnisse des Mikrozensus 2009, Fachserie 1, Reihe 2.2, Wiesbaden.

Steinhardt, M.F. 2009. The wage impact of immigration in Germany – new evidence for skill groups and occupations, *HWWI Research Paper* No. 1–23.

Stokke, T.Aa., S. Evju and H.O. Frøland. 2003. *Det kollektive arbeidslivet.* Oslo: Universitetsforlaget.

Woolfson, C., C. Thörnquist and J. Sommers. 2010. 'The Swedish model and the future of labour standards after *Laval*'. *Industrial Relations Journal* 41(4): 333–50.

Chapter 9

Importing Skills: Migration Policy, Generic Skills and Earnings among Immigrants in Australasia, Europe and North America

Tomas Korpi

1. Upgrading the Workforce

Rapidly increasing international economic integration and technological and organisational changes are believed to have led to increased demand for highly skilled workers. While the extent to which skill requirements have in fact risen and the importance of potential drivers are still being debated, the view that labour demand has shifted towards high skill workers has intensified policymaking in the area of skill supply. Arguing that an increase in the supply of skilled labour is necessary to remain competitive in the global labour market, governments' primary remedy has been to expand education and attempt to improve educational attainment.

A similar approach has been taken to migration policy. Here, the targeted provision of work permits and visas to highly skilled foreign workers has been put forth as a way to prevent possible skills shortages. In Europe, the Blue Card introduced in 2009 aimed at simplifying immigration for well-educated foreign labour from outside the European Union in order to attract skilled labour to promote competitiveness and growth. Moreover, the Blue Card had important national precursors, such as the German Green Card for IT professionals launched in 2000 and the UK Highly Skilled Migrant Programme from 2002. Such policies are of course not new, but echo the demand-based labour migration policies emphasising education, employment experience, and language skills traditionally pursued by, for instance, Canada (Shachar 2006).

Migration to Europe in recent decades, in contrast, has included a large proportion of people migrating for social or humanitarian reasons. Family-related migration and forced migration due to calamitous events in the country of origin may bring immigrants with a different set of skills from those discussed in connection with the Blue Card. This may of course still be beneficial to the destination country, as less skilled immigration could bolster growth, for instance by providing cheap and flexible labour (Holzer 2011). Nonetheless, the skill structure of the migrant population may be of great importance for how migration affects the receiving labour market and the position of the immigrants themselves

(Constant and Zimmermann 2005; Borjas 2007). Indeed, this is the premise on which demand-based migration policy is built.

Our knowledge of how differences in migration policy affect the skills of migrant populations is nevertheless fairly limited, being restricted largely to comparisons of the educational level of immigrants and natives. This obviously is an important characteristic, but we know little about how the skills of immigrants in fact compare to those of natives, and how migrant skills differ according to migration policy. This by extension also applies to the links between migration policy, immigrant skills and the labour market integration of immigrants, for instance in terms of earnings.

The purpose of this chapter is to explore these issues focusing on a specific set of generic skills, so-called 'literacy skills'. Generic skills are skills applicable across a wide range of jobs, and therefore crucial for labour market success. Although literacy is sometimes equated simply with the ability to read and write, the literacy concept used here is wider and the measure more complex. In addition to reading and mathematical skills, it also captures complex reasoning and problem-solving abilities and should therefore be seen as a measure of broad generic skills. The underlying hypothesis explored here is that differences in migration policies should lead to variations in the generic skills of immigrants to different countries, differences that in turn should be associated with differences in economic integration in terms of earnings.

The data come from the International Adult Literacy Survey (IALS), a large-scale comparative survey of literacy skills carried out in 23 countries in the years 1995 to 1998. Data from nine countries are used here; Canada, Germany, Great Britain, Ireland, New Zealand, Norway, Sweden, Switzerland and the USA. These countries have a wide range of migration policies and immigration histories.

2. Migration Policy, Skills and Integration

Immigration policies vary widely across countries and also over time.[1] The traditional immigration countries, such as Canada, New Zealand and the USA, have a history of large-scale immigration. As is well known, for a long time they relied on a relatively limited set of sending countries, mainly those of (Western) Europe and in particular Ireland and Great Britain. In the case of Canada and New Zealand this focus on source countries has since been replaced with an immigration policy focusing on desired labour market characteristics. In 1967, Canada adopted a points system within the framework of which immigrants are ranked according to their ability to meet the needs of the Canadian labour market. Canadian immigration policy distinguishes three broad categories of immigrants; social (family reunification), humanitarian (refugees) and economic (business

---

1   The following discussion is based on Bauer et al. (2000) and Shachar (2006), and focuses on the evolution of migration policies prior to the IALS surveys in the mid-1990s.

migrants, dependent migrants and assisted relatives). It is only dependent migrants and assisted relatives that are subjected to the points system, which gives preference to well-educated migrants with work experience and proficiency in English or French. The proportion of immigrants going through the system has varied, declining from over 70 per cent in the mid-1970s to around 15 per cent a decade later. The trend then reversed, the numbers increasing to roughly 50 per cent (Bauer et al. 2000).

New Zealand's immigration policy has developed in a similar manner, albeit with a significant time lag. Following the Second World War, New Zealand continued its previous policy of strongly favouring immigration from Great Britain, targeting specific skills and occupations. However, after roughly a decade of negative net migration, a change in policy led to the introduction of a points system similar to the Canadian one in 1991 (Phillips 2011). As was initially the case in Canada, around 70 per cent went through the points system after its enactment (Winkelmann 2005).

In contrast, the USA is alone among the traditional immigration countries in its current emphasis on family reunification rather than labour market skills. The source country quotas put in place in the 1920s were in 1965 replaced with a system that de facto prioritised family reunification. The changes also allowed for allocation of visas according to employment preferences, predating the Canadian policies but without the points system; however, these have remained a small share of all immigrants. During the late 1980s and 1990s, for instance, around 10 per cent of all immigrants entered as employment-based immigrants (US Immigration and Naturalization Service 2000).

Other countries have a more recent immigration history, related to either post-colonial immigration or post-war labour recruitment. Following the Second World War, Great Britain and some other European countries experienced a wave of return migration by colonists and of native immigration from the former colonies. This was relatively unrestricted, in that it consisted primarily of each country's own citizens. However, the long period of low unemployment that commenced in the late 1950s led to substantial labour shortages in these countries. This spurred active labour recruitment, which also occurred in countries such as Germany, Sweden and Switzerland. Much of this took the form of migration from southern to northern Europe, often institutionalised in bilateral agreements, but there was also migration from other parts of the world. However, Great Britain differed in that it never had a period of labour recruitment and instead continued to favour migration from the former colonies.

In all countries, this demand-driven immigration came to an abrupt halt in the mid-1970s in connection with the rise in unemployment triggered by the oil crises. Nevertheless, despite the recession, little return migration occurred and immigration continued in the form of family reunification. This inflow was in some countries also supplemented by a flow of political refugees from repressive countries around the world. The most recent stage in European migration history arrived with the fall of the Iron Curtain in 1989. West European countries, including

Germany, Norway, Sweden and Switzerland, experienced a drastic increase in the number of refugees and asylum seekers, an east–west migration induced by the turbulence in the post-communist countries in general, and the wars in the former Yugoslavia in particular.

Finally, some European countries have developed into receiving countries only very recently. This applies to Ireland, a country that traditionally has seen many more leave than arrive. Annual net migration was generally negative until the early 1990s, but this turned into a substantial net inflow in the mid-1990s as Ireland began to experience rapid growth. Many of the arrivals – around 50 per cent – were return migrants (Ruhs 2009). A similar reversal of migration flows took place in a number of southern EU countries in the 2000s. Because of their histories of emigration these countries lacked immigration policies of their own. Instead they by default adopted those of the European Union, which regulated intra-EU migration as well as refugee policy.

As should be clear from this brief review, migration policy has varied substantially across and also within countries over time. The variation over time complicates cross-country comparison, but a rough ranking according to the prominence given to labour demand and skills still seems possible. Canada's migration policy has undoubtedly had the strongest labour demand focus. The points system was put in place early, and although its importance has varied over time, a substantial fraction of immigrants have gone through the system. Despite its late introduction of the points system, New Zealand's continued emphasis on demand considerations would seem to place it second. Labour demand has also at times been an important part of migration policy in Germany, Switzerland and Sweden. Here, however, immigration during the years preceding the survey was dominated by refugees from various parts of the world, in Germany supplemented by immigrants of German descent from Eastern Europe. Great Britain would seem to rank sixth, as their labour demand following the Second World War was met not by active recruiting but rather through immigration from the former Dominions. Great Britain is followed by the US, which had demand-related migration policies on a small scale. Norway brings up the rear, with very little labour recruitment and recently fairly substantial refugee arrivals. Ireland, finally, constitutes a category of its own, as it basically lacked a migration policy.

It is of course difficult to say what migrants would have come to a given country if it had applied a different migration policy. Comparisons of countries with different migration policies therefore serve as approximations of the counterfactual – that is, changes in policy regimes – and motivate comparisons of migrants' human capital in the points system countries Australia and Canada with that of migrants in the USA and Europe. These typically focus on the educational attainment of the migrant population and show that immigrants to OECD countries generally are less educated than natives (for example, OECD 2000 and 2007). However, the limited transferability of educational qualifications makes this an imprecise indicator of immigrants' human capital (Chiswick and Miller 2007). It is therefore interesting to examine indicators of locally valued skills, and for a general assessment of the human capital acquisition associated with immigration these indicators should, moreover, be measures of generic skills.

While less frequently examined in the context of migration policy, such indicators of generic skills are available in the large-scale international surveys of literacy, mathematics and science skills that have been conducted since the mid-1990s. Most of the surveys target compulsory school students and are therefore less relevant in a migration context since children are not the direct focus of migration policy. In contrast, the International Adult Literacy Survey (IALS) examined generic literacy skills in the adult population, and can therefore provide important insights into the link between migration policy and human capital import.

The focus on attracting highly skilled migrants has often overlapped with attempts at promoting migration within a specific language community. The policies of countries such as Canada and New Zealand traditionally centred on attracting migrants from other English-speaking countries (and also French in the Canadian case). Although culturally motivated, this amounted to selection on language skills. Even after the replacement of a source-country focus with a points system, destination-country language skills continued to be seen as an asset. Likewise, the post-Second World War policy of free mobility of labour between the Nordic countries to a large extent involves mobility between countries with closely related languages. In contrast, with some exceptions migration to European countries requires overcoming language barriers. This holds for both migration within Europe and migration to Europe from countries outside the continent. Comparing generic skills of immigrants who are native speakers of the language of the destination country with those who are not will therefore provide evidence of the possibilities for general skill import, that is from outside a language community, as envisioned by proponents of, for instance, the Blue Card.

This is also of crucial importance with regard to the link between migration policy and the economic integration of immigrants. In addition to factors such as gender, education and age, language proficiency has consistently been found to be extremely important for the economic status of immigrants (Chiswick 2008).[2] Little attention has been paid to how migration policy is related to the integration of immigrants through its relationship with language skills, however. Is it, for instance, the case that demand-oriented migration policies generally provide for better immigrant outcomes in terms of employment, wages or earnings (for example, OECD 2007)? Or is it simply that they have tended to emphasise language as a selection criterion? Exploring the links between migration policy, the generic literacy skills of different migrant groups and their earnings relative to the native population will provide evidence of the differential impact of different migration policies.

---

2   Language skills may, however, also be a consequence of labour market attainment (Chiswick 2008).

3. Generic Skills Data and Analysis

Large-scale comparative studies rarely have access to direct data on skills of any kind. One exception is the International Adult Literacy Survey (IALS), a survey encompassing 23 countries conducted in the mid-1990s with around 3,000 respondents per country. Although only a cross-sectional survey, the data set has the advantage that it includes immigrants, has fairly extensive information on various background factors, as well as data on earnings, and, most importantly, contains detailed measures of generic literacy skills.

Literacy is sometimes conceived of simply as the ability to read, but as used by the IALS measures it encompasses a broader set of generic skills. The survey defined literacy as 'the ability to understand and employ printed information in daily activities, at home, at work and in the community – to achieve one's goals, and to develop one's knowledge and potential' (OECD 2000, x). The survey thus examined comprehension of different types of text, distinguishing between the following three domains: prose, document and numeric literacy. The three types of literacy correspond to understanding prose material, extracting and interpreting information from diagrams, maps and so on, and carrying out arithmetic operations based on information located in text and documents. To assess individual skills in these domains, respondents were asked to complete around 45 tasks, each corresponding to a specific level of complexity and type of literacy skills (Myrberg 2000). To illustrate the types and varying complexity of the task, we take three examples from the prose domain provided by Kirsch (2001). One of the simplest tasks involved deducing from the label of a medicine container the maximum number of days the medicine should be taken. Another, more difficult task involved determining whether the seat of a bicycle was in the correct position using information from a page in the manual. The most difficult task required respondents to list two ways in which a particular employee support initiative aids individuals who lose their jobs because of departmental reorganisation, based on an announcement by the personnel department. Basically, simple tasks demanded a direct match of an individual piece of concrete information with few distracting elements, while the most difficult tasks necessitated higher-level inferences, the management of conditional information and sorting out credible distracting information.

Since the IALS literacy measure captures task complexity it may be seen as an indicator of cognitive skills. Although not discussed in these terms in the final report, frequent references to cognition may be found in the background report (NCES 1998). An argument for such an interpretation certainly can be made with respect to the native population, although it should be remembered that the cognitive aspects surveyed are limited to understanding and employing printed information. However, an interpretation of literacy as general cognitive skills seems less permissible in the case of the foreign-born. The crux is of course that for many immigrants the language in which the tasks were conducted was not their mother tongue. They may, in other words, have been perfectly capable of completing higher order tasks if the language of the survey had been different. The literacy measure should therefore be interpreted as *problem-solving ability in the language of the country of destination.*

This, however, makes the skill measure particularly relevant from a migration-policy point of view. If the goal of migration policy is to attract highly skilled foreign labour it is precisely problem-solving in the destination language that is central. Literacy skills in the language of origin are, in contrast, less pertinent. This would also seem to apply to individual labour market integration, as employers primarily would be expected to be interested in applicants' skills in the local language. The IALS' literacy measure is, in other words, of fundamental importance from both a societal and an individual point of view.

The literacy estimates derived from the survey responses can be related to the five pre-defined levels of literacy below (Kirsch 2001).[3]

Five Levels of Literacy

- **Level 1** indicates persons with very poor skills, where the individual may, for example, be unable to determine the correct amount of medicine to give a child from information printed on the package.
- **Level 2** respondents can deal only with material that is simple, clearly laid out, and in which the tasks involved are not too complex. It denotes a weak level of skill, but more hidden than Level 1. It identifies people who can read, but test poorly. They may have developed coping skills to manage everyday literacy demands, but their low level of proficiency makes it difficult for them to face novel demands, such as learning new job skills.
- **Level 3** is considered a suitable minimum for coping with the demands of everyday life and work in a complex, advanced society. It denotes roughly the skill level required for successful secondary school completion and college entry. Like higher levels, it requires the ability to integrate several sources of information and solve more complex problems.

---

3   To save time and costs, each respondent completed only a selection of tasks. Scaling methods from item response theory (IRT) were then used to transform the results into a common scale. Since each individual completes only parts of the survey a 'series' of more or less likely estimates of individual skill on the common scale are generated. For each individual, five different equally valid estimates from the domain-specific skill distribution were then drawn randomly (cf. NCES 1998). To obtain valid point and variance estimates, all five plausible estimates of domain-specific literacy have been used, together with the so-called replicate weights required by the sampling schemes. The measure of overall literacy skills used in the descriptive analyses consists of the simple average score across the 15 estimates of literacy level. In the regression analyses, each plausible value has been treated as an equally valid estimate of skill and separate regressions run for each and the results then averaged. To obtain unbiased variance estimates a jackknife estimator utilizing the replicate weights provided with the data has been used (see Westat 2007 for details).

- • **Levels 4** and **5** describe respondents who demonstrate command of higher-order information processing skills.

    Source: OECD (2000, xi).

In the subsequent analyses of literacy differences between the immigrant and native populations we focus on the working age population, that is, respondents between 16 and 65 years of age. The definition of 'immigrant' here relies on information on country of birth, with immigrants defined as those born outside the country of interview. Another important variable is mother-tongue. Information was gathered on the first language spoken, with each country having separate lists of the languages most often spoken by the foreign-born in that country. This has then been used to create three different indicators of the similarity between an immigrant's mother tongue and the language of destination. Same language indicates that the first language was identical to that spoken in the country of destination. Related language indicates that the first language belonged to the same language family as the destination language, although not identical. For example, in the case of English the related languages are the other Germanic languages. The last category, distant languages, refers to all other languages, including the category 'other/unspecified'.

With regard to earnings there is information on annual gross wage and salary income, a convenient comprehensive measure of economic integration as it represents the combined outcome of wages and employment. The IALS public use file provides only grouped earnings data: more specifically, data in which each respondent is placed in a particular quintile of the country's earnings distribution as determined from outside sources. This relative crudeness should be kept in mind in the subsequent analyses of immigrant earnings. In particular, although the earnings measure is identical in the various countries, it should be remembered that the substantive importance of quintile placement will depend on the underlying level of inequality in the countries. In other words, while a position in the second rather than the fourth quintile in all countries implies that one's earnings belong to the bottom 40 rather than the top 40 per cent, the actual, absolute difference in earnings between the quintiles will be greater the more unequal a country is.

Finally, other variables included in the analyses are total years of education, gender and age. For Canada, age is available only in 10-year intervals, in which case age has been set to the mid-point of the interval. In addition, there is information on date of arrival for all countries except New Zealand and Norway. In most cases the information refers to the year of first arrival, but in the Canadian case the information on first arrival is provided only for 15-year intervals: year of immigration have here again been set to the mid-point of the interval. This information has then been used to calculate the variable 'years since migration'

Apart from the lack of longitudinal information, the survey also has other drawbacks. One problem is the massive non-response in some countries. While there are no clear-cut rules regarding inadmissible non-response, a response rate of at least 50 per cent has here been deemed acceptable. This disqualifies Italy, Belgium and the Netherlands from the analyses (see Table 9.A1 in the appendix). In addition, although the sample sizes are relatively large, meaningful analyses focusing on the plight of immigrants are still not always possible. The immigrant sample size is on average around 8 per cent of the total, ranging from 25 per cent in Switzerland to 0.5 per cent in Chile. Since an analysis of immigrants' labour market position requires a sufficient number of foreign-born respondents, a second exclusion criterion of an immigrant sample of at least 5 per cent of the country total has been adopted. This leaves us with nine countries: Canada, Germany, Ireland, New Zealand, Norway, Sweden, Switzerland, Great Britain and USA.[4]

4. Immigrant Skills

The generic literacy skills of the native- and the foreign-born are examined in Table 9.1 which shows mean and variation in skill levels within and across countries. Literacy skills are measured as a simple average over the items capturing literacy in the prose, document and quantitative dimensions. In the table, countries are listed from top to bottom according to our assessment of their use of demand-based migration policy.

Starting with the skills of the native-born population shown in column 1, the results in the table suggest that the countries fall into three clusters. Norway and Sweden have scores around 3, clearly higher than the other seven; 3 was also the level the IALS survey team considered to be a suitable minimum in modern societies (OECD 2000). Then there is a middle category made up of Canada, Germany, the USA and Switzerland with values of around 2.7. Finally, there is a trailing cluster encompassing Great Britain, Ireland and New Zealand. The literacy skills of the latter group average around 2.5, that is, halfway between the suitable minimum and a level at which one can manage in everyday life but may have problems when facing novel demands. It may also be noted that the difference between the top (Sweden) and the bottom (Ireland) is almost a whole level of literacy, quite a substantial gap.[5]

---

4   A tenth country, Slovenia, also meets the 5 per cent criterion. However, it seems that the vast majority of Slovenian immigrants never immigrated, but were born in other parts of the former Yugoslavia and moved to Slovenia while it was still part of the republic. Moreover, of those who arrived after independence many are likely to have come as refugees from adjacent war zones. Migration to the former Yugoslavian republic is, in other words, likely to differ substantially from the other countries, and Slovenia was therefore also dropped from the analyses.

5   It may also be noted that there are also important differences with regard to dispersion. The standard errors are much larger in, for instance, Germany and Switzerland than in Great Britain and Sweden, evidence of much greater disparities in the literacy skills of the native population in the two former countries.

Table 9.1　　Mean literacy level among 16 to 65 year olds by country, country of birth and mother tongue. Standard error in parentheses, sample size in brackets

	Native	Foreign-born				Diff. col. 3–2	Diff. col. 5–2
		All	Same language	Related language	Unrelated language		
	1	2	3	4	5	6	7
Canada^	2.75 (0.05) [4175]	2.49 (0.31) [325]	3.23 (0.44) [154]		1.94 (0.24) [171]	−0.26	−0.81***
New Zealand	2.56 (0.06) [2726]	2.39 (0.06) [575]	2.80 (0.09) [344]	2.77 (0.24) [35]	1.77 (0.10) [196]	−0.16**	−0.79***
Germany	2.73 (0.15) [1900]	2.23 (0.24) [162]	2.29 (0.28) [51]	2.20 (0.85) [5]	2.20 (0.24) [106]	−0.50***	−0.53***
Switzerland	2.70 (0.14) [3071]	1.92 (0.12) [1040]	2.53 (0.19) [422]	1.99 (0.14) [179]	1.53 (0.09) [439]	−0.79***	−1.18***
Sweden	3.15 (0.04) [2403]	2.43 (0.12) [241]	2.92 (0.17) [40]	2.88 (0.46) [4]	2.32 (0.14) [197]	−0.73***	−0.83***
Great Britain	2.49 (0.03) [3564]	2.12 (0.11) [247]	2.51 (0.14) [105]	2.76 (0.75) [7]	1.82 (0.16) [135]	−0.36***	−0.67***
USA	2.72 (0.06) [2336]	1.84 (0.08) [579]	2.75 (0.21) [65]	2.19 (0.42) [13]	1.64 (0.08) [501]	−0.88***	−1.09***
Norway	2.91 (0.08) [3064]	2.59 (0.14) [243]	2.96 (0.14) [93]	3.26 (0.20) [40]	1.93 (0.19) [110]	−0.32***	−0.98***
Ireland	2.35 (0.08) [2227]	2.53 (0.12) [142]	2.51 (0.12) [129]	3.44 (0.55) [4]	2.43 (0.44) [9]	0.18	0.08

Notes: International Adult Literacy Survey. ^ Canada only distinguishes between the languages English, French and Other. ***, **, and * indicate significance at the 1%, 5% and 10% levels, respectively.

Moving on to the mean scores of the immigrant population in column 2, we again find a certain clustering. The highest immigrant literacy scores are found in Canada, Ireland, Norway, New Zealand and Sweden. The level of literacy among immigrants in these countries is around 2.5. A second group with literacy levels of roughly 2.2 includes Great Britain and Germany, while Switzerland and the

USA trail the others with levels in the vicinity of 1.9. Here too there is almost a full skill level's difference between the high (Norway) and the low (USA) scoring countries.[6]

These results can be discussed from a number of different perspectives. First of all, as is evident from column 6, there tends to be a significant difference between the literacy skills of natives and of foreign-born immigrants. This is not particularly surprising; the tests are, after all, conducted in a language that most immigrants only began to master as adults. However, Canada and Ireland differ in that no significant difference can be established. In the Canadian case, the point estimates do indicate that foreign-born persons have lower skills than the native-born, but the standard error for immigrants is so large that the difference is not significant. Ireland, in contrast, is very singular: this is the only country for which there are indications that immigrants are more proficient than natives. However, as indicated by the Irish sample sizes almost all the Irish foreign-born have English as their mother tongue, reflecting the substantial migration from Great Britain.

Interesting also is the size of the within-country differences. Disregarding Ireland momentarily, the immigrant–native difference is relatively small in Canada and New Zealand and, as noted, non-significant in Canada. A second group of countries consists of Great Britain and Norway, while in Germany and, in particular, in Sweden, Switzerland and the USA the immigrant population has sizeable skill gaps. The gap is greatest in the USA, where the average immigrant score is almost a full level below that of the native-born. The comparison of the latter three countries also indicates a complex relationship between the relative position of immigrants and the skill level of the native population. The Swedish skill gap is only slightly smaller than the Swiss and the American, even though Swedish immigrants have among the highest scores and clearly above the other two. In contrast to Switzerland and the USA, where immigrants have a very low level of literacy, the reason for the Swedish skill gap is of course the high level of literacy in the Swedish native population. Conversely, although Canada, Ireland and New Zealand are among the countries with the highest immigrant literacy scores, the low gap in these countries is not primarily the consequence of particularly high immigrant skills but rather of low or medium skills among the native populations.

Relating these scores to the differences in migration policies outlined above, it is noteworthy that Canada and New Zealand do not stand out as having particularly highly skilled immigrants. Norwegian and Swedish immigrants stand up fairly well in comparison, and from the standpoint of skill importation their relatively high scores could be judged a success. However, the Swedish immigrants still lag far behind the native-born, simply because literacy skills in the native population are so high. In contrast, the results for Canada and New Zealand suggest that the

---

6   As is evident from the standard errors there are also large differences in the spread around these means, with the smallest dispersion in New Zealand and the largest in Canada.

points system may actually succeed in picking immigrants with a good fit to the local labour market.

Nonetheless, as suggested by the Irish case, the composition of the migrant group is crucial for the observed skill differences, and for the evaluation of migration policy a comparison of the skills of the non-native-speaker immigrants is particularly interesting. The proportion of the foreign-born having an unrelated mother tongue varies widely, from 6 per cent in Ireland to around 85 per cent in Sweden and the USA. With the exception of Germany, with 65 per cent, most other countries have proportions in the 40–50 per cent range. There are also stark differences in the proficiency levels of the native speakers (and of related languages) and of those having an entirely distinct linguistic background. The former categories tend to have literacy scores at least on a par with the native population, while the latter have clearly and often dramatically lower ability levels.[7] In most countries, the literacy scores for those who grew up speaking a distant language are below 2.0.[8] The migrants have clearly lower skills in the language of destination than the native population, skills that range from very poor to a level which enables them to 'manage everyday literacy demands', but not much more. The gap to the native population is also often close to 1, putting them at an unequivocal disadvantage.[9]

These results can, again, be viewed from the perspective of migration policy, and this raises questions regarding the general success of migration policies

---

7   An exception here is Germany, where native-speaking immigrants have relatively low scores. Although there is no direct information on this, it is likely to be related to the immigration of Eastern Europeans of German descent. A large part of the German-speaking immigrants in the survey come from Poland, Romania, the former Soviet Union or the former Yugoslavia, and this group is known for its limited German knowledge. As for the high scores for non-native-speaking Irish immigrants, they are based on too few cases to be considered reliable.

8   Note here that the Canadian score in column 5 is likely to be an overestimate. It includes immigrants speaking a related language, who in the other countries perform much better than those speaking an unrelated language.

9   The differences in Table 9.1 may of course also reflect differential learning processes among the immigrants in the different countries after arrival. This would primarily be related to length of stay, but also age at arrival. The importance of these two factors for the differences observed is examined in Table 9.A2, showing results from literacy regressions with and without the two variables 'age' and 'years since migration'. Panels A and C in Table 9.A2 basically reiterate the results from Table 9.1, with the slight difference that the categories 'same' and 'related language' here have been combined. Panels B and D show the results including the new variables, and although both 'age' (negatively) and 'years since migration' (positively) are strongly related to skills, the pattern evident in Table 9.1 appears to be stable. The immigrant variables now indicate the skills of a newly arrived migrant relative to that of natives. The most noteworthy differences in relation to Table 9.1 is that the British skill gaps decrease and the German and Swedish ones increase. Canada remains in the middle, followed by Switzerland and the USA. The low correlation with the initially hypothesised ranking remains.

employed by countries such as Canada and New Zealand. Despite their selective systems the skills of the non-native speakers are not particularly high – they are roughly average. This also applies to their skill gaps, which also are around average. Instead, Germany stands out as the country with highly skilled non-native-speaking immigrants, as well as a fairly small skills gap. Sweden would seem to place second, also with highly skilled immigrants but with a greater gap. Canada, Great Britain, New Zealand and Norway are about equal, while the USA and Switzerland seem to have the biggest problems. This ranking obviously deviates quite substantially from our initial expectations, indicating the difficulties involved in using immigration policy as a strategy for upgrading the labour force. The indications in Table 9.1 of successful 'cherry-picking' on the part of Canada and New Zealand (and Ireland) instead hinges on the availability of a large pool of English speakers. This, in turn, suggests that the possibilities for applying similar systems in other countries are limited.

5. Immigrant Earnings

How do these results relate to immigrants' economic integration? To examine this question we now turn to analyses of immigrants' earnings relative to the native population. Recall that earnings in the IALS refer to annual gross earnings and that the data are provided in quintile form. The quintile form implies an interval scale (each unit increase of the dependent variable thus involves an equidistant relative earnings boost), and we will therefore make use of standard OLS regression. We have estimated a basic earnings model in which quintile placement has been regressed on the variables sex, age, age squared, years of education, immigrant (or sub-groups) and a constant. In some models, we also include years since migration.

Panel A of Table 9.2 shows the results for all countries combined, as well as for each of the nine countries separately. As is clear from the leftmost, pooled, model, those born abroad tend to earn less. The point estimate of –0.25 indicates that immigrants in the nine countries on average are located a quarter of a quintile below natives in the earnings distribution, that is, around 5 percentile points. This result is expected, as native-immigrant earnings gaps have been documented in a wealth of country studies.

However, the country-specific results evince a fair degree of variation in the earnings gap. Most startling, perhaps, is the finding that in Canada, Great Britain, Ireland, New Zealand and the USA there is no clear evidence of an immigrant–native earnings gap. For Canada and New Zealand, the estimates are also close to zero, suggesting that there is indeed no immigrant earnings disadvantage. Great Britain and the USA display higher but insignificant point estimates. The point estimate for Ireland is actually relatively close to the cross-country average, only much less precisely estimated. In contrast, immigrants in Germany, Norway, Switzerland and Sweden earn clearly less than natives. The German and Norwegian earnings gaps are particularly large, around a half-quintile or 10 percentile points.

Table 9.2   Earnings regressions by country. Standard errors in parentheses

	All	CA	NZ	GE	SW	HE	GB	USA	NO	IE
PANEL A										
Immigrant	-0.25***	0.02	-0.02	-0.43**	-0.24***	-0.21***	-0.09	-0.11	-0.55***	-0.19
	(0.08)	(0.20)	(0.07)	(0.20)	(0.08)	(0.08)	(0.10)	(0.11)	(0.10)	(0.16)
PANEL B										
Immigrant	-0.11	0.06	0.02	-0.37*	-0.18**	-0.15*	0.00	0.03	-0.49***	-0.19
	(0.08)	(0.18)	(0.07)	(0.19)	(0.08)	(0.08)	(0.09)	(0.12)	(0.10)	(0.16)
Literacy skills	0.23***	0.17**	0.22***	0.13***	0.10***	0.13**	0.21***	0.20***	0.10**	0.25***
	(0.04)	(0.08)	(0.03)	(0.04)	(0.04)	(0.06)	(0.04)	(0.05)	(0.05)	(0.05)
PANEL C										
Same/Related language	0.04	0.05	0.16*	-0.49**	-0.18	-0.12	-0.00	0.04	-0.36***	-0.15
	(0.12)	(0.18)	(0.08)	(0.22)	(0.25)	(0.09)	(0.12)	(0.18)	(0.11)	(0.16)
Unrelated language	-0.38***	-0.01	-0.43***	-0.40	-0.26**	-0.31**	-0.20	-0.15	-0.83***	-0.67
	(0.09)	(0.28)	(0.12)	(0.25)	(0.11)	(0.15)	(0.17)	(0.12)	(0.12)	(0.47)
PANEL D										
Same/Related language	0.06	0.06	0.14	-0.45**	-0.16	-0.10	0.02	0.06	-0.34***	-0.16
	(0.10)	(0.18)	(0.08)	(0.22)	(0.25)	(0.10)	(0.12)	(0.17)	(0.11)	(0.16)
Unrelated language	-0.19**	0.06	-0.26**	-0.33	-0.19*	-0.21	-0.04	0.02	-0.72***	-0.53
	(0.09)	(0.27)	(0.12)	(0.24)	(0.10)	(0.16)	(0.16)	(0.13)	(0.13)	(0.42)
Literacy skills	0.22***	0.17**	0.21***	0.13***	0.10**	0.13**	0.21***	0.20***	0.10*	0.25***
	(0.04)	(0.08)	(0.03)	(0.04)	(0.04)	(0.06)	(0.04)	(0.05)	(0.05)	(0.05)

Notes: International Adult Literacy Survey. Dependent variable earnings quintile rank. OLS regression with jackknife standard errors. In addition to variables shown, all models also include the variables gender, age, age squared, years of education, and a constant. *** , ** , and * denote significance at the 1%, 5% and 10 % levels, respectively.

One interpretation of these results is that, with the exception of the USA, the countries lacking an earnings gap also have relatively small literacy gaps, suggesting that similar skill levels could be associated with similar earnings. A direct way of examining this conjecture is of course to explicitly take skill differences into account in the analyses, and Panel B of Table 9.2 presents results from analyses in which the literacy measure has been added to the models of Panel A. The leftmost column again shows the result from the pooled analyses, and it is clear that the skill differential is important for the earnings differences. Increasing literacy in the destination-country language is positively related to increasing earnings, a one-level increase in literacy skills is associated with an increase of earnings equal to a fourth of a quintile. Moreover, in this pooled model no immigrant earnings gap remains after controlling for literacy differences. It would appear that the literacy differential explains all of the earnings disparities.

These average results also to some extent carry over to the individual countries, as skills are positively related to earnings in all countries. In all countries, controlling for skills – that is, comparing individuals with identical skill levels – also tends to decrease the immigrant earnings disadvantage. The changes in the point estimates are relatively small, however, although the level of significance drops in Germany, Sweden and Switzerland.

Skills are thus important for the economic integration of immigrants, but there is no obvious link between national migration policies that target skilled migrants to different extents and integration. Canada and New Zealand have been successful in the sense that immigrants have the same earnings as natives, but this is also the case in Great Britain, Ireland and the USA. This, moreover, has little to do with the skills of the migrants, as the results for the Anglo-Saxon countries are similar irrespective of whether one controls for skill differences or not. The disparity is instead between the Anglo-Saxon countries and the other four. This could be a result of differences in migration policy, as Germany, Norway, Sweden and Switzerland have admitted a substantially larger number of refugees. This could explain the disparity to the extent that refugees have greater difficulties in integrating in the local economy. On the other hand, any such difficulties would appear to be independent of the skills of immigrants, as their disadvantage only diminishes somewhat after skills differences are taken into account.[10]

---

10 It may be recalled here that the dependent variable measures relative position in an earnings distribution rather than earnings per se. In principle, an identical absolute disadvantage may therefore show up as a relative disadvantage only in the four countries with a more compressed earnings structure. An attempt at assessing the importance of this issue has been made using the Luxemburg Income Study (LIS). The LIS contains roughly comparable income information for most of our IALS countries from around the time of the IALS. Using the Panel A models, the expected earnings percentile of males with mean years of education and age have been calculated for both natives and immigrants. The nominal values of the percentiles from the LIS, and exchange rates from around the time of the surveys, suggest expected earnings differences of around 750 USD in the USA, 1350 USD

One way of exploring the importance of refugees is to look at the two immigrant sub-groups, since in these countries refugees are most likely to belong to the 'unrelated language group'. This is not an ideal approach as the unrelated language group also includes many migrants arriving for other reasons; however, the data provide no direct information on reasons for migration. The leftmost column of Panel C again presents results for all countries combined, and it is evident that immigrants with unrelated mother tongues are at the greatest disadvantage on the labour market. While immigrants speaking the native language or some variant thereof have the same earnings as the natives on average, those coming from other backgrounds have clearly lower earnings. The point estimates in the country-specific regressions also show that, with the exception of Germany, those speaking a language markedly different from that of the new country do tend to earn less than other migrants. However, the difference is generally small and not significant (significance tests not shown), and it is only in New Zealand and Norway that immigrants speaking an unrelated language clearly trail immigrants speaking the native language. While there may be a difference between the two groups of immigrants, the difference is not as clear-cut as could be expected. As shown in Panel D, this conclusion does not change if we take literacy skills into account.[11]

These mixed results are of course interesting from a migration policy perspective. Canadian immigrants integrate well, both English- and French-speaking and others. In contrast, the relative success of New Zealand's approach turns out to be related to the fate of their English-speaking immigrants; despite their demand-based selection other immigrants clearly fare worse. Moreover, a demand-oriented migration policy is not a requirement for integration, as is evident from a comparison with the other, equally successful, Anglo-Saxon countries. As noted, the earnings measure may complicate comparisons with the other European countries, but migrants to these countries do undeniably worse than the native-born. This does not seem to be related to the composition of the immigrant group, however; it is only in Norway that the two migrant groups clearly differ from each other. Again, it is not clear that a demand-oriented migration policy is associated automatically with markedly better immigrant integration, nor that substantial refugee immigration necessarily poses serious integration problems in itself.

---

in Sweden, and 3500 USD in Norway. Although these estimates are crude, do not cover all the nine countries and depend on, for example, which year of the LIS is examined and the exchange rate at the time, they nonetheless do not indicate that the differences in the spread of the earnings distributions offset the differences in earnings rank found here.

11   Again, the differences in Table 9.2 may reflect differences in integration processes among the immigrants in the different countries after arrival, and one factor beyond those already included is length of stay. However, in the analyses presented in Table 9.A3 it is only in Britain and the USA (and sometimes Ireland) that the variable is significant. These are also the countries evincing the biggest changes in relation to Table 9.2. Newly arrived immigrants (irrespective of language) are thus at a clear and quite sizable earnings disadvantage. The effect of residence is generally positive, implying that the disadvantage tends to decrease over time in all countries, but most markedly in Great Britain and the USA.

6. The Possibility of Successful Skill Importation

Recent European debate on immigration and immigration policy has been based on the premise, implicit or explicit, that stricter selection of immigrants, primarily according to various labour market criteria, will produce a pool of skilled immigrants, simplify their economic integration and boost national economies (see, for instance, Constant and Zimmermann 2005). The analyses of locally valuable generic skills presented here seriously question this assumption. Indeed, if anything these results imply that there is no obvious way to obtain highly skilled immigrants or a self-evident path to their integration.

First, one immediate reflection regarding immigrant literacy is that the group of countries with relatively high immigrant literacy skills consists of countries with substantial immigration from places sharing the same linguistic heritage. Great Britain, Canada, Ireland and New Zealand have profited from migration within the Anglo-Saxon (and also French in the case of Canada) language community, while Norway (and to a more limited extent Sweden) has benefited from labour mobility among Scandinavian countries. That such a selection of immigrants has a positive impact on immigrant literacy skills is not particularly astonishing. With the exception of Sweden, they also belong to the countries with the lowest literacy gaps and could be said to have secured a migrant workforce with a relatively close fit to their labour markets.

Such mobility is in part likely to be the outcome of self-selection among migrants; it is for instance clearly simpler to move to a country in which one is familiar with the language. It could, however, also be seen as a consequence of an active migration policy: Canada and New Zealand, as well as Norway and Sweden have promoted migration within their language communities by various means. In Canada, this has primarily involved attaching weight to language skills under the points system introduced in the late 1960s. This has also played a role in New Zealand since 1986, and prior to this Great Britain was a favoured country with respect to immigration. In the Norwegian and Swedish cases, the gradual removal of mobility restrictions culminating in the creation of a common Nordic labour market in 1954 obviously simplified intra-Nordic migration. Seen in this light, a policy of successful skill import would seem to consist primarily of an emphasis on migration from countries belonging to the domestic language family.

Clearly, however, for most European countries this is not a viable policy option, and in many countries a substantial part of the immigrant population comes from countries outside their language communities. Given the emphasis placed on migrant selection, it would seem surprising that immigrants speaking a distant language do not perform better in Canada and New Zealand. Their small overall immigrant–native skill gaps are in part related to the low skill level in the native population and in part to the relatively high skills among a large native-speaking immigrant group. Their success in securing highly skilled migrants from unrelated language groups, on the other hand, appears no more than average. (Recall that the Canadian estimate in column 5 of Table 9.1 is likely to be an overestimate.) Instead, proficiency among immigrants with an unrelated mother tongue is greatest in Sweden, Germany and Norway. Strict migration policies might also affect the distribution of skills, but although immigrants in New Zealand have relatively few low skilled the dispersion in Canada is fairly large. A migrant population with substantial generic skills may in other words be obtained in different ways.

Second, immigrants in Canada and New Zealand do not integrate better than other migrants. Not that they do poorly: on the contrary, there appears to be no difference in the earnings of native and foreign-born workers in these countries. But similar results are also obtained for other countries, with drastically different migration policies. In Great Britain, Ireland and the United States there is also no clear immigrant earnings gap. The fact that the relative position of immigrants is similar in all five countries, regardless of their very different migration policies, suggests that economic integration can be achieved through various means and not only through the introduction of immigration programmes based on stringent labour demand considerations. For instance, the British and US results indicating a gradual earnings convergence despite substantial initial disadvantages point to the importance of labour market integration *after arrival*.

A particularly interesting case is of course the USA, where immigrants have been found to achieve earning levels similar to natives despite having the lowest skill levels among all immigrant groups and also being at a substantial skills disadvantage. How this comes about is beyond this chapter, but one potential explanation is that roughly half of the US immigrants in the survey are Spanish-speaking. Many parts of the USA, in particular along the Mexican border, now have substantial Spanish-speaking minorities, so large that they may have developed ethnic economies in their own right. If this is the case, a lack of one generic skill (English literacy) may be compensated by another (literacy in Spanish).

If the advantages of a demand-based migration policy are somewhat ambiguous, the lower earnings of immigrants in Germany, Norway, Sweden and Switzerland would seem to suggest that extensive social and humanitarian immigration may be difficult to handle. Nonetheless, while the data prevent us from focusing directly on refugees, the results in Table 9.2 suggest that more distant migrants need not inevitably fare worse than others. Moreover, with the exception of Norway, the results presented here suggest that the difficulties these groups have had in closing the earnings gap is at least in part related to their lack of this type of generic skills. This would seem to be an obvious area for remedial action (see, for instance, Myrberg 2000, for a discussion of how to develop literacy skills among migrants).

Taken together, these results call into question the general importance of migration policy for the possibility of skill import. Although there are large differences in the generic skills of immigrants in the nine countries, these differences do not appear to be related to migration policy in any systematic manner. Of course, migration policy is but one element of the long chain of events leading to permanent resettlement. This selection process starts with the question of who migrates, when and to which country, and continues with integration and potential return migration. Different factors may thus influence this process in numerous ways at various stages, and there may be differences between individuals in how relevant a specific factor is. The role of migration policy in this process may in fact be quite limited.

Appendix

Table 9.A1   International Adult Literacy Survey: sample sizes and response rates by country

	Number of respondents	Response rate (per cent)	Number of respondents, age 16–65		
			Native	Foreign-born	Share foreign-born
Canada	5660	69	4175	325	7.2
New Zealand	4223	74	2726	575	17.4
Germany	2062	69	1900	162	7.9
Sweden	3038	60	2403	241	9.1
Switzerland	4140	52	3071	1040	25.3
Great Britain*	3811	63	3564	247	6.5
United States	3045	60	2336	579	19.9
Norway	3307	61	3064	243	7.4
Ireland	2423	60	2227	142	6.0

Note: * The response rate refers to the UK, as no separate rates are provided for GB and Northern Ireland.

Table 9.A2   Literacy regressions by country. Standard errors in parentheses

	NZ	CA	GB	USA	IE	GE	HE	SW	NO
PANEL A									
Immigrant	-0.16**	-0.26	-0.37***	-0.88***	0.18	-0.50***	-0.79***	-0.73***	-0.32***
	(0.08)	(0.31)	(0.11)	(0.09)	(0.13)	(0.12)	(0.07)	(0.10)	(0.10)
PANEL B									
Immigrant		-1.03**	-0.33	-1.40***	0.39	-0.75***	-1.11***	-1.12***	
		(0.48)	(0.22)	(0.15)	(0.24)	(0.14)	(0.14)	(0.17)	
PANEL C									
Same/Related language	0.25***	0.48	-0.04	-0.08	0.19	-0.44***	-0.32***	-0.23	0.15*
	(0.07)	(0.45)	(0.14)	(0.21)	(0.12)	(0.17)	(0.09)	(0.17)	(0.09)
Different language	-0.79***	-0.82***	-0.67***	-1.09***	0.08	-0.53***	-1.18***	-0.83***	-0.98***
	(0.14)	(0.23)	(0.16)	(0.08)	(0.44)	(0.14)	(0.09)	(0.12)	(0.16)
PANEL D									
Same/Related language		-0.02	-0.13	-0.68**	0.40*	-0.68***	-0.48***	-0.73***	
		(0.59)	(0.22)	(0.29)	(0.24)	(0.20)	(0.16)	(0.22)	
Different language		-1.14**	-0.55**	-1.39***	0.21	-0.77***	-1.30***	-1.14***	
		(0.49)	(0.23)	(0.14)	(0.51)	(0.16)	(0.14)	(0.17)	

Notes: International Adult Literacy Survey. In addition to the variables shown, Panels B and D also include the variables age and years since migration. In New Zealand and Norway, no information was collected on date of immigration and these countries are consequently left out of these analyses.

Table 9.A3   Earnings regressions by country. Standard errors in parentheses

	CA	GB	USA	IE	GE	HE	SW
PANEL A							
Immigrant	-0.43	-0.88***	-0.58***	-0.42**	-0.71***	-0.21***	-0.35***
	(0.65)	(0.25)	(0.17)	(0.21)	(0.27)	(0.08)	(0.13)
PANEL B							
Immigrant	-0.34	-0.81***	-0.35*	-0.39*	-0.64**	-0.26*	-0.25*
	(0.63)	(0.22)	(0.19)	(0.20)	(0.26)	(0.14)	(0.15)
Literacy skills	0.16*	0.22***	0.19***	0.26***	0.12***	0.13**	0.10**
	(0.08)	(0.04)	(0.05)	(0.05)	(0.04)	(0.06)	(0.04)
PANEL C							
Same/Related language	-0.45	-0.85***	-0.62*	-0.43**	-0.87***	-0.26*	-0.31
	(0.67)	(0.30)	(0.34)	(0.19)	(0.28)	(0.14)	(0.34)
Different language	-0.42	-0.90***	-0.58***	-1.06*	-0.68**	-0.43***	-0.35***
	(0.66)	(0.25)	(0.17)	(0.55)	(0.30)	(0.18)	(0.13)
PANEL D							
Same/Related language	-0.39	-0.87***	-0.49	-0.40**	-0.82***	-0.20	-0.24
	(0.64)	(0.27)	(0.32)	(0.19)	(0.29)	(0.15)	(0.35)
Different language	-0.32	-0.77***	-0.35*	-0.84*	-0.60*	-0.30	-0.25*
	(0.64)	(0.22)	(0.19)	(0.47)	(0.28)	(0.18)	(0.14)
Literacy skills	0.16**	0.22***	0.19***	0.25***	0.12***	0.13**	0.10**
	(0.08)	(0.04)	(0.05)	(0.05)	(0.04)	(0.06)	(0.04)

Notes: International Adult Literacy Survey. Dependent variable earnings quintile rank. OLS regression with jackknife standard errors. In addition to variables shown, all models also include the variables gender, age, age squared, years of education, years since immigration, and a constant. ***, **, and * denote significance at the 1%, 5% and 10% levels, respectively.

Bibliography

Bauer, Thomas, Magnus Lofstrom and Klaus F. Zimmermann. 2000. 'Immigration policy, integration of immigrants and natives' sentiments towards immigrants: evidence from 12 OECD countries'. *Swedish Economic Policy Review*, 7, 11–53.

Borjas, George. 2007. 'Immigration policy and human capital', in Harry Holzer and Demetra Smith Nightingale (eds), *Reshaping the American Workforce in a Changing Economy*. Washington, DC: Urban Institute Press, 183–200.

Chiswick, Barry R. 2008. *The Economics of Language: An Introduction and Overview*. Institut zur Zukunft der Arbeit, IZA DP No. 3568.

Chiswick, Barry R., and Paul W. Miller. 2007. *The International Transferability of Immigrants' Human Capital Skills*. Institut zur Zukunft der Arbeit, IZA DP No. 2670.

Constant, Amelie, and Klaus F. Zimmermann. 2005. 'Immigrant performance and selective immigration policy: a European perspective'. *National Institute Economic Review*, 94, 94–105.

Holzer, Harry. 2011. *Immigration Policy and Less-skilled Workers in the United States: Reflections on Future Directions for Reform*. Washington, DC: Migration Policy Institute.

Howell, David and Friedrich Huebler. 2001. *Trends in Earnings Inequality and Unemployment across the OECD: Labor Market Institutions and Simple Supply and Demand Stories*. CEPA Working Paper Series I, Economic Policy Analysis, Working Paper No. 23, New School University.

Kirsch, Irwin. 2001. *The International Adult Literacy Survey (IALS): Understanding What Was Measured*. Research report RR-01-25, Educational Testing Service, Princeton, NJ, USA.

Myrberg, Mats. 2000. *The Foundation for Lifelong Learning*. National Agency for Education, Report No. 188, Stockholm.

NCES. 1998. *Adult Literacy in OECD Countries: Technical Report on the First International Adult Literacy Survey*. National Center for Education Statistics, NCES 98-053, Washington.

OECD. 2000. *Literacy in the Information Age*. Paris: OECD.

OECD. 2007. *Jobs for Immigrants*. Paris: OECD.

Phillips, Jock. 2011. *History of Immigration*, Te Ara – the Encyclopaedia of New Zealand, updated 13 August 2009. Available at: http://www.TeAra.govt.nz/en/history-of-immigration (accessed 3 May 2011).

Ruhs, Martin. 2009. *Ireland: From Rapid Immigration to Recession*. Migration Policy Institute. Available at: http://www.migrationinformation.org/Profiles/display.cfm?ID=740 (accessed 3 May 2011).

Shachar, Ayelet. 2006. 'The race for talent: highly skilled migrants and competitive immigration regimes'. *New York University Law Review*, 81, 148–204.

U.S. Immigration and Naturalization Service. 2000. *Statistical Yearbook of the Immigration and Naturalization Service, 1998.* Washington, DC: U.S. Government Printing Office.

Westat. 2007. WesVar 4.3 User's Guide. Rockville, MD, USA.

Winkelmann, Reiner. 2005. 'Europeans in the Antipodes: New Zealand's mixed migration experience', in Klaus F. Zimmermann (ed.), *European Migration – What Do We Know?* Oxford: Oxford University Press, 601–31.

Index

For Product Safety Concerns and Information please contact our
EU representative GPSR@taylorandfrancis.com Taylor & Francis
Verlag GmbH, Kaufingerstraße 24, 80331 München, Germany